# JULIUS ROSENWALD

Julius Rosenwald

# Julius Rosenwald

## THE LIFE OF A
## PRACTICAL HUMANITARIAN

BY

## M. R. Werner

HARPER & BROTHERS PUBLISHERS
NEW YORK AND LONDON
1939

Julius Rosenwald

Copyright, 1939, by M. R. Werner
Printed in the United States of America

FIRST EDITION

I-O

# Contents

v

# PREFACE

## I

"MEN are only interested in a man when that man is interested in humanity," wrote George Sand. This statement may explain why Julius Rosenwald received so much public attention during his lifetime and why there was such a spontaneous outpouring of condolence and regret at his death. His career was distinguished by the accumulation of great wealth in a colorful undertaking, the mail-order business, and the disposal of much of that wealth in acts of great generosity, intelligently conceived, for the well-being of mankind.

Other men in the United States were far more brilliant merchants than he, and other men gave away more money, but few philanthropists seemed to capture the love of the people they helped quite so completely. His sense of personal duty was usually stirred when he perceived social distress, and his sympathy was almost invariably enlisted when he came in contact with individual difficulty.

During a period of American history when the expanding nation developed the means of satisfying its craving for material well-being, Rosenwald, through his part in the development of Sears, Roebuck and Co., prospered greatly. He made much more money than he or his relatives could use and he gave much of it back to society. He had a passion for personality and he banked heavily on men and women whom he considered good; and he was always ready to supply large sums of money impulsively when ideas were presented to him. And what appealed to him was the cause which seemed to have the seeds, at least, of a fundamental social reform.

In the first place [he once said] philanthropy is a sickening word. It is generally looked upon as helping a man who hasn't a cent in the world. That sort of thing hardly interests me. I do not like the "sob stuff" philanthropy. What I want to do is to try and cure the things that seem to be wrong. I do not underestimate the value of helping the underdog. That, however, is not my chief concern, but rather the operation of cause and effect. I try to do the thing that will aid groups and masses rather than individuals.

Professor Charles S. Johnson, of Fisk University, said of him after his death:

The spell of his personality always intrigued close observers into the emotional indiscrimination of a lasting friendship. His disarming frankness, his rugged simplicity made him all too human to be linked with the momentous forces moving in the world today. Yet he was contributing to them with an insight so rare, so unusual as to have been scarcely discerned. That generosity by which he became so justly famed overshadowed the shrewd social intelligence and prophetic wisdom which gave it direction.

Because of the position which he gradually attained in philanthropic circles, he was looked upon as a leader among Jews and as a force in American life. By virtue of his sympathetic interest in their troubles, he became a counselor of the Negroes, and an adviser in countless movements and endeavors for social welfare. Those who came to him for his money, sometimes remained to take his advice. Thus a man who had started humbly and kindly to give away some of his surplus funds found himself gradually becoming the mentor of two groups and the standard for many types of philanthropy.

"Enclosed herewith I am sending you by Mr. Rosenwald's direction his check for," was a phrase innumerable organizations became accustomed to from Rosenwald's secretaries. The number of organizations, settlements, charitable efforts, associations and societies which received $100 a year or less from him are literally countless. The number of organizations which received $1,000 a year or more was very large. And there were numerous sporadic contributions made on the spur of the moment when he met friends and acquaintances who told him of causes and distress. Hundreds of people thought of him first whenever they heard of an individual in need or a worthy cause, and in a remarkable number of cases he responded promptly and fully to their demands. In the course of his life he gave away approximately $63,000,000.

The amount of money which he gave away personally was not, however, the full measure of his philanthropic influence. Realizing early in his career as a philanthropist that no man could hope to make much impression on a great need by personal gifts, he used his money to stimulate large donations by other men and to get government appropriations. By virtue of his interest in humanity and his generosity, he exercised a profound effect on movements and causes in several parts of the world. Although a conservative in politics and economics, he was fully conscious of the fact that government must take responsibility for social welfare in its larger aspects. The most that private philanthropy could do, he believed, was to initiate hitherto novel or unpopular projects and to stimulate government to support them permanently after their value had been proved. By making his money a stimulus, he thus raised many more millions of dollars than he himself possessed for the causes he thought of enduring worth. The strategic placing of his millions where they would create the greatest public interest and community activity was a great contribution to the welfare of people in this nation and abroad.

Although he put conditions on some of his offers, he seldom tied strings to his gifts. His outstanding contribution to the progress of philanthropy was the promulgation of his theory that perpetuities were harmful, and he kept up a persistent propaganda against the current practice of establishing perpetual endowments for charitable and educational institutions. He was firmly opposed to any effort at control of the future by the dead hand of the past. By virtue of his own example and his persistent preaching, he exerted a wide influence on other givers and prevented in many important instances the waste of great gifts because of the hampering restrictions which less thoughtful givers might have placed on them.

Rich men in Chicago came to fear his calls. One of his friends, in refusing an invitation to a luncheon, wrote that Rosenwald's luncheons usually cost too much money. But he was proud of his role of beggar for humanity and made strenuous efforts to induce others to give money to worthy causes. Once when he visited a very rich citizen of Chicago to ask for money for a large project, the man objected that he had not made money that year. "Well, give it out of last year's profits," Rosenwald replied. The man did not like that idea, and Rosenwald insisted: "But what possible difference can it make to you? It is only a figure on the books." He enjoyed getting money out of other people for causes almost as much as he did contributing himself, but there was no horse trading in his charity. He never said to a man that he would give to his charity if that man would give to one in which he was interested. His own interests soon came to be regarded as so important that it was easy to get others to attend a philanthropic function in Chicago, if it was known that he would be there.

Rosenwald was amused by the charge that came back to him once that he was practicing philanthropy for self-advertisement, and he told the man who brought the accusation that if he heard it again, he should reply that Rosenwald was too good a business man for that and could buy publicity much cheaper. He suggested that such people be told: "We have a lot of publicity to sell on your argument for much lower rates. How much are you going to buy?" Rosenwald believed in publicity for philan-

thropic gifts in order to stimulate others to give, and he was
opposed to anonymous gifts almost as much as he was to the
attempt to purchase immortality with charity. He steadfastly
refused to have his name attached permanently to institutions
to which he gave money.

## II

Julius Rosenwald was actively engaged in the acquisition of
wealth during the greatest period of American commercial expansion. Laissez faire economic principles were the rule, and
social consciousness was only beginning to be born as the opportunities of a pioneer civilization grew more constricted and
the inequities of an industrial civilization became more obvious.
In another connection, H. G. Wells has strikingly labeled the
four periods in world history which marked the boundaries of
Rosenwald's career: "The Imperialist Optimism of 1900"; "The
Futile Amazement of the Great War"; "The Self-Complacency of
the Fatuous Twenties"; and "The Frightened Thirties."[1]

During the eighteen-eighties, when Rosenwald came to maturity, the concentration of great wealth and the spread of social
unrest were simultaneous phenomena. He saw during his lifetime
the tremendous expansion of transportation and the great development of merchandising methods. He took part in an amazing number of the important movements and projects of that
period, and he tried hard to understand his duties and obligations in relation to them. His part was that of the practical business man, actively engaged in the industrial struggles of the
time, who had a social conscience which stimulated him to
use his money for humanitarian purposes. His business philosophy
was the rugged individualism of his contemporaries, and his
political principles were more nearly represented in national
affairs by those of the Republican Party than by any other group.

By the time of his death in 1932 it was evident that economic

[1] Wells, H. G., "Earth, Air and Mind." *Survey Graphic*, Dec., 1937.

expansion had reached a turning point, and that laissez faire principles in both industry and social welfare had become obsolete. Housing, medical care and educational opportunity were becoming increasingly impossible without state support. Rosenwald's own efforts had demonstrated clearly the need for such support in all three of these social endeavors. Toward the end of his life it seemed as if the era of tremendous personal fortune perhaps was closed. The railroads were built and consolidated; the natural resources were being consolidated as rapidly as they were exploited; industry was organized and finance coordinated; radio and air transportation, the newest big businesses, became quickly concentrated in control; mail order was largely in the hands of the two large houses, Sears, Roebuck and Co. and Montgomery Ward and Co. The days when large corporations were developed with enormous profits to their pioneers had given way to those in which millions of people were trying by means of stock ownership and speculation to participate in the continuous profits of corporate industry. The stock market collapse, in which he played a generous and dramatic part, was a symbol of impending change. The span of his life was a great one, and the scope of his interests enormous.

When he died, the usual moral about the young man of humble origin who had attained great wealth and renown by his efforts and thrift was not generally drawn in the editorial praise which came from all over the country. He himself had effectually forestalled this platitude by his insistence throughout his life that his own efforts were not the sole cause of his great wealth, and that a wealthy man was not necessarily a great one. He did not believe that every American boy could attain what he had, and he seldom lost an opportunity to stress the part that luck had played in his career.

Professor Charles S. Johnson said of him, "He taught self-emancipation, which embodies social growth and education, in the very act of sharing. . . . He was an apostle of social justice, but an apostle who never preached, nor who, indeed, had any faith in the magic of words alone for changing the deep convictions of men." Chief Justice William Howard Taft wrote in 1921: "Julius Rosenwald is a great national asset." Adolph S. Ochs, of the *New York Times,* wrote to him in 1912, on the occasion of his fiftieth birthday: "I know of no one else about whom so many people feel that they are glad he was born." On the occasion of his death, Representative A. J. Sabath, of Illinois, said on the floor of the House of Representatives: "I am certain that so long as philanthropy remains one of mankind's cardinal virtues, his name will be enshrined with those of the greatest benefactors of all time." Rosenwald himself was fond of remarking: "I have my generosity under complete control."

### III

William H. Herndon loaned Abraham Lincoln a biography of Edmund Burke in 1856. After reading a little here and there, Lincoln closed the book and threw it on the table with the exclamation: "No, I've read enough of it. It's like all the others. Biographies as generally written are not only misleading but false. The author of this life of Burke makes a wonderful hero out of his subject. He magnifies his perfections—if he had any— and suppresses his imperfections. He is so faithful in his zeal and so lavish in praise of his every act that one is almost driven to believe that Burke never made a mistake or a failure in his life." Herndon, in recording the incident, added: "He lapsed into a brown study, but presently broke out again, 'Billy, I've wondered why book-publishers and merchants don't have blank biographies on their shelves, always ready for an emergency; so that if a man happens to die, his heirs or his friends, if they wish to perpetuate his memory, can purchase one already written, but with blanks. These blanks they can at their pleasure fill up with rosy sentences full of high-sounding praise. In most instances they commemorate a lie, and cheat posterity out of the truth.' "

This book is an effort to establish the truth about Julius Rosenwald and his period. Those who worshiped him and those who criticized him may differ from some of my interpretations of his acts and motives. He himself would have been among the last to be interested in sycophantic eulogy. This book has been accomplished at the request of the Rosenwald family, with the financial subsidy of members of the family, and with their complete cooperation. The members of the family, however, have not dictated what should be included or what should be omitted from the book, and they are in no way responsible for any statements it contains. The sons and daughters of Julius Rosenwald have insisted from the first that they were more interested in a portrait of their father than in a purchased panegyric, which would only immure him in deadly platitude.

My thanks are due to Mrs. Adele R. Levy, Mrs. Edith R. Stern, Mrs. Marion R. Stern, Lessing J. Rosenwald and William Rosenwald, the children of Julius Rosenwald, for their interest, aid and cooperation. I am also indebted to Dr. David M. Levy, Mr. Edgar B. Stern and Mrs. Lessing J. Rosenwald for much valuable aid. Mr. Nathan W. Levin, Mr. A. C. Roebuck, Mr. Edwin R. Embree and Mr. Leonard M. Rieser have been of invaluable assistance, as have also innumerable employees of Sears, Roebuck and Co. and of the Rosenwald family, as well as the host of friends and admirers whom Julius Rosenwald gained during his lifetime.

M. R. W.

# PART 1
# BEFORE THE WAR

## CHAPTER I

# SMALL TOWN

I

JULIUS ROSENWALD was born on August 12, 1862, at Springfield, Illinois, where his father, Samuel Rosenwald, and his mother, Augusta Hammerslough Rosenwald had settled after some years of traveling in search of business opportunity.

Samuel Rosenwald arrived at the port of Baltimore on May 12, 1854, on the *Wilhemine* from Bünde, Westphalia, Germany, where he was born on June 18, 1828. He was the second of four sons of Bendix and Vogel Frankfurter Rosenwald. The children were educated at the Hebrew school in the village of Bünde, where their parents kept a small general store, selling clothing and household wares.

While Samuel Rosenwald was growing up, the town of Bünde was declining in economic importance. The flax and linen trades which had been carried on there were diminishing, and the machine was displacing weaving by hand. Some relatives maintained that Samuel left Germany because he hated military service, and that he had served several weeks in the army before emigrating. Others said that he had served five years of military service and hated German militarism ever afterwards. It is likely, however, that he emigrated primarily because of the lack of economic opportunities. His father had died when he was a child, and his mother was trying to support her family on the meager proceeds of her small shop. In the year 1854, when Samuel arrived, 427,833 immigrants poured into the ports of the United

States. The number was unprecedented and was twice as large as the number that arrived in the following year. The Crimean War, a dearth in Europe's food supply, and a falling off in manufactures were considered the main causes of this extraordinary exodus.

When he arrived at the port of Baltimore, he was twenty-six years old and was listed on the ship's manifest as a merchant. He had a total capital of twenty dollars, and he became a peddler on the old Winchester trail in Virginia. Many years later his son Julius heard some important business associates mention Winchester. He looked at them thoughtfully and remarked, "I've heard that name somewhere," and then after a moment of reflection, added: "Oh, yes, that is where my father was a peddler." According to a traditional family tale, Samuel remained a peddler until he could buy a horse and wagon for his work. Then, in about 1856, he became associated with the Hammerslough brothers, who had been in the clothing business in Baltimore for about ten years.

The four Hammerslough brothers had besides their Baltimore headquarters, a clothing establishment in Springfield, Illinois, and connections in New York City. Samuel Rosenwald married their sister Augusta, a short, amiable, affectionate girl. And in September, 1857, a month after their wedding, he became manager of the "Baltimore Clothing House," in Peoria, Illinois, which his brothers-in-law had established in the previous spring.

Augusta Hammerslough was born in the village of Bederkäse, near Bremerhaven, Germany, on July 20, 1833. Her father owned a small shop there, and, like the Rosenwalds in Bünde, lived with his family back of the store. The Hammerslough sons began emigrating to the United States as soon as each boy became thirteen years old, and they settled first in Baltimore, where they had distant relatives. Augusta joined her brothers in 1853, when she was twenty years old. She traveled in a sailing vessel, which took seventy-seven days to make the journey, and she often told her children of the perils and discomforts of a trans-Atlantic journey in those days.

Those fugitives from the defeat of liberalism in Europe in 1848 and from the economic constriction which followed the revolutions of that year enjoyed a peculiar advantage over the immigrants who had preceded them and over the men and women who were to follow. The spade work involved in laying the foundations of American prosperity was far advanced. Politically, the nation was formed, and though its greatest struggle for unity was to come within a few years in the form of civil war, the republican base was firm. Economically, the United States had developed vastly in the seventy-five years between the end of the American Revolution and the beginning of the Civil War. Land was being cleared and sold in huge tracts. President Franklin Pierce noted in his message to Congress in 1854 that six million more acres had been sold in that year than in the previous one. There was much land still to be cleared and many railway lines to be laid, but there were already numerous opportunities in the small towns which were growing rapidly into cities and in the villages which were becoming towns. Jewish merchants, who still found their privileges restricted in many parts of Europe, could thrive with a minimum of social prejudice in the cities of the East and in the new settlements of the Middle West and the Southwest. Most of them, like Samuel Rosenwald, had slight resources, and they had to exercise strict economy, but they could breathe freely and expand widely in a vast country which needed them and which they needed. Those who followed in the eighteen-eighties, nineties and early nineteen-hundreds found the land more restricted and the need for capital greater.

Augusta's first child was born in Peoria and died in infancy. The Peoria clothing store was sold out not long after and the

Hammersloughs sent Samuel and Augusta to Talladega, Alabama, in 1860. Their first son, Benjamin, was born there on July 23, 1860. They disliked Talladega because of the heat, the vermin and slavery, and they moved to Evansville, Indiana, later in 1860. The Hammersloughs established the Oak Hall Clothing House in Evansville in the name of S. Rosenwald & Co., and they advertised a new stock of clothing, gents' furnishings, hats and caps, trunks, boots and shoes. On May 16, 1861, about a month after the Civil War broke out, they had the following advertisement in the Evansville *Daily Journal*:

> Never behind the Times: As good money is very scarce at present S. Rosenwald & Co., at the Oak Hall Clothing House, No. 73 Main Street, informs the public that he is willing to take Illinois and Wisconsin money at a very small discount. We have a very large and extensive stock of ready made clothing and gents' furnishing goods which have to be disposed of in a very short time. This is a very good opportunity for those who have any of this money to get rid of it.

This was not a false sale. Samuel Rosenwald had to get rid of his goods in a short time, for the Hammersloughs needed him in their Springfield establishment, where they had begun to do a rushing business in uniforms for the troops. In the early summer of 1861 he closed the Evansville store and moved his family to Springfield.

The Civil War changed the clothing business in the United States from a minor trade to a large-scale industry. At first the government could not get enough uniforms in the United States and had to buy some of them in Prague and Vienna, but soon shops were set up by the government and by private industry to fill the large war orders. Workers began to pour into factories from tenements, and to work on the clothing in their sweatshop rooms.

II

In 1860 Springfield had a population of 9,320. It was situated on a beautiful prairie in fertile Sangamon County, where the corn crop was famous, and the town was becoming an important packing center for hogs. By 1856, when the Hammersloughs established the "Capitol Clothing House" on the north side of Capitol Square, Springfield had enjoyed railroad facilities for only seven years. There were twenty-three dry goods stores in the town, and trade was bad until the outbreak of the Civil War. Competition was strenuous and the Hammersloughs advertised their clothing intensively in the local newspapers; they hooked up the comet of 1857, the coming of the circus, and the gold rush to Pike's Peak with their goods.

President Lincoln called for 75,000 volunteers on April 16, 1861, and troops began to congregate in Springfield. The change in trade during 1861 was illustrated in the diary of John Edward Young, a farmer in Menard County, who went to market frequently in Springfield during the Civil War years:[1]

April 3 (1861). . . . Came home from Springfield this evening Business is very dull. A number of our banks are throwen out by the broakers and are uncurrent. This makes business men catious and suspicious.

July 20. . . . Stoped in Springfield three or four hours. Business lively and the town full of people and teames. The Menard company of soldiers went up to camp Buttler yesterday. This company numbers about 90 men.

Sept. 13. . . . Father & I went to Springfield with fruit got $1.25 per bus. for Pears and 60 cts for Peaches and 30 for Apples. Trade is pretty lively and people are beginning to gain confidence in each other and look to the future with more confidence.

Nov. 12. . . . I don't think that I have ever seen so fine a fall for business.

The Hammersloughs announced on July 26, 1862, in the *Illinois State Journal*, that they had built an addition to their store

[1] Journal of John Edward Young in the *Journal of the Illinois State Historical Society*, vol. 26, pp. 70-135.

because of increased business and to accommodate a new custom clothing department. "Officers and other military men," the notice said, "would do well to give them a call, as they have a splendid stock of military clothes, etc. which they are prepared to make up at the shortest notice."

By that time Samuel Rosenwald had moved from the Chenery House into the home at Seventh and Jackson Streets, one block west of the home of Abraham Lincoln. In this house on August 12, 1862, his second son, Julius, was born.

In August, 1863, the first anniversary of Julius Rosenwald's birth, the Hammersloughs were advertising that they had received their "first arrival of goods *direct from France*, purchased by our *Edw. Hammerslough*, now at Paris. . . ." Their competitors retaliated with the notice that they did not bother to send a man to Paris, for American goods were good enough for them. In March, 1864, the firm announced that it had had the honor to fit out the noble 10th Illinois Cavalry "from top to toe," and on April 16 they advertised: "Their military trade has assumed a fabulous dimension; their names are known to all the western armies, by each corps, division and by most every soldier."

Farmer Young noted in his diary that same spring of 1864: "War news and the troubles of the country seem to engross the whole attention of the people. They can think of nothing else they can talk of nothing else, either young or old." But he also noted that he got seventy-five cents a bushel for apples, which had been a drug on the market in the previous year, and he was buying government bonds and collecting five per cent interest on them in gold.

On April 10, 1865, Farmer Young noted the universal joy and excitement in the North at the news of Grant's capture of Lee's army. There was equally universal gloom in the North the next week at the news of Lincoln's assassination.

Hammerslough Bros. offered in May, 1865, "thirty thousand

mourning badges to be wholesaled at manufacturers' prices" for Abraham Lincoln's funeral in Springfield. On May 8 the store "was tastefully draped in black and white and underneath a portrait of Lincoln was the motto: 'Millions bless thy name.'" Julius Hammerslough who had been acquainted with Lincoln in Springfield, took an active part in the movement to raise a monument to the President there, and he made an appeal for funds to the Jews of the town.[2]

In September, 1866, the Hammersloughs advertised that they were manufacturing their own goods in the East and were prepared to sell both wholesale and retail clothing from their large stock. The firm announced in April, 1867, that Mr. Rosenwald, a member of the firm, had just returned from New York with a large, well selected stock of fine cassimeres, children's clothing, etc. By this time Samuel was making two trips a year to New York, and the firm was buying bankrupt stock of other clothing merchants in Springfield. An old document shows that total sales of the Hammerslough business in 1865 had been $280,473.

The *Illinois State Journal* for March 29, 1868, announced the dissolution of the partnership of Hammerslough Bros., and that Samuel Rosenwald was the firm's successor, effective February 1, 1868. The notice stated that he had purchased the entire interest of Messrs. Julius, Louis and Edward Hammerslough, and thereafter the firm advertised under the name of S. Rosenwald, "The C.O.D., one-price clothier." When the Springfield Board of Trade was organized on July 13, 1869, to promote Springfield, Samuel was a charter member and a member of the Committee on Trade and Commerce. His balance sheet for February 1, 1869, showed that his business was worth $32,866. He wrote to his German relatives who were still living in Bünde on February 15, 1872:

I have to do a very large business to meet my expenses. In the first

[2] "Lincoln and the Jews," by Isaac Markens in American Jewish Historical Society Publications, No. 17, 1909, pp. 128-129.

place it costs me $3,000 for my small family. May God keep them all well. My expenses for the store are approximately $4,000. That has to be earned. And if one does not make a fairly good business one has soon lost out. But really I must not complain. If God continues to grant me his blessing everything will be all right.

Samuel and Augusta had a family of six surviving children. There were four sons, Benjamin, Julius, Morris and Louis, and two daughters, Selma and Sophie.

### III

"I remember as a boy watching the wagons of the early pioneers going through Springfield on their long journey west," Julius Rosenwald wrote in 1929. He attended the Fourth Ward School at the age of six. As he grew older, he waited on customers in his father's store on Saturdays, selling paper collars, which, he remembered, almost everyone wore. He carried satchels for travelers and earned twenty-five cents in the paper money of the time for pumping the organ in the Congregational Church. Occasionally, he earned small sums working for the circus.

On October 15, 1874, the monument erected in memory of Abraham Lincoln at Springfield was unveiled. An advertisement appeared the day before in the *Illinois State Journal* which read: "Wanted 199 live active energetic boys to sell The Illustrated Description of the Lincoln Monument. Call at the offices of the publishers at 9 o'clock this morning. Edwin A. Wilson & Company. Monroe St. near Sixth." Julius was one of the small boys— he was then 12 years old—who sold these pamphlets, and he remembered in later years that he earned $2.25 on that historic occasion. He also remembered that President Grant was there for the dedication. "I remember seeing him in an open barouche and, in shaking hands with him, I was particularly impressed because he had on yellow kid gloves. He was the first man I ever saw who wore kid gloves."

In his spare time Julius also went from house to house selling lithographic chromos, which were new at the time. When he was fifteen, he worked during the summer vacation in the "Boston 99¢ Store" operated by C. W. Squires and received $2.50 a week as an errand boy and salesman. He managed to save about twenty dollars during his summer of work, and he and his brother bought their parents a china tea set on their twentieth wedding anniversary. One of Rosenwald's old friends recalled that he had told her that when he was a boy he felt so sorry for his cheerful little mother because she had to spend so many hours at the ironing board, that he used to pull the shirts from under the ironing board under the impression that he was lessening her chores. He used to tell his mother that when he grew up he wanted to make money so that she could have all the luxuries possible.

Meanwhile, the clothing store was prospering steadily. Samuel Rosenwald took another floor in the building he occupied and then moved to larger quarters on the west side of the square in September, 1876. He had also bought in 1869 a residence on Eighth and Jackson Streets, opposite the Lincoln home. Writing to relatives in Germany on December 11, 1880, Samuel told them that what was needed for his business was a cold and dry winter. He wrote that his profit was usually 30 to 33-1/3 per cent. "But if one has six children," he added, "and wants to educate them that also costs something. I am writing you this so that you may see that we have enough to live on. It has taken a long time, and my dear wife and I have been very economical; otherwise we would not have gotten so far."

In another letter to the family in Germany, he wrote on June 23, 1881:

I quite forgot that you wanted to be exactly informed about the Jewish question, although there is not much *Riches* [anti-Semitic prejudice] here, yet we are not on the same level with the Christians, especially since one reads so much in the papers about Russia. In business one hardly ever hears anything like that, but the children often hear about it, and that is unpleasant enough. That is all that I want to write now.

Samuel Rosenwald took part in the Jewish life of the community. He was a trustee of Emes Lodge of the Independent Order B'nai B'rith, and he was president of the B'rith Sholem Congregation from 1867 to 1873, and after that became vice-president of the building committee for a new synagogue, which was dedicated with ceremony in 1876. The congregation had previously worshiped since 1858 in a rented room on the third floor of an old building. The chairman of the building committee, B. A. Lange, in a speech at the dedication of the new synagogue said that the reason it had taken so long to establish a permanent building was that "the more rational members of our congregation were unwilling to contribute even a dollar toward building unless they had the guarantee that this new Temple should be devoted to worshiping our Heavenly Father, not in the orthodox, but in the reformed style which alone would satisfy them and their children, and which alone could instill into their minds a renewed interest in Jewish matters."

In a speech which he delivered on November 26, 1920, at a meeting of the Union of American Hebrew Congregations in Cleveland, Julius Rosenwald said:

Even though not a student of the subject of religion—I might lay claim to being especially consecrated to the Jewish faith because not only was I *Barmitzvahed* at 13, but it so happened a year later our congregation in Springfield, Illinois, dedicated a new reform Temple with confirmation exercises and I was also confirmed.

He added at that time that though his mother said her prayers in English almost every day, "my parents were not at all Orthodox as we understood that term."

Augusta Rosenwald took part in the German and Jewish charitable enterprises of the small town, and was an active member of the Ladies' Benevolent Society, which sewed for the unemployed during one of the hard winters of the early eighteen-eighties. She was a woman with strong family affection and a set Teutonic character. She was not a woman of the world, any more than her husband was a man of the world. Moses Newborg, one of Julius Rosenwald's early friends, described Samuel as: "A typical, upright, principled, hard-working successful small town merchant." Augusta was a warm, lovable person with an intuitive understanding and a delightful sense of humor. She had shared her husband's local problems, and in later years she proudly accepted her Jule's more national splendor. His love for this little old woman was strong. He was frankly sentimental about her and proudly proclaimed her to acquaintances and newspaper interviewers. His early letters to his wife always contained injunctions to show them to his mother.

Julius attended the high school in Springfield for about two years, and then in 1879 he went to New York City to serve an apprenticeship in the clothing business with his uncles, the Hammersloughs, who were then among the leading clothing merchants of New York. On the occasion of his fiftieth birthday anniversary, he said: "I have often regretted that I was deprived of a college education." This lack was, perhaps, one reason for his great respect for those who could write books, or even good letters, and who engaged in educational or other intellectual pursuits. In spite of his limited opportunities for education, however, Julius Rosenwald's letters indicate that he had, throughout his lifetime, an easy command of a vigorous style for the expression of his own ideas and for the criticism of the many projects presented to him.

IV

While Julius was a boy, the discontent of the farmers was increasing throughout the country and was particularly prevalent in Illinois. They were beginning to complain bitterly of the low prices paid for their farm produce and the high prices charged for the goods which they had to buy. The farmer knew that the railroads were discriminating against him by giving the expanding trusts special rebates and cut rates, while the farmers and small merchants were charged all that the traffic could bear. Getting no satisfaction from the Republican Party, in power, or the Democratic Party, seeking power, the farmers determined to organize for the promotion of their rights and formed the Order of Patrons of Husbandry, better known as the Grange.

The Grange movement was a combination lobbying organization, cooperative buying association, fraternal secret order and political party. It had its degrees, like the Masons, and it had its representatives in manufacturing centers for the purchase of goods, as well as its agents in legislative halls. One of the great efforts of the Grange was to educate the farmers to pay cash for their manufactured goods whenever possible and thus get cheaper prices. Exorbitant prices on reapers, threshers, wagons, sewing machines and other farm and home equipment were thus forced down.

The Civil War had taught the American people to think nationally and to organize on national lines, and policies adopted during the war and units organized for its prosecution had remained after the war was ended. The currency, the banks, the railroads, and labor had begun to be organized on a national rather than a local basis. One of those who was thinking in national terms with the specific purpose of satisfying the farmer's demand for goods was A. Montgomery Ward, a native of Chatham, New Jersey. Ward had been born there on February 17, 1844, the descendant of Captain Israel Ward, who had fought under General Washington in the colonial and Revolutionary wars. In 1865, when Julius Rosenwald was three years old, A. Montgomery Ward went to Chicago, where he worked for Field, Palmer & Leiter, later Marshall Field & Company, for a salary of $600 a year. Then he went into the wholesale dry goods business and later became a traveling salesman. While traveling as a dry goods salesman and buyer of merchandise, he learned the farmer's needs and ways. He also came in contact with the growing Grange movements.

Ward thought that a merchandising house which sold its goods through the mail by means of a catalogue and circulars would prove successful, especially among the farmers. He talked over his idea with his brother-in-law, George R. Thorne, of Kalamazoo, Michigan, who liked it so much that they decided to go into partnership. As they were getting ready to start their mail-order house in Chicago the great fire of 1871 occurred, and Montgomery Ward lost almost everything he possessed. He came out of the fire with sixty-five dollars. By early spring of 1872, however, he and Thorne had managed to scrape together $2,400. They started Montgomery Ward and Co. in a room twelve by fourteen at 825 North Clark Street, Chicago. They purchased a small stock of goods and issued a sheet eight by twelve inches offering those goods for sale. There were about fifty items in this price list, which all sold for one dollar or less. Soon they obtained permission to advertise themselves as the "Original Grange Supply House" and received the recommendation of the National Grange to its members. Ward and Thorne addressed Grange meetings and explained their new mail-order plan to farmers. Mailing their short list to a small number of farmers, they quickly sold out all of their merchandise for cash. During the first two months the two partners did everything themselves, buying goods, unpacking merchandise, preparing advertising, and shipping the goods. Their business increased so rapidly that in the following year, 1873, they had to move to larger quarters. By 1875 they were issuing a seventy-two page catalogue with a few woodcuts, including a "Grange" hat, a bed spring, a farm wagon and a line of trunks and valises. This catalogue guaranteed that money would be refunded if the customer was not satisfied. In 1876 Montgomery Ward and Co. issued a catalogue of 152 pages, and the firm had to move to still larger quarters. Montgomery Ward and Co., early in its career, operated a private railroad car with a troupe of entertainers, consisting of two or three minstrels, a clog dancer and a singer. The train stopped at small towns, gave a free entertainment and a lecture on the company and the advantages of mail order. The catalogue was then distributed. This advertising was later discontinued because it was considered undignified.

Some of the arguments used by Montgomery Ward in the effort to sell the farmers the new idea were these: "We don't pay Forty Thousand a year Rent. . . . We don't sell Goods to Country Retailers on six months' time. We buy for Cash and sell for Cash. . . . We don't employ any middleman to sell our Goods." The farmers were permitted to order the goods, open them after they arrived by express, and if they were not satisfied, they could decline the shipment. The company also offered to sell grain for them.[3]

While Julius Rosenwald was finishing his schooling and Montgomery Ward was developing his mail-order business, a young boy named Richard Sears was learning telegraphy and working on the railroad in Minnesota. Another boy, A. C. Roebuck, was beginning to learn how to clean and repair watches in his birthplace, Lafayette, Indiana.

[3] *The Centennial History of Illinois,* vol. IV, "The Industrial Estate," 1870-1893, by Ernest Ludlow Bogart and Charles M. Thompson. Chapter IV, "The Farmers' Movement."

## CHAPTER II

## CLOTHING MERCHANT

### I

JULIUS ROSENWALD arrived in New York on March 15, 1879, and went to live with his uncle, Edward Hammerslough. He wrote many years later of his mother's family: "They all lived in much finer surroundings than I had been accustomed to." The town was busy, active, noisy with the clatter of horses' hoofs and the clang of horsecars up and down Broadway and the Bowery. More than a million people worked, struggled and enjoyed themselves in Manhattan alone, and another half million occupied Brooklyn across the East River.

Rosenwald went to work as a stock boy for his uncles, at a salary of $5 a week. On Saturday nights he worked in Rogers, Peet & Company's store at Broome Street and Broadway and earned an extra $2. He also worked in his spare time for Carhart, Whitford & Company, retail clothiers at Canal Street and Broadway. After he had learned the trade, he sold goods for the Hammersloughs, in suburban towns near New York.

Moses Newborg, a friend of his at this time, related that he, Rosenwald and their young friends used to enjoy themselves after work at Tony Pastor's variety theater and other vaudeville shows in the cheap seats. Among his other friends besides Moses Newborg, whose father sold Rosenwald's father clothing, were Henry Goldman, later head of Goldman, Sachs and Company, bankers, and Henry Morgenthau, later a lawyer, financier and ambassador.

While Rosenwald was learning the clothing business, the

United States was passing through the greatest wave of prosperity
it had ever had. The crop of 1879 was the largest ever raised in
the United States, and that of Europe was one of the worst on
record. Gold began to pour into this country, and the United
States had in the year 1879 the most favorable balance of trade
in its history up to that time, $264,661,666. There was a sanguine
feeling in the air, and men were beginning to forget the terrible
conditions during the panic of 1873. Prices soon rose, and labor
became dissatisfied with its share in the economy. But the middle
classes had more money than at any time since the Civil War,
and life was gay and carefree in the Hammerslough household
and among their prospering middle class friends and relatives.
Rapid development of industrial methods and agricultural settlement went hand in hand with financial speculation, monopoliza-
tion of natural resources and political corruption. Land granted
to settlers stimulated the development of the West, and the
farmer, the miner and the cattle raiser were followed closely by
the commercial traveler. Towns sprang up quickly, and obscure
villages grew in abundance. Exports of grains and food stuffs
and cattle increased amazingly, and the demands for new machinery, materials and merchandise increased accordingly. Two
million immigrants from Europe came into the United States between 1860 and 1870, and another two and a half million arrived
in the following decade. New inventions were effective and
numerous. The farmers, however, complained of the low prices
they received for their products and the workers of the low wages
they received for their labor.

With the spread of monopoly in some means of transportation
and in various natural resources, organizations developed by
which the farmers and the workingmen attempted to protect
themselves. A series of great strikes broke out on the railroads,
in the steel industry and in the clothing trade. Political movements in the interests of the unprivileged spread throughout the

country. Socialists, Populists, Greenbackers, Knights of Labor, Single-Taxers and Anarchists found men willing, at least, to listen to them.

There were few philanthropists in those days, for the money later to be used lavishly for philanthropy was being acquired painstakingly by energy, ingenuity, and sometimes fraud, while labor was being exploited to the limit of its endurance.

While Rosenwald was engaged in his apprenticeship in the clothing business, parts of New York were transformed by the huge influx of Russian Jews, who poured into the harbor after the ruthless pogroms in Russia, following the assassination of Tsar Alexander II in 1881. His successor, Tsar Alexander III, inaugurated a fierce reaction from the more liberal rule of his father, and the prime political scapegoat of the government was the defenseless Russian Jew. The pogroms of 1881 had deprived hundreds of Russian Jews of their lives, and the May laws of 1882 deprived all of them of freedom of movement and freedom of property ownership. Between 1882 and 1887, 89,097 Russian Jews arrived in the United States, and most of them congregated, at least in the beginning, in New York City.

The Jews who arrived in New York had little money, little technical training and lacked the physique for manual labor. They turned naturally to the growing clothing industry, which required less capital than heavy industry and less skill than many other forms of manufacturing. No huge machinery was needed, and the quarters for the manufacture could be located almost anywhere, for there were no rules of sanitation and no labor standards. Some immigrants became cigar manufacturers under similar conditions. The Russian immigrants rapidly became the laborers in the sweatshops and garment rooms, while their German predecessors, who had accumulated some capital, became the jobbers and retail distributors of the clothing which the more recent immigrants made. During the eighteen-eighties in the clothing industry a man and his entire family working twelve to fifteen hours a day averaged $15 to $20 a week.[1]

The clothing business, as we have seen, received its great impetus from the large government orders for uniforms during the Civil War. During the war statistics were gathered on standard style sizes while soldiers were being measured. It was noticed that men who had a certain size chest usually had another certain size waist and legs, and that fat men and thin men had definite standards of size and weight. With this great accumulation of data on sizes, garments could be made in standardized quantities and sold in various markets. Division of labor, with lower production costs and lower prices for goods, followed quickly. After the war, manufacturers began to make ready-made clothing on a large scale and ship it everywhere on the extending railways. The hundreds of thousands of returned soldiers needed civilian clothes at once and created a huge demand. In 1872 a steam driven cloth-cutting machine was introduced by two mechanics, Albion and Wurth, in their factory on Staten Island.[2] Elias Howe had invented the sewing machine in 1846, and Isaak M. Singer had perfected it in 1851. These inventions and later developments of them increased tremendously the scope of the clothing trade.

II

Julius Rosenwald, whose relatives had gradually risen from peddling to retail trading and wholesale clothing manufacture, stepped into the status of clothing merchant himself, with the aid of his father's capital and his uncles' experience, not long after he had served his apprenticeship in New York. In 1884 he and his younger brother Morris, who had joined him in New York, started a business of their own at 24 Fourth Avenue between 6th and 7th Streets and lived together at 337 East 19th

[1] Report of the U. S. Senate, Committee on Education and Labor, 1885, I, pp. 421, 751.

[2] Humphrey, Edward F. *An Economic History of the United States,* p. 332.

Street. The firm name was J. Rosenwald & Bro. With their father's assistance the two young men had purchased the small clothing and tailoring business of Phillips and Van Derbugle. Their shop was a few doors south of Brokaw Brothers, who had the finest retail clothing establishment in the city at that time. It was Rosenwald's idea that if they opened a shop next to Brokaw Brothers they would get the overflow trade of the larger house.

At the end of May, 1884, their mother and father came to New York on their way to Germany, the first opportunity for thirty years they had to visit their relatives in that country.

There was a severe depression of short duration during 1884 and 1885, and Rosenwald and his brother were caught in its clutches soon after they opened their dark and narrow shop. The report of the United States Industrial Commission showed that in that year stocks fell from an index number of 112 to 75; there was a heavy decline in bank clearings, and a slight decline in bank loans.

While he was trying unsuccessfully to operate his own clothing business, Rosenwald had occasion to buy summer clothing from Alfred Benjamin & Co., who were large manufacturers of seersucker and alpaca garments. In some biographical notes which he dictated in 1927 he said:

One of the partners remarked to me that they had received over sixty telegrams for goods that day which they were unable to supply and that the demand was increasing constantly for such goods as they were supplying. I did not give it much thought at the moment, but during the night I awakened and thought of what he had told me and the opportunity entered my mind of embarking in the same sort of business. The idea took such hold of me that there was no more sleep that night for me and the next morning I presented my plan to my uncles who thought it might be a capital idea to open a business for the manufacture of summer clothing in Chicago. My cousin, Julius E. Weil, was employed in the manufacturing department of my uncles' business and together we planned to go to Chicago and begin the manufacturing of summer clothing. After several months planning he and I left for Chicago toward the end of

September, 1885, and rented a second floor loft in the Farwell Block, 185 Market Street, October 1st.

The two Rosenwald brothers and their cousin lived in one room at the Matteson House in Chicago when they went there to establish their business. Samuel Rosenwald put up $2,000 and Julius Weil's father put up $2,000 to finance the new Chicago clothing firm of Rosenwald & Weil. Their uncles, the Hammersloughs, gave the young men credit and guaranteed their purchases with other firms.

Chicago, by the time Rosenwald started in business there in 1885, was in the full exuberance of its reconstruction after the disastrous fire of 1871. Tall buildings, America's first skyscrapers, were rising rapidly. A new city hall and a new court house were being built. The Art Institute had opened its galleries one year before. The McCormicks, the Cranes, and Marshall Field were flourishing. Laborers were demanding the eight-hour day. Charles E. Yerkes was getting a strangle-hold on the city's transportation system. Carter Harrison, Sr., had been elected mayor for the fourth time in the previous April by 375 votes. The city had a population of 665,000, a real estate valuation of $107,146,882. Cable cars were authorized shortly afterwards, and electric street lights were planned within the city limits. Large hotels and mansions in imitation of the architectural styles of foreign cities were interspersed between rows of stolid dwellings with bay windows, towers and iron fences. Iron, steel, lumber, meat-packing, brick-making, railroad cars and equipment, distilled liquors, flour and grist mill products, clothing, carriages and wagons, soaps and candles and agricultural implements were being turned out in huge quantities. Illinois had great natural resources of its own, and by virtue of the quick development of Chicago as the railroad center of the country, it was in a position to draw on the huge raw materials of the West and the Northwest. Within a night's ride of Chicago on the railroads there was a population of forty million people.

Other young men had recently settled in Chicago who were to become important in the city's future development, when Rosenwald arrived there. The Rev. Jenkin Lloyd-Jones, pastor of All Souls' Church, a leading intellectual of the period, had recently taken in his young nephew, Frank Lloyd Wright, who had run away from his Wisconsin home to become an architect. Louis H. Sullivan and Dankmar Adler were planning the Chicago Auditorium, a combined theater, hotel and office building as a commission for Ferdinand W. Peck, who wanted to give performances of opera there. Daniel H. Burnham, the big business man of architecture, was developing contacts and putting up buildings together with his partner John Root. Rabbi Emil G. Hirsch and Jane Addams were meeting occasionally at the Rev. Jenkin Lloyd-Jones's house to discuss social problems. Theodore Thomas was giving concerts in the old Exposition Building, which Frank Lloyd Wright in his reminiscences called "a rank, much-domed yellow shed on the lake front." What Wright called "General Grant Gothic" was the prevailing mode of architecture of the period. Wright in his autobiography gave this picture of the city at the time:

Chicago. Wells Street Station: Six o'clock in late Spring, 1887. Drizzling. Sputtering white arc-lights in the station and in the streets, dazzling and ugly. I had never seen electric lights before.

Crowds. Impersonal, intent on seeing nothing.

Somehow I didn't like to ask anyone anything. Followed the crowd.

Drifted south to the Wells Street Bridge over the Chicago River. The mysterious dark of the river with dim masts, hulks, and funnels hung with lights half-smothered in gloom—reflected in the black beneath. I stopped to see, holding myself close to the iron rail to avoid the blind hurrying by.

I wondered where Chicago was—if it was near. Suddenly the clanging of a bell. The crowd began to run. I wondered why: found myself alone and realized why in time to get off but stayed on as the bridge swung out with me into the channel and a tug, puffing clouds of steam, came pushing along below, pulling at an enormous iron grain boat, towing it slowly along through the gap. . . .

Drifted south.

This must be Chicago now. So cold, black, blue-white and wet.

The horrid blue-white glare of arc-lights was over everything. . . .

Chicago! Immense gridiron of noisy streets. Dirty. . . . Heavy traffic crossing both ways at once, managing somehow: Torrential noise. . . .

A wide, desolate, vacant strip ran along the water front over which the Illinois Central trains incessantly puffed and ground, cutting the city off from the lake.

Terrible, this grinding and piling up of blind forces. If there was logic here who could grasp it?

To stop and think in the midst of this would be to give way to terror. The gray, soiled river with its mists of steam and smoke, was the only beauty. That smelled to heaven.[3]

Another sensitive architect, Louis H. Sullivan, described the spirit of the city at the time in these words:

For "Big" was the word. "Biggest" was preferred, and the "biggest in the world" was the braggart phrase on every tongue. Chicago had the biggest conflagration "in the world." It was the biggest grain and lumber market "in the world." It slaughtered more hogs than any city "in the world." It was the greatest railroad center, the greatest this, and the greatest that. It shouted itself hoarse in *reclame*. The shouters could not well be classed with the proverbial liars of Ecclesiastes, because what they said was true; and had they said, in the din, we are the crudest, rawest, most savagely ambitious dreamers and would-be doers in the world, that also might be true. For with much gloating of self-flattering they bragged: "We are the most heavily mortgaged city in the world." . . .[4]

Edgar Lee Masters, lawyer, poet, novelist and historian of the city, wrote of its builders:

These men of New York and New England, who were the pioneer fathers of Chicago, created that phase of the city which is swift and hard, executive and tireless, ambitious and selfish, but also public spirited and philanthropic, moralistic, censorious, exclusive and proud, given at times to witch hunting and mob appeals to the laws, and possessed of an unquenchable desire to rule and to shape the destinies of a people.[5]

[3] Wright, Frank Lloyd. *An Autobiography*, pp. 63-66. (1932)
[4] Sullivan, Louis H. *The Autobiography of an Idea*, pp. 200-201. (1926)
[5] *The Tale of Chicago*, p. 85.

Chicago had the largest men's clothing manufacturing firm in the United States and about one hundred factories and jobbing houses dealing in men's and boys' clothing during the period when Rosenwald established himself there. The sales of these establishments extended into Ohio and Michigan and to the Far West, the Northwest and the Southwest. A plentiful supply of sweatshop labor was pouring into the vibrant city.

Mrs. T. J. Morgan, a trade-union worker of Chicago, testified before a Senate Committee that men, women and children were employed by clothing contractors for not less than ten hours a day, and some worked eighteen hours in rooms about six by eight feet. About a dozen persons, on an average, worked together in these sweat shops. In one place in West Division Street she had found 39 girls, 11 men and 12 children employed in a room ten by forty, which was also occupied as living quarters by the clothing contractor and his wife. Cooking and sleeping went on in the same rooms. After working hours, which lasted far into the night, beds were made on the floor. The men, Mrs. Morgan testified, averaged $6 to $10 per week, the women $5.40 per week and the children $2. These wages were the highest she had found. Some were Russian Jews, some were Italians, a few Irish and some Germans. Other witnesses, clothing contractors themselves, testified to the same effect.[6]

Practically all the ready-made clothing manufacturers of the United States, located in the cities of New York, Chicago, Boston and Baltimore gave out garments on contracts at a specified price per garment to men who had their workshops in tenements and other primitive workrooms, where immigrant labor sewed the garments, sometimes by hand, and sometimes by sewing machines. Later some of the larger manufacturers established factories of their own with fair sanitary conditions. Rosenwald &

[6] *Investigation of the Sweating System.* U. S. Senate, Subcommittee of the Committee on Manufactures. March, 1892.

Weil, a smaller firm, naturally conducted their trade in the manner of their competitors, and competition was fierce.

Conditions in the cigar industry, the stockyards and other large and small industries were not, on the whole, much better than in the clothing business. A large majority of the population, foreign-born, performed the labor for a minority of men with capital and enterprise, most of them native-born, who felt that they had made the city and owned it.

In May, 1886, 80,000 men in Chicago went on strike, demanding the eight-hour day. On May 4, 1886, a bomb was hurled at a demonstration meeting in Haymarket Square, which not only killed a police sergeant and injured about sixty persons, but destroyed the eight-hour movement for some years. The police were accused of interfering with the meeting, and seven alleged Anarchists were arrested charged with complicity in the bombing. The press became hysterical and the police force dominant, while there was an approach to panic among the citizens. The sentiment whipped up against labor by the Haymarket affair and the ensuing trial and conviction of the Anarchists set the growing organized labor movement back many years and provided a large pool of docile labor for expanding industry.

Meanwhile, the two Rosenwald brothers and their cousin Julius Weil tried hard to make a living. In Springfield, Illinois, Samuel Rosenwald advertised his merchandise for final sale in November, 1885, preparatory to joining his sons in Chicago. The family took a house at 3233 Wabash Avenue, and their sons and nephew lived there with them.

A short distance away, on Wabash Avenue, lived Augusta Nusbaum, an attractive girl from Plattsburg, New York. She had been born there on December 27, 1869, and had come to Chicago with her family. Emanuel Nusbaum, her father, entered the clothing business in Chicago. She and Julius Rosenwald became engaged on January 6, 1890, and were married on the following April 8. Mrs. Rosenwald from the beginning of her home-building career took great interest in the welfare of those who surrounded her. She noticed that the colored mail carrier who served their house wore no overcoat in the bitter Chicago winter, and she spoke to him about it, asking whether the government did not supply him with one. When he replied that it did not, she fashioned a warm vest for him out of materials she managed to find in the house. Throughout a long life of usefulness, she continued to have great concern for the misery of anyone whose plight came to her attention.

During the eighteen-nineties Julius Rosenwald led the typical life of a middle-class clothing merchant. He went several times a year to New York to buy goods and made selling trips throughout the year to Western and Southwestern cities. He rose early and remained at his office until late. In his spare time he visited his numerous relatives and devoted himself to his mother and wife. Their first son was born on February 10, 1891, and was named Lessing, after Lessing Rosenthal, Julius Rosenwald's close friend, a Chicago lawyer and worker for civic reform. In July, 1892, Rosenwald rushed home from a buying trip to New York to be present at the birth of his first daughter, Adele.

Among Rosenwald's papers is a letter, dated December 31, 1892, signed by the eighteen office employees of the firm of Rosenwald & Weil, which reads:

> Messrs. Rosenwald & Weil
> City
>
> Gentlemen:
> We, the undersigned employees of your concern, after having enjoyed an evening such as was tendered to us last night, do wish to heartily thank you for the kindness and good will which you have shown. Knowing that same was given to permit us to see how much you appreciate our efforts in your behalf, we wish you to feel on your part the same as we do on ours, viz., that that confidence, which is so necessary in commercial business and is so beneficial to both the employee and employer, is mutual.
> At the dawn of both a New Year and a new place of business, we wish you such success as you have rightfully deserved.
> With due courtesy, we remain
> Yours sincerely,

In 1892 Chicago was preparing to open its great Columbian Exposition. In February, 1890, while he was en route to New York, Rosenwald was happy to read in the newspaper that Chicago had been successful in its long-prepared effort to capture the World's Fair from its competitors. He wrote to Augusta, then his fiancée, that he could imagine what sore heads there would be in New York: "Well dear, you never saw or heard of a 'sicker' lot of people than the N. Y.'ers are—they offer every nature of apology and excuse. It's glorious to see them."

While the excavations were going on for the World's Fair in 1892, Mrs. Julius Rosenwald's brother, Aaron Nusbaum, a clothing merchant in Chicago, was driving around the site in his buggy to see the new steam shovels in operation. He suddenly hit on the idea of obtaining the soda water concession at the Fair. By the time the World's Fair had closed, his profits were approximately $150,000.

Almost simultaneously with the public opening of the Chicago World's Fair, the terrible financial depression of 1893 began. The authors of the *Centennial History of Illinois* wrote: "Probably in no state in the union were the effects of this panic more far-reaching, and certainly in no city were they attended with more suffering than in Chicago."[7]

As in the case of most depressions there had been a previous period of great speculation. Men had been sanguine since 1885 that prosperity had returned permanently, and that any values would double and triple by natural laws. They overexpanded and were suddenly faced with a development of their financial desires more rapid than the pace of their economic accomplishments. In Chicago in 1892 business had slowed up. The first real shock, however, came with the failure of the Chemical National Bank of Chicago on May 9, 1893. Two days later the Columbia National Bank closed its doors. Then banks in Evans-

[7] *Centennial History of Illinois*, vol. V, Chapter XVIII, pp. 394 ff.

ton, Kankakee and other towns were forced to shut. Chicago savings banks followed, and the stability of eight state banks was endangered. There was a serious stock market crash in July, 1893. Money became dear and securities low in value. Prices of wheat collapsed in August after the failure of a "corner" to control them. Provision prices followed suit. Railway earnings fell off quickly; mills, factories, furnaces, foundries and mines shut down, and employees were out of work. Business confidence disappeared, and the failure of commercial firms increased by fifty per cent in Illinois between 1892 and 1893. In Chicago the inflation caused by the World's Fair exuberance had created speculative moods and acts, and the contraction during this financial panic was therefore correspondingly all the more severe.

The financial crisis of 1893 was followed by five years of depression. Transients roamed the streets of Chicago, where many men had come to find employment during the World's Fair. The warm corridors of the City Hall were filled with homeless men, who slept on the floors and on the stairs. W. T. Stead, who had come to Chicago that year, wrote in his impassioned pamphlet, *If Christ Came to Chicago,* that the Harrison Street police station in 1893, where homeless, unemployed men were mingled with criminals, prostitutes and men, women and children of all ages who had got into trouble, compared unfavorably with the House of Detention in St. Petersburg at the same period. Stead found the town and its citizens largely indifferent to the lot of the homeless unemployed. "The citizens," Stead wrote, "have acted each man of them upon the principle of 'each for himself and the devil take the hindmost.' They have made their fortunes if lucky, or they have failed if they were unlucky, but the devil has taken among other hindmost things the government of the city."

Rosenwald had not been extraordinarily lucky thus far, but he was managing to support his family in middle-class comfort.

In 1894 his father was stricken with paralysis. The clothing firm of Rosenwald & Weil, in addition to the interest which Samuel Rosenwald had in it, had to support the three families of Julius and Morris Rosenwald and Julius Weil. With the financial backing of the New York clothing firm of Newborg, Rosenberg & Co., Julius Rosenwald decided to form a separate firm, known as Rosenwald & Co.

Walking home to his Chicago house with Moses Newborg, of New York, one day in the eighteen-nineties Julius Rosenwald confided his ambition so far as wealth was concerned: "The aim of my life," he told his friend, "is to have an income of $15,000 a year—$5,000 to be used for my personal expenses, $5,000 to be laid aside and $5,000 to go to charity."

During the period before he became a wealthy man he attended a meeting concerned with Jewish charities in Chicago. Carried away by the account given by a speaker of a specific need, Rosenwald impulsively offered a contribution of $2,500. He left the meeting and went out into the cold street, worried at what he had just done, for he could not afford to contribute so much at that time. He was so worried that he walked all the way home and pondered about the best way to tell his wife what he had done. At home he began to hint that he had done something rash, and that he was worried. "What is it, Jule, tell me what you did?" Mrs. Rosenwald asked. He told her of his offer, adding that it would mean that they would have to economize. "Don't ever hesitate, Jule, to give money," Mrs. Rosenwald replied. "I will never stand in the way of any gift you want to make." That was Mrs. Rosenwald's encouraging attitude for the rest of their married life. Rosenwald always maintained that this was the largest gift he had ever made, for it was made at the time when he could least afford it. His opportunity to obtain wealth greater than he could possibly imagine or than he desired to retain was about to be presented to him.

### III

Richard Warren Sears was born at Stewartsville, Minnesota, December 4, 1863. He was the son of James Warren Sears and Eliza A. Benton Sears, who were of English ancestry. Sears's father had been a regimental blacksmith in the Union Army during the Civil War, and afterwards he established himself as a blacksmith and wagon-maker in Minnesota. The family moved to Spring Valley, Minnesota, about fifteen miles from Stewartsville when Richard Sears was a small boy, and it was there that he received his schooling, which extended through the first year in high school. When Sears was in his ninth year, Montgomery Ward, then twenty-eight, was establishing his mail-order business in Chicago. According to Richard Sears's sister, he was sending for catalogues and answering advertisements from the time he was able to write, and "the quantity of mail he received was a family joke." She added that "he ordered trinkets and notions and traded them to the boys."[8]

Sears's father bought a stock farm, which failed in 1878, and when Richard was sixteen he had to leave school and help support his family. He learned telegraphy and qualified for the position of telegraph operator, station and express agent. He served in those capacities at various stations in Minnesota and the Dakotas. He also bought fruit from an uncle who owned a grape vineyard in Illinois and sold it to the village merchants. In the fall he did some business in buying and selling wood with the money he earned in the fruit transaction. He then worked for a time as a clerk in the general offices of the Minneapolis & St. Paul Railroad at St. Paul, Minnesota. But Sears sought an opportunity to manage a railroad and express office in a smaller place where he might make money by trading on the side. In 1884 he became freight and express agent at the small depot at North Redwood, Minnesota.

[8] Letter of Eva Sears to Julius Rosenwald, dated July 29, 1918.

The railroad for which he worked gave Sears a special rate on wood, coal, lumber and other products, and he sold these to tradespeople in the neighborhood. He also shipped venison, blueberries and other products which he bought from the near-by Indians. He got to know the tastes and habits of the farmers in the neighborhood.

One day in the spring of 1886 a package of about half a dozen watches was shipped to a retail jeweler in Redwood Falls on consignment by a wholesale jewelry house in Chicago. It was the custom of wholesale jewelers at the time to attempt to establish business relations with small country town jewelers by shipping watches on consignment, in order to save the expense of sending out traveling salesmen to small towns. This particular package of watches was refused by the town jeweler, and Sears, instead of sending it back to the wholesale house, decided to sell the watches for that firm. He sent letters to the other railroad express agents along the line, describing the watches and offering them C.O.D., subject to examination. The express agents were to sell the watches to local residents for whatever they could get for them and keep all the profit above a price specified by Sears. During this period most farmers wished to own a "gold-filled, hunting-case watch," or a "yellow watch," as it was more familiarly called. Sears's express agents could afford to cut the local jeweler's prices and make a profit. According to the recollection of early friends, Sears paid $12 for his watches and re-sold them for $14. Watches of this type usually sold for $25 at local jewelers.

According to one account, Sears shipped watches C.O.D., to fictitious names in small towns, with the usual instruction to the express agent at the town to notify the consignor if delivery was not made in five days. On receipt of notification that the watch had not been called for, it was said, Sears would write the express agent and advise him that he was at liberty to sell the watch to someone else in the town and keep a commission of $2 for himself. If the sale was not made, Sears was said to have followed this letter with another offering a commission of $5. At the end of the first six months of his watch trade, Sears made $5,000.

The watch business was so promising that he wound up his other trading activities and moved to Minneapolis in the fall of 1886, where he established the R. W. Sears Watch Company. He hired a room there for $10 a month and bought a fifty-cent chair and a kitchen table, and he carried his stock in trade, consisting of his books and his stationery, back and forth from his office room to his bedroom in a tin box.

Early in 1887 he decided that Chicago was a better location for him than Minneapolis, and he established his watch company there at 51-55 Dearborn Street. Arthur Lawrence, who was a friend of his in North Redwood, Minnesota, and who had had more commercial experience and was older, was his assistant. His two sisters and a stenographer also helped him. On April 1, 1887, he put the following advertisement in the Chicago *Daily News*:

> WANTED—Watchmaker with reference who can furnish tools. State age, experience and salary required. Address T38 Daily News.

Alvah Curtis Roebuck, who was living then in Hammond, Indiana, twenty miles from Chicago, saw this advertisement and answered it. Roebuck was born in Lafayette, Indiana, in 1864. His father had died when Roebuck was twelve years old. Among his father's possessions was a silver hunting-case, key-wind watch with a 7-jewel Waltham movement. The boy was mechanically minded and decided to fix up this old watch. He did a good job of it with home-made tools, and then took to fixing watches for his schoolmates and local farmers. He soon got an assortment of watches, clocks, jewelry and parts of sewing machines to repair. When he wrote to a watch factory for spare parts, he was asked to send his business card. Roebuck managed to get access to a small self-inking printing press, and he printed himself business cards, letterheads and envelopes, and thereafter had no trouble buying supplies at wholesale and obtaining the catalogues, tools, merchandise and trade journals he required. He obtained most of his information from the trade journals and finally bought a used copy of Saunier's *Complete Treatise on Modern Horology* and the *Watchmaker's Handbook*.

Meanwhile, he studied telegraphy and set up a home-made telegraph wire in the neighborhood of his father's farm. He spent his evenings making and repairing things, buying, selling and trading. At seventeen he set up a small printing business, with his second-hand printing press, and printed gilt beveled edge floral name cards, which were very popular at the time. He also did carpenter and blacksmith work, was a member of the local brass band and sold books on subscription. But he preferred repairing watches, and his ambition was to get into the business for himself. Finally, a German who ran a combination delicatessen store and jewelry store in Hammond, Indiana, took Roebuck in for his room and board, also paying him $3.50 per week after the first few months.

When Roebuck first called on Sears, he showed him a sample of his work. Sears examined it, and then said: "To be frank with you, Mr. Roebuck, I am not a watchmaker and I don't know anything about this work, but I presume it is good, otherwise you would not have submitted it to me. You look all right to me, and you may have the position." Roebuck fitted movements into watchcases, did repair and engraving work and sent out orders. When Roebuck joined him, Sears had no other watchmakers working for him, but before the end of that year, the business of the R. W. Sears Watch Co. had grown so rapidly that Roebuck had eight watchmakers under his supervision.

Sears bought up discontinued lines of American watch companies, had cases and movements fitted together and offered them at low prices to railroad express agents throughout the country. They could sell at little more than the cost of watches to local jewelers and still make a good profit. Sears also began to sell watches to express agents on the installment plan, one-third in cash and the balance in promissory notes. There were about twenty thousand express agents in the United States at the time for Sears to circularize. During the winter of 1887 to 1888, he also began to advertise in country weeklies and other periodicals, offering watches for sale by mail-order. Then he added a line of watch chains, general jewelry, and diamonds. The diamonds he sold on the installment plan.

While operating his watch business in Chicago, Sears heard of the successful general mail-order business which Montgomery Ward had established there more than fifteen years before. In 1888 he also heard of a plan in Chicago, by which a club of thirty-eight members was formed, each paying one dollar a week. Each week by drawing lots one member would receive a watch, and at the end of thirty-eight weeks each member had a watch. Sears catered to this trade and put in a special department to handle it.

During this period Sears was in the habit of arriving at his office at seven o'clock in the morning and remaining until eleven o'clock at night. The business was not only growing profitable but burdensome, and Sears, always conservative and cautious, decided to cash in on his success when the favorable opportunity came along. In March, 1889, he sold the R. W. Sears Watch Co. to Moore & Evans of Chicago for $72,000, and he also sold the right to go into the watch business under his own name for three years. This transaction did not include the Canadian branch of the business, and Roebuck purchased one-half of that business, Sears retaining the other half interest. Sears accepted an equity in Chicago lots which Roebuck owned and Roebuck's notes, to be paid from the profits of the business.

Sears was now twenty-five years old. He invested $60,000 of the $72,000 he had received for his Chicago business in farm mortgages and retained the rest for living expenses and business ventures. He went to Iowa, with the intention of becoming a banker, but the business was not congenial to him. In the summer of 1889 he was back in Chicago, where he sold watches again under the name of The Warren Company, his middle name, and sewing machines under the name of Henry Hoverson & Co. Hoverson had been a bookkeeper for the R. W. Sears Watch Co. Sears and his mother and sisters, however, did not like living in Chicago, and in the fall of 1889 he moved The Warren Company to Minneapolis.

In November, 1889, Sears put the following advertisement in the rural weeklies:

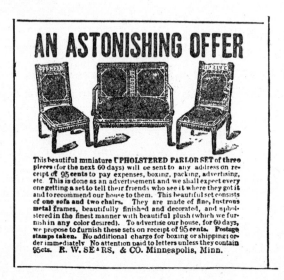

The farmers who accepted this offer received a set of doll furniture. It was true that the advertisement did say "miniature" in the first sentence, but the farmers who opened their packages on which R. W. Sears & Co. had generously paid "boxing" and "shipping" had expected something they could sit on and not something for the children to play with. They complained to the Post Office Department, which considered prosecution of Sears, but the case was never brought to court. Some years later

Sears used to say to Rosenwald: "Honesty is the best policy—I know because I've tried it both ways."

One day a customer came into Sears's office with a watch covered with mud. He explained that he had dropped it on a rock and that it had fallen into a puddle. Sears handed the customer a new watch. The man protested that the accident was his own fault, and that he had only brought the watch in for a joke. "We guarantee our watches not to fall out of people's pockets and bounce in the mud," Sears replied. This incident was widely circulated, and it was estimated to be worth many thousands of dollars in advertising to him. There are people alive today who bought watches from him in the late eighteen-eighties and who boast that the watches are still keeping good time.

By November of 1890 Sears was tired of the watch business again, though he was making money. He wrote to his friend, Roebuck, who was then in Canada, that he had sold $47,000 worth of goods during October. He declared his intention of going out of the watch business forever because of the great competition. In December he arranged to sell Roebuck the other half interest in his Canadian watch business and subsequently he also sold Roebuck The Warren Company, of Minneapolis, as well. But after about one week without a business, Sears was eager for one again, and he took back a two-thirds interest in his watch company.

While he was in Chicago, in 1892, he heard of an organization which was selling baking powder throughout the country by using school children in small towns for its agents and offering premiums for sales. He was enthusiastic about this scheme, and he suggested to Roebuck that they go into it. Roebuck suggested that they choose another commodity instead of baking powder in order to avoid direct competition, and they chose toilet soap, which they sold under the name of A. Curtis & Co. Curtis was Roebuck's middle name. The entire investment, however, was Sears's. The soap business was not successful and was closed after a few months with a loss of $20,000. Another company, the Alvah Manufacturing Company, for the sale of sewing machines was established with Sears's capital in 1892. Alvah was Roebuck's first name.

Meanwhile, the Minneapolis watch business was continued under the name of A. C. Roebuck Inc. until August 26, 1893, when the name was changed to Sears, Roebuck and Co. The agreement which Sears had made not to enter the watch business under his own name for three years had expired several months before. In 1893 they began to add clothing, sporting goods, buggies, harness, baby carriages and other general merchandise to their stock of goods. In 1892 the net sales of the firm had been $276,980, and in the bad year of 1893 they were $388,464. Even during the ensuing hard times the sales increased, and the business began to expand rapidly. By 1896 the annual sales were $745,595.

The company found it difficult to ship heavy goods from Minneapolis to the states from which the greatest volume of orders were coming, Pennsylvania, Georgia, Texas and Iowa, and it therefore opened an office and shipping depot at West Van Buren Street in Chicago in December, 1893. During 1893 and 1894 Sears, Roebuck and Co. also ran a retail city sales store in Minneapolis, selling watches, clocks and jewelry. Toward the end of 1894 it became apparent that there were great disadvantages in having the business in both Minneapolis and Chicago, and early in January, 1895, the entire business was removed to 161-175 West Adams Street, Chicago, in a five-story and basement building. There was more space than the company needed, and it rented the two top floors to a storage warehouse and opened a retail store on the ground floor.

Although the annual sales had increased, the depression which began in 1893 affected the structure of the company. The additional expense of moving the business to Chicago and of putting in new lines of merchandise had been a drain on its resources.

The net assets of the company had been reduced from $79,149 in 1894 to $56,245 in August of 1895. The liabilities had increased to $76,488, which was more than three times the amount allowed by the charter of incorporation. This made the directors individually responsible for the excess, and Roebuck, who was not wealthy, was worried about his possible liability. Sears, whose money was invested largely in farm mortgages in his mother's name, was not so much concerned. Roebuck was in ill health because of the burden of work involved in carrying on the rapidly expanding mail-order business. Sears was adding many new departments, which required additional capital for their proper expansion, and he was unwilling to furnish this new capital from his own private resources. Once again he wanted to sell his business. Roebuck decided in 1895 to retire from the firm and he arranged with Sears to place his stock interest in trust with him, to be disposed of as soon as there was a satisfactory opportunity. After existing excess liabilities were paid, Roebuck was then relieved of further financial responsibility for any debts of the firm. This was the last partnership share in Sears, Roebuck and Co. which Roebuck ever owned. Many years later he rejoined the company as an employee.

Sears, Roebuck and Co. had been purchasing clothing from Newborg, Rosenberg and Co., the New York company which owned one-half of Rosenwald and Co., Julius Rosenwald's new Chicago clothing business. One day in 1895 Sam Hayman, salesman for Newborg, Rosenberg and Co., called on Richard Sears. Sears asked for a price on 10,000 suits of clothes, which he wished to sell to the farmers through the mails. This was a colossal order and Hayman wrote to Moses Newborg about it. He then went to Chicago to see Sears. Sears told him that he wished to sell the suits to the farmers for about $10 a suit, and Newborg agreed to give them to him for $6 each. He then suggested that it would be more practical if Sears were to buy his clothing from Rosenwald and Co., their Chicago branch, and he introduced Richard Sears to Julius Rosenwald.

In the meantime, Aaron Nusbaum, Rosenwald's brother-in-law, had been looking around for a profitable use for the $150,000 which he had made from the soda water concession at the World's Fair. He had come into contact with officials of the Bastedo Pneumatic Tube Co., which made pneumatic tubes for transmission of cash and slips in department stores, which was then a new device. Aaron Nusbaum joined this company for a time and sold the system to many large department stores. While he was engaged in this enterprise he heard one day at the Standard Club in Chicago of Richard Sears, who was building up a tremendous mail-order business by his advertising. Nusbaum called on Sears in the summer of 1895, ostensibly to sell him the pneumatic tube system, but really to size him up. The upshot of the visit was that Sears agreed to sell Nusbaum one-half interest in Sears, Roebuck and Co. for $75,000. The original agreement, written in pencil on the stationery of the "Chicago Stock Exchange Restaurant and Buffet" and dated August 7, 1895, read:

Mr. A. E. Nusbaum
Dear Sir:

After our several interviews I believe we have arrived at an understanding concerning my business and I take pleasure in submitting to you the following proposition.

I will admit you into the firm of Sears, Roebuck & Co. on the basis of $15,000.00 for the good will or in other words, the business to be based on $15,000.00 more than the net assets which at present is about $60,000.00, the understanding is that the money be used to increase the capital, and the firm be reorganized with the new capital added, you to take one-half interest in the business and immediately assume an active part in the management, the capitalization to be approximately $135,000.00 paid in full. I will guarantee the correctness of the inventory and become responsible for same in every way. I hold this proposition open until Aug. 17th, 1895.

Very truly,

Richard W. Sears.

Although Nusbaum felt that he had made a good deal, he did not wish to risk the whole of the $75,000 investment in Sears, Roebuck and Co. himself. According to his widow, he first tried to interest his brother-in-law, Edward Stonehill, in taking half the investment. Mr. Stonehill at the time was making $25,000 a year as a clothing salesman for the large house of Sonneborn in Baltimore and was content. He tried to interest Louis E. Eckstein, who was later the entrepreneur of Ravinia Park, but Mr. Eckstein did not take advantage of the offer. Then Nusbaum interested his brother-in-law, Julius Rosenwald, who decided to accept the proposition.

At the time Rosenwald did not have the $37,500 necessary to purchase a one-quarter interest in the business. By agreements in his files, we know that his interest was financed in part by his family's clothing business, Rosenwald & Weil, and in part by his New York backers, Newborg, Rosenberg and Co.

The offer made to Nusbaum by Sears was acknowledged as accepted in a letter of August 13, 1895, from Sears to Nusbaum. The arrangement was that Aaron Nusbaum should become actively associated with the management at once, and that Julius Rosenwald should come into the firm as soon as he could conveniently wind up his association with the clothing business. Many years later Rosenwald, discussing his good fortune with an interviewer, said: "An opportunity opened before me. I didn't create it. . . . I accepted the opportunity more in behalf of a relative than for myself." He never considered that he was clever or farsighted in grasping this chance. At the time no one could have predicted that the opportunity was a tremendous one. Sears, Roebuck and Co. had an expanding business, but it still was subject to great hazards and required creative management.

Richard Sears, the dominant factor in the business, was a great advertising man. He created new ideas in advertising and early realized that volume of advertising of an appealing nature was necessary. He was constantly planning advertising and sales campaigns, and he would come to his office after a week end with his pockets bulging with manuscript, frequently forty or fifty handwritten pages. During the late eighteen-nineties Sears was writing copy for between $50,000 and $60,000 worth of advertising each month, and he placed it in rural weeklies with a combined circulation of about thirty million copies. His advertisements still stand out boldly from the crumbling pages of *Comfort, The Home Monthly,* and *Home and Country.* In addition, he was issuing in 1895 a mail-order catalogue of 527 pages, practically all of which he wrote himself.

Sears was a sales visionary and an advertising pioneer, but he was not a merchandiser and he was always doubtful of the future of the colossus which was growing up around him. He was frequently tempted to realize in actual cash the large figures which were mounting on his books. The mail-order business was to him an unnatural thing, and he felt that it would only last so long as new and startling sales schemes were hatched. The quality of his goods was in the early days of his business career a subordinate consideration with him, so long as he managed to keep up the quality and quantity of his advertising.

Even in his advertising Sears was no plunger, in spite of the great amount of space which he bought. He studied results carefully and watched them conservatively. If a new advertising plan did not work, he discarded it quickly. His early associate Roebuck said that Sears's habit of devoting himself exclusively to business, with almost no recreation, combined with his tendency to push his business beyond its resources, kept him in a constant state of worry, which in turn made him despondent and willing to sell out when offers came. When Nusbaum and Rosenwald were first considering investment in Sears, Roebuck and Co., Sears is said to have blurted out to them: "I'm going crazy. Here I've got the most wonderful business in the world, and it is running away with me."

The business which Richard Sears had established and stimulated by advertising was, towards the end of the century, sprawling and floundering. He wanted not only capital for its expansion, but he needed ingenuity for its management. More, perhaps, than anything he needed the aid of other hard-working men. The disorderly plant was painfully in need of organization. Wasteful methods of assembling goods for shipment and primitive means of shipping them were used. An insufficient number of two-horse wagons took the merchandise to railroad depots. On one side of each wagon was a large globe and the words "Cheapest Supply House on Earth." There were no inter-departmental telephones, and young boys ran all over the place with messages and orders. The number of orders received in 1895 was said to be about 2,000 a day. Men worked overtime, nights and Sundays in a vain attempt to take care of the flood of business brought in by Sears's advertising. There were between two and three hundred employees at the time, and one of these, J. A. Falconer, who started in as a clerk in the grocery department in the basement in 1896, wrote many years later: "I might mention that every time it rained hard the sewer backed up and practically flooded the basement. To play safe, everything was kept about fifteen inches off the floor, and many a time during these floods we used to walk around on raised planks to keep our feet out of the water while we were filling orders." Many of the desks used were packing boxes and dry goods cases. Goods were scattered about everywhere; the stock of guns was kept in a cabinet, the glass of which was broken.

An early employee of the clothing department recalled the days of 1895:

The whole stock consisted of possibly three or four hundred suits in three different classes of material. It was very amusing for us to fill such orders which we received out of a stock of incomplete and broken sizes. All coats and pants were only what is termed "Regulars" and if we got an order for a coat with long sleeves, for pants over about 33 length, we used to make them as long as possible and let it go at that.

The impression I gained at the time was that we were doing business on the plan that there is a sucker born every minute.

In about two months after I started, Mr. Sears wrote his famous ad. "Costs Nothing—for $4.98 we will send C.O.D. subject to examination etc. a fine black cheviot suit." This ad I believe was really the making of the clothing business of Sears, Roebuck, as I believe some 25,000 suits were sold, although we did not have one in stock when the ad went out. And at the beginning the buyer went down town and bought up what he could and at night all of us, including Mr. Sears and Mr. Roebuck, filled the orders as far as the purchase went.

The three men who started at the end of the century to organize with the aid of others this huge mail-order business into the greatest in the world were of different dispositions. Sears, portly, dark, genial but reserved, was an imaginative advertising promoter of creative ability. Henry Goldman, the banker, later said of him: "I think he could sell a breath of air." Aaron Nusbaum was a meticulous, capable business man, with an organizing ability that was of great value and with a degree of self-assurance that got on Sears's nerves. He was handsome, wore a dignified Imperial beard and was carefully dressed. Rosenwald, amiable, stout, and stubborn, with an optimistic outlook on life and on business, had had less training in larger business affairs than either of the others. He possessed a simplicity which Nusbaum came to regard as guile and which Sears learned to appreciate as sincerity. Associates agree that Rosenwald had then, and later throughout his extraordinarily successful career, a quick business acumen, a shrewd judgment of the worth of other men and an acute appreciation of the value of their ideas and projects. Sears was brilliant, Nusbaum was competent, and Rosenwald was a man of insight and diligence. He never lost faith in the business once he embarked in it and learned its possibilities, nor did he desire to dominate or to hamper the activities of other men. He said in later years:

The big successes are largely due to opportunity. Many men with quite exceptional ability never get a chance. I never had exceptional ability and there are in Sears today many men who are much cleverer than I. To say that I had vision and foresight in going into Sears is nonsense. I went in simply because I saw a good chance, in other words, for precisely the same reason that other young men change their jobs. I had no idea that Sears would develop into five per cent of its present size. It was simply a lucky chance that the business developed along such a scale. We ran it efficiently and worked hard and it made money. There is the whole story. The subsequent economic developments of the country have made it into what it is. . . .

## CHAPTER III

## BIG BUSINESS

### I

ROSENWALD wrote to his wife from New York on October 25, 1896: "My day has been spent largely in talking politics and hearing people make all sorts of offers to bet and no one to accept them. You never saw such a hotbed of McKinleyism." Following the defeat ten days later of William Jennings Bryan, who was considered by financiers and manufacturers as unsound, by William McKinley, who was cherished by big business as safe, the country strode out of the depression which had lasted since 1892 into a period of unprecedented expansion.

Public needs, deferred during the drastic depression, clamored for satisfaction. Loans made by bankers increased 44.4 per cent between 1896 and 1900 and money in circulation increased 36.9 per cent. The cotton crop was the largest up to that time. The price of wheat reached $1.12 a bushel in April, 1898, the highest since 1891. In the iron and steel trade prices increased more than one hundred per cent during the year 1899, and the growth in textile manufacture was enormous. Farm mortgages were paid off, savings bank deposits increased, building began again. Factories could not fill the mass of orders. Railroads were overburdened with the flood of freight.

The New York stock market was booming, and new issues of securities were being floated. Promoters and underwriters were flourishing. Holding companies came into being. During the ensuing years super-trusts were formed, including the giant United

States Steel Corporation. Groups of financiers began to control chains of banks. Immigration rose rapidly during the succeeding decade. In 1898 there was a favorable balance of trade of $615,-432,676, "more than double the largest balance at any time in the preceding history of the country."[1]

For ten years from 1897 business continued with almost undiminished prosperity, and it was during those vital ten years that Sears, Roebuck and Co., under the management of Sears, Rosenwald and their assistants laid the foundations of great fortune. The development of the mail-order business was another step in the tremendous nationalization of commerce in the United States which followed the Civil War and which was accelerated after the Spanish-American War. Rosenwald and Sears were too busy to realize just why they were growing so rich so suddenly. They were part of the force of consolidation, and their particular organization began to gather to itself large portions of the miscellaneous merchandise business of the rural areas of the country. It had competition in Montgomery Ward and several other smaller mail-order houses, but it quickly outstripped these by reason of Sears's superior advertising ability and the development of the firm's efficient management for the filling of orders.

Because of the volume of its trade Sears, Roebuck was able to buy goods cheaper and to sell them cheaper than its country competitors. It was also able to set up factories of its own for the manufacture of some of the goods it sold, and to take a financial interest in other factories, by means of its surplus profits. The small merchant found it difficult to compete with this colossus, but the mail-order house also had its disadvantages. People liked to shop for the goods that they bought and to see them in reality, rather than pictured in a catalogue. It took a great deal of aggressive advertising to break down the natural resistance of people to send their money before they saw their goods. Small department stores continued to exist in towns and

[1] Report of the U. S. Industrial Commission, 1902, vol. XIX, p. 31.

huge department stores developed in cities, simultaneously with the expansion of the mail-order trade in the rural areas, where goods were scarce and retail merchandising inefficient. The mail-order house, unlike some of the trusts, could not try deliberately to drive out individual competitors, even if it would, for its catalogue, the basis of its business, had to be priced for the nation, and it could not offer special prices for specific towns. It drove out much competition, but could not plan to do so deliberately.

The phenomenal growth of the mail-order business during the first fifteen years of the twentieth century was caused by the preponderance of rural and small town population in the United States and the difficulties in the way of satisfying the needs of this large population by local merchants. Distances were great and roads poor. Country stores were small and poorly stocked. Soon after the system of purchasing by mail became familiar it developed into a national rural habit. After the rapid development of the automobile and the consequent improvement in state and local roads, shopping by eye again became a national habit in rural areas. But so accustomed had large numbers of people become to buying some products at cheap prices from mail-order houses that the catalogue trade still remained a considerable part of the mail-order houses' activity even after they went into the chain store business.

When Julius Rosenwald and his brother-in-law, Aaron Nusbaum, went into active partnership with Richard Sears, a new Illinois corporation was formed on August 23, 1895. Sears remained president and controlled one-half the stock of the company, 750 shares; Rosenwald became vice-president with 375 shares; and Nusbaum became treasurer with 375 shares. The total capitalization of the company was $150,000. Sears contributed the inventory and the good-will of the old corporation for his stock. Nusbaum and Rosenwald, as we have seen, each contributed $37,500. The inventory was valued at $56,245.56.

When Aaron Nusbaum took over the duties of general manager, while Rosenwald was still winding up his clothing business, he found such a great need for additional employees in the growing business, that, according to the recollections of members of his family, he stood on a soap box outside the company's offices and hired men as they came along. By March, 1896, fourteen months after Sears had removed his business to Chicago from Minneapolis, more space was required, and the company moved to a building at Fulton and Desplaines Streets, where it remained for nine years. During that time the business expanded so rapidly that additional space had to be obtained all over the surrounding neighborhood. It was impossible to organize the business compactly in those early years because the rapid expansion of the trade made organization systems obsolete before they could be inaugurated. Until the scope of the business became evident, the costs of rigid organization would have been too great and the results inadequate.

In 1897 Rosenwald first became active in the management of the company. His first duties were concerned with the expanding clothing department because of his previous experience in that field. This department, though potentially profitable, had been suffering from inattention to customers' orders and inadequate stocks of goods. Early in his work there, Rosenwald found a complaint from a southern customer that he had received a heavy suit when he had ordered a 16-ounce one. When Rosenwald asked the man in charge why he had sent a different suit, the man said that there was no lighter model in stock. "Why didn't you send a watch?" Rosenwald asked tartly. From the first, Rosenwald realized that the company's success would depend basically on the satisfaction of its distant customers, and he devoted much attention to supervising the careful fulfillment of orders. It was particularly important to put the clothing department on an efficient basis, for the company was suffering heavy losses from the large number of suits returned, suits that did not fit, were badly made or were not as satisfactory as the catalogue represented them to be.

Sears was selling goods by his advertising faster than they could be bought for delivery. When Rosenwald or Nusbaum criticized either the character or the quantity of his advertising, he would hand over to them the bulky proofs of his catalogues or newspaper advertisements and suggest sarcastically that they handle the department themselves. The result was always that they begged him to take back the job. On one occasion he was voted down on his plan to advertise additional Clay worsted suits when the company had more orders for them than it could fill. That night he worked the composing room overtime, sent out his advertisements and took the next train to California for a much needed rest.

Rosenwald made strenuous efforts to change some of Sears's advertising methods. While Sears was still actively in control of the advertising and the largest stockholder in the business, Rosenwald was not able to accomplish all the reforms he had in mind. He wanted to make the catalogue an exact representation of the goods and to eliminate questionable products, such as patent remedies. The electric belt, a shiny contrivance, which was advertised as a sure cure for rheumatism and other ailments, had been sold to thousands of credulous farmers. Many of them succeeded only in burning themselves with the contraption, and they wrote indignant letters of complaint to the company. Rosenwald ordered that the money sent in should be returned to all dissatisfied customers who had bought electric belts, and he insisted that they receive compound interest from the time they made the purchases. In later years he also succeeded in stopping the sale of revolvers and ammunition. The company had been criticized because it was impossible to determine the use to which the revolvers were put. Although they still sold hunting rifles and ammunition, they gradually liquidated the revolver business.

He also developed simple policies for the benefit of the business. He urged that the company must sell for less by cutting its costs and reducing the cost of getting merchandise from the producer to the consumer, but must always maintain the highest quality possible for the price. By buying in quantity and paying cash it was possible to buy for less and sell for less than competitors. He made the company's guarantee of money back if the customer was not satisfied, the keystone of its business policy.

Sears originated devices for capturing customer interest rapidly. He was the first man in the United States to put in large type at the beginning of his advertisements the arresting sentence: "SEND NO MONEY." Others soon copied his technique, but he was constantly changing his advertisements, and his advertising always stood out from that of his competitors because of its simple ingenuity. In the welter of advertisements by others for gold watches, trusses, magic lanterns, remedies for loss of manhood, stammering, deafness and rheumatism, Sears wrote effective copy for vitreous white china, substantial stoves, glistening bicycles and lithe buggies. For many of these he used simple, effective woodcuts as illustrations. In one issue of *The Home Monthly*, a rural journal, the company had twenty-five double page and single column advertisements for patent medicines, sewing machines, milk cans, musical instruments, wall paper, pianos, baby carriages, bicycles, stoves, dishes, buggies, guns, "a rational body brace," talking machines, gasoline engines, shoes, carpets, men's suits from $4.50 to $7.50, a bedroom suite for $8.95 and the questionable electric belt.

II

Sears advertised his mail-order catalogue extensively. This huge book, which by 1898 contained 1,206 pages, was proclaimed to be the "Consumer's Guide." During the early years of the company's history it was sent to customers for 15 cents to cover part of the cost of postage. In one of his advertisements Sears wrote: "Tells just what your storekeeper at home must pay for everything he buys and will prevent him from overcharging you on anything you buy." Sears also gave many extracts from newspapers and magazines praising the virtues of the catalogue.

The mail-order catalogue has been classed with good roads, the telephone, rural free delivery, the automobile, the magazines, moving pictures and the radio as one of the greatest broadening influences in American rural life. It was the forerunner of most of these, and its pages from 1896 to date are an invaluable guide to the changes in national tastes and customs as well as the variations in prices of hundreds of commodities. The catalogue offered men, women and children every article of use for every phase of their existence. Babies' goods and tombstones were displayed in its pages. Food, clothing, recreational products, medicines, religious books and materials, vocational implements and household necessities were offered from the huge stock accumulated in the company's warehouses. In 1896 the catalogue declared that the company sold 9,000 suits of clothes a day, or four suits a minute, a buggy every ten minutes, a watch every minute.

The products advertised in the Sears, Roebuck catalogue were described in concise, vivid and careful English. A technique was developed for presenting the most impressive information in the least possible space. A page in the catalogue was of great potential value to the company, and no space was squandered on products whose appeal would not justify so much attention. By trial and error a system was developed for economical use of catalogue space so that each line would be of most value to the potential customer and of greatest advantage to the company.

The catalogue in the early years contained at the bottom of each page epigrams, anecdotes, news, homely advice and miscellaneous information about the world. It stirred the aspirations and imaginations of millions of men, women and children throughout the country. They sat at night under oil lamps turning over its glittering pages and wishing for money enough to satisfy their wants. On cattle ranches in the Far West "catalogue parties" were held soon after the new Sears, Roebuck books arrived. Cowboys from miles around came in on Saturday from near-by ranches, and a dance was held in the evening, with a big supper. Next day the catalogue was brought out, and the ladies had first choice. The ranch foremen handled the negotiation of the orders.

Customers who were ashamed to buy cheap goods at their local stores sent to Sears, Roebuck for tea siftings and other cheap commodities. The impersonality of the mail-order catalogue was a great factor in its success. Persons ordering from it were free from discrimination because of race, color or social position.

In the early history of the company the reluctance of customers to trust the distant mail-order house with their money had to be broken down. Sears inserted bank references and other testimonials from satisfied customers in his early catalogues. The catalogue also invited customers to visit the plant when they were in Chicago, and it offered them facilities for checking their parcels and writing letters. The company provided guides to take the many visitors through the growing plant. On one of these trips the boy who was acting as guide was asked what two large water tanks contained. "Ink, to write up our customers' orders," he replied. Many of the visitors wanted to see Mr. Sears in person. At first he used to greet them, but the burden became too great, and a portly clerk impersonated him. On one occasion a man came in to complain about the plow he had bought. He was offered a new one at once. "No, you don't," he said, "you're too damned square." He added that he had got into an argument with his neighbor, who said that the company would not make good on the plow which had broken down and was fixed without trouble.

People finally came to rely on the integrity of Sears, Roebuck as a merchandise house and also to entrust to the company many collateral duties. Many customers sent in their savings "to be kept till called for." Alaskan miners sent in gold dust. One Ecuador adventurer shipped in two thousand stuffed birds. One man sent a check for several hundred dollars with this note: "I am a confirmed bachelor, but I want to give some presents to my niece. Please get one of your typewriter girls to select the presents, and if the money is not enough draw on me for more." In later years one woman who ordered a prefabricated house, asked for careful attention to her order and plenty of materials of good quality. She ended her letter: "I am enclosing 25 cents extra for you to buy some good cigars with, so that you will be sure to treat me right and put in a little extra lumber, and to make you feel happy so that you will load me extra good grades."

The company always sent condolences whenever customers mentioned accidents, illness or death in the family. One woman wrote in for a black dress but gave the catalogue number of one in navy blue. She returned the blue dress and stated she wanted a dress suitable for a widow, adding that the company should rush the order as her husband was very ill and she wanted the dress to arrive in time for him to see it. One customer who ordered a cheap suit from the catalogue but was not quite sure about it, asked that Mr. Sears try on the suit, and if it looked well on him, the customer would be satisfied. A letter from a husband read:

Up to date this morning, we see no signs of goods ordered on the 4th. The good wife feels bad over it. You may see her there soon, walking from here to have a quarrel with you. I am not in it, bless my stars. If she reaches there, both of you may compromise as she wants to sue you for damages. How much that will be, I don't know, but can say the desire of a woman is greater than the mountains so you and she for it. I have washed my hands of the fight.

In the early years of the company's expansion when correspondence fell behind and letters were piled up in wash baskets, customers, irritated at delays, wrote angry or jocular letters. One customer who had ordered a baby carriage asked that the order be changed to two plugs of chewing tobacco and a double-barreled shotgun, as the boy was growing up. Some of the goods shipped were not always accepted by customers. One frantic freight agent wrote to Sears, Roebuck and Co. begging that no more sewing machines be sent to his depot. He stated that the ticket office, the waiting room and the cellar of his own home were filled with uncalled-for sewing machines. A Sears, Roebuck truck driver and a Montgomery Ward truck driver were overheard arguing about which company did the most business. The Sears, Roebuck man finally exclaimed: "Hell, we get more goods back than Montgomery Ward ships!"

Customers frequently hid jewelry in shoes, and on returning them to Sears, Roebuck forgot to take it out. All returned shoes were finally searched for valuables. The item on which money had to be refunded to customers most frequently was that of diamond engagement rings for ladies, returned by their rejected suitors. A jealous customer wrote to inquire whether a certain lady of his neighborhood had bought "a man's belt about last May and had the initials — engraved on the buckle," whether she had ordered a pair of men's gloves the following September, and a man's travel kit just before Christmas. He added:

If these things have been ordered from you by Miss ——— will you tell me if she orders anything else from you for a man between now and this time next year? Any information you can give me in regard to these things will be greatly appreciated, and will be kept strictly to myself. I guarantee you that.

The company regretted that it could not divulge the contents of its customers' orders. Lone ranchers wrote in for wives, and some men asked to be introduced to girls who posed on particular pages of the catalogue. Children wrote in for baby brothers and sisters. One woman wrote:

Gentlemen: I am about to become a bride and I am ordering my trousseau from you and want to ask that you make the selection for me. I am to be married next week. Some lady in your place might do better than the men in picking out these things. Will describe myself in order that you will know just what will best suit my type; I am tall, weighing 106 lbs., and very slender; have dark complexion, brown eyes that are large and expressive, and my hair is golden yellow or auburn. I am 35 years of age.

Please select youthful styles for me but, not too daring, as I am no "flapper."

I want to be married in a white chiffon dress with black straw hat and black slippers. Want lace slippers with low heels (size 8½). Also want a black pocketbook with some lovely initials on it.

From the underwear department please send me several pairs of bloomers in yellow or purple with trimmings of other colors. Do not send any "step-ins" or "step-outs," or whatever they are called, for I am a modest woman and I wear bloomers with elastic in the legs. Also send some ruffled petticoats with some brassieres. Will order my corset later on so you need not send it now.

Owing to the depression and the high price of house rent in the city my husband (to be) and I will not go to housekeeping here but will buy a tent and camp out this summer in the woods and green pastures. Please select some cute calico pajamas for me to wear when camping. Or do you think overalls may be better, but I want some handsome pajamas anyway. Say one pair of overalls and one pair of pajamas. . . .

I can't give the numbers on all these goods as I have misplaced my catalogue. You know how excited you are when you are about to be married, and as this is the first time for me I am unusually nervous. We are to be married next Friday so you see it is less than a week and the suspense is terrible.

Please be good enough to make the best possible selections as I may never be married a second time and a girl always wants to look her best on such a rare occasion.

I send a check in this letter. I am just guessing at the cost of the things as I haven't the catalogue here. If it is too much you will send me back the difference, and if it is not enough, let me know and I will pay you.

Less innocent customers sometimes wrote in for narcotics, brass knuckles and counterfeiting tools. Hundreds of orders for stills had to be refused when Prohibition came into force. Some customers wished the company to name their children. One father wanted the company to inform him if the young man who had eloped with his daughter should send in an order. Parents tried to locate runaway children through the mail-order house. Advice was asked on how to keep a husband's love and how to deal with unruly children. Some people wrote just to tell their troubles. Others asked for the name of a good lawyer or the company's opinion of a political candidate. Aspiring authors sent in rejected manuscripts requesting that they be published in the catalogue free of charge. One of Rosenwald's favorite stories about the catalogue concerned the teacher of a Sunday school who asked a little girl, "Where did we get the Ten Commandments?" "From Sears and Roebuck," she replied promptly. In telling this story Rosenwald used to add the alleged comment of a competitor: "They must have sold them, for they don't keep them."

The following is a sample of the company's extra-business correspondence:

Sears Roebuck and Co.
Dear Sirs:
   Will drop you a few lines and would like to know which sounds the best for children to call their parents, Father, Mother, Papa, Mama or Daddy?
   I have a girl who likes to write with her left hand. Would you train her to write with the right hand? I think it looks better to write with the right hand. What would you do? Train her to use the right hand or not and why?
   What is the meaning of rhythm? What are physics? Have you a book for sale that explains how words are pronounced?
   Which color of trimming looks well on wine color? And what trimming on orange color?
   I am sorry to trouble you but I hope you will write and tell me.

Another customer wrote:

   I am a farmer living near the town of ————— and have a good farm but I never got married because the girls here are sure stuck up. Am 42 years old but friends say do not look a day over 39 or 40. Would appreciate if you should ask your young lady (blonde) on page 42 upper left hand if she would like to get married if so she can get me at ————— and I will write. Am considered good looking. Can she cook she will not have to do no hard farm work just cook and feed the chickens and take care of the house and do a little churning and washing as I have a hand and his wife who do all the field work.

The catalogue was used in many ways for which it was not primarily intended. In Georgia a country school used the Sears, Roebuck catalogue while awaiting its textbooks. The pupils did their arithmetic by adding up purchases, practiced drawing from the illustrations and learned geography from the postal zone maps. Thomas F. Holgate, dean of Northwestern University, wrote to Rosenwald in 1925 that the Korean servant of his family was using the catalogue to improve his English. Rosenwald replied: "Some time ago, a man wrote me that the prisoners in the jail got more real pleasure from making up imaginary orders from the Sears, Roebuck catalogue than from anything else, and that they worked at it for hours at a time. He advocated our distributing the catalogue freely among prisoners for their diversion." An order came in one day for five hundred wagons, two hundred trucks and several hundred sets of harness to be furnished at once for cash. The correspondent who received it was excited, but he suddenly found attached to the letter a slip which read: "According to law, we are compelled to mail all letters written by the inmates of this asylum."

Writing in the *New Republic* for April 2, 1924, Charles Merz stated that he had heard in London from a British captain stationed at the Afghan border, that the Amir of Afghanistan spent hours turning over the pages of the Sears, Roebuck catalogue. He could not read a word of it. "But he would cluck contentedly as successive pages felt the moist touch of his thumb, and a bewildering array of go-carts and fly-swatters, inner tubes and potato mashers trekked across the printed page beneath his oriental eye." The catalogue was the chief source of entertainment for the Amir on a rainy day. "If I were going to try to get into the country," the British captain had said, "I should send him a new catalogue to pave the way. You know, of course, that only a half dozen white men have succeeded in crossing the frontier in the last twenty years. The catalogue he's reading now must be at least half a decade old." When Rosenwald heard of this, he had a copy of the latest catalogue bound in leather and with the inscription embossed in gold on its cover: "To His Majesty the Amir of Afghanistan, with the respects," etc. Mr. Merz sent this special catalogue into Afghanistan from Rawal Pindi and waited for an invitation to visit the country, but none came. Later he learned that the Amir Habibullah Khan "had been assassinated some two years before, and had been succeeded by his son Amanulla Khan, whose tastes were other than his father's."

Once Rosenwald handed a copy of the catalogue to a visiting author with the remark: "I am prolific, too, in a way. You may find my book a trifle disconnected, but there is some good stuff in it." On another occasion a distinguished visitor from Europe was dining at his home. He mentioned that he had never seen the Sears, Roebuck catalogue. Rosenwald sent his Japanese butler, Kiku, to get one. After a long time he came back with a Montgomery Ward catalogue and the information that it was the only one in the house. Rosenwald loved to tell this story.

The mail-order catalogue was not received with acclaim everywhere. The retail rural merchant, who felt that it was ruining his small trade, was bitter against its inroads. Rosenwald maintained that his mail-order house did not put the small country merchant out of business, but the small country merchant felt differently. Rosenwald's argument was that the mail-order houses actually created business for their competitors in small towns because they stimulated the desire for goods, which enterprising local merchants could cater to, if they were able to keep a good stock of fresh and attractive goods, which they sold at a fair profit. But the small merchants contended that they did not have the capital to compete with the growing mail-order houses and the large chain store groups which began gradually to penetrate the countryside.

The small rural merchant blamed most of his troubles on the large urban mail-order houses, and he tried to retaliate. Home town clubs were organized for community buying. Speakers were sent out to persuade people of the disadvantages of long-distance buying. They spoke of the money which left the local communities in that way and went into the hands of the Chicago capitalists and the New York financiers. They stated that mail-order buying led to personal extravagance and would ruin the fiber of the nation. They warned the housewife against buying perishable goods in quantity, and they pointed out the loss of time in delivery and the inconvenience of adjusting erroneous orders. Magazines were published during the first part of the twentieth century whose sole purpose was to attack the practice of selling by mail. In some towns local storekeepers offered prizes to people bringing in the largest number of mail-order catalogues for destruction. Ten cents each was paid in some places for the books, and a big public bonfire was held to celebrate the destruction. A candidate for mayor in Warsaw, Illinois, as part of his campaign for re-election declared that he would discharge any city employee who ordered goods from a mail-order house. In later years the secretary of the chamber of commerce in one small western town advertised in the local newspapers that, with the cooperation of the local moving picture house, children who came to the theater with a Sears, Roebuck catalogue would not have to pay the price of admission.

As early as 1902 Sears, Roebuck attempted to combat local community pressure on its customers and advertised in its annual catalogues that it made every transaction with its customers strictly confidential. The statement added that the company shipped its goods in boxes and packages which did not bear its name and address, so that no one in a local community could know where his neighbors bought their goods. The advertisement also suggested that merchants and manufacturers could buy from Sears, Roebuck, at cheaper prices than elsewhere and re-sell the goods.

Local merchants often insisted that their home town newspapers should refuse Sears, Roebuck's advertising or be boycotted by local advertisers. When the great dam was being built at Muscle Shoals, the company tried to sell its goods to the thousands of workmen suddenly assembled there. The newspapers in the neighborhood declined to publish the company's advertisements. Sears, Roebuck's representative, however, managed to get the addresses of the men who were working on the dam and sent them catalogues. The company also succeeded in placing its catalogue in the bunk houses of the unmarried workers. Lumber merchants once stimulated hundreds of people to write to Sears, Roebuck for estimates on barns and houses, and then refuse to order. It was thought that this maneuver would cause the company to abandon its new home building department.

The opponents of mail-order stirred up racial and religious prejudice in the effort to fight the company. Stories were circulated in the South that Sears and Roebuck were both Negroes. These stories began as early as 1897 and are still prevalent. Photographs of Sears were sent out in some of the catalogues to disprove the rumor, and the company went to the trouble to trace the genealogy of both Sears and Roebuck and made it public. Julius Rosenwald's later extensive interest in Negro philanthropy led to the story that he, too, was a Negro. In other communities the fact that Rosenwald was a Jew was used against the company. When the chain stores of Woolworth, Penney and Kresge became national institutions, the story that their owners also were Negroes was circulated.

In 1903 the country merchants objected vigorously to the extension of the Rural Free Delivery system by the U. S. Post Office Department. They were particularly disturbed by an order requiring postmasters to post lists of residents of rural routes, for they wished to keep these names and addresses from the mail-order houses. When farm organizations brought pressure on Congress to enact a parcel post system in the United States, the retail country merchants also objected vigorously. The mail-order houses themselves were not particularly interested in a parcel post system at first. They made their greatest profit on large orders, shipped in bulk by freight, and they were afraid that the inauguration of parcel post would cause their customers to order in smaller quantity at greater handling cost. The company had been encouraging farmers and small-town customers to club together and order jointly, so that they might enjoy the lower freight rates on orders of 100 pounds or more. The company was also afraid at first that a parcel post system would cause confusion in the minds of its customers concerning the correct amount of postage to include with their orders.

A parcel post act was finally passed and approved by President Taft in 1912. Soon Sears, Roebuck and Co. became the largest single user of the system, and within fifteen months of the inauguration the company was sending out an average of 20,000 parcels a day through the mails and paying postage of $6,000 a day. Customers took readily to the parcel post system, and it opened new channels of trade for the company.

As early as 1903 the country merchants complained that the mail-order houses had practically a monopoly of the rural trade in tea, coffee, chocolate, flour, canned goods, dress goods, wagon tires, cooking utensils and ready-made clothing. Over a long period of years Sears, Roebuck's sales were approximately 2 per cent of the farm income of the United States. In 1928 Rosenwald said: "Practically all that I possess is to a considerable degree dependent upon the farmers' prosperity."

In the years just before the World War, Sears, Roebuck began to take an active interest in agricultural aid for the farmer. On May 10, 1912, the company offered to contribute for the promotion of better agriculture. Dr. Seeman L. Knapp, of the U. S. Department of Agriculture, had inaugurated a group in the South of county agricultural agents to aid the farmers with advice. In order to expand this service to other parts of the country, Sears, Roebuck offered to contribute $1,000 to any county in the United States which would raise enough additional money to pay a trained agricultural expert for its county. The maximum payment by the company was to be $1,000,000. Counties to the number of 110 in the states of Illinois, Wisconsin, Iowa, Indiana, Ohio and Michigan took advantage of this offer. In 1914 Congress passed the Smith-Lever Act, carrying an appropriation of federal funds to be matched by state funds for this work.

The company also established an Agricultural Foundation, which supplied farmers with simple information on marketing, farm economics and production. It organized national seed corn shows and national single stalk cotton shows, with prizes for the best specimens. The company offered to dispose of raw furs for trappers, and in 1928-1929 they purchased more than $4,000,000 worth of raw furs and they held a national fur show in Chicago with prizes for the best cured pelts.

When agitation for a pure food and drug act was being carried on throughout the country, Sears, Roebuck was operating a large grocery department. It was suggested by one of the executives that they label all their food products with complete information concerning their ingredients, as was later required by the act, which went into force in 1906. This appealed to Rosenwald's sense of integrity, and the policy was carried out before the law was enacted. O. C. Doering, vice-president in charge of operations, suggested that the same policy be inaugurated for the fur department. The term "electric seal" was a common one for furs in those days and was applied to any skin from rabbit to skunk. Mr. Doering suggested that the character of the fur be described exactly in the catalogue and in other advertising. Rosenwald and his associates agreed to do this, though they anticipated that the fur sales that year would drop off considerably. To their great surprise the fur business was larger than ever before, due to the customers' confidence in the company's integrity.

In 1912 Sears, Roebuck established the first testing laboratory for merchandise used in this country. Laboratory workers tested every article in the catalogue for durability and supplied the advertising department with accurate material for descriptions of the goods. In addition, the laboratory tested the materials which factories used in goods manufactured for the company, and developed new designs and new materials for products, with a view to longer wear and lighter carriage. As the living habits of the nation changed from those of homesteaders to those of apartment dwellers, lighter materials of better appearance and smaller size were needed, and the testing laboratory devised many changes in the production of common household goods.

In 1897 soon after Rosenwald joined in the management, they discussed the possibility of increasing business by reducing prices. They decided to try out low prices by making great reductions in one of the special lines and sewing machines were chosen. Standard sewing machines had been selling at that time for from $35 to $55 and higher. The company had been offering machines for $16.55, $17.55 and $18.55, depending upon the number of drawers they contained. It was decided to reduce the five-drawer sewing machines from $17.55 to $13.50. The cost to the company of this machine was $10.50. Full-page advertisements in the mail-order papers were placed by Sears, and the response was enormous. The price was then cut another dollar and during the month of October, 1897, orders came in for more than 19,000. The cost to the company had been reduced to $9.50 by the manufacturer in view of the volume of orders. It was estimated that the advertising cost of this sale was $1 a machine, the overhead cost $1, and the profit $1.

This policy of lowering prices to increase volume of sales was quickly extended to buggies, harness, wagons, bicycles, and the business became phenomenal in volume. The cost to the company of handling many smaller articles of low price was great, and in 1897 they tried discontinuing some of these minor goods. But it was soon discovered that when people could not get the smaller, low-priced merchandise from a mail-order house, they did not order the larger items, and the low-priced articles were quickly restored to stock.

By 1897 the total annual sales of the company had increased to $3,020,557 from $1,273,924 the year before. In 1899, when the annual sales were $8,505,577 it surpassed its nearest competitor.

Richard Sears was credited with being the first man in the United States to make the bicycle, the sewing machine and the cream separator available at low prices. When Sears brought out a low priced bicycle, the company sold 100,000 of the one million bicycles sold in the United States that year. Sears was also the pioneer salesman of the cheap automobile. The "Sears Buggy," as this cheap automobile was called, was sold in 1907 in models varying in price from $370 to $525. In order to induce farmers to buy the new-fangled automobiles, Sears had them designed with a hood as nearly as possible to resemble the old-fashioned buggy. Some of the Sears automobiles are still running. The automobile business, however, proved to be too complicated to handle as a sideline. There were service problems and the problem of replacement of parts, as well as the need for new models of modern design. Sears abandoned the automobile business after a few years of successful operation.

In 1904 he also started one of the first chains of retail food stores in the United States. The grocery department of the mail-order house had been doing a huge business, and Sears thought a chain of food stores would be profitable. This, too, required special attention, however, and could not be operated as a sideline, so the food stores were closed after a short time.

In its early history the company tried a policy of selling goods C.O.D. Orders poured in, but it was discovered that many of them came from children, who ordered for the fun of it and could not accept the goods when they were shipped. The total value of C.O.D. orders refused or not called for was $800,000 to $900,000 before they changed back to requiring cash with orders. Many customers got out of the habit of sending cash with orders, and renewed propaganda at great cost to the company had to be resorted to in order to convince them of the necessity of doing so.

Sears, Roebuck charged fifty cents a copy for its catalogue in 1901 and for several years thereafter. The cost to the company of printing and distributing it always varied between sixty and eighty-five cents a copy. In 1904 Montgomery Ward increased its business rapidly by sending its catalogue free of even postage charges, and Sears, Roebuck quickly adopted this policy, to which it has adhered ever since. The big catalogue goes out twice a year to approximately six and a half million customers, and it takes the services of about one hundred thousand people to compose and distribute it. Today the catalogues list about fifty thousand separate items of merchandise. In addition to the big semi-annual catalogue, the company issues special mid-season catalogues and sales bulletins. About forty million of these smaller advertising items are issued each year. Including all catalogues, special advertising and other mail the company handles approximately 75,000,000 pieces of mail every year.

III

During the crucial period of 1895 to 1900 when the company was being reorganized and made more efficient, the clashes of temperament which frequently occur among partners in a nerve-racking enterprise took place. As we have seen, Rosenwald did not always approve of Richard Sears's advertising methods even though he had great admiration for his genius. But he managed to keep his criticism on an impersonal level. Aaron Nusbaum and Sears disagreed on policies and also found it difficult to get along personally. Finally, Sears insisted that Rosenwald and Nusbaum must buy out his interest or that he and Rosenwald must buy out Nusbaum's. He left the plant for a few days in order to give the other two partners an opportunity to come to a decision. In the meantime, Sears visited his former associate, Roebuck, and suggested that in the event that Nusbaum and Rosenwald decided to buy him out, he and Roebuck should re-enter the mail-order business together. Rosenwald decided to remain in association with Sears and in 1901 they bought Nusbaum's interest for which he had paid $37,500 in 1895, for $1,250,000. Aaron Nusbaum became connected with the Inland Steel Company and was very successful.

Shortly before Nusbaum retired he and Rosenwald went to visit their lawyer early one morning. The lawyer had not yet arrived at his office, and the two men stopped in to see their friend August Gatzert, who suggested that they use his lawyer, Albert H. Loeb, who, he said, was "the best lawyer in Chicago." Loeb was already in his office when the partners called. Sears and Rosenwald became so much impressed with Albert Loeb's personality and ability that after Nusbaum retired, they asked him to join them as secretary of the company.

Until the time of his death Loeb remained an intimate friend and close adviser of Rosenwald's and was always one of the most important and best beloved of the company's executives. Loeb was born in Rockford, Illinois, in 1868 and was educated at Johns Hopkins University. He taught in the night schools of Chicago, studied law, and was admitted to the bar in 1899. As the senior partner in Loeb & Adler he practiced law until he became secretary of Sears, Roebuck.

He was easy-going, jolly, kind and not so realistic or firm as Rosenwald. He had a knack of getting people in the company to work together, and the executives and department heads got into the habit of bringing their troubles to him. He soon took a leading part in the financial transactions of the company and he also exercised much influence in the formation of general policies.

The business was growing so rapidly that Sears and Rosenwald had little time to build up traditions and formalities. Executives and buyers had to devise new methods of obtaining cheap merchandise and distributing it rapidly. Men in charge of departments were given wide authority as soon as they proved capable. Among the other early executives was J. F. Skinner, who organized the buying departments and became merchandise manager. In the early days of the rush of orders Mr. Skinner had frequently to buy goods from the large Chicago department stores in order to satisfy customers' demands rapidly. Skinner had started with the company as a clerk at $5 a week, and he remained merchandise manager until his death in 1918. Otto C. Doering joined Sears, Roebuck in 1895 as chief clerk, after having worked for Montgomery Ward. He became operations manager, and established the schedule system of filling orders efficiently every ten minutes and shipping the assembled orders in rotation on a ten minute schedule. Max Adler, Rosenwald's brother-in-law, joined the firm in 1898. He had operated a music store in Chicago, and he was asked to reorganize the company's musical instrument and sheet music business. He later became one of its leading executives and its merchandise manager.

Elmer L. Scott, Louis E. Asher and William Pettigrew were valuable assistants to Sears in the advertising department, and Mr. Scott played an important part in the early development of mail-order methods. In 1911 Rosenwald's eldest son, Lessing, joined the company in a menial capacity. After a thorough training in varied phases of the business, he developed on his own merits into one of the outstanding executives of the company and finally became chairman of the board, until his retirement in 1939.

A good indication of the vast increase in the volume of the business since its inception, was the change in numbers of its employees. In 1897 the number of employees was 475. This increased to 700 in the following year, and to 1,720 in 1899. By 1901 there were 2,500 employed, and by 1906, when the company removed to its present Chicago plant, it was employing 9,290 men and women. In 1938 the company employed more than 50,000 people, and this despite the fact that by 1918 technological improvements had increased to the point where the same number of men could handle twice as many orders as they could have handled fifteen years before.

The annual sales increased prodigiously in the years before the war. From more than eleven millions in 1900, the gross sales of the company rose to more than fifty millions in 1906, and by 1914 they were more than one hundred millions. Then, with fluctuations during the after-the-war depressions, the net sales reached $537,242,400 during 1937.

By 1904 the company had outgrown its old quarters on Fulton and Desplaines Streets, and its goods were distributed wherever warehouse space could be obtained in various parts of Chicago. They decided to build a huge, modern mail-order plant. A site on the west side of Chicago in a section which was still prairie land, about five miles from the center of the city, was chosen. The land was on the link belt line of railroads, which connected with more than thirty railroads coming into Chicago, and was ideal as a shipping point for a mail-order house. Rosenwald took personal charge of the negotiations for the new plant. He had had no previous experience, except with the residence he had built for his family, but he quickly learned to supervise contracts for huge sums of money and enormous quantities of materials.

The news that Sears, Roebuck intended to build a plant was published in the trade papers of the building industry, and Louis J. Horowitz, of the Thompson-Starrett Company, went to Chicago to get the contracting job. Rosenwald had already selected Nimmons and Fellows as the architects. They had designed Rosenwald's Ellis Avenue home. Mr. Horowitz saw Rosenwald just after another representative of a contracting firm had talked with him, and he told Mr. Horowitz that still another was waiting to see him. Rosenwald admitted that he was confused because each company's representative offered different terms and gave different arguments. Horowitz said that he could understand Rosenwald's confusion, and he proposed that Thompson-Starrett put up the Sears, Roebuck plant for a fee of $250,000. But the contracting firm would make a legal contract for a fee of $1, and if Rosenwald and his associates were not satisfied with the plant when it was built, they would be obligated to pay only the cost of the materials and $1. Rosenwald looked at him sharply and said: "Do you mean that?" Horowitz assured him that he did. Rosenwald asked him to step outside for a moment, while he conferred with his associate, Albert Loeb. In about fifteen minutes he called him into his office again and said that they had decided to accept his proposition, but that their lawyers had advised that the agreement should be made for a fee of $40,000 instead of $1.

When Horowitz returned to New York with this contract E. T. Bedford, one of the directors of the Thompson-Starrett Company said to him: "Young man, can you afford to do business at a fee of one per cent?" Horowitz replied that he did not expect to do business at one per cent, but at five per cent, for he confidently looked forward to getting his fee of $250,000. "When you are as old as I am, young man," Mr. Bedford said, "you will realize that if you can get your client to live up to his contractual obligations, instead of exceeding them, you will be doing well." Mr. Bedford added that if Thompson-Starrett collected the $250,000 there would be a flag-raising on top of its Wall Street building, and that he would be happy to raise the flag personally. However, the Thompson-Starrett Company wanted the job in order to show what it could do with a large industrial plant, and the contract was signed on December 22, 1904. Nimmons & Fellows, the architects, and their successors, Nimmons, Carr & Wright, who have designed all of the Sears, Roebuck plants and retail stores never signed a contract with Rosenwald, so confident were they of his integrity.

The plan for the plant in Chicago naturally took into careful consideration the special character and needs of the business. The buildings cover more than three million square feet of floor space for the storing and handling of merchandise. The Merchandise Building, where the orders are assembled and shipped is three city blocks long and one block wide, and is nine stories high. A large Administration Building for clerical and executive offices was another main unit of the plant. As the business emanated from the mail-order catalogue, and the catalogue was then printed by the company itself, the Printing and Advertising Building was an important unit. A railroad freight depot more than four hundred feet long ran inside the main building, where forty freight cars could be handled at once under a huge skylight.

Seven thousand men worked day and night to put up this huge plant. The work started on January 24, 1905, and the company began to occupy some of the buildings nine months later. The entire plant was turned over to the owners on January 15, 1906, and was fully occupied by January 22, 1906, one year after the excavations began. The company moved its huge stores of merchandise in about 200 wagons and continued to ship out orders in the meantime.

After the work was finished, Rosenwald sent a letter to Horowitz, who opened it with trepidation. It contained three checks: one for $40,000, the contracted fee; one for $210,000, the verbal fee agreed upon if the owners were satisfied; and a third check for $50,000 because the owners were so well pleased with the work. Horowitz took the checks to E. T. Bedford's office. Mr. Bedford looked at them with delight and then said, "Young man, don't let this be a precedent."[2]

The solid buildings of the new plant gave an impression of substantial strength. Recreation grounds and athletic fields for the employees were provided on the plant site, and there were also a sunken garden, with a lily pond, a pergola and walks with flowers and plants.

Soon after the large plant was completed, it had to be enlarged to accommodate the growing business. Richard Sears said to the architects: "If this business gets any larger, it will blow up!" When the company was installed in its new plant, the catalogue for the following year announced that the new Merchandise Building contained a stock of varied goods worth more than seven million dollars.

Throughout his lifetime Rosenwald was fascinated by the marvelous mechanics of Sears, Roebuck's routine, and he enjoyed nothing better than to show people through the large, efficient plant. His eyes glowed as he described to his friends the system by which thousands of orders came in during the morning, were routed rapidly through the plant and were on their way in the mail or by express and freight by nightfall.

While the new plant was being erected, there was considerable delay at first in making enough bricks available for the army of bricklayers at the proper time. O. C. Doering, Sears's operations manager, worked out a schedule system by which he could calculate just how many bricks would be needed every day and then made arrangements to have that number available. From this system he evolved the routine by which merchandise was assembled and shipped every ten minutes during the day. Conveyor belts and chutes were built, torn down and improved; time and

[2] Interview with Louis J. Horowitz by the author. Mr. Horowitz stated that he had never before made such a contract and had never since in his long experience as a contractor. When asked why he had done so in Mr. Rosenwald's case, he remarked that he liked Julius Rosenwald's personality and trusted him instinctively.

motion studies were made; machines were invented and improved.

Orders arrived at the plant at the rate of about 100,000 a day during the busy season just before Christmas. Each morning the mail sacks were weighed, and the approximate number of orders in a pound of mail was calculated. Experience showed that there were usually forty orders to a pound of mail. The company had developed the first automatic letter openers used in industry, and they opened twenty-seven thousand letters an hour. As soon as a letter containing an order was opened, it was given a number. The time when the merchandise ordered was due in the shipping room was then stamped on the order, and a bin in the shipping room was reserved for each particular order for fifteen minutes and no longer.

After remittances and items ordered were checked, and the orders had been filed for future reference and labels made out, these were separated into their specific items and tickets for each item were sent to each department. The first mail arrived at the plant at six in the morning, and by eight o'clock when the main body of the employees arrived, the earlier shift had estimates for the managers of each department of the number of orders that department would probably be called upon to fill that day. The merchandise was stored in numbered shelves, which bore the same numbers as those for the item in the mail-order catalogue. Boys and girls selected the correct items of merchandise. Gravity conveyors and conveyor belts carried the merchandise to assembly points, where it was dropped through chutes into the shipping rooms. Mechanical conveyors carried the packed orders to loading platforms, where the heavier items went out by freight and express or to desks where girls rapidly stuck pre-canceled stamps on them. As many items, such as furniture and stoves, were shipped directly from factories to the customers, the executives had to institute a schedule system in many of the factories with which they did business, as well as in those the company owned. During its early history the company had been in the habit of storing the original orders sent in by the customers. The storage problem became overwhelming, and one of the executives suggested that as customers' orders were indexed by items in the customer index file, it would be better to send back the original order to the customer, so that he could compare it with the goods received. This system has been followed ever since.

IV

Before their new plant was finished Sears and Rosenwald needed money to finance the large building operation and to buy the new equipment they needed. The whole cost of the construction of the plant had been $4,282,000, and with the equipment needed the final cost was $5,600,000. In the spring of 1906, when the company had occupied its new plant for some months and was opening a branch mail-order house in Dallas, Texas, Henry Goldman, senior partner of the New York banking firm of Goldman, Sachs and Co., received a telegram from his boyhood friend asking for an appointment for himself and Mr. Sears. The partners explained their financial needs to Mr. Goldman and stated that they wanted to borrow five million dollars. Goldman suggested instead that they make their business a public company and issue preferred stock, based on the net assets of the company and common stock, based on good-will and future prospects of the business. The flotation of the stock of mercantile organizations was a new enterprise in 1906 in the United States. Railroads, steel companies and large manufacturing units were selling stock to the public in this way, but only a few general merchandising organizations had issued securities.

It was agreed that Goldman, Sachs and Co. in conjunction with Lehman Brothers should underwrite an issue of ten million dollars worth of the preferred stock and thirty million dollars of common stock, the preferred stock to bear cumulative interest at seven per cent per annum. In June, 1906, Rosenwald formed a Sears, Roebuck Stock Syndicate in order to give some of his relatives and friends opportunity to participate in the flotation of the new stock issue of the company, and he advanced the money needed. On January 1, 1907, he also advanced about $90,000 to permit some of the older employees to purchase the new stock of the company.

The public bought the stock with avidity. The preferred stock had a par value of $100 and sold for $97.50. The common stock sold for $50 a share. A purchaser who had bought 100 shares of the common stock in 1906 for $5,000 and held it until November 14, 1928, would have had stock of a market value of $282,-057.65, and he would have received cash dividends of $29,775.99. The total value of his $5,000 investment of 1906 would thus have been $311,833.63 in 1928. One share of Sears, Roebuck stock purchased in 1906 for $50 was worth $2,820.58 in November, 1928.

As a result of this stock flotation the company received plenty of fresh capital with which to finance its building operations and repay its loans at banks. Rosenwald and Sears each received $4,500,000 in cash for their previous stock holdings. When Rosenwald came to New York to discuss the details of this issue with bankers, he kept his customary habits of thrift and modesty. He had taken a small hotel room, as usual, and Herbert H. Lehman, of Lehman Brothers, recalled that he and Rosenwald sat on the bed in Rosenwald's room to discuss the details of this large transaction, as there was no other place to sit.

v

Early in 1909 Sears retired from the presidency of the company. His wife had met with an accident and had to have her leg amputated. His own health was poor, and, weary of the strain of the business, he sold his stock interest to Goldman, Sachs and Co. for $10,000,000. Henry Goldman offered Rosenwald an option on some of these shares, but he declined them, although he was always anxious to buy all the shares of the company's stock he could afford. He said that he did not want it to be possible for anyone to say in the future that he had profited at the expense of his former partner, even though Sears had been willing to sell. The interest which Sears sold in 1909 for ten million dollars was worth more than two hundred million dollars in 1928.

After he retired at the age of forty-six, Sears invested some of his money in lumber, land and railroad properties in Florida, Minnesota and the Dakotas. In Redwood County, Minnesota, where he had first developed his watch business as a boy, he went into partnership with William H. Gold, a country banker. They planned to raise cattle, hogs and sheep and sell them by advertising and mail-order methods. In 1910 he also developed a scheme for selling bonds and other debentures by mail, but he abandoned the idea. He finally became interested in the Emerson Typewriter Company, of Woodstock, Illinois, and bought it.

Meanwhile, A. C. Roebuck had become interested in magic lanterns, photography and motion picture machines after his retirement from the company in 1895. He formed the Enterprise Optical Manufacturing Company, in which Sears, Roebuck later had an interest. He had also developed a motion picture machine of his own and became one of the three principal manufacturers of motion picture machines and accessories for theaters in the United States.

In 1911 Sears induced him to join him in the typewriter business, and Roebuck made improvements on the Emerson machine. Sears changed the name of the typewriter to Woodstock. The two men were getting ready to expand the business when Sears died on September 28, 1914, at the age of fifty. According to the newspapers at the time, he left an estate of $17,500,000.

His personality faded quickly from the American scene after his death, and when people saw the name of Sears, Roebuck and Co., they thought of the huge catalogue which Sears had made so vivid, or the vast organization to which they sent their orders. Many people when they heard the name also began to think of Julius Rosenwald, for the national and international scope of his philanthropies soon transcended even the glamour of his business.

After the death of Sears, Roebuck went back to the motion picture business. He sold his business in December, 1924, and went to Florida, where he became interested in real estate and the construction of homes. This business became unprofitable after the collapse of the Florida real estate boom, and in 1933 he became an employee of the organization he had helped to develop, visiting the retail stores and talking with customers, who were interested to meet the original Roebuck of Sears, Roebuck.

After Sears had retired from the presidency of the company in 1909, Julius Rosenwald, the new president, called a meeting of the department managers. He told them that from then on the mail-order catalogue was to contain statements which were not only restrained and truthful, but which would also give customers a clear impression of the exact content of the goods they might wish to order.

When Rosenwald first entered the mail-order business its standard of integrity was not considered high in the business world. By his insistence that goods must be exactly as represented, he and his associates raised the level of that business. By his insistence that his company meet all of its moral obligations, even when it was not compelled to do so legally, he increased the confidence of the manufacturers who dealt with the company and the credit of his business with bankers. He came to regard the huge organization with much the same personal feeling that he had had for his small clothing business. In his letters to his family and in conversation, he always referred to the plant as "the store."

In his business, he never had any use for windy ostentation, and he was always accessible to anyone in the organization who had anything to say to him. He was kindly to his associates, but not sentimental in his business dealings. He did not favor enormous salaries for his executives, nor did he pay more than the prevailing rate of wages to the thousands of men and women and boys and girls who worked in the mechanical jobs. Rather than large salaries he preferred to give the executives bonuses and to make it possible for them to purchase stock on easy terms. From about 1910 and for many years thereafter, he made it a practice to sell stock to minor executives and take their notes, payable five years after date with interest at five per cent. He held the stock in their names, and they paid for it out of the dividends it earned. He guaranteed these men against any loss, and if at any time they did not wish to take up the stock, they could relinquish it and receive back whatever they had paid for it on account. He also did this for a large number of people who were his friends or whose unselfish services in philanthropic, governmental and educational endeavors he came to admire. For the company's laboring thousands, he and his associates later developed one of the best profit-sharing systems ever inaugurated in the United States,[3] and they also introduced health and recreational benefits for the employees.

Rosenwald used to have his hair cut in his office while he carried on his business activities at the same time. He would sometimes tear two shares of stock out of his perforated book and give them to John King, the company barber, for a tip. These tips were later worth $300 each on the stock market. Whenever he ate lunch at the plant, he sat at a large round table in a corner of the long company lunchroom, where he enjoyed hearing the clatter and din of the personnel, as he joked with department managers or carried on business conferences. Ten or more people would usually sit down to lunch with him, and he made it a custom to pay for the lunch of anyone who was invited to his table.

[3] See pages 159 to 163.

He hated nepotism as much as he abhorred extravagance and waste. When, in 1911, he took his oldest son, Lessing, into the business, he made efforts to see that he was treated with no special favor, and that his advancement depended entirely upon his own merits. Max Adler, the only other relative in the company's employ, also owed his advancement to his own abilities, rather than to the fact that he had married Rosenwald's sister. Rosenwald preferred to help his relatives by making it possible for them to own Sears, Roebuck stock rather than by taking them into the business.

Between 1900 and 1914 the industry and commerce of the United States expanded tremendously. Invested capital increased from about nine billion to more than twenty-two billion dollars. During this period when Rosenwald's personal fortune was increasing rapidly by millions of dollars, there was no federal or state income tax, and his accumulations became huge. Simultaneously, with the enormous growth of his wealth, he was making strenuous efforts to distribute his money wisely to innumerable causes, movements and organizations which he considered worthy of support.

## CHAPTER IV

## A CHARITABLE MAN

### I

DURING the first decade of the twentieth century, while the great fortunes of Rosenwald and other men were pouring in without transfusion from the individual to the community via the income tax, philanthropy became a social design. Men with large fortunes, far too great for their personal needs and far beyond the needs of their descendants, were looking for means of disbursing their surplus. John D. Rockefeller and Andrew Carnegie, with larger resources at their disposal than anyone else, were creating machinery for the distribution of wealth to charitable and educational endeavors. Education, particularly, became a natural pursuit of philanthropic energy, because, presumably, it would fit mankind for more effective life and remedy some of the social evils. Older educational institutions received wider patronage as wealth accumulated, and new cultural receptacles were established. Lesser millionaires confined themselves to supporting the innumerable organizations and associations which had grown up for the general welfare and to aiding individuals who made constant appeals to their good nature.

With the emergence of modern industrial capitalism, charity was a side line during the struggle for acquisition of wealth, but it attained more and more importance as the human wreckage of industrial exploitation increased and had to be cared for. Leadership in charity gradually passed from the church and the state to the business man, who preferred individual initiative to governmental action.

The motives of men who, after accumulating large fortunes, began to give part of them away, have often been questioned, and private philanthropy has been branded as an attempt "to drown revolution in free soup." "Frequently the very givers who have attempted to do most for their fellows," Professor Arthur J. Todd wrote, "have been put upon the defensive and subjected to ridicule, suspicion, and abuse. Their motives have been questioned, their judgment attacked, their integrity befouled." In view of the fact that much wealth in the United States was accumulated rapidly by some men, frequently at the expense of many, it is natural that the motives for its dispersion should be questioned by those who did not profit.

Rosenwald remarked to a friend one day in his later years: "I really feel ashamed to have so much money." He never felt that he had to apologize for anything he did in acquiring his wealth, but he always considered that he had an obligation to society to use it for the benefit of mankind.

Among the Jews there was an ancient tradition of charity. Talmudic injunctions and Biblical exhortations had taught the Jews to give part of their wealth to the poor, and in every town and city where they congregated during the centuries of their history organizations were soon formed for taking care of unfortunate, poverty-stricken or disease-ridden people. Rosenwald, beginning, in the traditional fashion, to contribute small sums to the traditional institutions, gradually enlarged the scope of his benefactions as the magnitude of his possessions increased. He had as examples to lead him in charity his co-religionists, Baron Maurice de Hirsch, and Sir Moses Montefiore in Europe and Jacob H. Schiff in the United States. He also had in his home a constant source of inspiration and encouragement in his generous endeavors to do good.

Mrs. Rosenwald was a woman of great spiritual susceptibility, and without the continuous play of her domestic influence, it is possible that Julius Rosenwald would not have become the important humanitarian force into which he developed. But his own impulsive interest in humanity was so warm and amiable that it is difficult to imagine limits to the wise generosity which he had acquired from his mother and which was nurtured by his wife. A woman of more worldly and less unselfish motives than Mrs. Julius Rosenwald could easily have diverted some of the stream of well-used riches into personal possessions and into social ostentation and vain display. But she readily exercised an influence towards generosity on her husband, because she had the same impulse so strongly in herself. She had as much instinct for the spiritual things in life as her husband had for personal relations.

The home on Ellis Avenue, together with those of his mother and his married children near-by, were objects of intense attraction for Rosenwald no matter how busy he might be with his business or his philanthropic affairs. After a busy day at his office, he loved to stuff his pockets with letters he had received which he thought interesting or amusing, and he enjoyed reading them aloud to his wife and five children at the dinner table. This process often bored the children, but it gave their father so much pleasure that they endured it and realized later that it had constituted a valuable part of their education. Another educative influence for Rosenwald himself and the members of his family was the habit he formed of making a genial forum of his dinner table. He brought home guests who interested him because of their personalities or the importance of the work in which they were engaged, and Mrs. Rosenwald had a knack for drawing them out and getting them to discuss the problems and ideas with which they were wrestling. These men and women represented every walk in life and every class in society. Bankers and writers, singers and social workers, rabbis and actresses all came to the Rosenwald dinner table at one time or another, and in his later years scarcely a distinguished person who passed through Chicago was not present at his home. There were heated arguments in which the children were permitted to join, and the spirit was one of interest and festivity combined. The children recalled in later years that there was scarcely any petty gossip at their dinner table although there was plenty of happy jocularity. Their father was noted for his love of fun.

The Rosenwald home was the scene of parties for adults and children of the whole neighborhood, and the tennis court and lawn were common property for the friends and relatives who lived near-by. The children of the servants played together with those of the household, for Rosenwald tolerated no social distinctions. He always kept a closet in his house filled with toys, and no child left the house without some gift. When his own children visited the Sears, Roebuck plant surprises in the form of gifts from the toy department arrived for them every few minutes. The house on Ellis Avenue and the estate which the Rosenwalds bought in 1911 at Ravinia were always crowded with relatives, especially at Sunday dinner, and Rosenwald rarely seemed to tire of being surrounded by his family and innumerable friends. On Thanksgiving Day the furnace man, the garbage man, the street sweepers and other hidden functionaries were invited to the Rosenwald home for the baskets of food which Mrs. Rosenwald prepared for them, and the regular household help also received many attentions. Every Christmas a large party for the servants was held by the Rosenwald family, and anybody who ever had done anything for Mrs. Rosenwald was remembered at that time. Doormen at department stores and hotels received substantial gifts, and the chauffeurs, gardeners and household attendants received liberal checks. For days the household was busy preparing the thousands of pounds of candy which they distributed each year to children in institutions throughout the city of Chicago. Some schools received as many as five hundred of these boxes and cornucopias of candy which the Rosenwald family and their friends filled themselves from the large tubs sent over from Sears, Roebuck. Two days after Christmas the family itself had its gala winter function, on Mrs. Rosenwald's birthday. The children got up skits making fun of her foibles, those of their father, and other members of the family, to the great delight of the parents.

Rosenwald made every effort to teach his children philanthropy, and he was often worried that his great wealth would have a bad effect on them. He was niggardly about their expenditures and anxious to instill into them his own abhorrence of waste or extravagance.

His automobiles were known for their age and he resisted all attempts to replace them until they had literally fallen apart. Harry E. Kersey, Rosenwald's Negro chauffeur, recalled his first day with his employer:

At eight-thirty the garage door opened and there was Mr. Rosenwald. He tossed a bundle of papers into the car and told me to come over to 4935 Greenwood Avenue, his mother's residence, right away. . . . Mr. Rosenwald came out in about fifteen minutes arm in arm with his mother, a lovely, happy-looking small lady. He introduced me to his mother as his new chauffeur. After a very affectionate goodbye, he told me to go to 4711 Greenwood Avenue, there to visit his daughter, Mrs. Armand Deutsch, and Mr. Rosenwald's first grandchild, Armand Deutsch, Jr. From there, to 50th and Ellis Avenue, where we picked up a gentleman who was having a talk with the White Wing. This gentleman was Mr. Albert Loeb, Vice-President of Sears, Roebuck and Company. After another introduction, we headed for Sears, Roebuck and Company.

This routine was followed almost every morning while the family was in Chicago. Rosenwald rose early and played tennis. Then he would often walk with his two younger children to school and have his car meet him en route, pay his daily visit to his mother, and then go on to the plant. He often made two or three trips from the plant to the Loop district of Chicago during the day, and Harry Kersey described how his employer would rush down the steps of the Administration Building several at a time, run to the car, say where he wanted to go while rushing into the automobile, jump out of the car before it had quite stopped and rush into an office building. When he came out again, he would dash out of the building, put his two fingers into his mouth and whistle loudly for his chauffeur. His automobile was always filled with the latest editions of all the Chicago newspapers, which he read avidly, and his pockets were frequently stuffed with clippings. When asked why he read so many newspapers, he once said: "They tell stories of people." He much preferred them to books. He nicknamed himself a "newspaper worm," and anything of human interest in the papers he enjoyed as he did all other reflections of human personality. Once Mrs. Rosenwald inquired of Harry Kersey how far it was to the place where they were driving, and when he told her, she said: "Never mind the miles, how many Chicago *Tribunes* away is it?"

The chauffeur also recalled:

Mr. Rosenwald was strongly opposed to waste of material or time. My first experience in buying anything for him was to buy him some razor blades. He told me to buy some blades one morning at Sears. Naturally, I thought he bought plenty of anything and brought him in a box of blades. He took a look at them and said, "What do you think I would do with all of those blades? First, I would use them up too fast and waste them or probably lose track of them." I had to take them back and bring three packages. "And another thing," he said, "suppose the price would go down."

Rosenwald liked to do things for himself. He often drove his own car, although he did it badly and was frequently in trouble. He always refused to employ a valet, although Mrs. Rosenwald urged him to do so in later years in order to save himself energy and time. He hated to feel that his money might make him soft and dependent upon others for personal services.

The impression one carries away from the accounts of him by his family and friends is of a healthy, energetic man who was possessed by an immense social curiosity and a hearty urge to remedy social ills by any power within his material or spiritual means. He was a man who was so impatient of anything that he disapproved of that he had the impulse to remedy it, and in small matters he could get into purple rages with business associates and intimates who crossed his wishes. He was, however, always ready to listen to constructive ideas and to implement them by means of his personal attention and his wealth if he found them of social value. He was incisive in his judgments and had a passion for the succinct and the factual. Once a decision had been made and action taken, he seldom fretted if the results were unsuccessful, provided he was sure that honest efforts had been made in the direction he felt to be right.

In a speech which he once made as president of the Associated Jewish Charities of Chicago he said:

Shall we devote the few precious days of our existence only to buying and selling, only to comparing sales with the sales of the same day the year before, only to shuffling our feet in the dance, only to matching little picture cards so as to group together three jacks or aces or kings, only to seek pleasures and fight taxes, and when the end comes to leave as little taxable an estate as possible as the final triumph and achievement of our lives? Surely there is something finer and better in life, something that dignifies it and stamps it with at least some little touch of the divine.

My friends, it is unselfish effort, helpfulness to others that ennobles life, not because of what it does for others but more what it does for ourselves. In this spirit we should give not grudgingly, not niggardly, but gladly, generously, eagerly, lovingly, joyfully, indeed with the supremest pleasure that life can furnish.

Rosenwald wrote to one of his sons-in-law, congratulating him on a civic interest which he had undertaken, and stated that he was much impressed with the thought that if a business man waited until business permitted to take up civic work, "he will rarely do anything because the larger the business grows the more absorbing it becomes and the real joy of life is missed."

## II

"Seek ye the welfare of the city whither I have sent you, and pray for its sake unto the Lord, for in its welfare shall ye fare well," the prophet Jeremiah wrote. In the city of Chicago at the beginning of the century there were those who had an interest in the welfare of the community and its unfortunate citizens, and the Jews of Chicago before Rosenwald was born had organized religious and philanthropic societies. Among the Jewish clothing manufacturers, wholesale and retail merchants, bankers and lawyers who had settled in Chicago was a responsible group with human sympathies and religious impulses. But with the arrival of Dr. Emil G. Hirsch as rabbi of Sinai Congregation in 1880, an especially strong force for community service was introduced into the city.

Emil Gustav Hirsch was born May 22, 1852, in the Grand Duchy of Luxemburg, and was educated there in the public schools until he came to the United States with his family in 1866. He studied Hebrew and Jewish literature with his father and was graduated from the University of Pennsylvania. Then he went abroad and did graduate work in theology and philosophy at the universities of Leipzig and Berlin and became a rabbi. On his return to the United States he was rabbi of congregations in Baltimore, Maryland and Louisville, Kentucky, before he was called to Sinai Congregation in Chicago. Dr. Hirsch, like his father, was one of the leaders of Reformed Judaism in the United States.

To a practical American business man of German Jewish descent Rabbi Hirsch's religious teachings were bound to be congenial. He stripped Judaism of its obscure theological trappings, and he did so all the more effectively because, as a Hebrew scholar, he was acquainted with those trappings. But he also took cognizance of the advances of science and of the requirements of a materialist civilization. Those who had grown up in an American atmosphere of industrial progress could find little of spiritual comfort or intellectual interest in a Judaism which consisted of the unaltered legends of a pastoral civilization.

On the west side of Chicago, during the same period of the eighteen-eighties, there was growing up a large Russian and

Polish Jewish population, refugees from persecutions abroad. These people found Rabbi Hirsch and his Reformed Judaism anathema. They had brought with them their orthodox forms and ceremonies, and they were afraid that if their children lost them, they would lose their identity. The contrast was one that was to run through the Chicago Jewish community for the entire period of Rosenwald's lifetime there, as it did in other large cities in the United States.

Dr. Hirsch expressed the nature of Sinai Congregation best when he told his followers one Sunday morning: "If we come to consult really who are our co-religionists, we shall discover that we have much more in common with the Unitarians and Ethical Culture people than with the orthodox Jews. We shall not leave the orthodox Jews for the sake of establishing ourselves distinct from them, but we shall try and must try to bring them up to our own amplitude and see our own construction of Judaism. We must missionarize among them." But not many of his parishioners were the missionary type, and they left the orthodox to go their way, while they themselves took a more modern point of view on the relations of themselves to God and to other sects in society.

One Sunday in his later years Dr. Hirsch told his congregation:

When we were building here, none of us thought of an eastern oriental building because we felt that here was our home. We do not belong to the East and we will not go back to the East. We are not Palestinians, we are Americans, and that is expressed in this building by the architecture. Our building is flooded with light—from the outside, it looks like a library. That was the criticism passed by a pious Rabbi: "See they put up a building which looks like a Carnegie Library." A Synagogue must have turrets and cupolas, and must have God knows what. That speaks of the East and speaks of the architect as the pious Rabbi did. Nothing of that sort is in our Temple. It proclaims that Judaism is not at war with thought, that it is friendly to knowledge. It is founded on knowledge, on abundance of knowledge. This is a study room, if you choose, and what you call my lectures, they are not lectures, are talks intending to make you thoughtful, to give you certain information apt to correct your misapprehensions.[1]

Cross-eyed, irritable and sardonic, Rabbi Hirsch exercised his leadership by virtue of his knowledge and powers of intimidation. He could be gruff as a porcupine and insulting as a boor, but he had a powerful intellect that commanded respect. With the motive power of his irritability, he poured out each Sunday morning sarcastic and vituperative wisdom on a respectable congregation, which was stimulated at the same time as it was shocked. Using irony and adept human illustration, he appealed to his listeners often by berating them, and even those who fancied themselves as dispensers of social justice were hard put to it to attain in practice the heights of Hirsch's pragmatic idealism. Though he was sarcastic, Hirsch was never cynical, and he decried cynicism in his congregation. Though he was a modernist and made fun of what he considered fundamentalist errors and fetishes, he remained true to the deep principles of the Judaism which his scholarship enabled him to dig from the mines of Hebrew literature.

Rabbi Hirsch was concerned that the Jews over whom he exercised ethical and educational leadership should live a life of practical idealism. "If you want to prove you have a mission, live it, act it. If you think you are the chosen people, show by your conduct that you are the chosen people," he told them one Sunday morning. "That ends all argument," he added. Rabbi Hirsch began early in his career to stress unmercifully in his pulpit what he called "the duties which religion and ethics regard as the sole justification for private control of wealth and social resources."

Rosenwald sat at his feet almost from the beginning of his residence in Chicago. When he was in Chicago, he seldom missed a Sunday except on account of illness. Early in his career he had the habit of looking up to Rabbi Hirsch for ethical advice, in

[1] Hirsch, Emil G., *My Religion*, p. 128-129.

a different spirit, but much in the same manner that he took business advice from those in his organization whom he respected most. He was, for many years, vice-president of Sinai Congregation and a member of the finance committee.

Upon occasion Rabbi Hirsch would level his wrath at his friend Rosenwald's head. Once he asked him to contribute to a Jewish educational cause in which Rosenwald was not interested, and the request was declined. The following Sunday Hirsch rose in the pulpit and denounced Rosenwald by name, saying to the congregation that he was too ignorant to appreciate the virtues of the cause Hirsch was furthering and suggesting that his pockets were stuffed with money. But members of the congregation had grown accustomed to this sort of thing from their leader, and Rosenwald remained the helpful friend of Rabbi Hirsch until his death in 1923.

In addition to his position of spiritual leader in Reformed Judaism in Chicago, Rabbi Hirsch was a practical influence in civic and philanthropic movements there. He once told his congregation: "Our life, according to Jewish doctrine, the true Jewish doctrine, is worth living and God's kingdom is of this world, and if it is not, it may be made to be of this world, and it must be made to be of this world." He started the Jewish Training School in Chicago and preached the idea of federation for Jewish charities until that form of consolidation was accomplished in 1900 when the Associated Jewish Charities of Chicago was organized.

There were several other figures who had a deep influence on Rosenwald's charitable and civic activities. Among the most important was Judge Julian W. Mack. Judge Mack belonged to the group of social workers who found in Chicago a great need and great opportunities for useful work. In this group, all of whom Rosenwald came to know and respect were, Jane Addams, and her associates at Hull-House, Dr. Graham Taylor, of Chicago Commons, Mary McDowell, of the University Settlement, and Minnie Low, of the Bureau of Personal Service. These men and women were touched by the great misery they encountered in the stockyards and other industrial districts of Chicago, where men, women and children lived in a squalor that would have been considered indecent for modern cattle, and they were determined to do something to remedy the evils they could see, touch and smell. In that endeavor they had in Rosenwald a willing financial backer and an ardent personal supporter.

Rosenwald trusted Judge Mack's judgment on economic, political and philanthropic matters, and the two men became intimate friends and corresponded constantly after the Judge was elevated to the federal bench and left Chicago. Judge Mack brought worthy causes and worth-while people to Rosenwald's attention, and Rosenwald continually sought his advice on social welfare movements which wanted his support. At times they differed widely, particularly about Zionism, for Judge Mack became a staunch supporter of that movement, but their friendship and close association in welfare work never ended.

Jane Addams exerted a powerful and liberalizing influence on Rosenwald. There were practically no trained social workers in the city in 1889, when she, inspired by Toynbee Hall in England, established Hull-House as a social settlement in a slum area of Chicago. The depression of 1893 awoke some social-minded citizens to the necessity for coping with the problems of poverty. The Civic Federation, first suggested in 1886 by Lyman J. Gage, became a reality after the panic of 1893. It established agencies in every ward in Chicago for dealing with the philanthropic, educational, moral and political needs of the growing city. The City Club, organized in 1903, consisted of those who aimed to improve municipal conditions and to renovate civic politics. Jane Addams in her reminiscences told this story about the Club: "One day as I entered the elevator, the boy who knew me well said casually: 'What are you eating with today—with garbage or with the social evil?' I replied: 'Garbage,' with as much dignity as I could command under the circumstances, and he deposited me on the fourth floor where I found Mary McDowell, head of the University of Chicago Settlement, pinning on the wall blueprints of a certain garbage reduction plant."

Rosenwald was contributing to the work of Jane Addams's Hull-House as early as 1902. He was an active member of the board of trustees of Hull-House for many years, and he and Mrs. Rosenwald, who was a close friend of Jane Addams's, seldom missed the dinners which Miss Addams gave for guests who were important in the field of social work here and abroad. Professor James Weber Linn, Jane Addams's nephew and biographer, recalled that Rosenwald was always "gently punctilious" about keeping even minor social engagements, and if he had promised to attend a function at Hull-House or anywhere else he made great efforts to do so in an unpretentious way and without any patronizing spirit.

Once as they were leaving Hull-House together Rosenwald asked Professor Linn if he might walk along South Halstead Street with him. He added that he seldom got the time to walk along those streets in Chicago and see how people looked and lived in the poorer sections of the city, and he eagerly took every opportunity to do so. He once telephoned his friend Judge Henry Horner to ask him to dinner. Judge Horner said that he was dining with his friends Carl Sandburg, the poet, and Oliver H. Barrett, Chicago lawyer and Lincoln collector. "May I come along?" Rosenwald asked eagerly. Carl Sandburg had been attacking his capitalist ideology in his newspaper, *The Day Book*, but the two men got along very well together, and Sandburg became as conscious of Rosenwald's personal warmth and amiability, as Rosenwald did of the poet's charm and intellectual integrity.

Rosenwald valued greatly the important efforts of Miss Addams and her associates. He was one of those practical business men to whom Jane Addams referred in *Twenty Years at Hull-House* when she characterized them as those "to whom the practical world of affairs seems so supremely rational that he would never vote to change the type of it even if he could." But he differed from many of his contemporaries in the Chicago business world in his admiration for the honest theorist. Once after Jane Addams had dined at their house, he said to his wife, "One feels that it is a benediction to have her in the home."

On the west side of Chicago, where the majority of the poor Jews from Russia, Poland and other countries of eastern Europe lived, the Maxwell Street Settlement had been established in 1893. Among its early leaders were Jacob J. Abt, who later worked with Rosenwald in Washington during the war, and Minnie F. Low, who early became an influence on his charitable impulses. Minnie Low became head of the Bureau of Personal Service, an organization that aided poor families in Chicago to establish themselves on an independent basis. For many years the Rosenwalds gave her money each month to care for the cases she brought to their attention or sent cases to her and the money to aid them.

Another of Rosenwald's early interests in Chicago was the work of the Immigrant Protective League, in which Grace Abbott took a leading part. He realized the importance of setting up an agency for the protection from unscrupulous exploitation of immigrants who were unfamiliar with the tricks prevalent in the new nation of which they were becoming a part. He attended meetings of this organization faithfully, gave it money and helped with his influence to forestall efforts to set up a literacy test as a means of excluding economic and political refugees. His enthusiasm for this work was non-sectarian, and he took as much interest in the plight of non-Jewish immigrants as he did in those of his own religion.

Grace Abbott recalled that on one occasion she and Rosenwald were attending a meeting of the Immigrant Protective League on a snowy night. At the time Miss Abbott was actively engaged on behalf of the strikers in the great clothing strike in Chicago.

She had to hurry away from the meeting in order to make a speech, and Rosenwald stopped her and said: "You're going to that strike meeting, aren't you?" She said that she was, and Rosenwald said that he probably would not agree with a single statement she made there, but that he was going to see to it that she did not catch cold on the way. He took her down to the street, put her in his automobile and sent her to the strike meeting. None of his associates could recall any instance when he ever attempted to bring pressure on any individuals with whose economic or political principles he disagreed, no matter how radical they might be.

His ideals were stimulated by his wife and by Rabbi Hirsch; his social purposes were stimulated by Jane Addams and her associates; Judge Mack acted as a clearing house for the multitudinous causes and schemes which soon began to pour into his office at Sears, Roebuck and Co., after it quickly became known that a phenomenon of generosity was working in the city.

### III

In April and May of 1905 new pogroms against Jews took place at Kishinev and in other towns in Russia. In the three days of April 19, 20 and 21 forty-seven Jews were murdered in Kishinev, 424 were wounded and more than 700 houses were burned down. In May, 1905, a mass meeting was held in the Star Theater, Chicago, to protest against the Russian massacres, at which Jane Addams and Clarence Darrow were the principal speakers. The pogroms increased, and Jews were killed and pillaged at various times during the rest of that summer at Lodz, Odessa, Kiev, Tomsk and other places, until about 3,000 had been murdered and many more wounded and made homeless. Rosenwald made the largest individual contribution in Chicago to the relief fund quickly raised for the helpless sufferers.

In 1905 he first became interested in the work of settling Jews on the land. He was one of the directors of the Jewish Agricul-

tural Aid Society of America and became interested in the work
of the Baron de Hirsch Fund. Baron Maurice de Hirsch, a Jewish
banker, had taken the initiative in devising plans and making
them possible for the resettlement of Jews who were persecuted.
In 1887 he had offered to give fifty million francs for the establishment of elementary and agricultural schools in the Jewish
pales of settlement in Russia, but the government refused the
offer. He then came to the conclusion that emigration of persecuted Russian Jews and their settlement on the land in new countries was the only possible solution for their plight. While he had
been interested in railroad construction in Turkey, he was impressed with the work of Jews in agricultural colonies there. In
1891 he formed the Jewish Colonization Association with a capital of $10,000,000, all of which he contributed himself. A tract
of land in the Argentine Republic was chosen, and efforts were
made to settle Jews there.

In the meantime, Theodore Herzl, who had witnessed anti-
Semitism on the rampage when he was a Viennese newspaper correspondent in Paris during the Dreyfus Affair in 1894, formulated
in 1896 his dream of a Jewish homeland in Palestine. The project
for a Jewish homeland had been considered by various people
ever since the fierce Russian pogroms of 1881. After the disastrous May laws three thousand Jews landed at Jaffa and were
soon reinforced by new arrivals from various parts of eastern
Europe. In 1883 Baron Edmond de Rothschild, of Paris, aided
the settlement of Jews in Palestine with funds and encouragement, and he continued to found colonies for his co-religionists
there.

As early as 1891 in Chicago Rabbi Emil G. Hirsch had taken
a determined stand against Zionism. In March of that year the
Rev. William E. Blackstone, a Christian clergyman of Chicago,
circulated a petition to President Benjamin Harrison and his
Secretary of State, James G. Blaine, urging that they use their
good offices with the Russian, British, German, Austro-Hungarian,

Turkish, Italian, Spanish, French, Belgian, Dutch, Danish, Swedish, Portuguese, Rumanian, Servian, Bulgarian and Greek governments to hold an international conference for the purpose of giving Palestine to the Jews. His plan was suggested as a solution of the Russian Jewish problem. Rabbi Hirsch vigorously opposed the plan and he was opposed to restoration of Palestine as a "visionary" and "sentimental" scheme, and "a fool's errand." In his protests Rabbi Hirsch denied that Palestine belonged to the Jews and that their salvation lay in that direction. While Rabbi Hirsch was thundering against the Zionist dream in his sermons to his German Jewish parishioners, the Russian and Polish Jews of the ghetto on the west side of Chicago were endorsing it with enthusiasm. Rabbi Hirsch told his congregation one Sunday morning: "We are not Zionists. As long as I am in this pulpit Sinai Congregation will be unalterably opposed to Zionism. There is no cause for Zionism in America. Let those who favor a return to Jerusalem go there if they will."

At the Seventh Zionist Congress held in Basle, Switzerland, in 1905 the ardent Zionists committed themselves once for all to Palestine as the national homeland and proclaimed that they were not interested in other colonizing ventures. Rosenwald did not at this time take an active interest in the subject. His close friend Judge Mack was to become an active Zionist, and for many years he battled for Rosenwald's interest and aid. But Rosenwald always felt much closer to Springfield, Illinois, than to Jerusalem.

In 1906 a keen Jewish idealist, Dr. Schmarya Levin, came to Chicago and met Rosenwald, Judge Mack, Rabbi Hirsch and the other outstanding men of the Jewish community there. He saw Julius Rosenwald on subsequent visits to Chicago, and frequently argued Zionism with him. On one occasion, when he was dining at Rosenwald's home, he said to his host: "I could convert one member of your family to the cause of Zionism, but I would first have to remove your wife from her husband's influence." Mrs. Rosenwald, though deeply interested in the Zionist movement because of her close friendship with Henrietta Szold and other idealists who felt that a homeland in Palestine was the solution for the problem of Jewish misery, was never a Zionist herself. Her warm sympathies for people of high ideals naturally brought her close to the group which was interested in Zionism, and she enjoyed their discussions, but she never had enough conviction in the cause to wish to influence her husband in that direction. In the last letter which he wrote to Julius Rosenwald from a Chicago hotel in November, 1928, Dr. Schmarya Levin said sadly:

> I see that the center of gravity of our people will be removed by *outer* and inner forces to the East with Palestine as the focal seat. I would be the happiest man in the world if I possessed the moral and intellectual power to convert to my views a man of your quality, and I am suffering a great deal because of my lack of success. I cherished the hope of seeing your name written into the last chapter of the history of the present epoch of our people with golden letters.

Although he remained unconvinced of the value of Zionism for the Jews of the rest of the world, Rosenwald willingly aided Dr. Levin to found a Hebrew publishing house at Tel-Aviv and also agreed to contribute for the work of the Jewish Institute of Technology at Haifa, with which Dr. Schmarya Levin was associated and in which Rosenwald's friend, Jacob H. Schiff, was interested.

Another Palestinian arrived in the United States in 1909 and made a great impression on the Rosenwalds. He was Aaron Aaronsohn, discoverer of wild wheat, and passionate devotee of agricultural development for Jews in Palestine. His parents had gone there from Rumania when he was five years old in order to escape persecution. His grandfather had been hanged head downward from a tree, on the false charge of complicity in the disappearance of a Christian child and a mythical blood ritual murder. When he was thirteen Aaron Aaronsohn was superintending agricultural work in Palestine, and at seventeen Baron de Rothschild sent him to the agricultural school at Grignon, France, for four years. Afterwards Baron de Rothschild commissioned him to take charge of a Jewish agricultural colony in Palestine, when he was twenty-one years old. He rode unprotected through the colony of the Arabian sect of Druses and acted as peacemaker between them and the Jews. In 1903 Aaronsohn began to look for specimens of wild wheat in northern Palestine, in order to trace the origin of wheat in the world. While walking in a vineyard at the Jewish agricultural colony of Rosh-Pinah on June 18, 1906, Aaronsohn found a stalk of wild wheat in the crevice of a rock, and subsequently he found other specimens at the foot and on the slope of Mount Hermon. He came to the conclusion that wild wheat could be grown in hitherto barren, arid areas by selection and crossing. He wrote a bulletin on wild wheat for the Bureau of Plant Industry of the Department of Agriculture of the United States, and in 1909 he first visited the United States and was received enthusiastically by officials of the Department of Agriculture.

Aaron Aaronsohn had a letter of introduction to Dr. Cyrus Adler, President of Dropsie College of Hebrew and Cognate Learning in Philadelphia. Adler gave him a letter of introduction to Julian W. Mack, who was then a judge of the Appellate Court of Illinois. He called on Judge Mack one Sunday in 1909 in Chicago, and described the importance of his discovery of wild wheat to the world's food supply. Judge Mack was enthusiastic and particularly pleased that such an achievement had originated in Palestine. That same day he took Aaronsohn to call on Rosenwald and his family, who were fascinated by him. Rosenwald spent the day absorbed in Aaronsohn's stories of Palestine and its agricultural possibilities.

On his return from a conference on dry farming at Billings, Montana, Aaronsohn stopped off in Chicago. Rosenwald and Judge Mack took him to dinner with a group of botanists from the University of Chicago, among whom was Roscoe Pound.

He, besides being an important jurist, was once State Botanist and an authority on the subject. The botanists were so much interested in Aaronsohn's discovery that they asked him to deliver a lecture next day before the botanical society. Rosenwald took him to the lecture and listened to it with great interest.

For some years Aaronsohn had wished to establish an agricultural research institute in Palestine, and he now interested Julius Rosenwald, Jacob H. Schiff, Paul M. Warburg, Louis Marshall, Morris Loeb, Julian W. Mack, Cyrus Adler, Judah L. Magnes, Henrietta Szold and others in the project. The Jewish Agricultural Experiment Station was incorporated in 1910, with Rosenwald as president. The experimental station was located in Athlit, at the foot of Mt. Carmel, between Zichron Jacob and Haifa on land belonging to Baron de Hirsch's Jewish Colonization Association. Aaronsohn's aim was to demonstrate the capabilities of supposedly barren soil on allegedly exhausted land. By scientific methods he and his associates succeeded in producing more wheat, barley and oats than their neighbors, and he also carried on valuable experiments with date and vine culture, which were later used in desert lands of the United States. He developed a health bureau, with the aid of Nathan Straus, published agricultural bulletins for farmers in Hebrew and gave agricultural lectures in that language in Palestine.

Aaron Aaronsohn revisited the United States in the spring of 1913 to raise additional funds for his experiment station, and he saw Mr. and Mrs. Rosenwald frequently. It was at this time, apparently, that he persuaded them to visit Palestine, which they did in the spring of 1914. In a letter to Mrs. Rosenwald from Washington on June 12, 1913, he wrote:

Will your Palestinian trip make you a Zionist, you ask. Not necessarily. Zionism is becoming to a certain extent a formula; and dry formulas may be very helpful for masses, for meek individuals, but are like chains for individualities. But I have no doubt whatsoever that your Jewish self-consciousness will find reconfort [sic], tonicity in such a trip. What action will result? Let the future take care of himself.

When the war broke out, Aaronsohn joined the Young Jews and fought with the British against the Turks for the liberation of Palestine. Rosenwald became dissatisfied with him, for he felt that it was his duty to remain at his agricultural station and continue his important work for scientific agriculture into which so much effort had been put. The Jewish Agricultural Experiment Station was occupied by the Turks in October, 1917. Aaronsohn's specimens and twenty thousand books and pamphlets had been packed up by his old father and sealed by the American consul. The Turks, however, found most of the boxes and carted many of them away. They also destroyed the mineralogical museum and the chemical laboratory at the station.

When he was on a brief visit to the United States in December, 1917, Aaronsohn became exasperated with Rosenwald's lack of support for the Zionist cause. The Balfour Declaration guaranteeing Palestine to the Jews as a homeland had been published a month before. He wrote Rosenwald from Washington on December 21, 1917:

In my letter . . . I started to point out to you what wrong you were doing yourself, your posterity, your race in failing to respond to the call of the race, especially now, when the British Declaration and the conquest of Jerusalem have thrilled the souls, quickened the blood, stirred the hearts of millions and tens of millions of both Jews and non-Jews. . . .

Unfortunately you have reached the stage when you are afraid of being pickpocketed whenever anybody approaches you. It must be a very uncomfortable state of mind. But I can assure you of one thing: We Zionists are not after your money. Not I at least. It is the salvation of your soul we are interested in. . . .

I am afraid you will find a good deal of "Hurzpa" [nerve] in my letter. There very likely is. The time for persuasion is over. Every Jew who cares for himself or his children to remain Jews must join. They cannot escape it.

Mrs. Rosenwald feels already this way. It is up to you now.

The train is leaving and I have hardly time to thank you and Mrs. Ros. for your kind hospitality.

Cordially,

Aaron.

Aaronsohn himself was not acceptable to the Zionists in Palestine, and they had bitter quarrels. But now he was exuberant, as were all groups within the Zionist movement, over the supposed guarantee contained in the Balfour Declaration. Rosenwald met Aaronsohn again by accident in August, 1918, in the lobby of the Savoy Hotel in London. That was the last they saw of each other. In May, 1919, Aaronsohn was at the Peace Conference in Paris as adviser to Judge Mack, Professor Felix Frankfurter and others interested in Zionism and Palestine. He went to London to get some needed data and flew back to Paris on May 15, 1919, with an expert British airplane pilot. The plane crashed in the English Channel near Boulogne and both men were killed.

After Aaronsohn's death the experimental station, heavily damaged by the Turks, fell into decay. The wild wheat experimental fields were ruined, but some of the planting survived, including fig and carob trees, grape vines and rose gardens. There were money claims from Palestine residents against the station.

Dr. Judah L. Magnes, head of the Hebrew University in Palestine, wrote to Mr. and Mrs. Rosenwald on May 7, 1923, from Jerusalem:

Dear Mr. and Mrs. Rosenwald,

I am sending you two roses from Aaron Aaronsohn's grave. My wife and I drove there recently. The stately palms line the road into the Experiment Station's grounds, but the road itself is all overgrown with poppies and thistles and daisies and weeds, as though no one was so poor as to trouble to enter this graveyard of many high hopes. Camels and asses were grazing over the experimental fields, and the camels had nibbled off almost all the young leaves of the fig orchard. The windmill still stands, as do the buildings. In the lower rooms of one live a few Arab women, who gathered armfuls of flowers for us in their delight at having someone

come there. In the shed American farming implements are piled in disorder, useless, rusting. We climbed the rotting stairs and looked through
a boarded window where eleven years ago we had been happy and full of
plans over some cups of tea. There the test tubes were all in order along
the wall, and at the other end specimens of wheat, some of them strewn
along the floor. At the back of his house we gathered lavender and roses
from glorious bushes, and as we picked them Aaron never felt so near
or so dead.

Dear Friends: May I not appeal to you to do something to clear
Aaron's good name? He sacrificed everything—his debts, his name
signed to checks for the Experiment Station that have never been hon-
oured. I do not ask that you help re-create his work, although it would be
fitting that in his death he might have some part in the new budding life
here in the land he loved. Please help to pay his debts and keep his name
from ill-use and contempt. Do this, if for nothing else, for the sake of
those old days, so long ago, before that War filled men's souls with bit-
terness and disappointment.

Perhaps I am not the right person to appeal to you, and perhaps the
cause of Palestine has but little interest for you. Please do not let the one
thing or the other stand between you and the old and deep affection you
once had for Aaron Aaronsohn.

Yours truly,

J. L. Magnes.

After some difficulty and delay the claims against the Jewish
Agricultural Experiment Station were liquidated in 1926, and
Rosenwald contributed generously for their settlement.

On March 18, 1929, Knowles A. Ryerson, Senior Horticulturist
of the U. S. Department of Agriculture, wrote to Rosenwald
concerning the young men whom Rosenwald had aided at Aaronsohn's suggestion with agricultural scholarships so that they
might return afterwards to Palestine to take up scientific agriculture. He mentioned that he had met them in Palestine and
went on to say:

You may or may not have heard of their continued progress; your activities and interests have been so wide and so varied. Your far-sighted
interest in Aaronsohn and in these young men with whom he was in contact
has gone far in making possible a group in Palestine who combine prac-

tical common sense and business training in agriculture with their un-swerving idealism and loyalty, which alone can guarantee a practical working out of the problems facing that fascinating country. . . .

The part you played in encouraging and supporting Aaronsohn and making it possible for the future agricultural leaders of Palestine to secure thorough training is not known by many. I do not know just how closely you keep in touch with these human investments of yours, but as an outsider—though an interested one—I have wanted to tell you that they are a credit to the confidence and support you gave them, and that this group of young men, together with a few others of like mind who received training in Europe, are the hope of a rational agricultural development in that country. If and when a sound rural life develops in the plains and hills of Palestine, it will have been due in a large measure to your far-sighted comprehension of the problem and your quiet but vital support to its rational solution.

### IV

Rosenwald was anxious to do whatever he could to bring about a rapprochement between the orthodox and reformed Jews of Chicago, and in that connection he became a willing and heavy contributor to the Chicago Hebrew Institute. This organization had been established in 1899 by a group of Chicago Zionists for educational purposes, and plans were made later to expand its activities and establish a cultural center for both the Russian and Polish Jews of the west side of Chicago and the German Jews of the south side. Rosenwald agreed to lend the Institute $75,000 for a building and made other contributions to it.

Both Rosenwald and his wife were greatly interested in the work of the Associated Jewish Charities of Chicago, of which he became president in 1907, and to which he was the largest contributor for the rest of his life. In his work with this federation of Jewish charities he developed an idea which he carried out for the remainder of his philanthropic career, and which had a profound effect on philanthropy in America. He urged those who contributed to the federated Jewish organizations of the city to give their money without restrictions and in such form that the principal as well as the interest might be used within the discretion of the directors and trustees. This principle he later developed into an ardent campaign against the practice of perpetual endowments for philanthropic funds.

In addition to his work for the Jews he responded readily to appeals from organizations among Christians of the city. The United Charities of Chicago, which carried on general relief work, received his generous support from 1906 until the time of his death, and during that period he gave it approximately $120,000. Catholic, Protestant, and non-sectarian hospitals, schools and causes always found him willing to listen to their appeals and eager to contribute to those of which he approved.

For many years he also acted as the bellwether of Chicago charity, and one of his favorite occupations was soliciting other men for contributions to worthy causes.

On the occasion of his fiftieth birthday, on August 12, 1912, Julius Rosenwald announced public gifts of $687,500. In addition, he made various gifts on his own birthday to his relatives in the United States and in Germany.[2]

Among his fiftieth birthday gifts to institutions was one of $250,000 to the University of Chicago, towards a building fund for new campus structures. In May, 1911, he had been invited to become a trustee of the University. When he was first approached on the subject by Judge Jesse A. Baldwin, one of the trustees, he remarked that he was reluctant to accept because he did not wish to pose as an educated man, since he had never finished high school. Judge Baldwin remarked that that was a reflection upon

[2] Julius Rosenwald's fiftieth anniversary gifts in 1912 included $250,000 to the Associated Jewish Charities of Chicago for a new administration building; $50,000 to Hull-House for a country club for social workers; $25,000 to the Winfield Tuberculosis Sanatorium; $50,000 for a new gymnasium for the Chicago Hebrew Institute; $25,000 for the Marks Nathan Home for Jewish Orphans, provided that institution would become federated with the Associated Jewish Charities; $12,500 for the purchase of a farm for the Glenwood Manual Training School for Boys; and $25,000 to Booker T. Washington, for the work Dr. Washington had begun for the improvement of Negro schools in the South, a work which Rosenwald had become interested in during the previous year.

him, as he never had gone to high school at all. Rosenwald finally became a trustee of the University in 1912. This was the only university appointment he ever accepted, and he did so because of his deep interest in Chicago and its development, for he considered the University a most important part of that development. University officials agreed that he was one of the most valuable trustees the University had ever had the good fortune to possess. Not only did he give lavishly of his own money to the University, making it contributions of about four and a half million dollars, but he worked hard to obtain other funds for it and to see that its funds were utilized to the best financial advantage. He had a genuine appreciation of the proper relationship of trustees to a university and its faculty and never took the attitude, as did some business men, that the faculty were the employees of the trustees and should do as they were told. When Robert M. Hutchins became President of the University of Chicago, he presented a plan for its thorough reorganization, which had been approved previously by the faculty's senate. At the meeting of the board of trustees called to consider the plan, Julius Rosenwald asked the new president: "You say the faculty approve this plan?" President Hutchins, who had been worried about his trustees' attitude towards the radical reforms suggested, replied in the affirmative. "Then who are we to object, gentlemen?" Rosenwald asked his fellow trustees, and the plan was approved unanimously.

Newspapers, friends and strangers in various parts of the world telegraphed their approval of a man who preferred to give money away on his birthday rather than to receive luxuries from others.

Reuben Brainin, who was the guest of Rosenwald in 1912, wrote of him:

He was then in the prime of life. His personality radiated vitality and versatile interest. He was a very patient listener. When somebody tried to bring out an argument, he would not interrupt even if the speaker repeated himself indefinitely. His decisions were always clear-cut. He would not say: "I will try to do my best," but would state that "provided you do this or that I will do the following." He once told me: "I believe in the instinct of the majority. In my philanthropic interests I have adopted the principle of supply and demand. Show me that there is a genuine demand and I will endeavor to help you to provide an adequate supply. In relief campaigns, in charitable institutions, even in institutions of learning, I have found this motto to apply: Never would I want to be the sole supporter or sole creator of any institution. It is too autocratic. It would lack a raison d'être."

## CHAPTER V

## THE NEGROES

### I

ONE of Rosenwald's friends, Paul J. Sachs, used frequently to visit Sears, Roebuck during the early nineteen-hundreds as a junior partner of their bankers, Goldman Sachs and Co. Mr. Sachs, subsequently professor of Fine Arts at Harvard University and director of the Fogg Museum, recalled that whenever he and Rosenwald began to talk business together, they usually ended up by discussing social movements instead. Professor Sachs had come in contact with Mrs. William H. Baldwin, Jr., and he had taken an interest in the work of the urban leagues for aid to Negroes. He discussed this work with Rosenwald and solicited his support for it. In 1910 Professor Sachs sent Rosenwald a book which had just then been published: *An American Citizen, the Life of William H. Baldwin, Jr.,* by John Graham Brooks. Rosenwald always said that this book and Booker T. Washington's *Up From Slavery,* influenced him more than any two books he had ever read.

William H. Baldwin, Jr., a native of Massachusetts, had become a railroad executive after his graduation from college, and during the late years of the nineteenth century was general manager of the Southern Railway. Baldwin's father, head of the Christian Union of Boston, saw a Negro one day carrying some heavy bags in a Boston railroad station. He helped him by taking one of the bags, and thus became acquainted with Booker T. Washington. He gave Dr. Washington a letter to his son, and Baldwin became interested in the work of Tuskegee Institute and in the efforts Booker T. Washington was making on behalf of his race.

Baldwin was soon convinced that the great need of the Negroes was educational opportunity, and he devoted himself thereafter to promoting Negro education in the South. He was a practical Unitarian moralist. He had taken part in protests against oppression of minorities, and he was one of the leaders of a Christian protest against the massacres of the Jews in Kishinev. After studying the method of vocational training established at Tuskegee by Booker T. Washington, Baldwin became one of the trustees and worked hard for its welfare. He was instrumental in getting Andrew Carnegie to make a contribution of $600,000 to it in the early years of the twentieth century.

At a meeting of an educational association in Richmond, Virginia, in 1902, Baldwin elaborated his ideas on rural education for Negroes and whites in the South. He suggested rural schools for both with at least ten acres of grounds, teachers in residence in the neighborhood, a term of not less than eight months in the year, and training in agriculture and trades. He felt that the school should be the center of social activity as well as a vocational enterprise.

Among Baldwin's other interests, in the years before his death in 1905, was the corruption of finance and politics. This, too, concerned Rosenwald throughout his career, and it seems most likely that in Baldwin's life Rosenwald found an ideal, which he tried hard to follow.

II

It has been said that the Negroes have been cheated from the first, for they were the only unwilling immigrants to the United States. During the period of their slavery no thought was given to their education except for a few individual efforts. The Negro, in slavery, was regarded as having been ordained by God to a state of ignorance, and every effort was made to ensure that he would remain so. After the Civil War broke out, many slaves escaped and many others were abandoned when their owners left their plantations at the approach of Union armies. The Negroes crowded into the Union Army camps, and it was in these camps that the first systematic effort was made to educate them. In 1861 the American Missionary Association organized a school for Negroes in Virginia, and in the following year a similar school was started in South Carolina. Freedmen's aid and relief societies sprang up, and religious zealots from the North welcomed the opportunity for uplifting the Negro. They did valuable preliminary work, but these efforts were no substitute for government action.

During the painful reconstruction era, the political combination of carpet baggers from the North and emancipated Negroes forced the state governments in the South to appropriate some funds for Negro education. However, the defeated southern states were too poor to provide decent public education even for the whites, and the result was that Negro education was neglected wherever possible and was always subordinated to white education. Whatever Negro public schools existed were located in churches, ramshackle huts, lodge halls and small homes rented for the purpose. By and large, they were filthy, dilapidated and utterly inadequate for school use.

After white political control was completely reestablished, the Negroes were practically disfranchised throughout the South. Socially they were ostracized everywhere in the country, and economically they were reduced to a level approaching their former state of slavery, without so much as the slight security of having an owner.

Soon after the Civil War some institutions of higher learning and manual training for Negroes were established, and to a large extent these provided the leaven for general Negro education. Fisk University at Nashville, Tennessee, was started in 1865; Howard University at Washington, D. C., and Atlanta University at Atlanta, Georgia, were opened in 1867; Hampton Normal and Agricultural Institute at Hampton, Virginia, was established in 1868. It was at Hampton Institute, directed by the benevolent and capable General Samuel Chapman Armstrong, that Booker T. Washington, who was born in slavery, received the education which he tried so hard for the rest of his life to pass on to others of his race. By 1870 about ten per cent of the Negroes were getting some slight education in the schools established by the religious associations and the Freedmen's Bureau. Negro illiteracy was estimated at 79.9 per cent.

The legislature of Alabama in 1880 passed a law establishing the Tuskegee Normal and Industrial Institute at Tuskegee, Macon County, Alabama, and gave it an annual grant of $2,000. George W. Campbell, a white man, and Lewis Adams, a Negro, were the leaders in this movement for a school on the model of Hampton. They wrote to General Armstrong at Hampton and asked him to send them a teacher, and in June, 1881, Booker T. Washington was sent to Tuskegee. When he began his work there, Rosenwald was still learning the clothing business in New York City.

Booker T. Washington opened the new school on the fourth of July, 1881, in a rented shanty church with thirty pupils and himself as the sole teacher. In his autobiography he wrote:

I recall that during the first months of school that I taught in this building it was in such poor repair that, whenever it rained, one of the older students would very kindly leave his lessons and hold an umbrella over me while I heard the recitations of the others. I remember, also, that on more than one occasion my landlady held an umbrella over me while I ate breakfast.

During his first month in Alabama, he made a preliminary tour of the country districts and found wretched conditions prevailing among his people. In most of the primitive schools established in log cabins and run-down churches, no provision had been made for heat; a fire was built in the yard, "and teacher and

pupils passed in and out of the house as they got cold or warm."
The schools held sessions for three to five months during the
year, and the teachers were badly trained. No equipment was
available except a rough blackboard. Carter G. Woodson, editor
of the *Journal of Negro History*, which Rosenwald helped to
support, wrote: "The writer once attended a school in Virginia
in which a girl studied McGuffey's Fourth Reader for fifteen
years."

The Negro students whom Dr. Washington encountered were
eager to learn, but they felt that book learning was the only kind
respected in the white man's world, and therefore they resented
any other kind. In many cases the aim of the average student
was to get a diploma which would enable him to teach others
who wished to get a diploma to teach others. Some who knew
nothing about taking care of their bodies or of ways of making
a living were puzzling painfully over Greek and other advanced
subjects. Dr. Washington knew that about 85 per cent of the
population of the Gulf states was dependent upon agriculture
for a livelihood, and he therefore aimed to teach his students to
take their part in an agricultural life. He summarized his aims in
his autobiography as follows:

> We wanted to give them such an education as would fit a large propor-
> tion of them to be teachers, and at the same time cause them to return
> to the plantation districts and show the people there how to put new
> energy and new ideas into farming, as well as into the intellectual and
> moral and religious life of the people.

But this kind of education was far from the thoughts of the
ambitious, but completely uneducated Negroes who had received
their freedom from slavery less than twenty years before. They
felt that they had not come to school to work with their hands,
make bricks, dig foundations, erect buildings, tend livestock and
care for crops. Dr. Washington insisted that they do all of these
things in part of their time not used for cultural studies.

His first great need was for funds adequate to establish even a primitive school. The legislature increased its appropriation in 1884 from $2,000 to $3,000, but this was nothing compared with the need. Dr. Washington became the traveling salesman of Negro education and interested generous individuals throughout the country in his plans and his requirements. Boston ladies were among his earliest supporters, and southern whites in his neighborhood also began to help him. The Negroes helped themselves with work and small sums. Dr. Washington wrote in his autobiography:

Even as a youth, and later in manhood, I had the feeling that it was cruelly wrong in the central government, at the beginning of our freedom, to fail to make some provision for the general education of our people in addition to what the states might do, so that the people would be the better prepared for the duties of citizenship.

What the central government had failed to do adequately, groups of earnest educators and wealthy individuals began to undertake. Shortly after the Civil War, George Peabody, a banker, established a fund of $2,000,000 for the promotion of popular education in the southern states through cooperation with local officials. This fund aided in establishing public schools in towns and cities, and it helped to create sentiment for Negro education and to procure legislation. It founded George Peabody College for Teachers, affiliated with Vanderbilt University at Nashville, Tennessee. John F. Slater, a manufacturer of Norwich, Connecticut, in 1882 left a fund of $1,000,000 for Negro education. This fund supported normal schools, including Hampton and Tuskegee, denominational schools and town schools for Negroes, and specialized in vocational education.

Anna T. Jeanes established a fund in 1908 for rural schools. In 1902 John D. Rockefeller, Sr., gave his newly organized General Education Board an initial gift of $1,000,000, which he increased by additional gifts of $10,000,000 in 1905, $32,000,000 in 1907 and $10,000,000 in 1909.

The General Education Board, whose first chairman was William H. Baldwin, Jr., realized that the first effort must be directed towards improvement of economic conditions in the South before education could develop there. "School systems could not be given to them, and they were not prosperous enough to support them," the General Education Board reported.[1]

The Board decided that it must help to teach the farmer, black and white, how to farm. Dr. Seeman A. Knapp, of the U. S. Department of Agriculture, who had established a system of county agents in some parts of the South, a work which Sears, Roebuck and Co. sponsored elsewhere in the country, was called into conference by the General Education Board, and plans were made to extend through the South, his farm demonstration system, which had worked so well in combating the boll weevil.[2]

Negro farmers were quick to take to demonstration of better agricultural methods, and Tuskegee and Hampton Institutes helped to make them aware of its value. Agents and teachers traveled among the white and Negro farmers throughout the South, teaching them improved methods of farming.

The General Education Board then began to devote itself to aiding communities provide educational facilities, and from 1902 to 1914 it spent $699,781 for Negro colleges and schools, in addition to contributing towards the work of rural schools for both races. Local prejudices against public education had to be broken down, but by persistent propaganda and financial aid educational facilities were gradually established. The traveling teachers, supported by the Anna T. Jeanes Fund, visited country schools, gave lessons to teachers and pupils, and aroused the local communities to greater interest in improvement of rural schools for Negroes.

In effect, the various educational foundations and funds, supplemented by contributions from individuals to specific institutions such as Tuskegee, became national, central organizations for

[1] *The General Education Board, An Account of Its Activities,* 1902-1914.

[2] Dr. Knapp had been enabled to combat the boll weevil, because the boll weevil was officially regarded as an interstate pest, for at the time it was felt that the federal government had no authority to spend money on local projects in the states.

carrying out what the federal government had neglected to do. This was the situation of increasing attention to Negro education in the South which existed in 1911 when Booker T. Washington first came into contact with Julius Rosenwald.

III

No book could have been calculated to interest Rosenwald more than Booker T. Washington's autobiography. It was filled with the homely, courageous truths which Rosenwald admired and in which he believed. The ex-slave, working in Alabama to improve his race, with a conviction that practical training in industry and agriculture were essential for his people, attracted Rosenwald's sympathetic interest. The experiences of the two men differed widely but each could intuitively understand the aspirations and problems of the other. Rosenwald, a member of another minority group, had the advantage of being white and of having had greater financial credit. Dr. Washington, on the other hand, had had superior educational opportunities. Both of them believed that it was better for individuals to start life without too many advantages, for neither of them had had too many himself.

To help men who were working hard to raise themselves out of discouraging depths was always a great satisfaction to Rosenwald, and he loved to help individuals and institutions when he could do so without destroying their self-reliance. In the case of Booker T. Washington, the individual was obviously a person of character and distinction, who had gained the enthusiastic approval of such people as President Theodore Roosevelt, Seth Low, Robert C. Ogden, H. H. Rogers, Andrew Carnegie, and William H. Baldwin, Jr. The institution he guided was obviously one of potential value, which had proved its ability to survive great hardships during the thirty years of its existence before Rosenwald first became interested in it. The problem of the colored race was such a large one that there was no danger that the effort to improve its condition would ever hamper the efforts of its own people.

Nothing could have been calculated to impress Rosenwald more than this statement in Dr. Washington's autobiography:

My experience is that there is something in human nature which always makes an individual recognize and reward merit, no matter under what colour of skin merit is found. I have found, too, that it is the visible, the tangible, that goes a long ways in softening prejudices. The actual sight of a first-class house that a Negro has built is ten times more potent than pages of discussion about a house that he ought to build, or perhaps could build.

As a successful man, coming from a minority religious group, Rosenwald must have heartily agreed when he read in *Up From Slavery*: "The individual who can do something that the world wants done will, in the end, make his way regardless of his race."

The Negroes in the United States were American citizens, but they were deprived of the rights of American citizens and discriminated against economically and socially. When competition for jobs became acute, the tension often resulted in riots. Negroes were lynched for alleged personal offenses, just as the Jews had been massacred and deprived of economic opportunity in other lands. There was no special kinship between the Jews and the Negroes and it would be too much to say that Rosenwald took up their problems because he was a Jew. But it is true that because he was a Jew he understood better the rigors of Negro persecution and discrimination.

After he became interested in the problem, he made an effort to get economic opportunities for colored men and women, and to insure them educational opportunities. But he followed the dictum of Booker T. Washington that the Negroes should not try for social equality but for individual perfection and mutual trade among themselves. In the effort to obtain employment for them, Rosenwald was thwarted by the prejudices of other white men. He tried to get Negroes more chances for employment in his own company but found that the consensus of opinion among his associates and his employees was against it. He also met with quick opposition when he tried to substitute Negro help for white men in the office building which he owned in Chicago; the tenants protested against the change and pointed out to their landlord that the old faithful employees should not lose their jobs in favor of Rosenwald's protégés. In both cases he bowed to the will of the majority rather than allow an antagonism to develop against himself and the Negroes whom he was trying to help. He ended by concentrating on education to fit Negroes for those opportunities open to them and which they might develop among themselves.

Booker T. Washington was insistent on the importance of vocational, manual and agricultural training in the Negro's struggle to make a place for himself in the contemporary scene. At the same time he wished the members of his race to keep themselves apart so that they might avoid the social frictions which resulted in individual and group violence. He realized that the Negro would come into business and professional contact with whites on occasion, but he advised strongly that their contacts be limited to these necessary meetings. In his autobiography he told of his own efforts to avoid social intercourse except where it was absolutely necessary for the advancement of his job as solicitor of funds for educational improvement. His doctrine, in effect, was one of constant compromise on the question of social equality and as such was repugnant to more passionate spirits who wished to advance the social status of the Negro as well as his economic and professional position, and who felt that the one could not be attained without the other.

Booker T. Washington had been invited to make an address at the opening of the Atlanta Cotton States and International Exposition at Atlanta, Georgia, on September 18, 1895. It was the first time a Negro had been asked to speak before an audience of southern whites. Dr. Washington was by then well known for his achievements as the exponent of practical education for the colored people. Standing on the sun-lit platform at the Atlanta exposition hall, crowded with whites and blacks, Dr. Washington raised his hand with the fingers outspread, and said: "In all things that are purely social we can be as separate as the fingers, yet one as the hand in all things essential to mutual progress," and he drew the fingers of his hand together into a symbol of solidarity. Going on to discuss the Negro's intense loyalty and his potentialities for cooperation with his white neighbors, Dr. Washington said:

Nearly sixteen millions of hands will aid you in pulling the load upward, or they will pull against you the load downward. We shall constitute one-third and more of the ignorance and crime of the South, or one-third of its intelligence and progress; we shall contribute one-third to the business and industrial prosperity of the South, or we shall prove a veritable body of death, stagnating, depressing, retarding every effort to advance the body politic. . . .

The wisest of my race understand that the agitation of questions on social equality is the extremest folly, and that progress in the enjoyment of all the privileges that will come to us must be the result of severe and constant struggles rather than of artificial forcing. No race that has anything to contribute to the markets of the world is long in any degree ostracized. It is important and right that all privileges of the law be ours, but it is vastly more important that we be prepared for the exercise of these privileges. The opportunity to earn a dollar in a factory just now is worth infinitely more than the opportunity to spend a dollar in an opera-house.[3]

When Dr. Washington had concluded his famous address the audience went wild with enthusiasm. Governor Bullock, of Georgia, rushed across the platform, and the two men of antagonistic groups stood for some minutes with clasped hands as the crowd roared its approval. No speech of the period except Bryan's, "Cross of Gold and Crown of Thorns," made a greater sensation. Newspapers all over the country published it in full

[3] *Up From Slavery*, pp. 221-223.

and expressed their editorial approval. At first the colored people of the South and North were almost unanimously impressed, but after the excitement had died down, some were not so sure of Dr. Washington's point of view. As he himself expressed it, "Some of them seemed to feel that they had been hypnotized."

The more radical Negro thinkers advocated continuous insistence on equality, and Dr. Washington insisted on complete acceptance of duties. His critics felt that industrial education was not enough, and that economic opportunity would never be achieved without political and social equality. With this group Rosenwald had no more patience than he had with the uncompromising Zionists, who demanded a national and political state for the Jews as a solution of their problem.

Dr. Washington's policy naturally appealed to the white men of the South and to a majority of the white men in the North. At this time southern white men were watching intently to see which way Negro leaders were advising their people, and how northern politicians might seek to profit by an acute southern problem. The southerners were determined that the majority rule would not apply south of the Mason and Dixon line. The years immediately following the Civil War, when the self-seeking and revengeful in both North and South had taken full advantage of predatory opportunities, were still vivid to southern whites. And the recapture of power by the oppressive Ku Klux Klan was still vivid in the minds of the Negroes. The southern whites were ready, by riot if necessary, to exterminate Negroes rather than permit them to control even locally, and they quickly adopted a defensive attitude that Negroes could not be looked upon as people, even in a democracy. Dr. Washington's gospel that his people should attain skill and wealth first before they attempted to gain rights and privileges ostensibly guaranteed them under the Constitution reassured the South and comforted many Negroes who wished peace.

## IV

In the fall of 1910 Dr. Jesse E. Moorland, secretary of the International Committee of the Y. M. C. A., was invited by L. Wilbur Messer to come to Chicago to help raise money for a Y. M. C. A. building for colored people in that city. Rosenwald invited Mr. Messer, Dr. Moorland and William J. Parker to lunch with him and Albert H. Loeb at the Sears, Roebuck plant. He asked the men questions about their drive for funds, and after he had listened to their answers, said: "I will give you $25,000 for a Y. M. C. A. building for colored people in any city in the United States where an additional $75,000 is raised among white and colored people." The men were startled at this extraordinary offer. Rosenwald smiled and added: "Well, I guess you can't do more than one a month, but I hope you can."

Mr. Messer felt it his duty to explain to Rosenwald that the organization of the Y. M. C. A. was such that only Protestants could be associated with its direction. He answered:

I want nothing to do with the management. I have been studying the colored people and have come to the conclusion that they need help more than any other group, and I want to help them and encourage other rich Jews to do the same thing. I believe that the Young Men's Christian Association is the best medium I know for accomplishing what I would like to see done for colored men, and this does not mean that I am any less a Jew.

The public announcement of Rosenwald's offer won instant approval throughout the United States. Among those who wrote to congratulate him was President Taft. He invited him to the White House to ask him if he would permit his offer to apply to an uncompleted Y. M. C. A. building for colored people which had been begun in Washington a few years before, but on which work had been stopped because of lack of funds; Rosenwald readily agreed to the President's suggestion.

When he made his offer to contribute to Y. M. C. A. buildings for Negroes, he felt that such a cooperative effort would make for better relations between the two races. In Dallas, Texas, which was one of the cities to meet his offer, the gathering to raise funds was said to have been the first occasion on which Negroes and white men came together in a cooperative effort. There had been no previous recreational or dormitory facilities for Negroes in Dallas until this colored Y. M. C. A. was built. Between 1910 and 1920 the dormitory rooms in the Y. M. C. A. buildings erected in thirteen cities with the aid of Rosenwald's money were practically the only places where Negro educators, business and professional men and others could find comfortable or safe sleeping accommodations, outside the cramped homes of their friends or relatives. In many places, the buildings offered the only gymnasium and swimming pool for colored people, besides the usual Y. M. C. A. opportunities for cultural and vocational studies. The fact that Negroes succeeded in raising money among themselves to meet the conditions of the offer impressed the white people in many communities and aroused interest among them in the living conditions of their Negro neighbors. It also gave the Negroes more assurance and inspired them to create other community activities for their mutual welfare.

Besides these thirteen buildings, Rosenwald contributed $25,000 each for buildings for colored women in New York City, Indianapolis and Philadelphia. A survey of the work was made at his request, and in 1920 he renewed his offer. By this time the large migration of Negroes from southern rural communities to northern urban centers had made the work more useful than ever. The vocational and other educational courses were particularly valuable. The new offer required that a total of $125,000 instead of $100,000 be raised locally in each city, because of increased building costs, and in order to provide better buildings; Rosenwald contributing $25,000. His total contributions for Y. M. C. A. buildings amounted to $637,000, besides his contributions of $75,000 for Y. W. C. A. buildings. Twenty-five communities

finally took advantage of the offer, and almost six million dollars
was raised by white and colored people for the work. Fifty other
communities, unable to meet the offer, were stimulated by it to
build smaller branches. In this renewed Y. M. C. A. effort George
R. Arthur, head of the colored Y. M. C. A. in Chicago, worked
closely with Rosenwald and became one of his most valued advisers on Negro affairs.

In his address at the opening of the Wabash Avenue branch
of the Y. M. C. A. in Chicago, Rosenwald said:

You must realize that in the evolution of a race time counted by
generations is necessary. This is true of any race, white or black or yellow.

The leaders and the participants in all great reforms have their dark
hours, their discouragements; but let me bring you a message of hope.
Let me remind you that your cause is just, that the world moves forward
and God still is on his throne, and back of every righteous cause there
is an arm strong enough to bring victory to his side.

The man who hates a black man because he is black has the same spirit
as he who hates a poor man because he is poor. It is the spirit of caste.
I am the inferior of any man whose rights I trample under my feet.

Men are not superior by the accident of race or color; they are superior
who have the best heart, the best brain. Superiority is born of honesty,
of virtue, of charity, and above all, of the love of liberty.

Of one thing you colored men can rest assured; the most intelligent,
the grandest are on your side. The sympathies of the noblest are with
you. Your enemies are also the enemies of liberty, of progress and of
justice.

The white men who make the white race honorable believe in equal
rights for you. The noblest dead were, the noblest living are your friends.

In May, 1911, Booker T. Washington came to Chicago to raise
funds for Tuskegee Institute. It was then that he met Rosenwald,
who decided to give a luncheon for him at the Blackstone Hotel.
He sent out invitations to bankers, educators, public officials and
capitalists and a large number of them accepted. It was the first
time the Blackstone had had a colored guest.

One of Rosenwald's chauffeurs objected to driving Dr. Booker
T. Washington because his skin was black. Rosenwald made no

attempt to persuade him but simply told him that if he did not want to drive him, one of the other men would take his place. The chauffeur asked him whether he was going to ride in the car too. Rosenwald assured him that he was. "Well," he said, "if you can stand it to ride with him, I guess I can stand it to drive him."

In introducing Dr. Washington to his guests Rosenwald said:

Whether it is because I belong to a people who have known centuries of persecution, or whether it is because I am naturally inclined to sympathize with the oppressed, I have always felt keenly for the colored race.

My sympathies, however, remained more or less dormant until the book "An American Citizen"—the life of William Henry Baldwin, Jr., came to my notice. I had of course read Dr. Washington's "Up From Slavery" and later writings, but interesting as they were they did not for some reason or other make the impression upon me that did this book. Particularly was I impressed with Mr. Baldwin's contention that if the question of deportation—which I think all will agree is unworthy of serious discussion—is dismissed, it leaves the single issue that in some way the two races must occupy one country. They have to learn probably the highest and hardest of all arts, the art of living together with decency and forbearance. Nothing will so test the sincerities of our religion, our moral obligation, or even our common self-respect, as will the exigencies of this which is among the greatest of all our problems.

The wise, statesmanlike leader who is our guest today, is greatly serving two races, which, but for his *ministry of conciliation*, might drift into irreconcilable antagonism. He is helping his own race to attain the high art of self-help and self-dependence, and he is helping the white race to learn that opportunity and obligation go hand in hand, and that there is no enduring superiority save that which comes as the result of serving. His own rise from slavery as told by him with the simplicity of truth, to the place of guide of one race, and friend and counselor of two races, is prophetic of the widening opportunities of his people. Happy the race which follows his sane, wise earnest leadership! Happy the nation which, in the words of the late Judge Brewer, knows and honors a Washington, whether he be George or Booker!

That same evening he and Dr. Washington attended the Fifty-third Anniversary banquet of the Y. M. C. A., at which both

of them spoke. At this meeting an announcement was made of
Rosenwald's offer to contribute $50,000 toward a fund to be
raised to build a 1,200 room Y. M. C. A. hotel in Chicago for
white men and boys, to cost more than $500,000.

L. Wilbur Messer had taken up his idea for a Y. M. C. A.
hotel with Rosenwald after he had made an investigation of
the demoralizing effect on youth of cheap hotels and lodging
houses. The Y. M. C. A. had only recently completed a drive
for $1,000,000 and it was impossible to go before the public for
this additional $500,000. They decided, therefore, to confine the
appeal to wealthy men.

Rosenwald went to see John G. Shedd, of Marshall Field and
Company, and persuaded him to be one of ten men to contribute
$50,000 for the project. He also called on Cyrus H. McCormick
next day, and he agreed to contribute $50,000. The day after the
project had been announced at the dinner, N. W. Harris telephoned from the country and offered to contribute $50,000. A
week later, James A. Patten, the wheat operator, at Rosenwald's
solicitation agreed to make a similar contribution. In less than
two weeks half the necessary funds were raised. But it was not
until May, 1915, that the rest of the money was raised, because
the World War intervened; the project was enlarged and then
they raised more than $650,000. The building was opened on May
22, 1916.

v

Rosenwald hired a private railroad car in October, 1911, and
took a party of relatives and friends to Tuskegee Institute, among
whom were Rabbi Emil G. Hirsch, Professor Graham Taylor,
of the University of Chicago, E. G. Cooley, former superintendent
of schools of Chicago, and L. Wilbur Messer. They made a
thorough inspection of the Institute, and were enthusiastic about
its achievements and its possibilities. A meeting was held in the
chapel with the faculty and about two thousand students. The

students sang spirituals and Dr. Washington, Rabbi Hirsch, E. G. Cooley and Rosenwald made speeches.

If any one again claims [said Rosenwald] that colored men and colored women will not and cannot be as good citizens as there are in America, I shall ask him to come down to Tuskegee and visit the places we have visited, and I am sure that no other evidence will be required to prove to him altogether—the proof was not necessary so far as I am concerned—but to prove to any doubter that colored men and women are just as capable of good citizenship, or learning, as any of the white people who have come into my experience.

I am just going to say a word along the lines of the song you have just sung about "back-biting will soon be over." That is optimism and I believe that the colored people of this country have every right to be optimistic. I have always felt that there was a future for them, but never felt so assured of that future, or that it was so near at hand as has been proven in my experience with the new movement for building Young Men's Christian Association buildings for colored men in the large cities of our country. . . .

What I have seen here today has inspired me beyond words. I only regret that some of the gentlemen whom I wanted to bring with me were not able to see what I have seen in this glorious work. Your Principal, Mr. Washington, to my notion has done the greatest work of any man in America. How he can be so modest as he is with what he has accomplished is something unheard of, so far as my experience goes. If only more people knew!

After he himself became enthusiastic about Tuskegee he saw to it that more people knew of the work. Robert C. Ogden, a trustee, took a party every year from New York, and Rosenwald followed his example by taking one whenever he was able. When he could not go himself, he sent those of his friends who might be interested. On February 12, 1912, he was elected a trustee and remained one for the rest of his life. Other members of his family have also served. When he was elected, Seth Low was chairman of the board, and the other trustees were Robert C. Ogden, William G. Willcox and William Jay Schieffelin.

That same year Rosenwald visited other Negro schools and

offered to contribute to their work. Among these was Meharry Medical College in Nashville, Tennessee. It was founded in 1876 by the Meharry brothers. Samuel Meharry had been hauling grist from a mill in Kentucky along a country road when his wagon was mired in a ditch. An old colored man helped him and invited him to spend the night in his cabin. Meharry had no money at the time, but when he parted from his host, he promised that if ever he prospered, he would do something for the colored people. He kept his word, and he and his brothers contributed more than $30,000 for a medical, dental and pharmaceutical school for Negroes. Rosenwald made contributions to it for a number of years, and the Julius Rosenwald Fund later gave $252,000 for its support.

Rosenwald's first act as a trustee was to suggest to the board that steps be taken to relieve Dr. Booker T. Washington from the arduous burden of traveling to raise funds for Tuskegee. He gave $5,000 a year for five years toward a fund of $50,000 a year, and thereafter Dr. Washington was able to spend more time at Tuskegee making improvements in its work. In addition to his own contribution, Rosenwald successfully solicited money for this fund from Jewish philanthropic leaders in both New York and Chicago.

Mrs. Rosenwald took as much personal interest in the welfare of Tuskegee as her husband did. On their trips to the Institute, she noticed that the guest house needed china and glassware, and upon her return to Chicago she sent equipment for its kitchen and dining-room, which is still being used there. Mrs. Booker T. Washington wrote to her:

I want you also to know that we love Mr. Rosenwald and you for what you are to us and not for what you may or may not give.

The coming of you two into our lives here gives us new courage, more hope and greater faith. I am not alone in this. Just this afternoon a group of us met accidentally in the house and the conversation turned to you and Mr. Rosenwald. We ended by saying Mr. Rosenwald makes you forget all of the hard things in life. His presence takes off the *chill.*

The Rosenwald family soon became familiars at Tuskegee. Mrs. Rosenwald taught the colored girls how to bake, cook and turn their dresses. She and her husband were always particularly fond of the Children's House and kindergarten, and they paid two-thirds of the cost of maintaining this branch, which had had to be closed for lack of funds. They also paid the small tuition fees of fifty cents a month for those children whose parents could not afford to do so. Every Christmas they sent toys for the Children's House at Tuskegee as well as to the colored children in various elementary schools in the South.

When their special car backed up to the small railroad station in Alabama each spring, there was always a throng of students, cheering joyously. Sometimes, when they arrived at night, they were greeted with a flaming torchlight procession. Rosenwald and his guests would march in an irregular procession, led by a brass band, to the neat, red-brick buildings with their white Colonial columns, which Booker T. Washington and his students had built themselves.

During their visit the students gave demonstrations of their vocational work. The visitors saw cows being milked, chimneys constructed, pottery manufactured, tailoring, shoemaking and mechanical work being carried out in the classrooms. Finally, a large white horse would be brought out for the demonstration entitled, "How to Keep an Animal in Repair." Rosenwald was particularly fond of this practical demonstration feature of the annual program. But most of all he loved the singing of Negro spirituals by the superb Tuskegee choir. His favorite was "Walking in Jerusalem Just Like John." And once, when he and Mrs. Rosenwald were in Palestine and could not attend the annual exercises he sent a cable which read: "I'm Walking In Jerusalem Just Like John."

VI

In 1904 H. H. Rogers, of the Standard Oil Company, an early supporter of Dr. Washington's work, offered to supply the money for building rural schools in a few counties of Alabama. He suggested that Dr. Washington take two or three counties as an experiment, build good schools and watch the result. They agreed that rather than give schools to the Negroes, they should stimulate them instead to contribute to the work themselves, so that they might learn its value, and support the schools after they were built.

In five years forty-six school houses were built at an average cost of $700 each. The Negroes themselves raised about $20,000, but in 1909 Rogers died, and the work had to be discontinued.[4]

By 1912 Rosenwald had become so much interested in the education of the Negroes, and in their general welfare, that he was anxious to help Dr. Washington build rural schools in the South.

"There are some dangers to be guarded against," Dr. Washington wrote to him, "one to have the counties understand thoroughly that you would give a certain amount provided they would give a certain amount in the way of an increase over what is now being done. The temptation in some places would be for the counties to lean on you, and do even less than they are now doing instead of more." He also felt that much careful propaganda work must be done to make white people realize that it was to their interest to help educate Negroes. He added:

There is no work that I do in the South that I get more satisfaction out of than going through different states and talking directly to southern white audiences about the interest they should take in the education of the Negro. I have been surprised at the responses I have gotten. The southern white man likes to be talked to, but does not like to be talked about. Great care should be exercised to let the county officials feel as far as possible that they are doing the work—in a word, to place the responsibility upon them. . . .

[4] Washington, Booker T., *My Larger Education*, pp. 304-306; Woodson, Carter G. *The Story of the Fund*, MS. Chapter II, p. 10.

Of the $25,000 which Rosenwald gave Dr. Washington as one of his fiftieth birthday anniversary gifts, $2,800 remained, and Dr. Washington asked whether he might use this money to build rural schoolhouses near Tuskegee; to which Rosenwald consented.

The conditions of rural education for Negroes which Dr. Washington described to Rosenwald were appalling. In Alabama, where Negroes formed one-half the population, only twenty per cent of the colored children were enrolled in schools, as compared with sixty per cent of the white children, and no Negro rural schools operated for longer than five months during the year; the average was about four months, as compared with a seven-month term for the white children. One of Washington's famous remarks was: "The Negro boy is smart, but white folks expect too much of him if they think he can learn as much in three months of school as their boys can in eight." The school buildings were indescribable, the teachers poorly paid, and the elementary educational situation approximated that which had confronted Booker T. Washington when he first arrived at Tuskegee in 1881. Rosenwald felt that it was dangerous for ten million inhabitants of the United States to grow up in ignorance. At first Negroes in the South were incredulous when they were told by Tuskegee agents that a white man from the North was actually going to give money for Negro schools. "Does he want a mortgage?" was often their first question. To get something for nothing was a rare experience for them.

Six rural schools were built in Alabama. The work was carried on under the direction of the Extension Department of Tuskegee Institute and was under the personal supervision of Booker T. Washington. Rosenwald contributed $1,976.67, the Negroes, local white residents and the state of Alabama contributed the rest, $3,377.47.

Clinton J. Calloway, of Tuskegee, under whose personal direction Booker T. Washington carried out the school-building

program traveled by every possible primitive conveyance throughout the countryside, exhorting the congregations to give money
for their local schools. It was difficult at first to break down the
lethargy of the more old-fashioned Negroes. Some of them felt
that what had been good enough for them was good enough
for their children, and they rather liked the idea of holding school
in dilapidated church buildings. Change was as repugnant to
them as to other people, but when they saw the achievement of
the first schools with their own eyes, they became enthusiastic
about them. Dr. Washington's name behind the project was a
great asset in engendering confidence in the minds of both white
and colored people that the plan was not dangerous or radical.
Some of the Negroes were suspicious at first that the white
philanthropist in far-away Chicago might not make his payment;
others were suspicious that the county government would fail in
its promise. Some white people felt that there was no reason for
them to pay part of the expenses, and others were skeptical about
the advisability of educating Negroes at all. It was important to
consider these antagonisms, and schools were not built in communities where they were too strong, for there was always the
danger that the schoolhouses would be burned down to the ac-
companiment of race riots. Some Negroes and whites thought it
foolish extravagance to include cloak rooms, sanitary facilities
and other unaccustomed conveniences in the new schoolhouses.
They also thought in some places that it was a silly extravagance
to paint the buildings. By means of personal conversation, meetings, church functions, raffles and other community efforts the
construction of schoolhouses was stimulated by the Tuskegee
agents.

Communities made great sacrifices in order to obtain a Rosenwald school. The colored children in one village saved $54 by
depriving themselves of candy and other small luxuries and
brought their pennies to the fund for the school. Money was
raised by selling eggs, hens, corn, cotton, berries and other

produce. Some people pledged their cows and calves for the money to build a schoolhouse, and one old woman in Alabama roused a meeting by giving her only money, one copper cent, for the local school. In one backward community in Alabama, where there had never been a school, the colored people emptied their pockets on the table at the meeting. One old man who had been a slave emptied out his life's savings, $38 in nickels, dimes and pennies, from a greasy sack and placed them on the table. "I want to see the children of my grandchildren have a chance, so I am giving my all," he told the meeting. The Tuskegee agent had expected to get $10 but the village raised $1,365. This community finally built a school costing ten thousand dollars, employing five teachers and serving three hundred pupils. Some of the gatherings to raise money for schoolhouses had the religious fervor of revival meetings. In one place the farmers pledged a small area of land planted with cotton, which they called "The Rosenwald Patch," and devoted the proceeds to the school fund. In other localities Negro children kept "mite boxes" and saved pennies for the school fund. Some childless Negroes took an interest in the movement, and one of them mortgaged his farm to raise money for the school.

The land for each schoolhouse had to be deeded to the local school authorities, and the completed building always became a part of the public school system. Working with county superintendents of schools and Negro building agents, the state superintendent of education selected sites and approved plans. In some states no buildings were begun until the required funds had been collected and deposited. After completion each building was inspected by the state superintendent of education, who reported to Rosenwald's officials. They required a guarantee that the schools be operated for a minimum of five consecutive months during the year.

When Rosenwald visited the first schools he was so much impressed with the potentialities of the plan, that he decided to give Dr. Washington another $30,000 for the construction of one hundred additional schools in Alabama. Enough money to match Rosenwald's contribution could not be raised in Alabama alone and so some of these schoolhouses were built in Tennessee. In receipt of $13,000 for the rural school work Washington wrote:

I often wish that you could have time to hear and see for yourself some of the little incidents that occur in connection with this work. I wish you could hear the expressions of approval that now come from white people— white people who a few years ago would not think of anything bearing upon Negro education. I wish you could hear the expressions of gratitude uttered over and over again by the most humble classes of colored people.

Let me repeat, that we count it a great privilege to have some little share in this glorious work.

Booker T. Washington had been in poor health for some years. In November, 1915, Rosenwald was visiting Tuskegee, while he was in New York consulting physicians. He was taken fatally ill while making a promised address and when he was told that he had only a few hours to live, he set out at once for Tuskegee. He wanted to carry out the wish he had often expressed in his public addresses: "I was born in the South, I have lived and labored in the South, and I expect to die and be buried in the South." He seemed to his wife and companions to get stronger as the train went further south, but on the morning of his arrival, he died. He was buried on the school grounds in a brick tomb built by his students.

A memorial fund in memory of Booker T. Washington was inaugurated soon after his death to which Rosenwald gave $100,000. The fund was to be used to pay the Institute's debts and add $250,000 to its endowment.

Eighty rural schoolhouses had been built under Dr. Washington's supervision and with Rosenwald's aid in Alabama, Tennessee and Georgia. In 1916 the state of Alabama took a direct interest in the work and passed legislation offering state aid for rural schoolhouse construction for Negroes to the extent of one half the amount raised by local communities. By this plan, the state contributed $300, the local community $300 and Rosenwald $300 for a school with one teacher.

In 1916 Rosenwald offered to pay one-third of the cost of an additional 300 rural schoolhouses in the South. He also called a conference on schoolhouse construction and asked the advice of Abraham Flexner and Dr. Wallace Buttrick, of the General Education Board, Anson Phelps-Stokes, of the Phelps-Stokes Fund, and state educational agents from the South. He wanted to develop an extensive, orderly plan for construction of a large number of these schools for Negroes in all of the southern states. Other states in the South began to apply for Rosenwald's aid, and in time all of them were participating in the work.

When the building activities began to extend over a large part of Alabama and into other states, it was found that Tuskegee could no longer handle them. Detailed supervision to prevent mistakes in selection of sites and errors in construction was required. In some instances it was found that the completed schoolhouses were not being properly furnished and equipped. In May, 1920, Rosenwald met in New York with Abraham Flexner and Dr. Wallace Buttrick, of the General Education Board, Dr. James H. Dillard, of the Slater and Jeanes Funds, Major R. R. Moton, the new principal of Tuskegee Institute and Mrs. Booker T. Washington. The conference advised changing the headquarters of the work from Tuskegee to Nashville, Tennessee, and placing a white man in charge. In addition to the fact that the work had grown too extensive to be handled from the Institute, white contractors in the South resented the supervision of the Tuskegee Negroes.

In 1917 Rosenwald had formed the Julius Rosenwald Fund as a clearing house for some of his more important philanthropies, and a branch of this Fund was set up in Nashville, with S. L. Smith as general field agent, cooperating with the departments of public instruction of fourteen southern states. Mr. Smith had been state agent for Negro schools in Tennessee from 1914 to 1920 and had had a great deal of experience not only in teaching but in rural school administration and planning. On consenting to release Mr. Smith to the Fund, the state superintendent of education wrote to Rosenwald: "No greater work than yours is now being undertaken in the South and the Tennessee authorities are delighted at any opportunity to cooperate with you." Larger and more uniform schoolhouses were planned, and teachers' homes were also constructed in some communities. Hitherto teachers had been miserably housed and poorly trained. In the new homes they received both comfort and instruction from trained graduates of Negro normal schools. State building agents, with salaries paid half by the Fund and half by the state, inspected and supervised the construction of the schools and teachers' homes.

Under its enlarged plans the Fund stipulated that money would only be furnished for rural schoolhouses in localities where the school term was at least five consecutive months, and for teachers' homes where the school term was eight months or more. Every community that wanted a school had to guarantee enough land for playgrounds and agricultural work where it was considered necessary. Labor, land and materials furnished locally were counted as cash at current market values. The communities also had to guarantee to equip, furnish and maintain the schools. The aim was gradually to decrease contributions from the Rosenwald Fund and from individuals and to increase public support, with the hope that the whole problem would eventually be undertaken by public funds.

By the time of Rosenwald's death he had contributed to the construction of 5,357 public schools, shops and teachers' homes in 883 counties of fifteen southern states, at a total cost of $28,-408,520, of which he had contributed $4,366,519 or 15 per cent. Of the total cost $18,104,115, or 64 per cent, had come from tax funds. The Negroes themselves had contributed $4,725,871, or

17 per cent, in a flood of small contributions. Local white friends had contributed $1,211,975, or 4 per cent.

The Rosenwald schools had a profound effect in the small rural communities. In addition to their obvious benefit to the children, they improved race relations because of the cooperation of whites and Negroes in the community movements to obtain them. By his own disinterested benevolence Rosenwald had succeeded in shaming both the white and colored people of the South into doing something for the colored children.

The school program also raised the standard of living for Negroes in small communities, because the example of neatness and decency which the schools afforded encouraged other communal and individual improvements. It was noticed that where the new rural schoolhouses were constructed, improvements often followed in churches and in homes. Teachers, feeling more pride in their work with the better facilities for conducting it, made greater efforts to improve their qualifications. Many of them took summer courses at Tuskegee and Hampton Institutes. Negro teachers who had received their education in the North had avoided returning to the South if they could possibly get jobs elsewhere, because of the wretched conditions in the schools, but the increase in the number of Rosenwald schools gradually renewed their interest in southern education. Attendance at schools increased, and the terms during which the buildings were in operation were lengthened. Teachers' salaries tended to increase, and the presence of these neat buildings stimulated interest in education in general. Demand for libraries resulted, and in later years the Rosenwald Fund established a library service for rural schools in the South.

After the Rosenwald schools were built the white population in some of the southern counties was stimulated by the example of these new, neat buildings to establish better schoolhouses for white children. Some appealed to Rosenwald for financial aid, but he declined on the ground that he was compelled to limit himself and felt that the Negroes needed his money more than the white people, who received a much larger share of public funds for education. The plans of the Rosenwald schools, however, were made available for anyone who wished to use them, and they soon became standard in rural areas for schoolhouse construction for both white and colored children. The bulletins on schoolhouse construction issued by the Julius Rosenwald Fund were in great demand throughout the country, and many educators appealed to the Fund for advice and approval of their construction plans.

Rosenwald himself became an object of hero-worship among Negroes in many parts of the South. To many he was known as "Cap'n Julius," and his photograph, together with those of Abraham Lincoln and Booker T. Washington, adorned the walls of many schools, homes and shacks. In one of the schools a visitor noted that the teacher was teaching her arithmetic class in the following manner: "If Mr. Rosenwald had six dozen eggs and if Mr. Rosenwald bought four more eggs, how many eggs would Mr. Rosenwald have?" When the children had finished that problem, she asked: "If Mr. Rosenwald had a crib four feet long and three feet wide, how many square feet would there be in Mr. Rosenwald's crib?" On one occasion some members of the Rosenwald family visited a school and discovered the teacher conducting the arithmetic lesson on the blackboard by means of orders from a mail-order catalogue—but the mail-order company mentioned was Montgomery Ward.

When Rosenwald began his philanthropic efforts for the Negro, the belief that the Negro was incapable of profiting by education was widespread. When he undertook projects for the improvement of Negro health, the prejudice was prevalent that the Negro possessed inherent physical defects which could not be corrected. He braved both of these strong social prejudices and never flinched at the criticism of those who felt that he was undermining the social order or those who felt that he was futilely combating biological facts. His work demonstrated that both beliefs, like all social prejudices, were superstitions rather than truths. Professor Charles S. Johnson said of him in this connection: "The courage of Mr. Rosenwald was in the quiet fearlessness of his assumptions and in the daring to impute full humanity to a group that had not yet full stature. In venturing the mortality of his reputation he gained immortality for his name."

In a speech which he made in 1911 before the American Missionary Association, which had founded Hampton Institute, Rosenwald said:

Not only does the record of nations demonstrate beyond the question of doubt the folly of race prejudice, but its pages are filled with evidence that indulgence of this pet vice is itself a prime factor in the decay of nations, and in modern times I believe Russia is a living example of that theory. May our own country profit by Russia's example! In Russia the Jew is subject to a thousand infamous restrictions for no earthly reason except that he is a Jew and must be kept down. We Anglo-Saxons of course cry out against this as a barbarous outrage, and comment superiorly on the lowness of Russian civilization, and straightway turn around and exhibit the same qualities in our treatment of the Negro, which today is little less barbarous than is the treatment of the Jew in Russia. . . . To think that in this land of the free a condition should exist that, on account of a difference in color of skin, children should be denied sufficient school privileges and shut out from parks and playgrounds; that the youth should be barred from public libraries! . . .

No man or woman who encourages even the mildest phases of race prejudice can wholly escape responsibility for the horrors at which every decent individual shudders. . . .

Race prejudice is merely destructive; it offers nothing but a hopeless warfare and a blank pessimism. A nation divided against itself cannot stand; two nations cannot live side by side at daggers points with one another, and maintain a healthy state of progress in either. Perpetual feud destroys what is best and most helpful in both.

To my mind, no man can in any way render greater service to mankind than by devoting his energy toward the removal of this mighty obstacle. The destruction of race prejudice is the beginning of the higher civilization.

As an American and as a Jew, I appeal to all high-minded men and women to join in a relentless crusade against race prejudice, indulgence in which will result in the blotting out of the highest ideals of our proud nation.

## CHAPTER VI

## CIVIC SERVICE

I

ASSOCIATED as he was with those men and women in Chicago who were eager for better social conditions, it was natural that Rosenwald should also become involved in many movements to promote civic welfare and to combat vice and crime. In order to accomplish anything, it was necessary to take part in politics; but the political corruption in the city revolted him and he took an active part only sporadically in trying to remedy it. He was naïve in his attempts at political reform and in many of the campaigns which he aided with his money and influence, his side was beaten by the professional politicians, who knew the game and were concerned not at all with public morals so long as they won jobs and money.

During Theodore Roosevelt's second administration, reformers were aroused by the conditions under which masses of the people were living and working. The details of municipal stealing and monopoly marauding, of life insurance scandal and stockyards filth found their way into the pages of a few of the more enterprising magazines. New laws were passed, and reforms were made, but the people, easily wearied, cared little who made their laws so long as they could make a living and politics were soon back in the hands of politicians. The reform movement had brought some lasting benefits, but Theodore Roosevelt sounded its death knell with a phrase out of Bunyan, "The Man with the Muckrake."

Underneath the public indifference, however, protests went on in cities throughout the country, and Chicago was fortunate in having a large and vigilant group who worked continuously for its welfare. Rosenwald was not always active in this group, but he knew all of its members and supported many of their aims. Some of them were disappointed in him for not taking a more active and continuous part in the reform movement, but he was not fitted for the role. He hated waste, and politics was a game in which lavish spending and wasteful tactics were essential. He was also inexperienced in political tactics and uneducated in political history. He was used in campaigns by reformers, managers and politicians for his wealth, but very few troubled to inform him of the reasons for their defeats or victories, and once again he would return with relief to the work which he understood; business and philanthropy. However, he felt a strong sense of responsibility for his community, and he loved Chicago as he did no other place in the world, so that he could not completely divorce himself from the political life which he so much despised.

II

One of the first great civic activities in which Rosenwald participated was that of the Chicago Planning Commission. Mayor Fred A. Busse appointed 353 citizens of Chicago to the Commission, with Charles H. Wacker, who had been one of the directors of the World's Fair of 1893, as chairman. Daniel H. Burnham, the managing architect of the World's Fair, drew up a complete plan for improvements in boulevards and parkways. The Commercial Club of Chicago, of which Rosenwald was a member, raised funds for a publicity campaign to interest the people in improving the looks of their city.

The Plan included briefly: the improvement of the lake front; the development of a system of highways outside the city; the improvement of railway terminals and the development of a complete traction system for passengers and freight; the construction of a complete park system; the systematic arrangement of streets and avenues within the city; the development of centers of intellectual life and civic administration, "so related as to give coherence and unity to the city."[1]

The first project launched was for the widening of Twelfth Street, a great thoroughfare, running east and west through a sprawling part of the city's west side. Rosenwald offered to contribute $250,000, if the Commercial Club of Chicago would raise an additional $100,000 or $150,000. He made this offer with the intention of electrifying the public and starting the Chicago Plan off with enthusiasm. It was the largest single offer he had made to any cause up to that time. The offer was not taken up, because the project for the widening of Twelfth Street was finally carried out in the regular way as part of the entire Plan. Rosenwald completely forgot about it, and Edward B. Butler wrote to him in 1925, enclosing a copy of his letter of 1911 with the remark: "Most any other man would have remembered making an offer of $250,000 toward a great public improvement. . . ."

For more than twenty years the particular projects of the Chicago Plan were gradually carried out until some magnificent city improvements were made. The work is still going on along the lines first laid down, and Rosenwald never lost interest in it.

Some of his friends, and particularly his intimate friend, Lessing Rosenthal, were interested in municipal reform and took an active part in the work of the several organizations formed during the early years of the century. The Municipal Voters' League, of which George E. Cole and Lessing Rosenthal were leaders, kept reform an issue during elections. The City Club, organized in 1903, was a center for the discussion of public improvements, traction problems and civic corruption. In June, 1910, plans were made at the Club for the organization in Chicago of a Bureau of Public Efficiency. The Bureau was an outgrowth of the revela-

[1] Quoted from Plan summary in Lewis and Smith, *Chicago: The History of Its Reputation*, pp. 319-320.

tions made by the Merriam Commission, of which Charles E.
Merriam, then an alderman, had been chairman. Rosenwald took
a great interest in this first organized attempt to eliminate waste
in municipal affairs, and he consented to become the chairman of
the board of trustees of the Bureau of Public Efficiency and contributed towards the expense of its organization.

The Bureau of Public Efficiency became a permanent organization which scrutinized the expenditures of the innumerable independent taxing bodies of Chicago and Cook County. It suggested
plans for economy of administration and made itself admirably unpopular with the full-time politicians, who could stand
almost anything but economy. When the Bureau began to examine pay rolls, question the purchase of supplies and materials
and make public its suggestions for saving money for taxpayers,
the politicians grew fierce in their opposition. In 1913 the Bureau,
for instance, advised the public against the "ill-advised and extravagant contract" made for 1,000 voting machines for the city
of Chicago. The machines were declared by the Bureau to be
too expensive, costing $942.50 each, and to be at the same time
complicated and faulty. Rosenwald as chairman of the Bureau
wrote a letter advising against paying the bills on this contract.
In October, 1913, he and other members of the Bureau of Public
Efficiency started a taxpayer's suit as individuals against the voting machine contracts. In 1915 Judge Kenesaw Mountain Landis
decided against the voting machine company, which was trying
to collect $325,000 from the city.

For his activity in this matter Rosenwald was subjected to a
foolish attempt at retaliation by the enraged politicians. Soon
after the Bureau had advocated an investigation of the city's
expenditures and revenues, Rosenwald was denounced on the
floor of the Chicago City Council as a tax dodger by Alderman
Kunz, who claimed that he had not filed personal property tax
schedules for his ownership of Sears, Roebuck stock. A large majority of the residents of Cook County had always refused to

file personal property tax schedules, being unwilling to file untrue schedules and maintaining that to file true schedules made them subject to confiscatory taxes.

From time to time Rosenwald had been assessed on his personal property and had paid the taxes. In 1914, after the voting machine victory in the courts and the demand for an investigation of city finances by the Bureau of Public Efficiency, he was assessed on personal property valued at $2,500,000, although the year before his personal property had been assessed at $166,667. The indictment against him for failure to file a personal property tax schedule, which came at the end of 1914, said that he was the owner of "a large amount in value and certain sundry items of personal property, consisting of watches, clocks, household and kitchen furniture, and 147,701 shares in Sears, Roebuck and Co., of the value—to wit: the sum of $25,000,000, lawful money of the United States of America." The records of the county treasurer's office showed that he paid the largest individual personal property tax in Cook County. The maximum penalty for the alleged offense for which he was indicted was a fine of $200.

This indictment turned out to be a political boomerang for State's Attorney Maclay Hoyne, and it resulted in a wide newspaper defense of Rosenwald and an attack on the antiquated system of personal property taxation. The Chicago *Daily News* pointed out that State's Attorney Maclay Hoyne had repeatedly failed to file schedules of personal property himself, and that only six of the twenty-four grand jurors who had indicted Rosenwald had ever filed personal property tax schedules themselves. It was also pointed out that thousands of citizens of small means with savings bank deposits were subject to attack under the antiquated personal tax law. The Chicago *Tribune* remarked in an editorial on January 7, 1915:

If the indictment of a useful citizen is necessary to focus public attention to the extent necessary to bring about this crying need, one might philosophize that it is as well that a wrong was done to one whose reputation is so amply able to stand it.

The indictment was quashed in 1915 along with those which were subsequently returned against a few other rich men in Chicago.

Rosenwald became active in the spring of 1911 in the effort to elect Charles E. Merriam mayor of Chicago. He returned from Europe, especially to take part in this campaign. Charles E. Merriam had been a member of the department of political science of the University of Chicago and was an authority on municipal government. He had taken an active interest in the municipal finances of Chicago as early as 1905, and as a member of the charter convention of 1906 and as alderman in 1909 he had come into intimate contact with the city's problems. He ran as a candidate for mayor on the Republican Party ticket in the primary election of 1911 and won the nomination over the regular candidates of the party machine. In the election campaign which took place in April he was opposed by Carter Harrison II, who had been mayor of Chicago for four terms, and whose father had been mayor of Chicago for five terms. Harold L. Ickes, subsequently Secretary of the Interior in the administration of President Franklin D. Roosevelt, was Professor Merriam's campaign manager, and Julius Rosenwald and Charles R. Crane were his heaviest financial backers.

The regular Republican politicians in Chicago were lukewarm in their support of Merriam, because, his campaign being a reform movement, his managers could not promise patronage. The civic reformers and some enlightened business men were on Merriam's side, but many of the big business interests preferred Carter Harrison. The Merriam forces attacked Harrison as a slothful, drifting executive and claimed that their candidate was youthful, energetic and ready to lead the city to progressive advance. Their opponents branded Merriam as a "reformer,"

claiming that he would close the saloons on Sunday. Writing of
his campaign in his book on Chicago, Professor Merriam stated:

The truth was that the opposition succeeded in convincing many that
I was a "reformer," and I was unable to escape from the implications of
that pregnant term. In vain to protest against being classed as a Puritan
and to profess liberal views. . . . Was I not from a silk-stocking district?
Was I not in the University? Had I not pursued the grafters, and beaten
the machine? Was I not supported by many idealists and enthusiasts?
So, much against my will, I was hustled away into the camp of the rich
and the well-born. . . .

I thought of the time Horace Greeley tried to enter Girard College and
was stopped at the gate by the guard, who explained to him that under
the terms of the deed no clergyman would be allowed to enter. "The hell
you say," retorted Greeley. "Come right in," said the guard. But I could
find no equivalent formula.

Professor Merriam also quoted the remark of William Kent at a
beefsteak dinner of the Municipal Voters' League:

Fellow Reformers: Our problem is how can we make the other fellow
better, without being too damned good ourselves.

Rosenwald not only contributed about $30,000 to the Merriam
campaign fund, but he spent much time speaking at meetings
in the Jewish and Negro quarters of Chicago in support of the
candidate. It was thought that his offer of the previous year to
give money for Y. M. C. A. buildings would bring votes into the
Merriam camp, but the Negroes in Chicago voted the machine
way. He also wrote to friends and strangers throughout the city,
solicited funds and addressed his employees in a mimeographed
statement in favor of Professor Merriam. He persuaded Cyrus
McCormick, Victor Lawson and James A. Patten to give $10,000
each and collected smaller sums from other rich men.

In the election Merriam was defeated by Carter Harrison
by about 17,000 votes. Rosenwald wrote next day to his wife, who
was still in Europe:

I've just taken a few of the Merriam pictures off the windows of our house to lay them aside for four years—when maybe he'll try again. It's all over and we must console ourselves with having fought in a righteous cause. It has at least quickened the public conscience and will have a moral effect the value of which it is not possible to measure. . . . It poured all day yesterday which probably made some difference but nowhere near enough to account for 17,000 majority. . . .

He added to this letter later that evening:

Your cable expressing your dreadful disappointment also awaited me at the store. I feel better this eve., but it was an awful blow. I wrote Carter H. a letter of congratulation and told him I had no apology to make for my part in the campaign but wanted him to know that if I could do anything as a citizen for the good of Ch. he could have my cooperation.

Carter Harrison, however, made a better mayor than the campaign orations had predicted, and on December 22, 1911, Rosenwald wrote to him:

As a citizen who is greatly interested in the welfare of Chicago, I feel that I should express to you my gratitude for the magnificent work being done under your administration. In my judgment your courageous stand in regard to the Police Department, and the splendid backing you have given your Civil Service Board, is the greatest forward step toward good government that Chicago has ever known.

I shall do everything in my power to bring to as many citizens as I can the sense of their obligation to you for this and the other great movements which you have been instrumental in furthering. Surely the next three years are full of promise for the people of Chicago, for which no one is more grateful than is

Yours most sincerely,
Julius Rosenwald.

The defeat of Merriam discouraged Rosenwald for some years from active participation in municipal election campaigns.

In September, 1910, he attended a convention on conservation at which President Taft, ex-President Theodore Roosevelt, Governor Deneen of Illinois, and others spoke. This was his first important contact with national political affairs, and he was fascinated by the conversation of the men whom he met at that time. He wrote to Mrs. Rosenwald that he had "never met intimately so many interesting people in so short a time."

At the convention he met Francis J. Heney, San Francisco reformer, who had prosecuted the famous San Francisco graft cases in 1908. In an attempt to help him and people of his kind he wrote the following letter to Rudolph Spreckels:

I have just returned after attending the Conservation Congress at St. Paul, where I had the pleasure of meeting Mr. Heney. In speaking with Mr. Charles R. Crane, he informed me that Mr. Heney would be much more comfortable if he had an indebtedness of several thousand dollars out of the way, and I at once told Mr. Crane that I would be glad to send you $1,000 to that end. Enclosed find check for that amount.

It has often occurred to me that some arrangement should be made by which men of Heney's type should be so compensated that they would be able to continue their work without being hampered by the necessity of earning a livelihood. I believe there are wealthy men in this country who would be glad to join in creating a fund to be used for the purpose of paying a reasonable salary to men who are willing to sacrifice themselves for the benefit of the community or the nation. It is unreasonable to expect men of marked ability to deprive themselves and their families of the necessaries of life while devoting themselves to an unselfish cause. It is reasonable to suppose that there would be more men to assist in noble work of this kind if they were not called upon to make unreasonable sacrifices. I should be glad to have your views on this subject.

Mr. Spreckels thought the idea worthy, but he felt that such a plan of endowment for public service workers of the highest type might lead to a curtailment of their usefulness. Rosenwald carried out the plan on an individual basis by giving sums of money and Sears, Roebuck stock to people who had devoted themselves to worthy causes. Sometimes he made it possible for them to buy shares of stock and to pay for them out of the dividends.

President Taft visited Chicago in October, 1911, and made an address at the colored Y. M. C. A. building there to which Rosenwald had contributed. He had a political conference with Taft at this time and was present at a small luncheon Taft gave at the Blackstone Hotel. It was rumored at the time that Rosenwald would become Secretary of Commerce in Taft's cabinet if the President were re-elected. When asked by a reporter for the Chicago *Record-Herald* about this rumor, he was quoted as saying:

> I know nothing about it except what I have read in today's papers, and have received no communication from the President or anyone else on the subject; of course, I feel highly complimented to be mentioned for such an honor, but there is not an office in the gift of the President or the people that I would accept—all I ask is to keep my good health and to be allowed to live in Chicago among my friends. I greatly enjoy the work in which I am engaged.

He had been mentioned in 1910 as a good man for mayor of Chicago, but neither he nor anybody in Chicago politics took this movement seriously.

President Taft invited him to visit him at the White House and he spent two days there. During this visit he saw and admired an excerpt from a speech by Abraham Lincoln, which stood in a frame on the cabinet table where President Taft sat. Rosenwald obtained a copy of it, which he always valued. The excerpt read:

> If I were to try to read, much less answer, all the attacks made on me, this shop might as well be closed for any other business. I do the very best I know how—the very best I can; and I mean to keep on doing so until the end. If the end brings me out all right, what is said against me won't amount to anything. If the end brings me out wrong, ten angels swearing I was right would make no difference.

During dinner at the White House Rosenwald made a disparaging remark about the attitude and activities of Theodore Roosevelt. Taft ceased smiling and said gravely: "I can never forget the great obligation of gratitude that I am under to Theodore. Neither can I ever forget the years of pleasant, affectionate, personal intercourse between us." Then the President smiled again and added: "Theodore's idea of government is that of the

Oriental Cadi about whom we used to read in the 'Arabian Nights.' He would like to have every decision of government made without the hampering restraints of constitution or statute, but according to the manifest equities of the matter as they should be made to appear at the time. That idea of government is all right, provided you can unite in your ruler infinite wisdom and infinite goodness, but that combination might not occur again in a thousand years."[2]

Although a strong supporter of President Taft's, Rosenwald appeared to have no illusions about his chances of success, for he wrote in a letter to a friend: "Confidentially, however, I am very much inclined to the belief that no matter what is done or what is not done, Mr. Wilson will be the next President."

The political campaign in 1912 took place in a maelstrom of social reform and personal political controversies. Many of Rosenwald's friends were ardent supporters of the new Progressive Party, under the glamorous leadership of Theodore Roosevelt, but he himself swung away from the high hopes of the social reformers to the solid conservatism of William Howard Taft.

Jane Addams expressed the difference in opinion between people like herself and people like Rosenwald when she wrote in her autobiography that she and her colleagues were "ready to give up the short modern role of being good to people and to go back to the long historic role of ministration to basic human needs." She added: "After all, we asserted, our philanthropies have cared for the orphans whose fathers have been needlessly injured in industry; have supported the families of the convict whose labor is adding to the profits of a prison contractor; have solaced men and women prematurely aged because they could find no work to do; have rescued girls driven to desperation through overwork and overstrain."

[2] Rosenwald Papers. Letter of Judge Frederick A. Henry, of Cleveland, Ohio, to Julius Rosenwald, dated June 7, 1923. Judge Henry was a fellow guest of Rosenwald's at the White House at the time.

Though he differed from Miss Addams, Rosenwald did not cease to aid her in her work at Hull-House. It was in that same summer of 1912 when the Progressive Party was first organized in Chicago that he sent her a check for $50,000 for a country club for social workers. In the accompanying letter he wrote:

In order that you may leave for the East with a trifle freer mind, Mrs. Rosenwald and I desire to drop the enclosed into the Hull-House treasury to add to the joy of my 50th birthday celebration.

We hope you will get the benefit from your well earned vacation.

May I take this opportunity to say that in choosing the political course you did, against the advice of your friends, I have no hesitancy in admitting that I now believe that you acted wisely, and that I was mistaken?

Sincerely and cordially yours,

Julius Rosenwald.

### III

The city of Chicago had long been the seat of an active traffic in girls, which extended into near-by states and throughout the rest of the country. Politicians profited by the trade, and civic officials ignored it. In 1907, Clifford G. Roe, then Assistant State's Attorney, decided, after he had prosecuted several cases of white slavery, that the traffic was enormous and should be eliminated. During the spring he began convicting procurers of girls at the rate of about one a week. In order to obtain proper legislation and to fight the evil at its source, the Joint Club Committee was formed, with Mr. Roe as chairman, and representatives of various Chicago clubs as members. The Joint Club Committee succeeded in getting the legislature to pass the Illinois Pandering Law in the spring of 1908, the first law of its kind in the United States.

Business men decided to form a committee and asked Mr. Roe to resign from the office of Assistant State's Attorney and lead the fight against white slavery, which he consented to do. An office was established for the purpose of carrying on the fight against vice, and for its first half year the Chicago *Tribune* financed the work. Afterwards Julius Rosenwald and Henry P. Crowell, of the Quaker Oats Company, were its leading backers, and other wealthy men in Chicago contributed to the cause. When this group began to put detectives on the trail of procurers and to prosecute them in the courts, public officials could no longer safely ignore the situation.

Mayor Fred A. Busse appointed the Chicago Vice Commission on March 5, 1910. Dean Walter T. Sumner was its chairman, and Rosenwald was appointed as one of its members. At the time of the appointment he wrote to his son Lessing, then a student at Cornell: "If you look in Sunday's *Tribune* you will notice that I was appointed on the Vice Commission. This is a thing, however, which I believe should be in the hands of people who have made a study of it more than I have, and I shall attempt to be released as soon as possible, provided I can get the Mayor's consent." At the request of Dean Sumner and others, however, he consented to remain a member of the Commission.

The Chicago Vice Commission sent detectives into almost every resort in the city and prepared an exhaustive report. Rosenwald was not very active in the work, although he attended meetings from time to time. He wrote to his wife who was in Europe: "I just came from a Vice Comm. meeting—about the last we will have as the report is about ready and I think will be a fine one—not due to me at all, so I can compliment it."

The report of the Commission caused something of a sensation, and its distribution through the mails was forbidden. It found that the proceeds of vice in the city ran to more than fifteen million dollars a year, and that about 5,000 women were engaged in prostitution. Among its general recommendations the Commission suggested:

An intensive study should be made of the working conditions and wages paid by those establishments in Chicago which depend upon the labor of girls and women. This investigation should also ascertain living conditions, cost of living of different groups, and decide on what constitutes a "living wage" for each group.

It was suggested that such investigation be carried on not by public bodies but by "philanthropic and other organizations." Under the heading, "The Economic Side of the Question," the report read in part:

The life of an unprotected girl who tries to make a living in a great city is full of torturing temptations. First, she faces the problem of living on an inadequate wage: Six dollars a week is the average in mercantile establishments. If she were living at home where the mother and sister could help her with mending, sewing, washing, where her board would be small—perhaps only a dollar or two towards the burden carried by the other members of the family—where her lunch would come from the family larder—then her condition might be as good as if she earned eight dollars per week.

The girl who has no home soon learns of "city poverty," all the more cruel to her because of the artificial contrasts. She quickly learns of the possibilities about her, of the joys of comfort, good food, entertainment, attractive clothes. Poverty becomes a menace and a snare. One who has not beheld the struggle or come in personal contact with the tempted soul of the underpaid girl can never realize what the poverty of the city means to her. One who has never seen her bravely fighting against such fearful odds will never understand. A day's sickness or a week out of work are tragedies in her life. They mean trips to the pawn brokers, meagre dinners, a weakened will, often a plunge into the abyss from which she so often never escapes.

Hundreds, if not thousands, of girls from country towns, and those born in the city but who have been thrown on their own resources, are compelled to live in cheap boarding or rooming houses on the average wage of six dollars. How do they exist on this sum? It is impossible to figure it out on a mathematical basis. If the wage were eight dollars per week, and the girl paid two and a half dollars for her room, one dollar for laundry and sixty cents for carfare, she would have less than fifty cents left at the end of the week. This is provided she ate ten cent breakfasts, fifteen cent luncheons and twenty-five cent dinners. But there is no doubt that many girls *do* live on even six dollars and do it *honestly*, but we can affirm that they *do not* have nourishing food, or comfortable shelter, or warm clothes, or any amusement, except perhaps free public dances, without outside help, either from charity in the shape of girls' clubs, or friends in the country home. How can she possibly exist to say nothing of live? . . .

Are flesh and blood so cheap, mental qualifications so common and honesty of so little value, that the manager of one of our big department stores feels justified in paying a high school girl, who has served nearly one year as an inspector of sales, the beggarly wage of $4.00 per week? What is the natural result of such an industrial condition? Dishonesty and immorality, not from choice, but necessity—in order to live. We can forgive the human frailty which yields to temptation under such conditions —but we cannot forgive the soulless corporation, which arrests and prosecutes this girl—a first offender—when she takes some little article for personal adornment.

After the clergymen, the social reformers and the public-spirited citizens had finished with the subject of vice, the politicians took it up and decided to defend themselves publicly for their own negligence by conducting their own investigation. The city officials tabled and shelved the report of the Vice Commission, but in February, 1913, the Illinois Senate passed a resolution providing for a committee to consist of Lieutenant Governor O'Hara, as chairman, and four state senators, "to investigate the subject of white slave traffic in Illinois."

The sessions of the committee began on February 28, 1913, when several women who had been forced to earn their living by prostitution testified to their experience, and several social workers testified concerning general conditions in Chicago. Mrs. Josephine Schell, of the New Future Institution, a home for girls, testified that payment of low wages was one of the first causes of prostitution in Chicago in 1913, "that most of the girls working are underpaid," and that the lowest wage a girl could maintain herself virtuously on, in the city of Chicago, in 1913, was $10 a week. "That covers it very closely," she added. One of the witnesses, who had been a prostitute in Chicago, when asked by Senator Beall how much it would take for her to live "an honest and straightforward life" answered: "It would take at least $12 a week to live right." The committee decided to divert its inquiries temporarily "to investigate the matter of wages paid to girl workers and the possible connection of low wages with the spread of immorality." The first employer of labor called to testify before the O'Hara committee was Julius Rosenwald.

In answer to questions, he said that Sears, Roebuck for the week ending March 8, 1913, had 4,732 girls and women in its employ, and that the average wage paid them was $9.12 per week. He testified that the lowest wage paid to the girls under sixteen years of age was $5.00 per week for the first three months or less and $5.50 per week after three months' employment. One hundred and nineteen girls between the ages of sixteen and sixteen and a half received $5.00 per week, and 1,465 received less than $8.00 per week. He also testified that the company made it a point not to hire any girl at less than $8.00 per week who did not live at home. G. H. Miller, manager of the employment department, testified that the highest wage paid to women employees except department heads at that time was "about thirty-five dollars a week," and the twenty-three higher paid women employees received an average of $26 per week. The highest paid woman department head received $3,000 per year. An investigation conducted by the company in 1911 had revealed that it would cost girls between $7.50 and $9.00 a week to live in Chicago, and the committee of the company investigating the cost of living for employees recommended a minimum wage of $8.00 per week at that time.

"Now, Mr. Rosenwald," Lieutenant Governor O'Hara asked, "you are a public-spirited citizen and a benefactor widely known; may I ask you if you think that low wages have anything to do at all with the immorality of women and girls?"

"I would answer that as I said before the vice commission," Rosenwald replied, "that I think the question of wages and prostitution has no practical connection. I think there is no connection between the two." . . .

"Do you remember any occasion upon which any individual or any organization or any organized society with which you were affiliated has associated the question of low wages with vice?"

"The only one I remember is the vice commission."

"Do you believe that self-preservation is the first law of nature?"

"Well, as to that I should say yes."

"Do you believe that some crimes are committed because of want?"

"Yes."

"Do you believe that a girl who wants to live respectably and support herself can live on less than $10.00 a week?"

"I wouldn't want to answer that question offhand."

"What is your opinion, Mr. Rosenwald?"

"As I stated, I believe that the question of wages has no connection with the question of prostitution. I believe that the number of girls that come from proper homes and proper environments are just as liable to become prostitutes as other girls, whose wages range from $8.00 up as from $8.00 down and from $10.00 up to $10.00 down."

"Do you know, Mr. Rosenwald, if a girl has ever worked in your establishment at low wages and had to get money in other ways because of necessity?"

"That would be a very difficult thing to say whether it ever happened."

"In your judgment, Mr. Rosenwald?"

"I don't believe that those cases have any connection with it. The girl that gets $10.00 a week would be just as likely to use that as a subterfuge as the girl who gets a less wage."

"Then you think the employer who pays the girl less than a living wage has no moral responsibility in her down-fall, if down-fall there be?"

"I would say that one had no connection with the other."

"And that the employer had no moral responsibility for her down-fall?"

"I would say that so far as her pay is concerned."

"Then it would be wholly proper and morally right for any man to pay women and girls less than living wages?"

"That is another question. I am referring entirely to the question of prostitution. I say the question of wages isn't a moral question. It ought to be treated on an entirely different basis. I wouldn't combine the question of prostitution with wages. I say in my opinion there is no connection between the two."

"Mr. Rosenwald, if you knew that women employed by your corporation could not decently exist on the wages paid, what would you do?"

"We would raise their wages."

"Have you ever done so?"

"Many, many times."

"Do you think $5.00 a week is sufficient for any woman to live on?"

"If she lives at home, yes, sir, I do."

"It is sufficient?"

"For a girl of sixteen or under, if she lives at home and probably has the help of her family."

"And $8.00 would be sufficient for a woman of twenty-five years if she were living at home?"

"Yes, sir; and possibly if she were not living at home. She could be honest and might live on $8.00 a week."

Chairman O'Hara then brought out by questioning Rosenwald that the net profits of Sears, Roebuck during 1911 had been over $8,000,000, and Rosenwald admitted that dividends could still be paid on the stock if $2,000,000 of the profits were added to wages of employees. He refused to answer what his personal income from the company amounted to during the year.

> "Could you, Mr. Rosenwald, live on $8.00 a week?" Senator Juul asked.
> "That is pretty hard to tell without trying."
> "Have you ever tried?"
> "No, I don't think I ever tried."

Rosenwald testified that the girls under sixteen worked eight hours a day, and those over sixteen worked eight and three-quarters a day. The maximum was nine and one-quarter hours a day. Rosenwald invited the committee to visit the Sears, Roebuck plant and to question any of the employees. He added that all employees who were at work for five years or more received anniversary checks of from five to ten per cent of their annual earnings. "I would also like to state for the benefit of the committee," he said, "that over one thousand of our women employees have saving accounts, and a goodly number are stockholders in the company." He denied the knowledge of "drivers" who urged the girls to harder and faster work in the plant, and he did not know of any such persons as "official scolders."

> "Now, Mr. Rosenwald," Senator Juul asked, "do you figure that there is any good reason why a young woman, any more than a young man, should give her entire time during the entire week to your or any other concern in the City of Chicago, for wages for her services for less than

she could keep herself clothed and properly fed and have a comfortable bed to sleep in?"

"I should say there are reasons, that is, competition that might bring about such a condition. I would not say it was wholesale."

"What I want to lead up to," Senator Juul continued, "looking at this statement of your earnings of $8,500,000 and where you pay a dividend and there are one hundred girls each receiving $5.00 per week, suppose it would take $260,000 per year to give one thousand girls $5.00 a week— would you say in view of that statement that this $260,000 added to the wages of the employees would materially interfere with the profits or dividends declared by your company on the $8,500,000?"

"I would say that we should be glad to do that if that should be permanent."

"That is right, but would you say that that additional payment of $260,000 in one year to one thousand girls would materially interfere with the earning capacity of your concern or prevent you from meeting competition with similar concerns in the United States, when the earnings show $8,500,000—would you say that competition comes into that proposition at all?"

"I think it does."

"To what extent?"

"Because in years when we might make these earnings we might be able to afford it, but in years when we might not make these earnings we could not afford it."

"Well, would you say that taking $8,500,000 as the earnings for the stockholders, would you say that in using $260,000 to pay one thousand girls an additional $5.00 a week, to keep the girls off the streets and to give them a good living, would you say that would be reasonable?"

"I would say it would be entirely in our province to give all our earnings to our help."

"That isn't the question, Mr. Rosenwald. Let us be fair with one another. I mean to be fair with you."

"I shall try to be fair."

"We are not here to annoy you and we do not mean to. I want to try to see what the condition is in the City of Chicago, and to find out what is right. What I want to find out is this: Would it be possible to take the lowest wage earners in your institution and take care of them by paying the lowest paid girl or woman $5.00 a week?"

"We pay no woman $5.00 a week, nothing but girls under sixteen years of age." . . .

Rosenwald was asked whether a minimum wage agreement in Illinois would cripple his business or any business. He replied that it might not cripple his business, "but it might cripple others," and put them in a position where they could not compete with business men in other states. He added that his business would not suffer from competition under a national minimum wage law.

"You don't think, Mr. Rosenwald, that your concern would be one of a number, seriously to contest a minimum wage bill if a minimum wage bill were enacted and came within reasonable lines?" Senator Juul asked.

"Our policy has been and now is," Rosenwald replied, "not to attack any legislation that would benefit our help or that would benefit the community. I cannot say that that would be an injustice to anybody."

In March, 1913, the O'Hara committee visited Washington to urge President Wilson to make the eradication of vice a national issue and to help enact a national minimum wage law for women. At this time Rosenwald wrote to Wilson:

I notice that our Lieutenant Governor and his Commission are expecting to call on you, and I deem it in line with my duty to express to you my views regarding this Commission.

In my opinion the Lieutenant Governor is not in the least interested in the question of the minimum wage, except as it affects his political ambition and the use he can make of it to gain votes. I say this without the slightest desire to injure him in any way, but I conscientiously believe that he has done more to injure the good name of the women of this country than any man has ever done or probably will ever do. He has led the women wage-earners of this country to believe that they are justified in leading an immoral life if they do not earn a certain wage. He has given the mothers of these young women justification for condoning immorality in them for the same reason. His object in connecting the question of wages and vice was to bring about a sensation which would have been lacking had he tried to urge the minimum wage after the same manner that Massachusetts and Wisconsin have done. I sincerely trust that he will have no encouragement from you in working along these lines.

I make bold to state that no one in this country is more desirous for justice to the wage-earner than the writer, nor is anyone willing to do more to bring about this condition along lines that will in the long run, serve that end, but I earnestly condemn the basis upon which this investigation is being made, since to my mind it is most harmful to the good name of the women of this nation.

The whole question of vice in Chicago or any other large city cut deeply across the entire social system in the United States. Employers in 1913, subject to competition or carrying the competitive spirit into their affairs long after it was necessary to do so, felt it a duty to themselves and their stockholders to pay the current rate of wages. In some cases those wages obviously resulted in prostitution, though low wages were not the sole cause. The O'Hara Committee brought out valuable data which established the connection between the two in the minds of people who had preferred not to look at that side of the costs of business enterprise.

Rosenwald was outraged at the implied accusation that he, a reputable citizen of excellent intention, had been causing prostitution. He had been brought up in the clothing business, which, as we have seen, was a trade admittedly based on sweatshop labor. Men who had grown up in the economic jungle, where they fought other men for money, power and prestige did not stop to consider the effects on the underlings who helped to perform the daily tasks. Rosenwald was sincerely concerned with the welfare of his employees, but he never believed in paying them higher wages than they could get elsewhere.

His case stood out from those of his contemporaries because he was more philanthropic as well as wealthier than most of his neighbors. It was an ironic fact that because he gave away such large sums of money, he was singled out as a target for politicians. But he could not escape his share of the blame. The wage policy of the businesses in which he had been engaged, while no worse than those of their contemporaries, was also no better. He had been reared in a school of business which considered it foolhardy and dangerous to pay more for labor than was absolutely necessary, and when he gave away his money, he did not give it away in the form of high wages to those who helped to create his wealth.

It may well be argued that the choice should not have been placed in his or any other man's hands. A national effort to create minimum standards of living and wages was the duty of the entire community, and such an effort might have made much philanthropy superfluous. But it was an effort that no one man, however rich, could initiate, though individual employers could and did approach higher standards than the average. From his competitive training, Rosenwald had acquired the distinct feeling that it would be unfair to others to make a humanitarian institution of his business and he always enjoined others never to mix philanthropy with business. He believed firmly in paying the market rate for labor and in giving it paternalistic benefits.

Rosenwald stuck to his determination to keep his business free from such forms of idealism which he felt might hamper its growth and development. Jane Addams argued with him frequently against the practice which Sears, Roebuck indulged in along with other large companies of buying some prison made goods. Rosenwald argued that he must do and would do what his contemporaries did in this matter. There were only a few items of prison made goods, such as rough tables and chairs for summer porches, in the Sears, Roebuck stock, but Rosenwald refused all pleas by Miss Addams that he forbid the practice of buying and selling these goods, which she considered were unfairly depressing the labor market by their cheap labor cost.

He was deeply interested, however, in the efforts of his company to provide its employees with health and recreational facilities. He was proud of the Sears, Roebuck athletic fields and clinics, its rest rooms and gardens. Whenever he was in Chicago, he loved to attend the athletic field days held at the plant.

On February 11, 1915, Mrs. Joseph T. Bowen, who was closely associated with Rosenwald as a trustee of Hull-House, wrote to him:

I had hoped to see you this past week to talk over with you a matter which has been troubling me, but as I have not been able to go anywhere I am writing although it is not half as satisfactory.

As a stockholder in Sears, Roebuck and Company holding seven hundred shares, I am wondering if it would not be possible at the annual meeting of the stockholders on February 23d to consider the question of appropriating a part—perhaps a small one—of the stock dividend, for the use of the employees of the Company; either to be added to the Pension Fund or as a bonus to be divided between them.

As a stockholder I am, of course, glad that the Company has had such prosperous years that it can afford to pay me such a large return upon my investment, but I must also confess to a feeling of responsibility as a stockholder—and perhaps some sense of guilt—that in these hard times so large a sum is to be distributed among the stockholders and that the employees are to have no share whatever in it.

While I have not talked with any of the other stockholders I believe that I am voicing the sentiment of many of them who feel the same responsibility, and who believe that some distribution of the profits would not only tend to better the feeling between employer and employed, but would redound to the interest of the Company in better service, as the employee would feel that he was not merely a cog in a machine but a participant in the profits of a business created by his work.

This is, in no sense, intended as a criticism; I presume that the question has already been discussed. But it is perhaps a kindly protest, addressed to you as a friend, against the distribution of so large a sum to the stockholders without some participation by the employees.

Mrs. Bowen never received any reply to her letter. But in 1916 Rosenwald and Albert H. Loeb worked out for Sears, Roebuck an employees' profit-sharing plan, which was one of the first in the country and the most comprehensive and generous of any in operation during the period.

By this profit-sharing plan, every employee was eligible to

participate after three years of service with the company, and participation was entirely voluntary. The employees who wished to do so deposited five per cent of their annual wages in the Employees' Savings and Profit Sharing Pension Fund. The company agreed to deposit a sum equal to five per cent of its annual net profits (without deduction for dividends paid to stockholders). No employee was permitted to deposit more than five per cent of his salary, and in no case more than $150 a year, so that the higher salaried employees were prevented from receiving too large a share of the fund. After ten years of service with the company, a depositor could withdraw all money and securities credited to his or her account, including the company's contribution. If a depositor wished to withdraw his account before ten years of service had elapsed, he could withdraw only the amount deposited plus interest at five per cent per annum compounded semi-annually. The difference between what the depositor received and what he had to his credit was in this case divided among the other members of the profit sharing fund. A woman depositor who left to be married after five years of service with the company, was entitled to withdraw all money and securities credited to her account, including the company's contribution. In the case of death of a depositor, the estate was entitled to all money deposited plus the company's contributions. If a depositor ceased to remain an employee of the company, he was compelled to withdraw from the fund. Loans were made to depositors against their accounts if the trustees of the fund decided that the circumstances warranted such action.

The Employees' Savings and Profit Sharing Pension Fund was administered by a board of five trustees, three officers or directors of the company and two employees. It was intended that so far as practicable all the moneys of the fund should be invested in the stock of the company, "to the end that the depositors may, in the largest measure possible, share in the earnings of the Company." The fund could be discontinued by announcement of the company at least six months before its final payment of its yearly contribution.

More than ninety per cent of the employees of the company decided to take advantage of this profit-sharing pension plan.

In 1923, when Rosenwald was considering a more liberal extension of the plan, Albert H. Loeb wrote to him:

Here you will have a few of my thoughts on profit sharing. This is old stuff for you but I think it best that we occasionally remind ourselves of the salient points.

First of all I fully believe that for *us* our present plan *is most ideal* in principle. It will be improved as we are now contemplating, making it more liberal in percentage distribution and withdrawing the limitation as to the higher salaried people. Outside of that it is most admirably fitted for *our business*.

The Crowell Publishing Co. made an intensive study of all kinds of plans, some of the brightest minds being engaged thereon, and after a prolonged survey of the whole field, they adopted our plan bodily, almost *verbatim*.

The peculiar thing about profit sharing and the scientific study thereof, is that it depends for its success on the particular kind of business involved—its organization—number of employees as compared with volume of profit, classification of male and female employees, young boys and girls, skilled and unskilled labor, etc., etc., and above all and *greatest of all* the confidence of the employees in the personnel of the management.

Most profit sharing ventures have been failures. What may be good for one business is not good for another. *You* have just about hit it right for *our business*. It was a most fortunate find and it has already proved itself—in the years to come it will be wonderfully effective.

Profit sharing should never be made a substitute in part for wages or a palliative for long hours or poor working conditions. True profit sharing gives the employees a share in the prosperity of the business *in addition* to a good compensation. It avails nothing, however, and is doomed to disaster unless these three elements precede any profit sharing:

1. A fairly liberal salary at least as good or better than the competitive scale of wages.

2. The right number of working hours, also based on what your neighbors are doing.

3. The right kind of working conditions. (In this division may be

included so-called welfare work, paid vacations, pay for sickness, accidents, etc.)

If, in any of these three departments, we should be ever so slightly under the "market" the employees would at once feel we have introduced profit sharing to get the best of them. This would be the result even though the profit sharing were quite liberal. It is in the nature of the human mind to think only of present benefits. This applies not only to the big fellows but also in greater proportion to the rank and file.

The girl asks her neighbor "How much do you get?" and if she gets *less* she tells her friend, "Yes, but I get a share in the profits," at which she is greeted with a sneer and a cynical laugh. Of course there are many exceptions but I think it holds true that most of us live in and for the present.

In that connection I was rather surprised to hear there is in contemplation an insurance feature in addition to the provisions of our present plan. The reason I am surprised is because in the early days I was rather strong for employees' insurance. You convinced me that it was not worth while. I remember one of the arguments you used when you asked me "How many of us would carry insurance if the agents did not pester us into buying a policy?" Very few go into life insurance voluntarily. Another proof of people living for the present. You especially pointed out that in our organization, composed of so many *young* men and women, the great majority would not be much interested in life insurance. . . .

The company increased its contribution to the profit-sharing pension fund from five to a minimum of seven per cent of the net annual profits without deduction for any dividends or federal income taxes. The new company contribution was to be one-third of the net earnings after deducting its outstanding preferred stock dividends and ten per cent of the par value of the common stock. But the minimum in any year was to be seven per cent of its net earnings without deductions. The employees still contributed five per cent of their salaries. They were divided into three groups according to length of service, and those who were with the company for one year were now entitled to share in the fund. The older employees, however, shared more extensively. The plan not only enabled the employees to share in the profits, but also made it possible for the company to retire super-annuated employees without leaving them destitute in their old age. Rosenwald told an interviewer for the Chicago *American* in 1930:

It is good business. We need not carry any dead timber in the organiza-tion. At the same time when leaving the company the employees go with something to carry them through. Business is business, and what we do here is not charity, or benevolence, but business. It is good business to treat people right.

During the twenty years between 1916, when the plan was in-augurated, and 1936 the report of Sears, Roebuck showed that 65,000 employees who had died, retired, left the company's em-ploy, or withdrawn part of their deposits, had deposited $10,-042,304 from their salaries and had drawn out cash and stock of the company valued at $45,203,989, or $35,161,685 more than they themselves had deposited. In addition there were still 19,000 depositors of the fund in 1936, who had assets to their credit of $44,205,568. In the twenty years of the fund's operation the em-ployees past and present had deposited $18,309,445 from their salaries, and the company from its profits had deposited $26,-402,000. The total assets including those withdrawn amounted to $89,409,557. The fund became the largest single stockholder of Sears, Roebuck stock.

An employee who earned $1,200 a year and had deposited with the fund for twenty and one-half years was credited with $17,819 in cash and securities, for which he himself had deposited $1,230.[3]

---

[3] In its analysis of the Sears, Roebuck profit-sharing plan in an article, "General Robert E. Wood, President," *Fortune* in its issue of May, 1938, stated:

"Admirable as the plan is, it has flaws. Labor leaders criticize such schemes gen-erally as devices to keep employees from organizing and quitting; as a pretext for paying low wages—on the excuse that if profits run high, the bonus will compensate; and as a scheme for sharing losses in bad years—on the argument that profits have been shared in the past. Where the Sears plan is most vulnerable is the 'eggs-in-one-basket' practice of investing in company stock, since it leaves the employee at the mercy of Sears's destiny. . . .

"Sears has earnestly sought to minimize the possibility of the fund's ever being used as a club. The employee is eligible to withdraw his own contributions, plus 5 per cent interest, any time, and the total credits after ten years' service (or, in the

Rosenwald also made liberal provision for the heads of departments and other major and minor executives. In his files there are many copies of a form letter to employees announcing the terms on which he was selling them shares of stock. These terms gave the men a period of five years to pay for their stock. They executed notes payable to Rosenwald for the purchase price of their stock five years after date with interest at five per cent. The stock was then issued in the employee's name and held by Rosenwald as collateral for the note. The employee could make payments on account at any time. If at any time the employee preferred not to take the stock, any payments on account were returned to him plus five per cent interest, less the amount of dividends he might have received. In other words, Rosenwald held the men free from any loss up to the time of the maturity of their notes. Stock dividends were held by Rosenwald as collateral for the notes, but the employee-owner of the stock could elect to have him sell any shares issued as a stock dividend, and the proceeds of such sales plus five per cent interest would be deducted from the face of the note at maturity.

Rosenwald, along with other citizens of Chicago, was enlisted during 1913 and 1914 in an effort to relieve the large number of unemployed in the city. A survey made by the United Charities of Chicago, with which he was closely associated, estimated that during 1913 there were 100,000 unemployed in the city, and by 1914 the Chicago *Tribune* estimated "that destitution due to unemployment has increased in the city by more than 50 per cent." Mayor Carter Harrison appointed an industrial commission in January, 1915, to study the problems of unemployment, and among the members were Julius Rosenwald, R. T. Crane, Jr., Professor Charles R. Henderson and others. Rosenwald and Crane announced that their companies would do work during the win-

---

case of a woman, leaving to get married, after five years). As for the 'eggs-in-one-basket' idea, General Wood said that the officers have debated buying government bonds, yet have never done so on account of the reduced income, and also because the step would contradict the main objective, which is sharing the company's profits."

ter which had been planned for the spring in order to create
as much employment as possible. A campaign was organized to
influence other men to do the same. This industrial commission
reported to the mayor:

This commission has endeavored to stimulate employment of the unemployed by private citizens. We shall continue to do so. We have used
all available means of setting the facts before manufacturers, merchants
and householders. The response has been courteous and serious, but has
not met the situation. Reports reveal a widespread distress. Many school
children are unable to study because they are weak from hunger.

We had thought of asking the public to provide a large fund from
private subscriptions that we might give some relief and pay something
in wages for labor in improving parks and cleaning streets.

This emergency relief work with charitable funds is at best a sorry
makeshift. Generally it is wasteful.

We recommend to the city government the following policy:

To enlarge municipal public works which will create permanent utilities for all the people—improvement of parks, streets, roads, subways, etc.

As soon as possible land owned by the city, county, and sanitary
district could be used for growing food and many persons could thus
find profitable occupation.

We ask the mayor and council to unite with us in petitioning the
legislature to assume its share of responsibility, to provide immediately
for useful public works on a large scale.

To prevent, if possible, a recurrence of these periods of distress we
call upon the city, county, state and federal authorities to cooperate with
the business world in a system of arranging plans and contracts for
public work, which will call for an increased labor demand when regular
business is depressed. We also call for systems of unemployment insurance by state or nation.

This report was made in February, 1915, but shortly thereafter the demand for labor increased because of the World War,
and the problem, temporarily, was ended.

Rosenwald also took an active part in the drive which the
United Charities of Chicago, the largest non-sectarian charity
organization in the city, conducted during the spring of 1913. At
a luncheon in the Hotel Sherman he told the prominent men

of the city who were to become house-to-house canvassers how
to go about it:

> While we are at it, I want to give the workers a tip on how to collect
> the money. Don't use the telephone. Meet them face to face and personally
> urge them that it is their duty as citizens to give a check for $500 or so.
>
> Flatter them by fixing the amount of their gift at a big figure, and you
> will get at least half of what you're after. The money is here in Chicago
> available for the poor. All you have to do is to go after it.

He was also quoted as saying on this occasion:

> They call me the king of beggars, and I guess they know what they
> are talking about, for I have been begging for the unfortunate ones of
> the city for years. If we can't manage this society as it should be managed
> and keep it afloat, we ought to go out of business. The town would
> soon be full of beggars, but if that is the desire of the people of Chicago,
> let them have it. They ought to put a shoulder to the wheel and give
> this thing a boost, for it is their duty.
>
> Don't go to the corporations. Get out and see the individual. Corpora-
> tions, you know, have no souls, and are not interested in a scheme of
> this kind. The individual, on the other hand, is deeply interested. Charity
> is an individual matter and we must see that the $125,000 is raised.

In that same year, in a speech before the Associated Jewish
Charities, to which he contributed a total $1,888,645 during his
life, he said: "Notwithstanding the splendid generosity of our
subscribers, I am still looking for the man who is giving more
than he can afford, for I believe you will agree with me that, as
a rule, we all have our liberality under control."

IV

While he was devoting himself to civic affairs, Rosenwald
maintained his close interest in Jewish activities throughout the
world. In October, 1913, Mendel Beilis, a Russian Jewish resident
of Kiev, was put on trial, accused of the ritual murder of a Christian boy. The world was aroused at this renewal of Russian anti-
Semitic activities. A huge mass meeting was held in Chicago, to

demand justice for Beilis. Rosenwald was a member of the committee on arrangements of this meeting, and he offered to help defray its expenses. Jane Addams, and many other social workers, as well as civic officials, judges, priests, lawyers, and professors took part in the protest. Two theaters had to be used to accommodate the crowds, and about 25,000 people took part, many of them Gentiles. Resolutions were adopted denouncing the charge against the Jews that they murdered for ritual blood purposes. Jane Addams, said: "These old superstitions must be dealt with by the same social control that eliminated the black plague and cholera. Nations must be taught that certain things once believed in because the world knew no better, can no longer be tolerated." Booker T. Washington made a plea for racial tolerance, and Rabbi Emil G. Hirsch, the only Jew on the platform, said: "The Jew has been handy in all countries of Europe and sometimes even in America as a counter-irritant when a ruler feels himself tottering and looks around for a means of diverting the attention of his subjects."

Rosenwald was also associated with the American Jewish Committee since its inception in 1906. This organization devoted itself to guarding the rights of Jews throughout the world. It took action against civil and religious persecution and discrimination. It was also active in the movement for a liberal immigration policy for the United States, so that Jews, subject to persecution abroad, might find asylum here.

In 1914 he took an active part in the effort to obtain justice for Leo M. Frank, a Jew who was charged in Atlanta, Georgia, with the murder of a fourteen-year-old girl, Mary Phagan. His trial had been held in an atmosphere of intense passion, fanned by rival newspapers eager for circulation. Frank was sentenced to death. Appeals were taken to higher courts, and Rosenwald was one of those who contributed money towards the expenses of those appeals.

Louis Marshall argued for Frank before the Supreme Court

of the United States. He wrote to Frank's Atlanta attorney at the time that he had pleaded with Justice Lamar of the Supreme Court to admit an appeal to that court and said: "I impressed upon him that I was not in the case as paid counsel, but that I had embarked upon it, because I felt that I owed a duty to the profession, to the cause of justice, and especially to the permanency of our institutions which are based on the supremacy of the law." Justice Oliver Wendell Holmes expressed doubt that Frank had ever had the benefits of due process of law, and leading lawyers throughout the country were convinced that Frank had not had the semblance of a fair trial. Judge Roan, who had sentenced him to die, admitted later that he could not decide from the evidence whether the man was guilty or innocent, "but that is a matter for the jury and not for me to decide." Newspapers, outside Georgia, came out in favor of Frank and some leading papers in other southern states maintained that to execute Frank would be to perform judicial murder. The Supreme Court of the United States denied a motion of habeas corpus, with Justices Holmes and Hughes dissenting.

On May 10, 1915, Frank was resentenced to die, and the only hope of saving his life now rested with Governor John M. Slaton, of Georgia, and the Board of Prison Commissioners. Rosenwald wrote to Senator Lawrence Y. Sherman, of Illinois, urging that he appeal for clemency for Frank, and to others whom he knew, including former President Taft and members of Congress. He also wrote a letter to James Keeley, editor of the Chicago *Herald*, of which he was then one of the leading financial backers:

I have read in this morning's *Herald* with a great deal of astonishment the editorial on "Capital Punishment," particularly the concluding sentence:

"We can rely on judge, jury and public sentiment in this day to see that justice does not err on the side of harshness."

It is beyond my comprehension how the *Herald* can justify this statement, when Leo M. Frank is under sentence to be hanged at Atlanta, Ga., next month, after a spectacular and widely published failure of the people's reliance upon judges, jury, and public sentiment in Georgia "not to err on the side of harshness." Furthermore, the editorial is inconsistent with previous utterances in the *Herald* about this case. The only trial judge before whom the facts were presented expressed doubt as to Frank's guilt. The Georgia State Supreme Court and the United States Supreme Court refused, on legal, technical reasons, to grant Mr. Frank's appeal for justice, though in each Court two able Judges dissented, and, in their opinion, stated unequivocally that Frank was entitled to legal relief.

Permit me also to dissent from the view expressed in this editorial that a would-be murderer "has a holy horror of the noose or the electric chair." I believe the idea of capital punishment is not a deterrent to such an individual.

Of course, I am well aware that you personally cannot pass judgment before hand on everything that goes into the *Herald*, but the editorial from which I quote is so at variance with the facts and with the *Herald's* previous policy that I feel compelled to call it to your attention.

Sincerely yours,

Julius Rosenwald.

P.S. Dear Keeley:

This reads a little stronger than I intended but I know you will understand. **J. R.**

In one week Governor John M. Slaton received 25,000 letters and telegrams urging him to act both for and against commutation of the death sentence. On June 22, 1915, the Governor commuted Frank's sentence to life imprisonment. Governor Slaton's term of office expired on June 30, and he realized when he acted in the Frank case that after mob anger against himself and his wife, carefully fanned by the demagogue, Tom Watson, and other yellow journalists, had subsided, he was condemning himself to political obscurity in Georgia.

Leo M. Frank wrote to Rosenwald from the State Prison Farm:

Allow me to assure you how profoundly grateful I am for the interest you have taken in my cause. I am cognizant of the fact that you have given unselfishly and so largely of yourself to the end that my preservation and vindication become actualities.

My life, thank God, has been denied the hue and cry of the unreasoning mob. I am in an environment which, through the kindness of the Warden and his staff, has been made as bearable as the circumstances will permit. I am gaining rapidly in health and strength, storing up vitality for the next phase of my battle against ignorance, prejudice and unreason to the goal of liberty and honor—justly mine, even now.

Surely the day cannot be far distant when Right and Justice holding complete sway, my vindication and the acknowledgment of my absolute innocence will of necessity result!

When all of these things are with us, you will know for a surety, that your kindly interest in me has been amply justified. May God speed the day!

With the assurance of my deep gratitude and profound respect, and with every good wish to you and yours, I am,

Very sincerely yours,

Leo M. Frank.

One week after he wrote this letter, another convict at the State Prison Farm, William Green, serving a life term for murder, attacked Frank from behind and slashed his throat, saying that he had a command from God to do so. While Frank was recovering from his wound, a mob of armed men broke into the Milledgeville prison soon after midnight of August 16, 1915, and took him from the cot where he was sleeping. They drove 170 miles to Marietta, the birthplace of Mary Phagan, and hanged Frank to a tree near her grave. No one was ever punished for the lynching.

v

In the course of his many activities for the benefit of Chicago and its citizens, Rosenwald took a deep interest in projects designed to promote the health of the people. He and his wife supported the work of the Visiting Nurses Association for many years.

Early in 1911 efforts were made by a few public-spirited dentists in Chicago to provide free dental clinics for school children there. It was estimated that about ninety-five per cent of the school children of Chicago had defective teeth. By January, 1913, six clinics had been established in the Chicago public schools with funds which Rosenwald supplied. After much difficulty the city government was persuaded to take over this work, although Rosenwald had to come to its aid whenever the politicians had not appropriated money for it.

In 1916 Abraham Flexner, of the General Education Board, took up with him a project for a modern medical center at the University of Chicago. "Let's talk it over with Gussie," Rosenwald suggested when Mr. Flexner first brought the matter up, and they went to Rosenwald's home for dinner, where he could get the benefit of Mrs. Rosenwald's point of view. She was enthusiastic about the idea and they both accepted Mr. Flexner's invitation to inspect the Rockefeller Institute in New York. On the steps of the Rockefeller Institute as they were coming out of the building Rosenwald offered to give $500,000 for a modern medical center at the University of Chicago. The Rockefeller Foundation and General Education Board had each pledged $1,000,000 for the project, and the aim was to raise a total of $5,300,000. Stimulated by Rosenwald's gift, others quickly made large contributions and the medical center gradually became a reality.

In the ten years before the outbreak of the World War, Rosenwald's name was attached to every important civic effort in Chicago. Although his experience with politics was unsatisfactory, he never let it intimidate him and he stood by his convictions in the face of his enemies as well as in the face of his friends. He gave generously and he gave, not because he wanted to please, but because he believed in what he was doing.

# CHAPTER VII

# WAR WORK

## I

EARLY in 1914 the Rosenwalds prepared to go to Palestine, partly because of the interest of their friends in Zionism and partly because Aaron Aaronsohn had made them want to see the country with their own eyes.

Rosenwald wanted, however, to make his position clear on the controversial subject of Zionism before he left and to that end wrote to Dr. Gottheil, Professor of Semitic languages at Columbia University:

I have personally not been greatly interested up to this time in Palestinian matters, and the causes which I have helped to foster there were from motives which could not be attributed to my affection for the country, but from altogether different motives. I refer to this because I have often been misunderstood in my attitude, and have been accused of inconsistency.

I therefore cannot enter into any discussion concerning matters which pertain to Palestine from a Zionist's standpoint without danger of having it unpleasant. I mention this for two reasons: one is in regard to what you say concerning a representative there, and the other is the matter of Miss Szold. [Henrietta Szold, the president of Hadassah, had visited Chicago that year, and she had become a close friend of the Rosenwalds.] I fully agree that Miss Szold is too valuable a member of society to be confined to the work she is doing for the Publication Society, but I imagine the only thing that would induce her to leave that work would be to devote herself to Palestine, and while I would not be in the least opposed to this, if I were to take an active part in bringing it about, my sincerity would be very much questioned, and it would leave me in a very uncomfortable position.

I would not be surprised if it would be difficult for you to appreciate my situation." . . .

They arrived in Palestine in February, landing at Jaffa; they inspected the new development at Tel-Aviv, the holy places, the modern schools and social institutions. They visited Aaronsohn's agricultural station and were delighted with it. Wherever they went, the people were enthusiastic and eager to show them their accomplishments and to welcome them.[1] They were greeted with fireworks and singing, and next to Baron de Rothschild, who was also in Palestine at the time, were treated as the territory's most distinguished guests.

On his return Rosenwald disappointed his Zionist friends by his conviction that the Jewish settlement there would never be successful from an economic point of view. He felt that the Palestine development would only endure so long as philanthropic funds were poured into it from the United States and from European countries, and he never was interested in large-scale projects which did not, in his opinion, promise to become self-sufficient. He remained for the rest of his life an interested observer of the Palestine development, but he resisted all attempts on the part of earnest friends and ardent Zionist workers to gain his philanthropic support. He was willing to relieve distress in Palestine, as he was elsewhere in the world, but he was never interested in Palestine as a national home for the Jewish people because he doubted the prospects of industrial and agricultural success.

When the European war broke out in the summer of 1914, Palestine settlers soon found themselves destitute. Suddenly cut off from the sources of capital in Europe and the United States, as well as from the markets for their products, the Jewish settlers had to appeal immediately for aid. Jacob H. Schiff promptly telegraphed to Louis Marshall, and a meeting of the American Jewish

[1] Information on this trip based on short diary kept by Rosenwald at the time.

Committee, of which Rosenwald was a director, was held on
August 30. The sum of $50,000 requested for relief in Palestine
by Henry Morgenthau, American Ambassador to Turkey, was
raised at once.

During the early months of the World War the position of the
Jews in various countries of eastern Europe rapidly became critical. An American Jewish Relief Committee, consisting of organizations representing orthodox Jews, reformed Jews and Jewish
working men and women, was formed, with a Joint Distribution
Committee to distribute the funds collected in the United States
for relief. This distribution agency worked through all available
agencies in Germany, Russia, Poland, Galicia, Rumania and
Palestine.

Rosenwald was firmly opposed in 1914 to a special Jewish organization for war relief. He felt that the problem should become
part of the larger one of general war relief, and he feared that
if it became known abroad that a special fund was being raised,
other war relief agencies would refuse to help Jews. He also
felt that if Jews were singled out for special assistance by their
co-religionists abroad, non-Jewish sufferers in war zones would
take violent action against them. The other leaders of the American Jewish Committee disagreed with him. They felt that the
existing agencies in warring nations would do nothing for the
Jews if they could possibly avoid it, and in any case would help
Jews last of all. They thought it was incumbent on American
Jews to come to the rescue of the European Jews as rapidly as
possible, as they had come to the rescue of Jews who had suffered in other calamities here and abroad. Rosenwald's objections
were voted down, but he continued to have his misgivings, and
during the early part of the war he refused to take an outstanding part in Jewish war relief work.

In November, 1914, Louis D. Brandeis visited Chicago in the
effort to interest Jews there in the fate of the suffering Jews of
Palestine. A meeting was arranged at Rabbi Hirsch's Sinai Tem-

ple, at which Mr. Brandeis and Rabbi Hirsch spoke. Rosenwald, who was in the audience, suggested that the war would last longer than anyone there anticipated and urged that small donations would not meet this large special emergency. He offered to pledge $1,000 a month for relief of sufferers in Palestine for the duration of the war and for one year thereafter, and he carried out this pledge during the remainder of the war. Although he was not a Zionist, his heart was touched by the predicament of these people in Palestine, wedged in between hostile armies and utterly unable to market their products.

Concerning the special war relief fund Louis Marshall wrote to him:

I had hoped to have an opportunity to see you long before this, for the purpose of rearguing with you the question as to the soundness of our action in attempting to raise a fund for the relief of the Jewish war sufferers. I am satisfied that, if you had been with us, we would have had a much larger measure of success than we have thus far attained. I am sure that we are right in our views, as is evidenced by the fact that other religious denominations are doing the very same kind of work that we are seeking to accomplish.

Rosenwald replied, enclosing a check for $10,000 and wrote:

While I have not changed my mind in the least concerning the wisdom of the plan for raising a fund for the relief of distinctly Jewish sufferers in the war zones and while, for that reason, I am not willing to publicly make a contribution to the cause, as such act might be considered to represent my views as being in sympathy with the plan, I desire, out of respect for the judgment of yourself and your co-workers, to contribute, anonymously, the amount of the enclosed check. Making anonymous contributions is contrary to my policy, since I have always urged that, as a rule, the personality behind the gift is far more valuable than the gift itself, and should be known, but in this case I can see no other means of accomplishing the desired end.

Acknowledging this gift, Louis Marshall expressed the opinion that in time Rosenwald would come to the conclusion that the opinion of the other leaders among the Jews was justified. He added: "I observe from the reports which come to us, that in the treatment which is accorded to the Jews in Poland, they are treated with equal rigor and hostility by the Russians, the Germans, the Austrians and the Poles."

Judge Mack came to Chicago in 1915 to help in raising Chicago's quota of $75,000 for Jewish war relief. Rosenwald consented to attend a luncheon for this purpose, but he warned that he had not changed his views. At the luncheon $40,000 of the $75,000 was quickly subscribed among those present, and Rosenwald said that although he disagreed with their views, he would contribute $15,000, provided the others present raised their contributions from $40,000 to $60,000, which was promptly done.

In the spring of 1915 Louis D. Brandeis suggested that a national Jewish Congress be organized in the United States to meet the Jewish minority problems which would arise at the peace conference as soon as the war ended. The aim was to have representatives of the various shades of opinion in the Jewish world meet in congress and resolve their attitude toward the important peace settlement in so far as it would affect Jews. The holding of such a congress was opposed by the conservative group who managed the American Jewish Committee. At a meeting of this Committee Jacob H. Schiff expressed himself as opposed to any American Jewish Congress because he feared that such action would be taken as an indication that the Jews wished to become a nation within a nation and that the holding of a Congress would be a suggestion "that we are Jews first, and Americans second." He believed that a conference of national Jewish societies was all that was required, and added: "As for the Congress, I am afraid that it will come whether we want it or not. It is probable that this is just exactly what some of the Jewish National leaders want." The leaders of the American Jewish Committee felt that as they had guarded the rights of Jews throughout the world since the committee was organized they should have the leading part in protecting the interests of Jews at any peace conference after the war. They also wished to avoid a congress which would commit them and the Jews of America to an endorsement of Zionism or "any general theory or philosophy of Jewish life, or any theoretical principle of a racial, political, economic or religious character, or which shall involve the perpetuation of such Congress."[2]

The advocates of the Congress felt, on the other hand, that the American Jewish Committee was dominated by rich Jews like Schiff, Rosenwald and Marshall, among others, and that it was not representative of other sections of Jewish life in America. They felt that these men were trying to establish a monopoly "in the accomplishment of Israel's work in America," and they wished representation for their own dissenting views on various problems. The Zionists and the more radical Jewish leaders of workingmen's circles wanted an American Jewish Congress, elected by popular vote of Jews throughout the United States, to represent the views of American Jewry on specific and important problems. After much hard feeling, unity of a sort was achieved, and a large convention was held in Chicago on January 23, 1916. This convention formed a coalition with the American Jewish Committee and the National Workmen's Circles and elections of delegates to an American Jewish Congress were finally held.

In the meantime, instead of peace and a peace conference, the scope of war increased, and it became more disastrous to the Jews of various European nations. A campaign was held in the United States to raise $5,000,000 for relief. It was estimated by the committee that in Russia alone 750,000 Jews were made homeless by the war and that in Vienna there were 300,000 Jewish refugees from Galicia. Rosenwald was finally convinced that funds for special Jewish relief work must be raised. He was in New York and he had an engagement to dine with Schiff before attending a meeting of the American Jewish Committee. Before going to

[2] Annual Report of the American Jewish Committee, 1915.

dinner he told Judge Mack that he had changed his views, and that he was going to suggest to Mr. Schiff that each of them donate $250,000 to the drive for funds. After the dinner, he met Judge Mack again. "Well, Julius, what about it?" Judge Mack asked. Rosenwald answered that Schiff had opened the conversation by saying that it was up to them to contribute $100,000 each, and that he had not felt like suggesting $250,000 instead, because it might look as if he were trying to take the leadership in the movement from Schiff. In addition to his contribution for this work he also contributed during 1914, 1915 and 1916 to the Belgian Relief Fund, the Salvation Army War Fund, to a fund for the relief of Armenians and Syrians, to a fund for the aid of German widows and orphans, as well as to a fund to fight typhus in Serbia.

II

Just as Rosenwald's attitude toward Jewish war relief had changed with the course of events, his general attitude on peace went through a gradual evolution as the development of the war altered the complexion of the world and the relationship of the United States to other countries. He had been interested in pacifism and supported many of the movements for peace even after the sinking of the *Lusitania*. But as the German submarine warfare continued, and the war drew closer to American interests, he became an advocate of the preparedness policies of Colonel Theodore Roosevelt. He wrote to him in 1916:

I am especially interested in, and deem of utmost importance, your plan for Industrial Preparedness and the necessity of universal service. The latter I believe is far more important as preparedness for peace than preparedness for war, in order that our young men may learn that they have duties as well as privileges. This seems to me to have been entirely forgotten.

He and five other Chicagoans gave $30,000 to establish a fund for furthering the cause of universal military training. They formed an organization to obtain legislation making universal military training obligatory and to issue propaganda in favor of such training. At the time of making his contribution Rosenwald made a public statement:

The need of defense is a subject on which my heart is very full. I feel that if the public continues in its present state of apathy towards means of defense and towards a higher national idealism, our children will live to see a different form of government rule these United States. The time is here for mobilization of our strength. There should be no age limit exemption clause. No man is so old that he cannot do something for his country or so old that there is not some able capacity in which he can serve it and give something out of his life to this country from which he has received so many benefits.

During the presidential election campaign of 1916 he favored Charles Evans Hughes, who was running against President Wilson on a platform calling for preparedness. At this time Newton D. Baker, Secretary of War, wrote to him:

I have been asked by the President to notify you that he has appointed you a member of the Advisory Commission, to be associated with the Council of National Defense, under the provisions of the Act of Congress creating that Council.

Your associates on the Commission will be as follows:

Mr. Daniel Willard, President Baltimore & Ohio R.R., Baltimore, Md.

Mr. Samuel Gompers, President American Federation of Labor, Washington, D. C.

Dr. Franklin H. Martin, Chicago, Ill.

Mr. Howard E. Coffin, Detroit, Mich.

Mr. Bernard Baruch, New York City.

Dr. Hollis Godfrey, Care Drexel Inst., Phila., Pa.

The Council of National Defense consists of the Secretaries of War, Navy, Interior, Agriculture, Commerce and Labor. At an early date the Council will meet and arrange an opportunity for a meeting for organization purposes with the Advisory Commission.

I have the honor to ask on behalf of the President your acceptance of this appointment and your participation in the important work for national preparedness which is committed to it.

Rosenwald was pleased at this mark of distinction, and accepted the appointment.

The idea of a Council of National Defense for the United States had been considered first in 1906. Dr. Hollis Godfrey, an engineer and an educator, was in England and had a discussion one night with Sir Henry Campbell-Bannerman, then Prime Minister. The discussion turned to the possibility of war between Great Britain and Germany, whose relations were disturbed by the controversy between France and Germany over Morocco. Mention was made of the fact that the British Council of Imperial Defense was being remodeled as a result of the experiences and difficulties encountered during the Boer War. When Dr. Godfrey returned to the United States, he was convinced that a war between Great Britain and Germany was inevitable, and he considered it necessary that the United States should be prepared, in case it was forced to take part. He lectured and wrote about the need for a council of national defense in this country.

When war broke out in 1914, he came to the conclusion that our participation was inevitable. He planned for this coming war, and determined that a new organ of government must be established or an existing organ of government reorganized for the purpose of correlating the defense of the nation. The main purpose of such a body, as he first conceived it, was to make surveys of resources and furnish the information to the executive branches of the government. He prepared preliminary charts to show what he thought such a group of surveys could accomplish.

In the latter part of 1915 many other men began to talk of preparedness, and former President Theodore Roosevelt was particularly vociferous in his attacks on President Wilson for his lack of preparedness policy. In the meantime, Colonel House took Dr. Hollis Godfrey's plan to President Wilson, who approved of it. A Council of National Defense was finally created by Congress and Wilson approved the bill a few days later, but he did not appoint the members of the Advisory Commission called for in the act until October, when the election campaign was nearing its end. The President was running for re-election as the man who had kept the United States out of war, and it seemed, perhaps, politically dangerous to appoint a council of national defense under the circumstances. But as the strength of the Hughes preparedness campaign was demonstrated, it may have been considered wise by President Wilson's advisers to announce the new body before election day in November.

### III

The Council of National Defense held its first meeting in Washington on December 6, 1916. The seven advisory members arrived in Washington with very vague conceptions of the function they were supposed to serve. They did not know whether they were supposed to prepare for war, and yet all had a feeling that peace could not be much prolonged. The first meetings were vague and general and discussion took place as to the best means of collecting data which might be useful. According to Dr. Franklin H. Martin, who prepared a digest of the proceedings, Rosenwald brought up the matter of universal military training at this first meeting:

Universal military training, which was on all tongues at that time, was brought into the discussion by Mr. Rosenwald, a strong advocate of the Plattsburg method. He bluntly asked the members of the cabinet if they favored it. There was some attempt at making distinctions on the subject, one suggestion being that there might be two points of view, viz., universal military training or universal military service. This led to the gradual taking of sides, the pacifists agreeing that military training might be admissible, and the more militant-minded asserting that universal military service should be established.

This was the first showing of hands. The Secretaries of War, Navy, Commerce, Agriculture, and Labor, and possibly Samuel Gompers, of the Commission, at that time still hesitated to commit themselves to a universal military service; but the other six Commission members indicated a distinct leaning to immediate commitment of the country to such a program. As time went on it was interesting to watch the gradual change of attitude on the part of the conservatives.[3]

In December and January, 1917, the Advisory Commission marked time and waited, as did the rest of the nation, to discover whether President Wilson intended to maintain peace or to recommend war. On January 23, 1917, Count Bernstorff, the German Ambassador to the United States, handed to the Secretary of State the note announcing unrestricted submarine warfare, and declaring that all ships, neutral or belligerent, would be sunk without warning if encountered in a zone drawn around the British Isles, France and Italy.

Now the Council of National Defense was able to organize more completely. At its meeting with the Cabinet members on February 13, the Commission recommended that it be divided into committees: medicine and general sanitation under Commissioner Martin; labor under Commissioner Gompers; transportation and communication under Commissioner Willard; science and research under Commissioner Godfrey; raw materials, minerals and metals under Commissioner Baruch; munitions under Commissioner Coffin; and supplies, including food, clothing, etc. under Commissioner Rosenwald. Each commissioner was to select members of his own committee from both civilian and military life, and each committee was to organize with representatives of trades and professions and to gather information on their ability to cooperate with the government for the national defense and welfare.

While he was waiting with the rest of the world for President Wilson's decision, Rosenwald was kept busy not only with the new contacts he had made in Washington but with philanthropic work which assumed dramatic proportions. Sears, Roebuck he

[3] *Digest of the Proceedings of the Council of National Defense during the World War*, prepared in narrative form by Dr. Franklin H. Martin. Senate Document No. 193, 73d Congress, 2d Session, 1934. This document is far from an objective digest of these important proceedings. It constitutes more of a world war diary of Dr. Martin, but contains valuable incidental information.

had temporarily turned over to Albert H. Loeb, but he was constantly receiving reports.

It was at this time that he made a magnificent offer which created a great impression throughout the country. It elicited the following tribute from Jacob H. Schiff: "I believe," he said, "there is no one who has done so much to make the name of Jew respected, to raise it, not only in the eyes of our countrymen, but everywhere, as Julius Rosenwald!"

The offer was occasioned by the desperate plight of the Jewish war sufferers in Europe. Plans were being made by Jewish philanthropic leaders in New York to raise $10,000,000, twice the amount solicited in the previous year. Jacob Billikopf was engaged in conducting the drive for funds. In a conference with Jacob H. Schiff, Felix M. Warburg, Leo K. Frankel and others, Mr. Billikopf made a suggestion that sounded like a fund raiser's dream. He wanted one wealthy Jew to dramatize the drive by giving one million dollars. He was delegated to go to Washington to see Julius Rosenwald.

Jacob Billikopf arrived in Washington the day of President Wilson's second inauguration in March, 1917. Rosenwald spent the day attending the inaugural ceremonies, but that night Billikopf caught him in the lobby of the Willard Hotel. He had been rehearsing to himself a dramatic plea. He never made it, for he found himself merely telling briefly of the new ten million dollar campaign and of the need for a powerful stimulus to start it off effectively. Rosenwald agreed readily to give ten per cent of every million dollars raised up to a maximum of $10,000,000.

When this offer was published throughout the country, the response to it was electric. Jews in other cities offered to give ten per cent of the money raised in their localities. The slogan for the drive was, "Be the Julius Rosenwald of Your City." In an interview published in the Chicago *American* one week after the Russian Revolution broke out, Rosenwald was quoted as saying:

No one can appreciate or comprehend the terrible plight of the Jews in Russia—for that is where the great majority of them live. Countless thousands of them are penniless and worse than penniless. They are homeless and hungry. What I have agreed to give is no more than I should give.

There is a new era dawning for the Jews in Russia. The revolution has made that clear. But the changes that will come, the persecution that will stop, will not be things of a day, a month, or a year. They will be gradual—a generation perhaps will be needed to accomplish them. Meanwhile there is urgent need. I hope that what I have agreed to do will spur others on to give freely. It is the duty of the Jews of America to look after the Jews in Russia. I am simply doing my duty.

President Wilson telegraphed him that his contribution served democracy as well as humanity. Two years before he had held the belief that Jewish war relief was unwise. Now he was its leading contributor in the world. Conditions had changed rapidly between 1915 and 1917, and it was now obvious that the war was becoming both more extensive and more catastrophic.

Schiff gave a dinner in New York in honor of Rosenwald, and Henry Morgenthau, Sr., at which more than $2,000,000 was raised. Schiff himself gave $100,000 with the stipulation that the sum be applied to the organization of a hospital unit to be presented to the Russian people by American Jewry in recognition of the emancipation of the Jews by the recent Russian Revolution. Julius Rosenwald spoke at this dinner and was quoted by the *New York Times* as saying:

I feel that the Jews of America have a serious duty that they cannot evade. These starving men and women and children must depend on us to do for them what we would expect them to do for us were the conditions reversed. We have been successful as we view success, but there are hundreds of thousands who have worked harder than we have and have been just as able, but it has been ours to have the opportunity that they lacked. And now it is our opportunity to aid them. We have had the good luck to live in this free country, the United States, and it is our duty to help those whose cradles happened to be rocked in Russia instead of here. They are no more to blame for their condition than our children would be if they were similarly situated. What we must do is to bring it home to the Jews of this country that it is our duty to aid the Jews of Europe.

To a meeting held at Sinai Temple to raise funds, Jacob H. Schiff telegraphed: "Would that there were more Rosenwalds in Chicago." When Rosenwald arose to speak. he said:

There is another Rosenwald in Chicago. My grandson has arrived within the last twenty-four hours. He is a most precocious young man. The first thing he suggested was a contribution to the fund. Being financially embarrassed, I lent him $500, which he hereby tenders to the fund.

He also announced at this meeting a gift of $150,000 from himself and Mrs. Rosenwald in addition to his pledge to give $1,000,-000 if $10,000,000 were raised.

By May fifty-one people had pledged ten per cent of the funds raised in their localities. Some men, including Governor Simon Bamberger, of Utah, Governor Moses Alexander, of Idaho, Adolph S. Ochs, originally of Tennessee, S. R. Travis, of Oklahoma, and E. M. Chase, of New Hampshire, offered to give ten per cent of all the money raised in their states. Local committees organized by the American Jewish Relief Committee in New York made efforts to locate every Jew in the United States and to present appeals for contributions. In a town in Wisconsin where there was only one Jew, the committee got $3,500 and the one Jewish family in a town in Pennsylvania sent in $7,000. The working people of New York's East Side contributed $1,-250,000 of their wages. The Jews in Sing Sing prison sent in $200. In spite of every effort the entire ten million dollars was not raised by November 1, 1917, the expiration date of Rosenwald's offer, but he extended the time until December 31. These fourteen days were labeled "Rosenwald Days," and an intensive campaign to meet the conditions of his offer was carried on.

In the end, after Rosenwald had been extremely liberal in the interpretation of the terms of his offer, permitting the auditors to count promissory notes and post-dated checks, the final amount actually collected was $7,789,252.79 and Rosenwald paid $778,-925.28 plus the $150,000 that he and his wife had pledged separately.

IV

In the meantime the atmosphere in Washington had become more tense, as the certainty grew that the United States would enter the war. Rosenwald had been pressing the other members of the Advisory Commission to express themselves in favor of universal military service and persistently attempted to offer a resolution on that subject. Samuel Gompers, who was not sure how labor would take to conscription, and who was planning to make the pill as palatable as possible, was reluctant to go on record as being in favor of such a measure. Daniel Willard, the chairman, managed whenever Rosenwald tried to offer his resolution, not to hear him or to recognize him. Finally, Rosenwald approached him after one of the meetings and asked why he could never seem to get his attention. Mr. Willard expressed surprise and asked forgiveness. Then he explained that it would be impolitic for the commission to go on record for such an important measure unless the vote was unanimous, that Gompers was not yet in a position to come out for conscription, and that the matter would be brought up at the earliest possible moment.[4]

The issue of universal military service was finally brought up at a tense session of the Council held at the office of the Secretary of War on March 24. The United States had not yet entered the war officially, but the Advisory Commission recommended to the Council of National Defense that an army of at least one million men should be organized, trained and equipped as soon as possible, and that the navy should be brought up to full war strength. Daniel Willard told the meeting what he had told

[4] Interview with Daniel Willard by the author, March 18, 1937.

privately to Rosenwald, and Rosenwald after some discussion, said:

> With all due deference to Mr. Gompers' position, it seems to me that we are stultifying ourselves by not expressing ourselves on this question, with it the main thing desired by the people. The people have a right to know our views.[5]

Secretary Baker responded that he regretted the necessity for universal service, as he believed that in a democracy there should be as few compulsions as possible, but that he would be "sorry to miss making such a suggestion to the President." Rosenwald's answer was:

> I'm afraid that we will be condemned if we do not recommend universal military service to Congress. I believe further that it is even more necessary for peace than it is for war.

This statement was followed by a long discussion in which some favored an army of volunteers and others opposed it as being unfair. The discussion ended with Secretary Baker's intention of bringing the views of the Commission to the attention of the President.

Walter S. Gifford, director of the Council, wrote to Rosenwald in 1925, recalling their war experience together, and said:

> My own recollection of the occasion is very distinct, and I feel that if it had not been for your insistence that no full discussion would have occurred nor would any action have been taken. As it was, 12 out of the 13 advisers of the President—that is, 6 Cabinet Officers and 7 Advisory Commissioners—reported themselves as in favor of a draft system. That information was conveyed to President Wilson. I have no doubt in my own mind but that it was one of the most important factors in influencing the minds of the President and of the Administration toward a draft in place of the volunteer system.
>
> I have often told the story to others and, personally, I feel that you can have a good deal of satisfaction in knowing that your determination and courage at that time was most helpful—in fact, it perhaps decided

[5] Minutes of Council of National Defense, pp. 32-33.

the question of this country's adoption of a sound and successful plan for raising an army. . . .

On April 2, President Wilson, escorted by a troop of cavalry, rode to the capitol and asked for a declaration of war. By the sixth the resolution was voted through the Senate and the House and approved by the President.

Men with varied ideas of just how to win the war were besieging Washington, and the Council of National Defense was the place to which thousands wrote offering their services and ideas. Rosenwald was besieged by men who wanted a chance to serve the country or to further their ambitions.

Congress had adjourned on March 3, 1917, without appropriating any special war fund, and the Secretary of War had only thirty million dollars at his disposal. Orders had been given for various supplies for an army of one million men before the United States declared war, in the belief that after it did, Congress would appropriate the money to pay for them. Some of the regular Army officers felt that the Secretary of War and they themselves would go to jail because they were exceeding their authority, but Secretary Baker assured them that their wives would no doubt bring them food in prison, and that he, for one, was willing to risk his freedom. As an instance of the prevalent bewilderment in the face of the huge reality, Frederick Palmer in a book based on the papers of Newton D. Baker, recorded a conversation with the chairman of the Senate Finance Committee, when Secretary Baker and Colonel Palmer Pierce went to the Senate to ask for three billion dollars.

"Three billions? What do you want it for?" Senator Martin asked.

"Clothing, cots, camps, food, pay, medical supplies, haversacks, blankets, slickers, cooking outfits, horses, mules, motor trucks, gun carriages, all forms of transportation, airplanes, balloons, marching equipment, guns, rifles, pistols, tanks, gasmasks—" Colonel

Pierce went on. And then he added: "And we may have an army in France."

"Good Lord!" the Senator said, "you're not going to send soldiers over there, are you?"

"That may be the only way to win the War," Colonel Pierce replied.

"Well, the three billions will be enough. You won't need any more, will you?" the worried Senator asked. Secretary Baker spent one billion dollars without the authority of Congress before the Emergency Appropriation bill was passed.[6]

Meanwhile, the committees formed by the Advisory Commission of the defense Council, suddenly assumed great importance. Among the most important was Rosenwald's Committee on Supplies.

A few days after he had been made chairman, he had written Charles Eisenman, an old friend, who was an expert clothing merchant, and asked him to become his first assistant. Mr. Eisenman accepted and became the most important executive under Rosenwald. A General Munitions Board had been set up in February, and Rosenwald or his assistant attended the meetings of this coordinating body, which aided the army, navy and the allied nations in establishing priority of purchases of munitions. Cooperative committees of the Committee on Supplies were soon set up by Rosenwald and Eisenman, and in that way constant contact was kept between the government and the leaders of the industries on which the army and navy depended for supplies. Committees were set up for cotton goods, woolens, knit goods, shoes and leather. It was soon discovered that one committee could not handle all clothing supplies and food and the latter was assigned to another branch of the government.

Two days after war was declared a conference was held at the office of the Secretary of War, the purpose of which was to discuss the manner in which supplies should be purchased, and

[6] Palmer, Frederick, *Newton D. Baker*, Vol. I, p. 120.

it was pointed out that the necessary supplies would be enormous; in some cases, beyond the productive capacity of the nation. Huge purchases by the Allies had depleted the supplies of some commodities, and prices had increased greatly. It was anticipated that prices would go still higher, and the problem was discussed of protecting the interests of the government and of people who required products for civilian use. At the same time it was necessary to stimulate production and offer inducements in the form of prices. The army and the navy had been in the habit of advertising for bids on supplies, but it was maintained at this conference that to advertise publicly for bids would create havoc in the market and would lead to attempts to corner the products which the government needed at any cost. It was felt that the huge purchases for the government should be made by contacts directly between manufacturers and producers of commodities and the representatives of the government. Rosenwald advocated this policy strongly as did Eisenman. As a result of this conference the Secretary of War issued an order abrogating the necessity for public bids for supplies during the war emergency.[7]

At a later conference between the Secretary of War, Quartermaster General Sharpe, Rosenwald and Eisenman, it was arranged that the Quartermaster General should deal directly with Rosenwald's Committee on Supplies and have as his representative on that committee Colonel H. J. Hirsch, who would sit with the committee in its hearings with producers and manufacturers in the effort to fix prices for materials needed by the army. It was arranged that the Quartermaster General should inform Rosenwald's Committee of the quantities of particular goods needed and the time when they would be required. The Committee would then consult the manufacturers and producers. The actual contracts for goods were negotiated by the Committee but signed by the representative of the Quartermaster Department.

[7] Sharpe, Major-General Henry G., *The Quartermaster Corps in the Year 1917*, p. 151 ff.

When the Advisory Commission was created, its members had never contemplated that they would themselves actually arrange for the purchase of huge quantities of varied supplies. But the regular departments of the army which ordinarily had these functions were not organized for the huge war time task that had to be undertaken. They were on a peace time basis, and when war was declared found themselves overworked and under-staffed, as well as hampered by regulations which were valuable during times of peace but which did not work in the unnatural situations created by war.

Early in April, 1917, Rosenwald sent telegrams to the principal Chicago meat packers asking them to come to Washington for a conference. He outlined the needs of the government in meat and hides, and they were asked to fix the prices at the closing prices for these commodities in Chicago the night before. The packers agreed readily, and fluctuations in prices were stopped. This same technique was then adopted in dealing with other producers and manufacturers. Secretary Baker told a Senate investigating committee in the summer of 1917: "We had, over-night, to pass from a market in which prices were regulated by free competition into a market in which the government was a monopolistic and exclusive buyer—a compulsory buyer, and in which competition was practically impossible as a regulator of prices."[8] The war orders which had occupied American industry before the entry of the United States into the war, while they consumed huge quantities of raw materials and finished products and seriously depleted supplies in some lines, also caused an im-mense expansion of industrial equipment at the command of the government.

Bernard M. Baruch wrote in his report after the war:

As attention turned to immediate preparations, it was soon felt that the problem of supplies was going to involve difficulties of the most far-reaching and important character. Private industry in this country was

[8] Investigation of War Department, p. 1639.

already making important contributions to the supply of the Allies, but without proper coordination in the supply of our own requirements and those of the Allies it could well have happened that our entering the war might have had the effect of impeding rather than stimulating the flow of supplies to Europe and thus actually hindering the progress toward victory.[9]

It was part of Rosenwald's work to maintain contact with representatives of the British War Office who were purchasing materials in the United States for the British government, and to exchange information with them and arrange for priority of orders on shoes, leather and other commodities in which there was a great shortage.

The merchandising methods used by his Committee were similar to those used by Sears, Roebuck. Instead of dealing with middlemen, the government went directly to producers and manufacturers, just as Sears, Roebuck made contracts wherever possible with factories for a large proportion of their output. When the Committee adopted the rule that it would not deal with middlemen, but only with producers, in order to create an orderly market and a fixed price, the middlemen became antagonistic and through their representatives in Congress made as much trouble as possible for Rosenwald and his associates. In order to reduce competition and prevent chaotic price changes, the Secretary of War, at the request of the Committee, ordered that the contracts made by the army for supplies should not be filed for public inspection until some time had elapsed.

Between March 5, 1917, and June 30 of that year the Quartermaster Department with the cooperation of the Committee on Supplies, which virtually made the contracts, placed orders for goods costing $766,284,489.93.[10] The quantities of goods purchased were staggering: five million blankets, thirty-seven million yards of bobbinette, two million cots, more than forty-five million yards of cotton cloth, more than twenty-one million yards

[9] Baruch, Bernard M., *American Industry in the War*, p. 17.
[10] Sharpe, p. 159.

of unbleached drilling, six million pairs of shoes, and 11,191,000 pairs of woolen socks. Rosenwald claimed that the government had saved $1,500,000 in the purchase of shoes alone by the policy of obtaining options on the raw materials first and then calling for bids on manufacturing. But the disappointed middlemen kept visiting their Congressmen and writing letters of protest.

Attacks on the merchandising methods were made on the floor of Congress as early as May, and rumors were spread that there was corruption and extravagance, and that some men were being favored above others for the contracts. Rosenwald said that to invite middlemen to participate would have caused prices of raw materials to soar when they began to compete with one another in an effort to obtain the means of fulfilling their contracts. In some instances he asked for bids from the leading organizations in an industry, and in others the work was given at once to the largest and best equipped plant.

Secretary Baker testified that in the nine months between April 1, 1917, and December 31, the armies of the United States had increased from 9,524 officers to 110,856, and from 202,510 enlisted men to 1,422,650. By the end of that year the army had made 4,650 contracts for supplies and spent more than $800,000,000 for them.

In order to house the huge army that was being trained and shipped to France, sixteen cantonments, which were little cities in themselves, were built, each one to house between 40,000 and 60,000 men. Rosenwald took an important part in the letting of these contracts by the General Munitions Board. At a meeting of the Munitions Board held on June 1, 1917, he offered a motion to the effect that in all contracts of $5,000,000 or over, the contractor was to receive as his compensation six per cent of the cost of construction, with the proviso that in no case was the compensation to exceed $200,000.[11]

Finally, cantonments and camps were constructed to shelter

[11] Minutes of General Munitions Board, p. 120.

about 1,800,000 men in the United States, and the expenditures for them were estimated to be about $818,000,000, or about twice the cost of the Panama Canal. Construction overseas was almost as great.[12]

The original war plans had called for sending no troops to France from the United States until March, 1918, but when Marshal Joffre visited the United States in April, 1917, he made clear the urgent need for men as soon as they could be transported. The government's policy was changed overnight, and the effort to supply the large numbers of troops suddenly drafted became increasingly difficult and urgent. Deliveries had to be speeded up and new orders rushed. Manufacturers, eager for orders, had overestimated their capacity to produce. Transportation facilities for freight and raw materials were heavily overtaxed. The winter of 1917 was unusually early and severe, and there was a shortage of clothing and supplies in several cantonments. Quartermaster General Sharpe testified before the Senate investigating committee that Marshal Joffre's plea for troops had complicated the problems enormously, as six months' reserve clothing and equipment had to be provided for those who were sent to France. He added:

"I think it has a very serious effect upon the people everywhere when they see that we are going ahead and have gotten 100,000 men or 200,000 men, or 1,000,000 men into the field. I think it is to our advantage to put as many men in the field as we can possibly get there, even if they have to suffer somewhat. . . . I think if we put them in only when we can fully equip them, we will make a mistake. I think the greater the number we have in the field the greater the effect will be upon the enemy. I look upon it very much, Senator, as if you or I were to get up in the middle of the night to go to a friend's house which was on fire. We would not stop and elaborately dress before we tried to save the lives of our friends."

"But the unequipped condition of these young men is costing their lives," Senator George E. Chamberlain, chairman of the Senate investigating committee said.

[12] Ayres, Leonard P. *The War with Germany, A Statistical Summary*, p. 59.

"I must confess that no one regrets that more seriously than I do," General Sharpe replied. "I think, however, that the effect upon the Germans will be worth it, even though a few lives are sacrificed in the cause." . . .[13]

When the factories and railroads became swamped for a time in this country, General Pershing was compelled to purchase clothing in England and blankets in Spain until the difficulties were overcome. Each soldier in the U. S. Army required twenty-nine regular articles of clothing. "Three days before our entry into the war, Julius Rosenwald reported that we could not clothe a million men before January 1, 1918," Frederick Palmer wrote in his book, *Newton D. Baker*.[14]

Meanwhile, Rosenwald was making every effort to cope with the problems that were thrust upon him and his associates. During the early part of his service in Washington, Mrs. Rosenwald, who was ill, remained in Chicago. Later they took a house in 16th Street. In addition to his work, Rosenwald kept in close touch with his extensive philanthropic interests, and in May, 1917, he became a trustee of the Rockefeller Foundation. He also took an active part in the Jewish War Relief drive for funds in 1917 and was active in the Liberty bond drive. He himself subscribed for one million dollars' worth of each of the Liberty loans, and he induced Sears, Roebuck and its employees to purchase additional bonds of more than one million dollars during each of the loan drives. His own business, meanwhile, was prospering. The net profits for 1917 were $19,758,000. These profits were not made on government orders, for Rosenwald had refused to permit Sears, Roebuck to sell any goods to the army and navy while he was head of the Committee on Supplies. On one occasion the government badly needed some sheepskin coats which his company had in stock. Rosenwald consented to the sale, but elaborate precautions were taken so that the government's request

[13] Investigation of the War Department, pp. 635-637.
[14] Vol. I, p. 109.

could never be interpreted as in any way connected with his activities as head of the Committee on Supplies. During the epidemic of influenza in 1918, the navy needed blankets badly at its Great Lakes Training Station. Sears, Roebuck had some blankets which were requested for the emergency. Rosenwald consented to the transaction, provided the blankets were sold to the navy at the cost price to the company. In addition, the Sears, Roebuck testing laboratory tested fabrics and commodities for the government free of charge, and Rosenwald frequently sent such goods from Washington to the Chicago plant for expert examination.

While he was in Washington on government service, he requested the board of directors to discontinue his salary as president of the company, even though he was not being paid by the government. The company was reluctant to do so, but Rosenwald insisted.

V

The rapidly improvised committees soon met with great difficulties as the demands for men, munitions, clothing and food increased during the spring of 1917. Serious economic, political and administrative problems developed, and the system by which a loose Council of National Defense with mere advisory powers tried to operate a huge industrial enterprise such as a war became unworkable. Daniel Willard, speaking of the Advisory Commission, told the Senate Committee on Military Affairs:

"The scheme itself is not a good scheme. This Council of Defense and the advisory commission is not in any sense a war measure. It was there when the war broke out, and it was made use of, because there was nothing else to fill the place and without a defined status it brought to the assistance of the departments I think the best business experience of the country. . . .

"We have here a board which is more or less unsatisfactory as an administrative agency reporting to the Council of National Defense which has no authority under the law, and through that Council to the President. . . . Six members of the Cabinet, and as a Council of National Defense have no authority at all. That is the law. Through them they go to the President. If this, instead of being a board were a man, and if the President were authorized to give that man such authority as he might need from time to time to deal with any question of the character we have been discussing, and to deal with it effectively, why this plan will work all right. . . .

"I would not have the Council of National Defense in it at all. I would have the man at the head of the War Industries Board report direct to the President."

"As a matter of fact," asked Senator Wadsworth, "Is there any necessity at all for having the Council of National Defense in here?"

"No, none at all," Mr. Willard answered.[15]

The economic confusion was accentuated by the fact that in spite of all efforts to maintain fair prices for war time goods, the prices of commodities "were," according to Baruch, "soaring out of all relation to the cost of production and were fluctuating with great uncertainty."[16]

Mr. Baruch added:

This condition was having a more menacing effect than the mere extravagance of paying high prices on the part of the Government. The present generation of business men had been accustomed, for three decades preceding 1915, to conduct their affairs, under steady and sober market conditions, with extreme price fluctuations in staples only at rare and extraordinary intervals. The rapidity of the rise from 1915 to the early spring of 1917 had already thrown great confusion and irregularity in the processes of trade. Commodities had begun to flow through unusual and ineffective channels, causing unbalanced and often retarded production. The final upward swing of prices during the spring of 1917 enhanced these unhealthy tendencies. Capital was turning in great quantities toward speculation and manufacturers were uncertain in their purchases of raw materials. "Cost-plus-profits" contracts brought adventurers into the field of production, who flooded the country with options and inquiries to cover their bids, and prices were being forced further and further out of joint while actual work and production were halted by the confusion.

[15] Investigation of the War Department, pp. 1816-1824. Mr. Willard was testifying in January, 1918, but the situation had begun as early as the spring of 1917.
[16] Baruch. *American Industry in the War*, p. 70.

American business could not make progress in the unaccustomed atmosphere and there was no relief in sight. Demand for goods was to increase rather than decline, and it would increase with ever more telling persistence. A war demand differs in its essential nature from the normal demands of peace. In ordinary times a rising price carries with it its own defeat. Purchasers will buy so long as they can make a profit or reap a satisfaction by doing so. This at least is true of everything except the most extraordinary luxuries. They will stop buying when the price reaches a point outside the range where the commodity can be turned over at a profit. The inflated price drops as a result. But war is economically the greatest and most scandalous of spendthrifts. No economic profit comes from the expenditure of an instrument of war and no economic profit is considered in connection with its purchase. The demand is absolute; the price is no deterrent.[17]

Rosenwald was faced with a situation utterly foreign to his past business experience. The scandalous spendthrift, war, was throwing all preconceptions out of joint. He had been accustomed as head of Sears, Roebuck to the expanding needs of peace and to making plans for their satisfaction. Now he was compelled to buy for the government at all costs, and yet costs had to be regulated to insure adequate supply and profitable production. The situation called for economic dictatorship and was being handled on lines of old fashioned laissez faire economics, with voluntary cooperation of industry and government. When the situation was one of buying by cooperative agreement with producers, Rosenwald was in his element, but within a few months the relationship between the demands of the war and the supply of the nation—complicated by the necessity of allowing for a stimulating profit and the necessity for keeping that profit within reason—became an impossible relationship. It was necessary to have dictatorial authority, vested in either one man or one group.

The situation was complicated in May and June by accusations on the floor of Congress against the men of the Council who felt that they were working day and night with honest intentions to cope with these problems. The political pressure of the

[17] Baruch Report, pp. 70-71.

middlemen became effective, and the clamor in Congress rose. In the effort to remedy unfairness to their constituents, Congressmen made accusations against the members of the Council and the other dollar-a-year men in Washington. One of the principal charges made in and out of Congress was that those who were determining who should get the profitable business of the government were buying from and selling to themselves. In order to prevent this, Congress was considering a rider to the food bill by which members of the Council were prohibited from giving any contracts to firms in which they were financially interested themselves. There was also opposition to the practice of letting contracts for goods without calling for public bids.

Rosenwald was incensed at the charges on the debate over the rider to the food bill that members of the Advisory Commission and its committees were profiting by sales to themselves, and he was outraged by the effort to prohibit these men from doing business with companies in which they might have any financial interest. He was in Chicago over the Fourth of July and telegraphed to President Wilson:

It is of the most vital importance that the rider in the Food bill referring to the Advisory Commission and its method of securing supplies be stricken out. To cast suspicion on men in many industries who without exception have been eager to serve the Government rather than themselves will destroy a spirit which should be encouraged. The Committees representing these industries have succeeded in instilling and securing a loyalty to the Government from many in their own lines that could never have been produced under the old system. Even at this early stage of the war the savings to the Government due to this desire to serve runs into many tens of millions of dollars. Having been intrusted with a responsibility to protect and serve their Government interests, a patriotism has been aroused in these men which is absolutely necessary to secure rapid production. It is probably impossible to devise any plan which is dishonest proof, but any man of standing in his profession or industry will sacrifice everything rather than be unfaithful to his trust. At any rate such has been my experience with the men who have served as advisors to the Commission which I have had the honor to appoint. The present system should not be destroyed until a better one is found. If changes in methods are desirable, they can be made after proper investigation. It is vital that the cooperation which has already been established should be maintained and, furthermore, it is of greatest importance that confidence exist between Government and Industry, and that suspicion which has existed on the part of both be eliminated.

While he was still in Chicago, Rosenwald gave an outspoken and politically indiscreet interview to the Chicago *Tribune*:

It is simply outrageous. Personally it would suit me very well to be relieved of my duties, so I could be back here with my family. That is, it would be much more pleasant here, but I am like the other men who are serving the Government at this time and doing it loyally, with the sole thought of helping this nation to go through as economically and efficiently as possible.

Congressmen under the Constitution cannot be interested in any contracts with the Government, and Congress now, it appears, has tacked a rider to the food bill, the effect of which, if passed, and not vetoed by the President, would be to legislate the committees of the defense council out of business by putting the members in the same class with Congressmen and Senators.

This is very stupid. It is shortsighted. It is nonsensical and foolish. It means a return to the old slipshod days of unloading on the Government— the days of rotten contracts in a time of great national emergency.

I do not like to say these things and have my name associated with them. That is, it is not pleasant, but I know what the several committees have been doing, and I know that a more loyal lot of men never got together to do the best they could for this Government. I say it is impossible to describe adequately the loyalty of these men. There is not a thought of self-interest on the part of a single member.

Take, for instance, the case of Howard Coffin, who is in charge of the aeronautics division. The commission has found that it would be greatly to the advantage of the Government if the automobile plant with which he was connected and in which he now probably owns stocks, could be taken over in part, at least, for government work. But Congress proposes to pass a law that will deny to the government the service of Mr. Coffin because he happens to own some stock in the company that will be called upon to provide certain supplies.

Could anything be more outrageous, more unfair, more stupid? The

Government needs the services of this man and needs them badly. But he doesn't happen to be a politician. That's the trouble.

Members of the council and subcommittees are not politicians. They are the biggest men in their several lines of industry in this country, men who don't depend on political favors for success. They are men who know how to do and just what to do, to bring to the aid of the Government the highest possible degree of efficiency and economy in the shortest possible time.

Why, if it hadn't been for the men on these commissions the Government would have been unable in this short time to provide supplies for a million soldiers without the slightest suspicion of graft. Never in this world would it have been done.

These committees have saved millions and millions of dollars for the Government. I guess that is one reason why they are not popular with some contractors.

If they destroy these commissions then surely they are putting the Government back to the rotten days of the Spanish-American War.

Of course, these men are interested in their own plants. That is, they still have their investments. But these men, also, are the biggest men in their line of industry. That is why they were chosen.

If it should be deemed advisable, because of the capacity to produce quickly what the Government wants, to ask a plant in which one of the members of the commission happened to be financially interested to take a contract, it would be done without hesitation. But what is wrong in that, when men of large experience and success are asking that it be done and know that it is best for the Government that it be done this way?

No member of these commissions, I repeat emphatically, is financially interested in a single contract in the sense that he has tried to take advantage in any way of the Government.

The day this was printed some of the Senators were very angry. James K. Vardaman, of Mississippi, said:

Mr. President. I am not inclined to criticize harshly this man. On the contrary, he challenges my sense of charity. His stupid utterances are but the emanations from a mind uninformed and a spirit inflated with the vanity of riches. They are but the manifestation of that contemptuous regard which the purse-proud individual usually entertains for an honest man in public life who dares to do his duty to his country. His conduct is the impudence of ignorance, the arrogance of great wealth—the bad

manners of a plutocratic vulgarian. I think it calls for action on the part
of the Senate. Senators cannot preserve their self-respect and have anything to do with such an ill-mannered coarsely bred creature, and I shall
be glad to vote for a resolution requesting that he withdraw altogether
from the Government service.[18]

Plans of reorganization, leading to more complete coordination of the vast war efforts of the government, were rife at this
time, and President Wilson was considering important changes.
There was divided authority not only in the purchasing of supplies but in the government's shipbuilding operations. The regular departments of the government and the emergency organizations which had been set up were in constant conflict. The
regular departments had the authority and the emergency organizations had the contacts with industry. The two were finally
merged in the new War Industries Board set up by Wilson in
July, 1917. Frank A. Scott, who had been head of the General
Munitions Board, was the first President, but illness finally compelled him to resign, and Bernard M. Baruch became the co-
ordinator of war industry. Rosenwald was made a member of
the Board, representing the Advisory Commission of the Council
of National Defense, but his functions as a purchaser of supplies
were gradually taken over by the new body, and his services soon
were limited.

The question of prices for war commodities was becoming
critical, and Wilson threatened to fix prices. Although there was
prejudice against government price fixing, there was also discontent among families whose earnings decreased when their male
members were conscripted, while their living costs were rising.
The President fixed the price of bituminous coal in August and
the price of copper a month later. Thereafter, the War Industries
Board, the Food Administration and the Fuel Administration
fixed prices regularly.[19]

By October, 1917, the position of the business men who had

[18] *Congressional Record*, July 3, 1917, vol. 55, Part 5, pp. 4656-4659.
[19] Baruch Report, p. 72.

acted in an advisory capacity was becoming both embarrassing and futile. Congress passed the resolution declaring it illegal for any person to participate in making contracts with companies in which he was financially interested. It also passed a resolution calling for an investigation of the War Department, with particular reference to its activities in the purchase of supplies. The result of the first resolution was to make the position of the business men who were cooperating with Rosenwald's Committee impossible, and they were forced to resign. After the members of his committee retired, Rosenwald's position was more ambiguous, and the feeling of futility which he and others were experiencing was accentuated. Gradually the War Industries Board and the regular government departments took over the work of the emergency war organizations. The coordination of all contract work in the new War Industries Board stripped the Advisory Commission of the Council of National Defense of power and purpose, and yet it was not abolished. The government having asked these prominent individuals to do patriotic work, found it difficult to admit that their services were not required any longer, and the individuals were placed in the position of being critical and "slackers" if they resigned. The subordinate members of the committees could resign quietly, but any resignations by members of the Advisory Commission would have gained widespread publicity and political attention.

In December the Senate Committee on Military Affairs began its investigation of the War Department. Rosenwald's Committee was a major target of attack. He, himself, was not called as a witness, but Charles Eisenman was grilled by the Committee. The center of the attack on Eisenman was based on accusations that he had made prices with the aid of people in trades who were, in effect, selling to themselves. A specific charge was made that in the matter of the Base Sorting Plant for salvage of cloth, he had urged that a contract be made with a private company at an exorbitant figure. It was also charged that he had changed the army specifications for uniforms and permitted shoddy wool to be used instead of pure wool. Eisenman defended himself successfully against these charges. In the matter of the Base Sorting Plant he maintained that the original figure of six cents a pound for clippings of wool cloth was set as an experiment, for there had been no precedent for this kind of work, and that when it was discovered that the figure was too high, the private operators of the plant had offered to reduce it. The Quartermaster Department finally decided to operate its own salvage plant for wool. Eisenman also maintained that there had been great danger of a shortage of wool and that the uniforms of part wool and part shoddy were adequate.

Rosenwald's Committee on Supplies and Eisenman's part in its activities were defended at the Senate investigation by the Quartermaster General, Henry G. Sharpe, by Daniel Willard and by Secretary of War Baker. Secretary Baker told the committee in January, 1918:

In the first place, Mr. Rosenwald is one of the biggest merchants in the United States. For the past eight months he has given his time, morning, noon and night, to the investigation of problems exactly like that problem [price fixing]. In the second place, Mr. Eisenman is a man of large experience in merchandising. Neither Mr. Eisenman nor Mr. Rosenwald has the slightest possible interest in the sale of anything to the Government. . . . Both of them are men of unimpeachable integrity and established reputation. They have had grouped around them a lot of experts and men interested in the trade. I do not think that is the best way to deal with the questions, but the only way at the outset, until you could collect the information of the industrial world. You were changing from a basis where competition fixed the prices down to where prices were fixed by arbitrary act. They gathered around them a lot of men who were expert in this business and asked them not to fix prices, but what the elements of cost were, what percentage labor bore to the aggregate product, and the cost of material, etc. and what the overhead expenses were, and out of that this committee undertook to arrive at prices, and Mr. Eisenman and Mr. Rosenwald, who, by reason of their lack of interest and business experience, were able to check up the committee's recommendations and determine whether they were fair recommendations, and the result is not at all what would be inferred from your question. But many, many questions have arisen in which Mr. Eisenman disagreed with the Committee and disagreed with the experts and disagreed with interested persons and required them to make lower prices, resulting in the saving of many tens of millions of dollars to the Government.[20]

Secretary Baker was fond of telling after the war of an incident in which Rosenwald was concerned. The Secretary was having a conference with a large manufacturer who was demanding a price for his goods which the Secretary felt was not warranted. As the manufacturer was leaving his office, Julius Rosenwald was on his way in to see the Secretary. The manufacturer, whom Rosenwald had never met, stopped and said: "Mr. Secretary, may I put my views before Mr. Rosenwald, who is an excellent business man and let him judge the proposition?" Secretary Baker consented, although he was pressed for time. Rosenwald listened attentively to the manufacturer's arguments, and after he had finished, turned to Secretary Baker and said in the presence of the manufacturer: "Mr. Secretary, I think the proposition is completely crooked." The manufacturer left the office of the Secretary of War in a hurry, and Mr. Baker sat back in his chair and enjoyed a hearty laugh at the quick results of his friend "J. R.'s" forthright decision.

Rosenwald was disheartened and annoyed at the attacks of the Senators and at the aspersions cast on himself and his assistant, Charles Eisenman. Once again politics had been too much for him. He was a naive, direct person who could not conceive that simple direct means were not always the best. When he said what he thought without regard to political motives and thereby let himself in for criticism and defeat, he was always surprised and bewildered. Because he could not understand political ways, he was hurt by them, particularly by slurs on his integrity.

The purchasing functions performed by Rosenwald and his

[20] Investigation of the War Department, pp. 1642-3.

committees were now divided between the War Department and the War Industries Board. The labor functions performed by Samuel Gompers were turned over to the Department of Labor as a part of its regular work. In other words, the Advisory Commission lapsed into the vague and general status which it had held during the first months of its existence before war was actually declared. Despite Secretary Baker's assurance that their work was of great value, some members of the Commission were anxious to resign, but the Secretary of War and the other members of the Cabinet still felt that it would be inadvisable for them to do so.

In January, 1918, Secretary Baker appointed General George W. Goethals, Acting Quartermaster General, and gave him wide powers. General Robert E. Wood, who had been chief quartermaster of the Panama Canal under General Goethals, was brought from France to become director of purchase and storage. Rosenwald was left with nothing but a secretary. At this time he was of the opinion that the government was contemplating buying much more material and commodities than the needs of an army of about two million men would require for a year. His protests to General Goethals and to Benedict Crowell, Assistant Secretary of War, resulted in an investigation with the result that many of the contemplated orders for millions of dollars' worth of supplies were not placed.

He felt keenly the futility of his position in Washington, and he wrote to President Wilson, pointing out that since the reorganization of the Quartermaster's Department he had been "practically marking time." He said that his services were available should the President desire to use them. Wilson replied warmly expressing his appreciation of Rosenwald's past services and said that he realized that Rosenwald and his associates were a bit thrown out of function, but he hoped that he realized that this was largely because of the excellence of the work he had performed in the past and which had been fully accomplished. He

added that he would keep Rosenwald's offer of his services in
mind and hoped that if he had any thoughts of his own on how
he might be useful that he would not hesitate to let him know
them.

VI

While he was marking time in Washington, Rosenwald was
able to take an active part in the new drive for Jewish War
Relief funds. The condition of the Jews in Poland and the
Ukraine had grown steadily worse. After the Bolshevik party
came to power in Russia, the Jews were denounced as bourgeois
by Marxists and as Bolsheviks in neighboring nations. Political
chaos in northeastern Europe brought outbursts of anti-Semitic
violence, and the Jews were used as scapegoats by various factions
seeking political power. More than twenty thousand Jews lost
their lives in pogroms in the Ukraine during 1918, and there were
also sporadic outbursts against them in the Baltic provinces and
in Lithuania.[21]

In Poland of the 340,000 Jews in Warsaw, 220,000 were dependent on charity. There were twenty-five Jewish soup kitchens
at which one meal a day was served, consisting of three-quarters
of a liter of soup, made of boiled water with some vegetables
and a few potatoes, and each sufferer was allotted one hundred
grams of bread. Forty thousand people were in line daily, and
the scanty meals were often divided between two or more persons. Adults had to stay at home, and children were kept out
of school, for lack of any clothes. Typhus was spreading and
the lack of bathing facilities was breeding other contagious
diseases.[22]

It was decided to attempt a campaign for $15,000,000. In this
campaign the help of non-Jews as well as Jews was solicited,
and they contributed liberally, as the Jews had done to non-

[21] Annual Report of the American Jewish Committee for 1918.
[22] Bulletin of the Joint Distribution Committee, March, 1918.

Jewish war drives. Rosenwald, Schiff, Judge Mack and others took active part in meetings to raise funds. In Wilmington, Delaware, at a public dinner which Rosenwald attended, Pierre S. du Pont offered to underwrite the $75,000 quota for Jewish War Relief which had been set for the city. They raised $73,000 over their quota. In Duluth a Negro newsboy turned over the proceeds of one week's work to the fund because he had heard that Julius Rosenwald was interested in it. When he was asked how he knew of Mr. Rosenwald, he said: "Ever since I was a little baby we always had two pictures in our house; one was Abraham Lincoln and the other Julius Rosenwald. My father said they were the best friends we colored folks ever had."

Chicago's quota was one million dollars, and Rosenwald offered to contribute twenty-five per cent of all funds contributed up to one million dollars. His offer amounted in the end to a contribution of $212,530.

The Jewish and non-Jewish war drives for funds became huge crusades, and every emotion to which men were capable of responding was carefully touched by planned publicity and personal persuasion. In these drives Rosenwald's famous generosity was of great value as a stimulus, and in addition to the large sums he gave, the worth of his influence was incalculable. He himself wanted no publicity. In December, 1918, he wrote to Jacob Billikopf, apropos of a book by M. E. Ravage on the Jewish War Relief work:

It should be distinctly understood that he is not to play up any person conspicuously, because nothing would hurt the book more than to have it appear that it was gotten up to attract attention to the wealthier donors. Much more emphasis, to my mind, should be laid on the sacrifices made by the working people and the people in the smaller towns. . . . So far as my name goes, I want it to be as inconspicuous as possible without injuring the story.

In addition to this work, he made contributions for the war work of the Y. M. C. A., and contributions for the aid of Negro troops. He was very much interested in the status of the Negroes in the United States Army during the war, and in Washington he cooperated with Emmett J. Scott, Secretary of Tuskegee Institute, who was made an assistant to Secretary of War Baker, in charge of Negro problems in the army.

While he was waiting for the Wilson administration to find something useful for him to do, it was suggested that he become the head of a government mission to Persia. He considered this project for a few days but finally decided against it. Another suggestion was made to him, however, which proved attractive. On June 26, 1918, Thomas S. McClane, chairman of the Overseas Entertainment Section of the Y. M. C. A., wrote to him saying that it was the purpose of the Y. M. C. A. to send representatives of American industry to France "who shall carry to the soldier the story of American ingenuity, the romance of business in all its fascinating ramifications." He asked that a representative of Sears, Roebuck be sent on such a mission, and he added: "The message your representative will carry will meet with the most splendid reception, and the memory will last long in the minds of these boys who are making such great sacrifices for us, and who ask nothing in return. It is an opportunity— but is it not also our duty?" Two days later Herbert L. Pratt of the Standard Oil Company of New York, who was interested in the Y. M. C. A. in France, wrote to Rosenwald:

From personal experience within the past two months in several of the camps in France, it is my opinion that no better work can be done for our boys "Overseas" than to give them a talk on a particular kind of business by a man who knows that business.

America is the great business nation of the world and most of our boys were in one or another line before being drafted. As the most interesting thing to you yourself is a business chat, just so is it to the boys.

To take and hold their minds from the dull monotony of their daily army or navy drill is to add just so much to the morale of our forces.

Can't you go yourself, or, failing that, send a substitute to tell the boys the story of your business and let them ask the thousand and one questions they will want to, about its workings?[23]

Although he was fifty-six years old and had heart trouble, Rosenwald eagerly grasped the opportunity to go abroad on a mission which appealed to him. At first it was apparently the intention that he should go to France under the auspices of the Y. M. C. A. as an entertainer, but instead Secretary Baker requested him to go as his semi-official representative. He wrote:

I want you to go to France, move around among our American troops, and avail yourself of every opportunity which arises to address our boys on the conditions at home, and particularly on the opportunities of American life as you have observed them in your own successful business career.

It is not unlikely that your chief opportunity will be among the men in the so-called Services of Supply, of whom there are great numbers, who are deprived of opportunity for service at the front to render valuable service in the lines of communication, upon which the safety and efficiency of the army at the front depends. You will find them filled with the spirit of service and sacrifice; you will find all our boys enthusiastic, intelligent, and brave. Your special opportunity of usefulness to them will be to take a message from home, pointing out how the country appreciates the services they are rendering and how great the opportunity will be for them to build up business and professional careers at home when once the menace of militarism has been removed from the world. Carry them a message from me, or rather from the people of the United States, for whom I venture to speak to them, this thought: that in a time of universal sacrifice they are having the heroic opportunity, and that their privilege is to vindicate again in the eyes of the world the wholesomeness and beauty of the principles upon which American liberty is based; that this war will free France and Europe, but that in addition to that it will free America, and that when they have helped to make men free everywhere the blessings and rewards of a finer civilization will be especially theirs to enjoy since they have so greatly contributed to their preservation.

When he decided to go to France, Rosenwald requested the department managers and oldest executives of Sears, Roebuck to

[23] Over the face of this letter Julius Rosenwald wrote: "This letter was the cause of my going abroad."

get up for him varied data about the business to be incorporated into his talks to the troops.

Officially, he was still a member of the Council of National Defense, but when he went to France, his position was peculiar, for he had no military status and at the same time he was the semi-official missionary of the Secretary of War. Secretary Baker offered him a commission with high rank in the army, but he refused to accept it, maintaining that he was not an army man and did not deserve the distinction. Secretary Baker pointed out that he would need some sort of uniform, as he would not be allowed to wander around among the troops in civilian clothes. He, therefore, agreed to wear a uniform without insignia of rank.

Secretary Baker liked to tell the story of Rosenwald's departure to France with a large number of packing cases, all marked "J.R." The officers in charge of the S.S. *Aquitania*, then a troop ship, had at first declined to load these boxes, as all travelers were limited strictly to the least possible baggage. Baker asked Rosenwald what he had in his crates. "Sears, Roebuck catalogues," he said. "I want to give them out in hospitals." He then explained that he was not trying to promote business for Sears, Roebuck, because it would be impossible to handle such business with the soldiers, but he said that the men, far away from home, would welcome the sight of the familiar articles they had been accustomed to in their homes and which were illustrated in the pages of the catalogue. Baker agreed to permit the experiment, and later when he went to France himself he learned from those in charge of the hospitals that Rosenwald's catalogues were the books in greatest demand.

VII

From the S.S. *Aquitania*, Rosenwald wrote his family:

Having no insignia I felt like an imposter or rather I felt others might think so—not knowing the circumstances. So I pinned the entertainment badge on my coat. It doesn't explain much and is not especially dignified but answers the purpose. I was saved a good deal though by the wearing of a life preserver which is like a coat and covers the place where the insignia is worn. Every one must wear these all the time when out of one's room.

From London he went to Paris and left four days later by motor car for the General Headquarters of the Army at Chaumont. He saw the battlefield of Chateau Thierry and the devastated towns near by. At Langres he had a ride in a war tank and witnessed other military activities. Returning to Paris he worked out with the officials of the Y. M. C. A. an extensive itinerary for a speaking tour in the cantonments and camps of the Services of Supply.

Howard Vincent O'Brien, intelligence officer, noted in his war diary on August 23: "Met Julius Rosenwald. Vigorous, wholesome type, not at all *avise*. As proud of his catalogue as any author of his novel. Don't know what he's here for. Neither does he. Who *does* know why he's here?"[24] The following Sunday Mr. O'Brien had lunch with him and noted afterwards in his diary:

Lunch with Julius Rosenwald. Crude, unpolished, naïve, but genuine and likeable and worthy of respect. Very friendly and democratic, stopping soldiers on street to introduce himself and get their names, so that he could write home about them. Not subtle, but refreshingly direct and honest. Disdainful of money, per se, but proud that world knows his business. . . .

Rosenwald seems so very wrong on so many things. But not smug. His soul not dead. Only those who are neither big nor right, shelled in their own contentment, worthy of being hated.[25]

He made his first speech to the soldiers at Brest, and wrote to his family from there:

Well I have made my start and so far it is gratifying. . . . My letters from the Governors and Senators make a great hit. Boys from each state call for the letters from their state and it is pandemonium. So I read those letters from states having largest representation, 12 or 15 and every one gets

[24] *Wine, Women and War*, by Howard Vincent O'Brien, p. 177.
[25] *Ibid.*, p. 180.

applause. Of course, I always read the Secy's letter also. First talk to them
awhile, 15 or 20 minutes.

So far business has not been touched upon. After I got through they
crowded around me to shake hands and wanted to see the letters.

He had taken the precaution to obtain from the governors and
senators of every state in the union letters of appreciation of the
services of soldiers from their states.

During September he often spoke five times a day to large
crowds of men in the open air. He also spoke at Y. M. C. A.
huts for white troops and at huts for colored troops. Whenever
possible he shook hands with boys from Illinois, and especially
Chicago, and he often took their names and addresses at home
and had his secretary in Chicago inform their families that he
had seen and talked with their sons and that they were well. In
one of his letters home in September he described two meetings
near Nevers:

Both places together about 4,000. Both right in the streets of the towns
with the French looking from every window and doorway, just as tho
they could understand and the kids playing around my improvised stand,
which was cartridge cases one place and three empty boxes piled one
upon the other in the next. . . . The treatment I received everywhere is
royal. I couldn't have believed it. Of course, it adds much to the enjoyment of the trip. Wherever I speak, the officers are delighted and enthusiastic, and say it does the men great good. I always or generally,
spend the last fifteen minutes to tell them of what they must make of
America when they return—a real nation all belonging to one another, and
they are demonstrating in the army that men from all places have their
faults and their virtues but all made of good stuff and the same way with
nationalities no more prejudices against peoples who come from any
country if they are Americans—etc., etc., and then other civic matters per-
taining to politics and often tell them what a disgrace to our country
is our treatment of the Negro and that it is not a square deal—they like
it—also tell them we must honor the men we elect to office and not
suspect them of improper motives if they want to serve the state or
nation. Of course, I inject some humor—but mostly serious.

In hospitals, at aviation fields, in front of barracks, in a boxing ring, and inside Y. M. C. A. huts Rosenwald told the men the glory of their task and offered them hope of a better world when it was finished. His was a sentimental journey, and there was plenty of evidence that both he and the soldiers enjoyed it. From August 28 until September 13 he made forty-eight speeches. Then, his voice being tired, he decided to visit his Chicago friend, Colonel Abel Davis, at the front.

I wish you could see the place where I am dictating this letter [he wrote to his family] taking advantage of my first opportunity to use a good stenographer. I am about ten feet below ground in a very comfortable dug-out where I slept last night in a room adjoining Colonel Abel Davis. . . .

I have been over one of the most famous battlefields in France where the Colonel is now located. I saw through a glass the front lines of the enemy. I have walked miles and miles through trenches and tunnels, and one about five-eighths of a mile long and as dark as pitch since it is at least twenty-feet below the ground, and wet and muddy all the way through. Nevertheless, a wonderful construction. The guns are going all day long, and I have seen any number of airplanes shot at from both sides of the line with anti-aircraft guns. I had a lesson in the wearing of the gas mask. It is necessary to carry one here at all times, also wore a steel helmet on about a four-hours' tramp. In the towns around this place there is not a semblance of a building standing. Of course, many of the things I saw I would not be permitted to refer to in a letter. . . .

In a place like this there is no opportunity to get the men together to speak to them. They are all on active duty in real war work and could not be together for any cause whatsoever, so my opportunities with people in active war duty is nil, neither is it necessary because these men are all full of pep on account of their activities and opportunities in the front area. . . .

The cannons have been within earshot and this is the nearest to the real thing I've seen, although it is comparatively quiet here at that and I have not been in the front trenches at all. Tonight no sign of activity. It is great to see airplanes being shot at, sometimes thirty or forty shells at one plane, and never hit one. In fact, only one shell in hundreds which they shoot all day long ever hit anyone.

On September 16 he walked for four and a half hours on a
"red hot day" in deep mud in the trenches with Colonel Abel
Davis and dined that night at the Brigadier General's headquarters in the St. Mihiel sector. Many of the troops in this division
were from Illinois, and he met two former Sears, Roebuck employees and took down names of all Chicago boys and had letters
written to their families. After dinner he sat out in front of
Colonel Davis's quarters and watched the signal rockets in the
German lines and heard the bombing of the airplanes.

After three nights and two days at the front, he visited General Pershing and lunched with him at his headquarters. He
recorded that Pershing was emphatic about the need for more
men and more supplies. At the time preparations were being
made for the war to last into 1919, although the Germans were
then retreating. The day after his return to Paris, he started on
a new speaking tour. He wrote his family: "I felt a little guilty
at having been absent from my work for nearly a week, having
made my last talk on Friday afternoon."

At Tours, where he was making speeches, he met Secretary
Baker. He described the scene in a letter home, and told of
standing in the line of "silver and gold leafed dignitaries" who
greeted the Secretary of War by announcing their rank and
names. "And there was I with a perfectly good uniform but
no insignia. When I came up to him I was standing between
two Generals and I said, 'This is General Merchandise.' He
roared and stopped to talk with me for a minute or two, compli-
menting the tailor and the belt-maker, by saying how well I
looked in soldier's clothes. He said that he hoped I would be
able to go home with him, but I told him that it would very
likely be impossible, for if the weather remained good enough
for me to continue my work I would remain at least for a week
or ten days longer than he would."

He continued speaking day and night in the neighborhood of
Tours. He wrote home: "It pelted rain all day yesterday and the

day before that. Both days I tramped about in mud up to my knees." He became ill and was put to bed at the camp hospital in Tours, suffering from a mild attack of pneumonia. He was able to leave for Paris, however, after a week in the hospital. Then he noticed a pain in his left foot and could scarcely walk a few hours after his arrival in Paris. The doctors prescribed rest and heat, and it was arranged that he should return to the United States with Secretary Baker.

Some of the families of men who had heard him speak in France sent copies of letters from their sons to Mrs. Rosenwald. Lieutenant Russell C. Gates wrote to his family from Issoudon, describing the scene:

After luncheon I dropped into the Y. M., there was a lecture going on and the place was packed. The enthusiastic cheering, whistling and clapping aroused my curiosity and I knew it must be something worth while to stir the fellows up so. I wedged in at the back of the hall. The speaker was a short, heavy man of middle age and he was in officer's uniform, had iron gray hair, a ruddy face, a little flushed because of the effort to make himself heard over the whole assembly, and perhaps due also in part to the enthusiasm with which his remarks were received by the boys. As I listened I was soon deeply impressed by what he was saying. He was an artist in touching just the right chord in the fellows and he talked in such a personal way and so whole-heartedly mixing in a few good stories now and then that he took the boys by storm. I turned to a mechanic next to me and said, "Who is he?"—"Dam fine, the fellows call him Rosy, he is a big bug from Chicago on the National Defense. He certainly is dam good." I stayed through to the end and joined in the three big cheers that were given him. It is the first time a speaker has been cheered in this camp since I've been here. A long line formed to shake hands with him, I couldn't resist the temptation to fall in line with the rest and as I stepped up I said, "You just touched the spot"—and "Where do you come from?" he said—"Montclair, N. J." I answered, "and your name is"—"Gates," I answered. "What Gates *Gates* —Are You Russell Gates? Well—well, I have been sending all over camp for you!" He gave me a big hug and turning to the assembled group he said, "I know this boy's dad and mother, his sister and his kid brother. I tell you there is no finer stuff in this world than this right here under my arm." I was a trifle embarrassed not so much so because they all knew he was a trifle optimistic after the big demonstration he had just received. We had a pleasant chat and I soon found him to be Mr. Rosenwald that father knows and told us so much about in connection with his great gifts to the University of Chicago and Belgian Relief. I was keen to take him for an airplane ride, he was such a good old sport. I went to see the officer in charge of training to get permission, but when he learned he was a civilian, he said that Pershing had issued orders forbidding it." . . .

Rosenwald's plea for fair treatment of the Negroes aroused the antagonism of some of the soldiers from the South, but most of the soldiers accepted his sentiments. In talking to Negro troops he assured them that their sacrifices during the war would undoubtedly result in better treatment for them when they returned home. While he was in France, he left sums of money for use in making life more comfortable for both white and colored troops. He also sent a cable from France subscribing to $1,000,000 in Liberty bonds for the Fourth Liberty Loan. The Chicago *Tribune* stated that he was the only man in Chicago to take $1,000,000 worth of the bonds of that loan.

On the night of October 3, 1918, Rosenwald, unable to walk without crutches, left on Secretary Baker's train for Brest. He noted in his pocket diary, "suffered all night—foot extremely swollen." On Sunday, October 6, after their boat had sailed, Secretary Baker came to Rosenwald's stateroom with the news that he had had a message from Admiral Wilson at midnight "saying a newspaper had a report that Germany had asked for armistice —based on Wilson's 14 points, etc. He was undecided at night whether to get off the boat and decided not to. He was inclined to credit the report. I was not." On October 9, news came of President Wilson's reply to Germany's request for an armistice that the Allies would not consider peace until the Germans had withdrawn from their soil.

Rosenwald was compelled to remain in his stateroom during most of the voyage. In the middle of one night, the dressing on his foot took fire spontaneously from the oil and lint. He managed to pour water on the sparks in his bed and on his pillow, which was smoldering, and then summoned help. He noted in his diary: "They had smelled smoke but could not locate it. I was put into another room until morning. A large hole had burned into both sheets, pillow and blanket. I was not at all excited—my foot was not burned as there was no flame all smolder—slept very little all night account pain. Was choked a little by smoke. Nothing of consequence." The report of his spontaneous fire got round the boat, and he had many visitors next day, including Secretary Baker. The next night an inch of water from an open porthole covered his stateroom floor, and he noted in his diary: "Fire followed by flood." The rest of the journey was uneventful, except for the severe and continuous pain in his foot. Upon arrival at Hoboken he made the last note in his diary: "I was offered a car both by Red Cross & by the Army— attention galore." This diary was packed with names and addresses of the officers and men whom he had met, so that he could write to their families that he had seen them in France.

VIII

The strain of his strenuous journey in France compelled Rosenwald to remain inactive for some months after his return to Chicago. His doctors ordered complete rest, and he was sent to Johns Hopkins medical center for a thorough examination. While he was still confined to his home, he learned that Colonel Harry J. Hirsch, the representative of the Quartermaster Department on the Committee on Supplies, had been indicted for conspiracy to defraud the government. Rosenwald expressed his willingness to violate his doctors' orders and go to New York at any time to testify in behalf of Colonel Hirsch, if his testimony would be considered desirable. Colonel Hirsch was acquitted in March, 1919, and the jury drew up a statement denouncing the indictment and expressing the opinion that there never had been any reason to indict. Rosenwald contributed to an expense fund raised by some of Colonel Hirsch's former army associates to pay his legal bills. He also sent a check for his personal needs to Colonel Hirsch, who was ill.

Secretary Baker wrote to Rosenwald, in March, 1919:

Since the cessation of hostilities it has been possible to see a little more clearly in perspective the work which was accomplished during the early days of the war. While it would be invidious to make any comparisons in the value of the work of the various agencies which came to the assistance of the Government in the emergency, I am sure that in any adequate appraisal the work of the Committee on Supplies, which you established, would be recognized as extraordinarily helpful. You and your associates on the Committee brought to the War Department the benefit not only of your wide experience and mature judgment in affairs, but of your detailed knowledge in fields of commercial activity in which the Government was necessarily to become for some time the dominating factor.

Most of the men who answered the call of the Government at that time have now returned to their peace-time pursuits. I cannot, however, let the occasion pass without a word to you expressing my grateful appreciation of the singleness of spirit with which you and your associates devoted yourselves to the great task which was placed in the hands of the Committee on Supplies.

I am writing a brief note to some of your associates who rendered unusual service, but I cannot refrain from adding this personal word to you who brought the Committee together and guided it through the difficult days of 1917.

In November, 1918, Jacob H. Schiff took up with Rosenwald again a great project which they had discussed together as early as 1916 for the restoration of the European nations after the war. When they had first discussed the matter, Rosenwald was enthusiastic about it and offered to contribute one million dollars. Recalling Rosenwald's earlier offer, Schiff suggested that the time was ripe to take the matter up with President Wilson, and he thought that each of them ought to offer to contribute a million dollars to a fund of $500,000,000 to be raised by the American people under the name of the "American Commission for Restoration in Europe." It was Schiff's idea that before the project was made public he and Rosenwald should attempt to interest other wealthy men who might be willing to donate one million dollars each before President Wilson's departure for the Paris Peace Conference.

When Rosenwald received Schiff's letter, he became greatly excited at the opportunity to use his money and influence in a constructive way, and he telegraphed to Schiff:

After serious deliberation I would be very glad to join you in the plan outlined in your letter of the twenty-first provided we as leaders in the movement would both be willing to multiply by five if not by ten the amount which I said at the time I would be willing to give. This program is fifty times as large as the original and consequently would have to be started on a much grander scale. To my mind this is an opportunity of a life time and I sincerely hope we can take advantage of it. I would be willing to meet you in Washington at the earliest possible moment that we could get an appointment.

Schiff replied:

My breath is evidently not as long as yours and I cannot see my way to do for the present more than I have suggested. This, however, ought not to restrain you from doing to the full what you so nobly propose. Do take the lead by all means and I shall be glad to follow after you in my slower pace. My suggestion is that in any event you consult the President before he leaves.

Rosenwald's physician and Mrs. Rosenwald were urging him to take the rest his condition required, but he told Schiff that such was his enthusiasm for this plan that he was willing to disregard their orders and go to Washington at any time. Schiff declined to permit him to jeopardize his health in that way and suggested that they defer action on their extraordinary plan until they had the opportunity to discuss it together more thoroughly. The two men met in New York later in 1918, but it is impossible to determine whether they ever took up their idea with President Wilson. Such a restoration fund was never attempted. Rosenwald and Schiff may have considered that it would be too difficult to raise $500,000,000 after the number of large war drives and Liberty loans for which the public had been solicited, or President Wilson may have considered this magnificent gesture inadvisable at the time.

After his return from France, unsuccessful efforts were made to interest Rosenwald in making large contributions to Palestine. Jacob H. Schiff was becoming more interested in Palestine as a ·refuge for persecuted Jews in Europe, and he and Rosenwald exchanged letters on the subject in December, 1919. Rosenwald wrote apropos of a report on the condition of Russian Jews which Schiff had sent to him:

The removal of these afflicted peoples in any numbers seems to me as unthinkable as it would be to remove the water from the Atlantic. We must enable them, if possible, to become respected members of the communities where they now are. Demand that their rights be respected in the various countries and that they—the Jews—adjust themselves to their surroundings. No matter what our desires may be—comparatively few can go to Palestine or elsewhere during the next fifty years at any rate.

To which Schiff replied:

I agree with you that, as far as possible, we should endeavor to hold our co-religionists where they are now to become respected members of their communities, which I am sure a great majority of the Jewish people always will be, if they are only permitted.

But we have learned by very hard experience that the cruel persecution of our co-religionists in the Near East and in Russia has little chance to cease or even to become greatly diminished. We have been actively at this for the past forty years and what have we accomplished?

It is true it will take considerable time until Palestine can absorb a larger number of those who *wish* to go there and who, moreover, can no longer go anywhere else, and the sooner we begin to make the land habitable, the sooner there will come light into the Jewish problem. Or, do you mean that we should do practically nothing, except expending these large sums for palliative purposes only, with the certainty that our children and their children's children will be no further than we are? I have absolutely no patience with the proposition of re-establishing a Jewish nation, but bitter experience tells me that we must make it possible for the unfortunate and unhappy Jew to go somewhere where he will be welcome, and where else can this be than Palestine in due time?

Some time, if not now, we shall learn through more bitter experience that it is an absolute necessity to stand together in order to work out the rehabilitation of Palestine, so as to prepare it for the reception of a larger number of our people. There need be nothing of a political nature in this.

At the Paris Peace Conference Louis Marshall, as head of a delegation of American Jews, worked hard to obtain guarantees of minority rights for Jews residing in the old countries of Europe and the new entities created at the Peace Conference. Rosenwald was very much interested in these efforts.

During the war Julius Rosenwald's abounding energy was at the service of the country in its great efforts towards victory. At the same time his purse was at the service of suffering humanity in every part of the world, and he used his wide influence to persuade others to give for the alleviation of the great misery caused by the war. After the war he harbored no resentments against any nation or group of peoples, and he exhibited magnificently his willingness to devote himself and his resources to any practical efforts for human and national restoration.

# PART II
# AFTER THE WAR

## CHAPTER VIII

## BUSINESS CRISIS AND CHANGE

### I

AFTER Rosenwald had recovered his health and become active again as president of Sears, Roebuck he was faced with the most serious problems of his business career. From October, 1916, when he went to Washington, until early in 1920 he had not been in direct touch with his business. During these years of the war boom the company's business along with that of the nation in general had expanded rapidly. Huge profits on large sales made men careless of the future, and in the minds of most of the people it was certain that this unprecedented prosperity would never end.

At the end of 1916, the net sales of Sears, Roebuck were $137,-200,802, and its net profit was $16,488,622. The net sales climbed quickly during the remaining years of the war, and the statement of the company for the year ending December 31, 1919, showed sales of $233,982,584 and net profits of $18,890,125. There was a surplus at that time of $33,574,919. In addition the company had set up reserves for income and excess profits taxes of about five million dollars. During these war years the common stock was paying dividends of eight dollars per share per annum, and in 1920 the company declared a stock dividend of forty per cent, making its total common stock one million fifty thousand shares of a par value of $105,000,000. Rosenwald and members of his family were credited with owning approximately forty per cent of the stock. As a matter of fact he never knew exactly how much he owned or how much money he was worth. He did know that he had a vast fortune, invested primarily in the stock of his own company, in Liberty Bonds, and in a few other securities sold to him by bankers who were his trusted friends. He used to say of his wealth, "Whatever it is, it's too much."

The end of the war brought not only a spiritual exuberance but a desire for material things. People throughout the world who had been schooled to do without sugar, bread, meat, clothing and luxuries demanded everything their money could buy, and in the United States many merchants, laborers, farmers and service workers had more money than they had ever had before.

In order to meet the huge demand for merchandise, Sears, Roebuck buyers ordered large quantities of goods and paid high prices for them in competition with the other merchants. The catalogue business required advance planning and purchasing, and large stocks had to be kept on hand to fill not only the flood of current orders but also to anticipate future demands. The inventory of merchandise in the company's warehouses went up from $42,685,776 at the end of 1919 to $105,071,243 at the end of 1920.

In the spring of 1920 prices of goods began to fall rapidly, and sales were diminishing. The mail-order house's best customers, the farmers, were the first to suffer. Unemployment increased, and men who had been accustomed to a continuous demand for their services at high wages found no jobs available at any price. Money was high, and factories began to close. Consumers went on a nation-wide buyer's strike in protest against the high prices. Sears, Roebuck, its warehouses loaded with goods, and the company committed to orders for great quantities of additional merchandise, found itself in the most dangerous position in its entire history. And as 1921 progressed the business situation throughout the world grew rapidly worse. The price of wheat declined from $3.45 a bushel to $1.42 during that year, and the price of corn fell from $2.17 to 59 cents. The gross value of all farm production fell from $24,025,000,000 in 1919-1920 to $12,894,000,000 in 1921-1922.[1]

By July of 1921 there were about six million men out of work, and those who were employed had been forced to accept drastic reductions in wages. During the first four months of 1921, 6,386 business organizations failed, and before the year was out more than 17,000 had gone into bankruptcy.

The market value of Sears, Roebuck stock had reached $243 a share at one time in 1920; during the following year it fell from a high of $98 a share to a low of $54.[2]

In October, 1920, the company sold serial notes, redeemable in three years, with interest at seven per cent, to the extent of $50,000,000. Rosenwald refused to take the suggestion of bankers that these obligations be paid back over a period of ten years, maintaining that the company would be able to repay the money within three years—or not at all.

During the fall in values of 1920-1921 there had been an unscrupulous rush on the part of merchants to cancel orders for goods as soon as the great break in prices had occurred. Rosenwald declined to join this stampede, and he was anxious that the credit of the company, which he had done so much to build up since the beginning of the century, should be maintained. There was, for instance, an order for 10,000 dozen overalls at the war-time price of $36 a dozen. The price dropped in 1921 to $17 a dozen. Sears, Roebuck did not want the overalls, and the only agreement for their purchase was a penciled note on the back of a piece of blotting paper. The man who had made this penciled note did not have authority to give the order. Rosenwald looked into the matter and decided that the manufacturer of the overalls was morally entitled to the difference between

---

[1] Department of Agriculture, *Crops and Markets*, July 1929, p. 253.

[2] Each share of stock was then equivalent to over four of the present shares of stock, for in 1926 four shares of no par value were issued for each share of outstanding common stock, and there were twelve one per cent stock dividends from 1928 to 1931.

$36 a dozen and $17 a dozen, although there was no binding legal contract to pay him anything, and he insisted that the order be carried out. He was furious at the sloppy way in which the order was issued in the first place and made efforts to see that only those in proper authority should thereafter issue orders for merchandise and that formal contracts should be drawn for these orders.

When he came back to the active management of the affairs of his company, he found that laxity had spread in the organization. Some of the executives had not only bought goods recklessly, but they had become careless about hours and vacations. Albert Loeb, who had been in charge during the war, was kindly and soft, and the company had become badly disorganized and needed tightening up. Once, at the suggestion of a friendly adviser, Rosenwald telephoned to about forty executives ten minutes after closing time and found none of them still in the plant. He took firm action with the personnel and insisted on drastic economy measures and thorough attention to the precarious condition of the business. He ordered executives to come in on time in the morning and to remain late, and he himself arrived at eight o'clock every morning and stayed at his desk until late in the evening. He reduced salaries and stopped all increases. His own salary, which had been $100,000 in 1916, he abolished altogether until 1924, when it became $60,000. He got rid of men whose work he felt had become unprofitable to the company. During this economy drive the staff of the company was cut by about ten per cent, and operating expenses were reduced during 1921 by more than twenty million dollars.

The overexpanded inventory was marked down drastically during 1921, and the goods disposed of as rapidly as possible at a loss. In September, 1920, all the large mail-order houses in Chicago announced reductions of between ten and twenty per cent in their catalogue prices on many lines of merchandise. Rosenwald announced in a newspaper interview at the time that prices generally throughout the country had to be reduced in order to stimulate buying and prevent the further closing of factories.

Meanwhile, the market value of Sears, Roebuck stock continued to decline, and rumors were flying about in financial and commercial circles that the company was in great difficulty and would fall into the hands of bankers. Other large mercantile establishments were rapidly going into bankruptcy or were being reorganized, with resultant loss of control on the part of their executives. Large personal fortunes were being wiped out, and few rich men felt secure.

Rosenwald, who had taken firm action to put the affairs of his company in order, also took generous action to preserve its small stockholders from distress and bold action to save the company from possible bankruptcy. In February, 1921, the regular quarterly dividend on the common stock was due. Scrip was issued instead of cash for these dividends, the scrip bearing interest of six per cent, and payable before August 15, 1922. Rosenwald was concerned for those small investors who would be compelled to sell their scrip to traders at discounts in order to obtain money for their current needs. He announced that he would purchase at par the scrip of all stockholders who held fifty shares or less of the company's stock. Some employees who were also stockholders had pledged their holdings of the company's stock with banks and with brokers for loans. Rosenwald guaranteed many of these accounts in order to save the individuals from heavy losses and in some cases from the destruction of their savings of a lifetime.

At the end of 1921 the company had an operating loss of $16,435,468. Dividends were due on the preferred stock to the amount of $559,188, and these could not be passed without serious damage to the company's credit. Albert H. Loeb devised a plan whereby Rosenwald might come to the rescue of his company's credit. Rosenwald agreed readily to Loeb's suggestion that

he make a donation to the treasury of the company of 50,000
shares of Sears, Roebuck stock, which would enable the company to reduce its outstanding capital stock by $5,000,000 with-
out causing loss to any of the stockholders except himself. When
he discussed this transaction with a friend, the man remarked
that it was a fine thing to do, but he suggested that Rosenwald
take an option to buy the stock back at par. Rosenwald thought
about this idea for a moment and then said that he was afraid
such an option requirement might interfere with the spirit of
the gift to the company. He finally was persuaded, however, that
his option to buy the stock back at par of $100 a share at any
time within three years would in no way alter the fact that he
was making his company a gift of $5,000,000, and he consented
to take such an option, which he later exercised.

In addition to this gift of 50,000 shares of stock, Rosenwald
took over the real estate assets of the company valued at $16,-
000,000 and paid into its treasury $4,000,000 in Liberty bonds.
For the remaining $12,000,000 he gave the company his notes,
secured only by a trust deed on the real estate, without personal
liability. The banks did not regard real estate holdings of a company as assets fulfilling bank requirements for loans, and at the
time the company owed banks more than one hundred million
dollars. In 1931 the company agreed to re-purchase its real estate
from Rosenwald by repaying him $4,000,000 in cash and can-
celing his notes for $12,000,000, thirty days after his death or by
December 31, 1936, whichever date might be later.

The result of this complicated transaction was that, in effect,
Rosenwald made to his company an outright gift of $5,000,000,
a loan of $4,000,000 and improved its credit greatly. After it was
completed, the company, instead of showing a deficit of more
than $16,000,000, could pay its dividends on its preferred stock
and showed a surplus of $1,745,607.

When this transaction was made public at the end of December, 1921, it received nation-wide acclaim from financiers and

newspapers. It was generally agreed that Rosenwald had rescued his company from possible disaster, in a way that was both upright and courageous. Editorials suggested that other wealthy heads of large companies would do well to fellow his example. C. W. Barron, the Boston financial expert, wrote to Rosenwald at the time: "I do not know of anybody in the United States in the mercantile line who today is held in higher esteem or sounder regard than you and your great enterprise." Stockholders wrote to him expressing their gratitude, and friends wrote of their pride in knowing him. He himself, although he was naturally pleased with the praise, felt that he had merely fulfilled his responsibility to the stockholders of his company, and that what he had done was not only in their interest but in his own as well. His own integrity and financial security were bound up intimately with the credit of the great company in whose development he had taken such an important part. To work for its cure when it required a credit transfusion, even at the expense of his own resources, seemed to him as natural as it would have seemed to sacrifice something for the health of his family.

Added to business worries at this time was a deep personal sorrow, for he suffered a great loss in the death of his mother. She died on February 24, 1921, at the age of eighty-eight. He had adored her all of his life and called on her every day when he was in Chicago. She had taken pride in the rise of her son to a position of nation-wide influence in varied philanthropies and in his reputation for integrity in the business world.

II

During 1922 the business of Sears, Roebuck gradually improved. Dividends on the common stock were passed, however, in that year and during 1923, but were resumed again in 1924. By December 20, 1922, Rosenwald could write to his old friend and former associate in the clothing business, Moses Newborg:

I am happy to be able to tell you that our company received more orders during the last two weeks than in any two weeks in its history and I know of no season when we did less to force business than we did this fall as we have been more watchful than ever of our expenditures in every direction, particularly in advertising. We are therefore very happy over this fresh assurance that our good will has not been impaired and that the prospects for the future are as bright as they were in "pre-slump days." The only money indebtedness we have now is our Serial Note Issue and we have enough cash on hand today to care for the larger part of that.

At this time when he was devoting the major share of his attention and his resources to preserving the huge business to which he had been devoted, he also cut down his philanthropic activities and contributions. There were numerous fixed commitments which he had made every year for so long that they became a habit with him and an expectation with the recipient organizations. His gifts, which had averaged about $500,000 a year since 1912, dropped in 1921 to $218,555 and in 1922 to $145,893. With the increased business of Sears, Roebuck and the improved position of its stock Rosenwald's contributions rose again in 1923 to $482,081.

During these three years of business anxiety, he continued to watch his organization carefully. During 1922, Albert H. Loeb had become seriously ill of heart disease, and Rosenwald's own health was never so good as it had been before his strenuous years in Washington and the exertions he had made in France during the war. The burdens of his great business were growing too heavy for him, and he felt that the entire organization, after the crisis of 1921 had passed, needed new and vigorous executive direction by younger men with creative policies designed to meet the changing economic trends of the country.

At the time of the crisis, it was predicted that the day of the huge catalogue houses was over. The great attraction of the mail-order business during the first fifteen years of the twentieth century had been that it gave the large and isolated farm community an opportunity to purchase a wide variety of goods at attractive prices without making long trips to near-by cities. Good roads, the amazing increase in the use of the automobile in rural areas as well as urban centers, and the great increase in national advertising of standardized products made the rural communities less and less dependent on the mail-order catalogues. At the same time, the farmers' share of the national income was gradually falling. Sears, Roebuck could always depend upon getting a large share of the farmers' purchases by means of aggressive advertising and merchandising policies, but it was now necessary to cater to the change in farmers' shopping habits and to compete for a larger share of the spending money of factory earners, railroad employees and recipients of corporation dividends, who lived in towns and cities.[3]

Rosenwald, whose faith in the permanence of his business was never shaken, was anxious to prove by aggressive and constructive action that the day of the mail-order business was not over. He did not consider that either he himself or any of the older people who were associated with him had the vigor or creative ability to bring about the necessary changes, and he kept looking carefully outside of his own organization for new executive strength. He had to find someone to take his own place and that of Albert H. Loeb.

Some of the executives within the company felt that their many years of service entitled them to preference in consideration for these positions. But in this matter Rosenwald again showed his disregard for sentiment in business. He respected ability first and put this respect before friendship or personal considerations. He once told one of his lawyers: "I have no time for 'seconds.' I want expert lawyers, expert charity people, expert merchants, expert plumbers, but no 'seconds.'" In his search for a successor to himself and to Albert H. Loeb, he watched various men care-

[3] "Some Short Time Interrelationships between Agriculture and Business," by L. H. Bean, Agricultural Economist of the U. S. Dept. of Agriculture. Mimeographed address, Dec. 1, 1927, pp. 3-4.

fully and created opportunities to acquaint himself with their abilities. The business continued to improve rapidly, and the company recovered from its post-war difficulties. In 1922 there was a net profit of $5,435,168, as compared with the loss of $16,435,468 of the year before. By the end of 1924 the profits had increased to more than $14,000,000. Dividends on the common stock were resumed, and all of the preferred stock was redeemed at a premium of $2,000,000.

At the end of April, 1924, Rosenwald and his wife returned to Chicago from a trip to Europe and were startled by the news of the Leopold-Loeb murder case. Richard Loeb was Albert Loeb's son. Nathan Leopold was the son of another of Rosenwald's friends. Albert Loeb, who had been at home, ill for some time, never recovered his health, and died on October 27, 1924.

Albert Loeb was a man of refinement whose quiet influence in shaping the policies of Sears, Roebuck had been great during the more than twenty years of his intimate association with the organization. Less in the public eye than Rosenwald, he led a more meditative life. His interest in the business, however, was intense, and his advice was always highly valued by Rosenwald. He was loved by the executives and employees of the company for his kindness. Less forceful than Rosenwald, he was the perfect associate for a man whose impulses towards participation in social welfare were so strong and whose own verve required the measured appraisal of one whose mind he respected and whose character he admired.

During the autumn of 1924 Rosenwald had been discussing with Charles M. Kittle, senior vice-president of the Illinois Central Railroad, the possibility of his becoming president of Sears, Roebuck. Mr. Kittle had made a conspicuous success in railroad work, and Rosenwald, ever since his close association on the Council of National Defense with Daniel Willard, president of the Baltimore & Ohio Railroad, had come to have a high regard for the efficiency in railroad administration. He was also firmly convinced that the important posts of president and vice-president should be filled by men who were young enough to have the necessary physical energy and progressive spirit, and mature enough to have had adequate experience.

In Washington Rosenwald had met General Robert E. Wood, who had been recalled from France to aid General Goethals in the reorganization of the Quartermaster Department at about the time when Rosenwald's Committee on Supplies had been shorn of its major functions. General Wood had served as chief quartermaster during the construction of the Panama Canal and later had been assistant to the president of the General Asphalt Company. After the war he was vice-president of Montgomery Ward for about five years. He had had disagreements with Theodore Merseles, the president of Montgomery Ward, and had resigned just about the time when Rosenwald was looking for a successor to Albert Loeb.

In October, 1924, Charles M. Kittle was elected president of Sears, Roebuck and General Robert E. Wood, vice-president in charge of factories and retail stores. Rosenwald was now able to relax somewhat, and to return to his varied interests in philanthropy. He continued, however, his watchful care for Sears, Roebuck and Co. until the day of his death.

### III

When Rosenwald had reorganized the personnel of Sears, Roebuck and Co., vigorous policies were inaugurated. After careful study, the company began to open retail stores and to establish branch mail-order plants throughout the country.

As early as 1906 a mail-order branch was opened in Dallas, Texas, in order to handle the southwestern trade more efficiently. This was followed in 1908 by a branch plant in Seattle, Washington, to take care of the trade in the Pacific northwest. In 1920 a branch house was established in Philadelphia. Rosenwald's son, Lessing, became associated with the Philadelphia mail-order plant and eventually was in charge of it. During the next few years branches of the mail-order house were established in Kansas City, Atlanta, Los Angeles, Memphis, Minneapolis, and Boston. By 1929 the company had nine large mail-order plants, in addition to the original plant in Chicago.

In February, 1925, the first retail store began to do business in Chicago, under the direction of General Wood. Two more stores were opened in Chicago that summer, and in the same year stores were started in Seattle, Dallas, and Kansas City, in connection with the mail-order plants in those large centers of population. In 1926 and 1927 stores were opened every other business day. Today the company has more than 490 retail stores scattered about in cities and towns of various populations.

The presidency of Charles M. Kittle was a disappointment. Mr. Kittle was a man of outstanding ability, but he was brusque and ruthless. He treated Rosenwald and the other executives of the company with little respect, but Rosenwald never interfered with his administration. In January, 1928, Mr. Kittle died, and it became necessary to replace him. Some of the older executives still felt that they should have the position, but Rosenwald persistently clung to his opinion that the business needed new and vigorous executive direction. He chose General Robert E. Wood as Kittle's successor. Rosenwald knew at the time that he was being criticized, but he had come to admire General Wood's abilities, and he insisted on the appointment.

General Wood had studied both population trends and the figures of mail-order sales. He realized clearly the progressive change in the proportions of rural and urban population in the United States. According to the United States census of 1880, the rural population was 71.4 per cent and the urban population 28.6 per cent. By 1920 the urban population was 51.4 per cent and the rural population 48.6 per cent, and the census of 1930 showed 56.2 per cent urban and 43.8 per cent rural.[4]

While the mail-order houses of the country were trying to adapt themselves to the changes in population and transportation, chain store mercantile establishments were also developing rapidly throughout the country. As there was duplication between Sears, Roebuck and Montgomery Ward in the effort to obtain a large share of both the catalogue and retail store business, it was natural that bankers and mail-order executives should consider a merger between the two companies at a time when mergers were prevalent in financial circles. Rosenwald, hating waste and duplication, was anxious for the merger. He took the matter up with bankers and other interested people and developed data to show the advantages of a merger to stockholders and customers. Negotiations finally broke down, however, because an agreement could not be made on the matter of management for the combined companies and on the problem of the fair ratio of exchange of Sears, Roebuck and Montgomery Ward stock.

The administration of General Wood and his associates was enormously successful. Not only was there great expansion in mail-order plants and retail stores, but capital was put into new factories, and old factories which the company owned or in which it had an interest were efficiently reorganized. Rosenwald and General Wood were able to cooperate fully, and everyone was pleased with the choice of a second successor. Rosenwald's decision to inject new life into the management of his changing business was perhaps the most profitable decision of his career. The company had come to a crucial point, and it could easily have lost control of its immensely profitable field by sticking conservatively to old methods and machinery. Rosenwald had the ability to recognize other men's talents and the modesty to realize his own limitations. He was able and willing to relinquish

---

[4] Those classified as urban lived in places having a population of 2,500 or over. If persons living in places under 10,000 are classified as rural, the percentage of rural population increases by between four and five per cent.

authority to other men and to permit them free scope for their ideas and projects. He was noted in both business and philanthropy for his flexibility of mind and his courage in action. Although he could be stubborn after he had reached a conclusion, his mind was not fixed in a conservative mold. There is also plenty of testimony to the value of his personal contributions to the business. Although he was not considered by his associates to be a man of wide and brilliant business conceptions, they all came to respect his intuitive judgments. One of his favorite remarks in discussions with other Sears, Roebuck executives was: "I can't tell you what's wrong with it, but I don't like it." In many cases his "hunch" was correct.

In 1929, long before the crash in stock market values, he shrewdly called a halt to the opening of any more retail stores. He realized that this department of the business was developing so quickly that the organization could not handle it. Competitors were opening stores in large numbers. Sears, Roebuck concentrated instead on the development of those stores already established. One result of this policy was that after the crash in the autumn of 1929, Sears, Roebuck was able to lease stores cheaply, while its competitors were committed to leases entered into at boom prices.

During 1928 and the first nine months of 1929 Sears, Roebuck stock, along with that of other companies, was mounting to extravagant levels on the stock market. Rosenwald realized clearly that the market value of his stock was not its real value, and when he pointed this out to bankers and brokers, he was assured genially that no one could foretell the limits of the current expansion. Inflated paper prices were considered at the moment to be real values, and those who had spent their lives in intimate contact with businesses were not considered accurate judges of their worth. Writing to his children in May, 1928, Rosenwald remarked: "Business is only moderately good. Whether it is due to the backward season, or unemployment, or some other cause, possibly several, it is difficult to say. . . . There seems to be absolutely no top to the stock market. The day of reckoning is bound to come, the only question is when." Rosenwald had been invariably optimistic about the continued rise in the value of Sears, Roebuck stock, and he had always advised friends and philanthropic institutions to invest in it, but he realized that its current rise was speculative and artificial. But he never speculated in the stock of his company, and he now made no attempt to turn any of it into cash.

When the crash in securities' values began with terrific force in October, 1929, he took courageous and generous action in the effort to prevent that disaster from sweeping away the life savings of his employees and his friends. His son, Lessing, who was in Los Angeles at the time, had telegraphed to all of the retail stores and guaranteed the stock accounts of Sears, Roebuck employees with brokers. His father, learning of his son's action, took over the responsibility himself.

It was announced by the Chicago *Herald-Examiner* on October 29, 1929, that Julius Rosenwald was "pledging without limit the millions of dollars of his personal fortune," to guarantee the stock market accounts of all Sears, Roebuck and Co. employees who required such aid. The guarantee held not only for their investments in Sears, Roebuck and Co. stock, but for their investments in other stocks as well, so that the employees who had bought stocks on margin would not be suddenly ruined. Describing the scene in Rosenwald's office at Sears, Roebuck and Co. that day in October, 1929, Edwin R. Embree, president of the Julius Rosenwald Fund, wrote after Rosenwald's death:

I remember well his zeal in the midst of the financial crash in 1929. He had been ill; nevertheless he was at the office promptly at 8:30 on that memorable blue Thursday of late October. As thunders and lightnings began to threaten the financial structure of America he placed two telephones before him, squared himself at his desk, opened the three doors to his office and began to "do business."

Streams of eager callers, previously sifted by a corps of secretaries and clerks, poured through those doors making three long lines right up to his desk. He took them in order from the heads of each line, snapping out decisions and clearing the business of the callers as fast as the lines could move forward. His actions were like the staccato of a machine gun mowing down the columns of eager questioners. He periodically called Washington and New York and answered a hundred telephone messages from Chicago. He made decisions for his company, gave advice to other corporations, came to the rescue of friends and associates and employees who were caught unprepared in the sudden market crash.

He sold many securities and also bought thousands of shares. In the course of one attempt to get an order through to a broker, the report came back that the telephone exchange for the whole LaSalle Street section had suddenly gone out of order; he burst into a gale of laughter at the absurdity of such an accident on such a day. He made not less than a hundred separate decisions in this one day, many of them of momentous implications. He saved hundreds of persons from immediate bankruptcy. He saw his own fortune in the collapse which culminated this day, reduced by a hundred million dollars. He saw his business and his personal affairs plunging inevitably into the most troubled waters. It was one of the happiest days of his life.[5]

Perhaps the main reason for Rosenwald's happiness on this dramatic occasion was that he was engaged in his favorite occupation—that of helping other people. He also liked activity, and illness had forced him to be quiet too long; the fact that he was once more needed made him happy. In addition to helping the employees of his company, he went out of his way to discover which friends, and associates in philanthropy, needed help. He loaned them shares of Sears, Roebuck stock to guarantee their stock market accounts and put up cash for them when it was necessary.

The wave of enthusiasm for his action in guaranteeing the accounts of his employees was nation-wide. Employees and former employees, strangers and public officials, bankers and educators wrote to thank him. His friend Henrietta Szold wrote

[5] Julius Rosenwald Fund, Review of the Two-Year Period, 1931-1933, by Edwin R. Embree, Chicago, 1933, pp. 3-4.

to him: "Such acts demonstrate that moral heights can be reached in our condemned commercial era as in the eras glorified by historians. When I read of it, I was proud to call myself your friend. I hope that my words will not seem presumptuous to you." The financial news services quickly picked up the story, and it was commented upon with hopeful enthusiasm in every banking and brokerage house in the country as an extraordinary thing for an individual to do. A member of Rosenwald's family telegraphed to him: "For a man who does not believe in speculating you did a marvelous noble deed." One employee wrote feelingly: "God if there were more like you." Eddie Cantor telegraphed to Rosenwald: "Understand you are protecting your employees on their margin accounts. Can you use a bright industrious boy in your office? I am ready to start at the bottom. Regards." To which Rosenwald replied: "Please come at once. Have a job awaiting you. Will meet you at station. Answer time of arrival. Warmest greetings." To Homer Guck, of the Chicago *Herald-Examiner*, who had first made Rosenwald's action public, he wrote on November 2, 1929:

Your great scoop in regard to my action for employees will, judging by my mail, probably make me President of the United States. Such an avalanche of messages from all over the country and letters and telegrams galore!

They are extremely embarrassing to me, because the importance of the action was exaggerated far beyond its deserts. On a number of previous occasions I have followed the same course, but this seems to have been an aggravated condition involving a great many more people. I never gave a thought to the possibility of its becoming public.

I do think this, however, that judging by what countless people have told me, the publication did help to establish confidence. Whether this is true or not can never be proven, but if what so many have told me can be relied upon, it surely seemed to have that effect and to that extent I congratulate you.

Altogether Rosenwald guaranteed approximately 300 stock market accounts held by his employees. Of these all but 117 were able to finance themselves. In order to centralize the trans-action and to take the employees' accounts over from the broker-age houses, Rosenwald borrowed seven million dollars from the Chase National Bank, giving his note, secured by Sears, Roebuck stock as collateral.[6]

After this work was finished, he was ill for several weeks with bronchitis. Upon his recovery he wrote the following letter to all department managers in Sears, Roebuck and Co., dated December 31, 1929:

I am writing this now, which should have been written some time ago, but was delayed on account of my illness.

At the time of the great decline in the stock market, I was given credit for protecting the accounts of the employees of Sears, Roebuck and Company.

Through some means unknown to me, the newspapers announced this fact, and it received nation-wide attention. I desire it known, especially to our employees, that my part in this was only a minor one. Mr. Lessing J. Rosenwald was in Los Angeles at the time and wired all the stores to see that deserving employees, who might possibly be in financial difficulty, due to market conditions, be taken care of.

When Mr. Higgins received Mr. Lessing Rosenwald's message, he brought me the names of those who had applied to him for help, and I telephoned the different brokers to protect the interest of these people.

The favorable comment which came to me as the result of the news-paper publicity was due almost entirely to Mr. Lessing Rosenwald, and I think it is only fair to him and to me that the credit go where it belongs. I would appreciate your informing the employees of your department of this communication.

Wishing you and them a Happy New Year, I am

Yours very truly,

Julius Rosenwald.

The years of depression which followed the crash were years of increased responsibility and worry for Rosenwald as for everyone else. His health was gradually failing, and his fortune

---

[6] Some of these guaranteed accounts were still outstanding at the time of Julius Rosenwald's death in January, 1932, and settlements were made with each employee separately on a mutually satisfactory basis.

was dwindling, but he felt that the organization was in capable hands, and that the opportunities for renewed prosperity were inherent in the nature of the combination mail-order and chain-store business. During the period of recovery after the business crisis of 1921 he concentrated more and more of his attention on the large-scale projects for human welfare with which he had been previously associated and on those new plans for social betterment which were presented to him.

## CHAPTER IX

## JEWISH PROBLEMS

### I

WHILE he was actively engaged in handling the business crisis which confronted him after the war, Rosenwald was also concerned with the critical problem of the Jews both here and abroad. And he embarked at this time upon one of the greatest philanthropic ventures of his career.

For many years the Tsarist regime had done nothing to prevent and much to encourage pogroms and persecutions, the horrors of which were only exceeded afterwards by the more efficient National Socialists in Germany. The overthrow of the Russian autocracy had caused a sigh of relief in many parts of the world. But war and revolution, followed by civil war and famine, had created tragic problems in Russia for Jews and non-Jews alike.

During the winter of 1921, efforts were made to interest Rosenwald in financing the less reactionary forces which were opposed to the radical Bolshevist government. Professor Paul N. Miliukov and Nicholas D. Avxentieff, leaders of the Provisional Government of Alexander Kerensky, were in the United States at that time to raise funds to use in propaganda for a democratic regime in Russia. Rosenwald met the two men when they came to Chicago and heard them speak at the City Club. He also examined the letters which they wrote him urging his support for their movement. He came to the conclusion, however, that he could not give them support and that it would be unwise for other Jews to do so. In meetings of the American Jewish Committee he urged that the Committee should not commit itself to support of a movement that was political in its nature and might have violent repercussions for the millions of Jews residing in Russia, if it were ever to become a counter-revolutionary reality. His firm action on this occasion prevented involvement of American Jews in a movement which would have destroyed the possibility of mutual confidence on the part of the Joint Distribution Committee and the Russian government when they began to cooperate a few years later on a great project for the solution of Russian Jewish problems.

During the devastating famine of 1921, the American Relief Administration, under Herbert Hoover, working with other American relief organizations, undertook to feed starving Russians, regardless of their creed or politics. The Joint Distribution Committee, operating in areas where Jews were numerous, made it a point to feed any Russian non-Jews who applied for aid, and by this non-sectarian attitude, the organization won good will among the Russian peasants for Jews during the ensuing years.

Among those who were taking part in this relief work was Dr. Joseph A. Rosen, a Russian-American agronomist, who was working on a vast resettlement scheme for Russian Jews. Before the Revolution the Jews had been restricted to fixed pales of settlement and to limited occupations. A few small agricultural colonies had been established in the Ukraine early in the nineteenth century and had been in operation ever since, but for the most part Jews had not been permitted to own or to till land, could not live in the villages and could not hold any government positions. The result was that most of the three million Jews after the Revolution were petty traders and small craftsmen.

The war had brought them exceptional hardships. Much of the fighting on the eastern front took place in those sections of Russia to which they had been confined. When the Tsar's generals were defeated, they made studied efforts in many instances to blame the catastrophes on the Jews. Many of them were executed as spies without evidence, and inhabitants of entire provinces were exiled to the far interior. White Army chiefs and guerilla bands which infested the Ukraine and White Russia practiced pillage and murder of Jews in the areas which they occupied. It has been estimated that between 150,000 and 200,000 Jews were killed in the course of these upheavals.[1]

After the failure of the various counter-revolutionary movements in Russia and the alleviation of starvation, it became possible to give some attention to the special problem of the Jews. It was necessary to give them both a status and a skill, and agriculture and artisanship were the only possible solutions in a country where trading had been outlawed. The Russian government was anxious to facilitate the movement of Jews to settle on the land, and the Joint Distribution Committee initiated practical projects in that direction.

Previously, the Joint Distribution Committee had been restoring some of the old Jewish colonies in the Ukraine and distributing seed, live-stock and tractor service in those areas. In addition, loan *kassas* were set up to aid Jewish artisans. In his report to Agro-Joint, the American organization in charge of the resettlement project, Dr. Rosen wrote:

There are thousands of people in small Jewish towns, especially, who would be glad to dig the soil with their fingers to eke out an existence for their families, but have absolutely nothing to do. The demoralizing and degrading effect of this enforced idleness, especially on the younger generation, is hard to picture. It is really heartbreaking to see the spiritual agony of these people. There are only three possible ways out of the situation:

1. Starvation.
2. Emigration.
3. Adaptation.

[1] Material on condition of Jews in Russia is based upon "Report of the American Icor Commission for the Study of Biro-Bidjan and its Colonization." Ms. report in Rosenwald papers.

Emigration was extremely limited, for in almost every country there were restrictions even on those who could support themselves and bans on those who could not give guarantees of support.

Dr. Rosen urged haste on the part of foreign Jews to supply capital for the settlement of these sufferers on land, while the Russian government was still inclined to cooperate by giving land free and aid for its development. He estimated that within three years it would be possible to settle between twenty and thirty thousand Jewish families on the land, comprising between one hundred and one hundred and fifty thousand individuals, and in the first year, Agro-Joint, under his direction, resettled more than 25,000 people.

The results of the first year's work were so encouraging that Felix Warburg, chairman of the Joint Distribution Committee, decided that funds should be raised in the United States to carry out Dr. Rosen's project on a large scale. He discussed the matter with Rosenwald on board ship coming home from Europe. While they walked the deck, Warburg told him the plan for farm settlements; that Russia would place desirable lands in the Crimea and the Ukraine at their disposal, and that they were aiming to collect $9,000,000 in America to be matched by the Russian government. To Warburg's surprise, Rosenwald offered, on the second day of the trip, to give $1,000,000 if the total amount should be raised.

On the train to Chicago, Rosenwald read a copy of Dr. Rosen's report and the day after he returned home, he wrote to Warburg:

En route, I read Rosen's report and, assuming that his statements will all be borne out upon investigation, also that the attitude of the Russian government toward Jews and agriculture will continue, I consider this a rare opportunity for constructive work—an opportunity that comes once in a lifetime. It seems to me that the other matters that are up for consideration at next Sunday's meeting are all palliative and might well be side-tracked rather than have them interfere in the slightest with the possibilities open to us in the Rosen plan.

The conference to which he referred was to be held in Philadelphia to consider European relief problems.

Rosenwald's enthusiasm was aroused to the limit by this large-
scale constructive plan. It was the kind of project in which he
had absolute faith, where, with contributions from private individuals as a stimulus, a government was induced to provide
for the welfare of large numbers of people in great need. In this
respect the Russian colonization plan resembled the rural schoolhouse program which Rosenwald instituted in the South. It also
offered a great opportunity to demonstrate a theory in which he
firmly believed that the Jews should be taken care of, wherever
possible, in their native lands rather than by transporting them
to Palestine or other foreign settlements maintained by outside
capital. When he suggested, however, that the Philadelphia conference should devote itself entirely to the Russian colonization
plan, he was reckoning without the Zionists, who sensed in this
scheme competition with their own settlement plans for Jews.

A bitter struggle took place between those who urged large-
scale Russian colonization supported by American funds and
those who opposed it. Rosenwald, Felix Warburg, Colonel Herbert H. Lehman, James N. Rosenberg, Louis Marshall, Dr. Joseph
A. Rosen were opposed by Dr. Stephen S. Wise, Jacob de Haas,
former secretary of the Zionist Organization of America, and
Joseph Barondess, of the American Jewish Congress. These men
felt that American Jewry should recognize the priority of the
colonization plans for Palestine and not embark on a large-scale
project in Russia. They were very much afraid that a new colonization plan would mean a movement of Jews to Russia instead
of Palestine, and they also resented the competition for funds
to which Palestine would be subjected. Their aim was a Jewish
homeland in Palestine, and they were suspicious of any movements for settlement of Jews elsewhere. There were delegates,
including Zionists, who opposed placing funds in Bolshevist
Russia. They said that the Soviet government would never keep

its word to the American supporters or to the Jewish settlers, that the government was unstable in any case, and that a succeeding monarchist government would dispossess the Jews from the land.

Dr. Rosen read his report on the resettlement work to date, and as soon as he was finished Rosenwald made an extemporaneous address in which he said:

Some of you may think that my arising on this occasion may have been staged or prearranged with the Committee. I want to assure you that, up to the time I entered this room I had not the slightest idea that I would speak. But I have been so impressed by what this wonderful man has told us that I am not willing to sit quietly by and permit this moment to pass. This is a subject that has interested me for many years. I have contended—whether rightly or wrongly—that the only way to help our co-religionists in these benighted lands, is to help them where they are.

My experience and what I have been able to find out from the experience of others shows that subsidized immigration, where you have to transport masses of people, is absolutely impracticable.

My friends in Chicago will vouch for what I say, that this is not an opinion that I have formed recently. My unwillingness to join in the Palestine movement was not at all based on my being opposed to Zionism. I am not opposed to Zionism. I have been willing to help any efforts made in Palestine for years and have done so, but I have never been a believer in subsidizing immigration to the extent of moving people in masses from one country to another and trying to establish them with funds which, to my mind, is impossible at the present time. I do not believe that it is possible to establish—and then not always successfully— a family in Palestine or in Argentine or anywhere else where land must be bought and the people taken care of until they are self-supporting, for less—and I think on the average it will be more as time goes on—for less than $5,000 a family.

I have thought and thought and thought about this subject, year in and year out, and particularly for the last six or seven months since I have given a greater amount of study to this Russian situation.

I am firmly convinced that the Jews have never had an opportunity to do a real constructive piece of work for their co-religionists, until this time. I have always felt that whatever they did heretofore has been palliative. During the war I was willing to go along and I was willing to give in a large measure for palliative relief.

I am willing no longer to give in any large measure for palliative relief. I believe that the people will always require assistance. This thing is going to continue. There will always be orphans and sick. There will always be poverty, but I believe those things have got to become local duties imposed upon the people who live in a community.

He then announced publicly that he was willing to make an initial contribution of $1,000,000 for the Russian colonization work, provided at least nine million dollars in addition was raised over a period of three years.

After he had finished speaking, other speakers denounced the Russian colonization plan on the ground that Russia had always had pogroms and could be expected to have them again. Dr. Stephen S. Wise questioned the wisdom of dealing with the Soviet government while it was still unrecognized by the United States, and if risks were to be taken, he felt that they should be taken for Palestine rather than in Russia. Other objections were that the Russian government was avowedly antagonistic to religion, and that it was unethical to settle the Jews on land which had been appropriated from its original owners. Louis Marshall, who was a firm opponent of the Bolshevist regime in Russia, pointed out that the revolutionary government in the United States had confiscated land of Tories during the American Revolution and disposed of it to other settlers.

Most of those who argued about the Russian colonization project neglected entirely Rosenwald's main point, which was that it was both more practical and more desirable to settle people on land in their native country than to uproot them and transport them hundreds or thousands of miles to new lands. He was not so much interested in the preservation of Judaism as he was in the preservation of Jews.

Although he was opposed to the principles on which the Soviet government was founded, he felt that it was essential to take a chance on the good faith of the government and on the ability of Russian Jews to work out their own salvation on the land.

He was not interested, however, in the autonomous Jewish colony set up by the Russian government at Biro-Bidjan in Siberia, because he felt that it was impractical to settle Jews so far from the central part of Russia. He told Dr. S. M. Melamed: "But, impractical as I consider this project, it is still, in my opinion, preferable to Palestine, for there at least they remain in their native country." To Dr. Melamed's question whether he considered the Soviet regime sufficiently stable to remove any apprehension as to the future of the Jewish settlers on the farms, he replied:

No, not necessarily. But I am willing to go into it in the spirit of speculation—and I consider it a fairly sound speculation—a good gamble. I believe that this colonization will prove to be a lasting contribution to the welfare of the Russian Jews. It will relieve them in their present state of privation, and that is something not to be regarded lightly. It may not solve the Jewish question in Russia, but this was never its objective.

Rosenwald was counting heavily, as well, on the extraordinary personality of Dr. Joseph Rosen, with whose ideas and methods he had been greatly impressed. As always in his large philanthropic and business endeavors he took into consideration the talents of individuals as well as the importance of their projects. Dr. Rosen, a trained agronomist and a patient administrator, had unusual gifts. He was able to conciliate both Soviet government officials and Jewish colonists. He succeeded admirably in getting the one to grant privileges and rights and the other to overcome obstacles and endure hardships. The Soviet officials respected and trusted him; the Jewish colonists came to worship him; the patrons of the enterprise in the United States quickly learned to place complete confidence in his judgment and his ability, for he was both a capable administrator of funds, and one who was able to create the projects for which the funds were used.

A compromise was finally reached between the Zionists and those who favored the Russian colonization plan. It was agreed that a joint effort be made to raise $15,000,000 to be expended by the Joint Distribution Committee for reconstruction work, agricultural settlement and relief in Europe. A resolution was passed approving the agricultural plan for settlements in Russia and also calling upon American Jews to support resettlement plans for Jews in Palestine. Rosenwald, however, made it a condition of his million dollar offer that all of the money he contributed should be devoted exclusively to the Russian plan.

By June of 1926, when the American campaign for $15,000,000 was completed, the Agro-Joint in Russia had settled 7,000 families on the land. In addition the organization Ort, with the cooperation of the Joint Distribution Committee, had settled 2,000 families in White Russia. A total of 50,000 Jews had been aided up to that time to establish themselves on the soil, and those who had already settled there had been given services and loans. Non-Jewish Russian peasants also received tractor service from the Agro-Joint, which plowed thousands of acres of land for them and gained their good will and gratitude. One hundred villages were established. Hospitals and schools were set up, and 4,000 Jewish boys and girls were learning factory trades in schools operated by Agro-Joint, the Jewish Colonization Association, and the Soviet government. Jews were cutting their own timber, working in stone quarries, and establishing cooperative stores and medical centers in connection with the colonies.

In the colonies in the Ukraine the Jewish settlers usually had allotments of land averaging forty-five acres, and in the Crimea seventy acres. The people settled in cooperative colonies, and they could thus share water supply, tractor service and other community enterprises, one well being sufficient for a settlement of fifty to sixty families. Fencing was not necessary, as the herds of cattle were cared for by herdsmen on communal pastures. Communal systems of crop rotation were introduced, and there was cooperative ownership of implements and machinery. The settlers shared in the proceeds of the crops according to the amount of labor each contributed, and besides had their own small private holdings for garden produce. The system of sharing the costs of settlement was similar to that in force in the Rosenwald school program in the rural areas of the South. Agro-Joint paid between 25 and 30 per cent of the cost, the Soviet government paid the same proportion, and the settlers themselves contributed the rest. It was estimated that the cost of settling each family was between $1,000 and $1,200.

In the summer of 1926 Rosenwald was anxious to visit the colonies in Russia, but his doctors and his family vetoed the plan. His son, William, went there that summer and Rosenwald was delighted with his reports of the success of the project. He wrote to him: "Keep an open mind and do not permit what I have done to influence you, because I may have been wrong, and if so I am as anxious to know it as any one."

Rosenwald was so impressed with the reports which came to him of the success of the colonies, not only from his son, but also from Dr. Rosen, James N. Rosenberg, Jacob Billikopf, and others that he offered to contribute another million dollars to the work, if four others would do the same. It was impossible to obtain the additional pledges but in March, 1928, he subscribed $5,000,000 provided a fund of $10,000,000 was raised for the continuance of the colonization work. To this campaign John D. Rockefeller, Jr. contributed $500,000 out of respect for Rosenwald's and Felix M. Warburg's interest in the work.

By May, 1928, Agro-Joint had settled more than 100,000 Jews on more than one million acres of land. Dr. Rosen also had plans for industrial aid to Jews in Russia, and after listening to him expound them, Rosenwald offered to subscribe $3,000,000 for this work in addition to his offer of $5,000,000 for the agricultural settlements. This second offer was conditioned on subscriptions from others totaling $5,000,000 to establish mills, workshops and other factory enterprises in which to offer employment for Jews living in cities. The Russian government had offered to contribute four roubles for every American dollar. The stock market crash of 1929 and the ensuing depression made it impossible to raise sufficient funds to meet Rosenwald's second offer.[2]

Upon the announcement of Rosenwald's unprecedented offer, Herbert Hoover, then Secretary of Commerce, wrote to him:

That is indeed a princely benefaction and I believe I know something of the great heart and the willing hand with which it is given. The dedication of that wealth to make it possible for a people who have been striving as petty tradesmen, to return to their ancient calling and become producers of the necessities of life from the soil, is a great experiment in human engineering, and you and I who have watched together the fruition of so many enterprises born of a realization that the welfare of other human beings is the concern of all of us, can entertain no misgivings for its ultimate success.

Rosenwald answered:

Your friendly letter commending my participation in the Jewish Russian colonization work is a treasured document which I shall preserve and some day pass on to my children.

It is especially prized coming from one who stands head and shoulders above any other human being in the preservation of human life. It is high honor indeed to have my name coupled with yours as you have been kind enough to do.

In 1929 more than 250,000 Russian Jews were tilling more than three million acres of land. The farms were brought into the government's collectivization program, along with those of other Russian peasants, and gradually the trade schools and medical work were also taken over by the government. The Jewish farmers suffered along with the rest of the population from the inability of the government to supply them with manufactured products in return for the products of their farms. Some of the colonists left and went to the large cities to engage in industry, but their places were taken eagerly by others. For the first time in recent Russian history the Jews were on a par with other

---

[2] Rosenwald's final contributions for the colonization of Russian Jews totaled approximately $3,600,000. The Russian government had offered the contributors bonds in return for part of their contributions.

Russians economically and politically. By 1931, Dr. Rosen estimated, only ten per cent of the Jewish population was without citizenship rights, whereas seventy per cent had been declassed before the colonization projects were started. He stated that if this plan had not been carried out, most of the Jews would undoubtedly have perished, for the government would not have undertaken the work without the outside initiative of the American supporters. And without the impetus Rosenwald had given the movement with financial backing, and without his faith in its value, it could never have attained the scale that it did.

II

In September, 1923, General Henry T. Allen, former commander of the American Army of Occupation in Germany, wrote to Julius Rosenwald asking him to lend his name to a national committee which aimed to raise money to feed starving women and children in Germany. Rosenwald not only lent his name but he gave the committee $100,000, and was instrumental in raising much additional money in Chicago.

At the time Hitler and Ludendorf were already beginning to spread anti-Semitic propaganda throughout Germany, and oppressions against individual Jews were taking place. After the public announcement of Rosenwald's gift, some Jews wrote to him suggesting that he insure that his money was not spent in Germany solely on "Aryan" women and children. Others felt that he should have accompanied his gift with a protest against anti-Semitism. To one of his correspondents who felt that steps should be taken to inform the world that the Jews were giving more than their share to feed starving Germans, he replied:

The fact that the Jews are "giving more than their share toward helping all the different creeds in Germany" is known and, to my mind, it is more helpful to give *without protest* which would make it appear that the money was given for the purpose of having the Jew-baiting stopped.

My opinion is that this disagreeable thing will subside of its own accord as rapidly as it would if any form of propaganda were resorted to.[3]

During the difficult years following the war Rosenwald did whatever was in his power to improve the relations of Germany and the United States as well as to relieve the suffering in Central Europe of Germans and Austrians. He was one of the largest contributors to the fund for the Carl Schurz Memorial Foundation, which aimed to promote intellectual intercourse between Germany and the United States. He contributed to the work of the Deutsche Hochschule fur Politik, an institution founded in Germany by Walter Rathenau, Dr. Hjalmar Schacht and others for the purpose of stimulating international cooperation with Germany and the growth of democracy in that country. In conjunction with Paul M. Warburg he made efforts to reestablish German industry and trade.

In 1927 Rosenwald became greatly interested in the dental clinics for children which George Eastman was establishing in European cities. He requested Dr. Harvey J. Burkhart, who was in charge of the Eastman dental projects, to investigate the possibility of establishing such a dental clinic in Berlin, and he offered to donate one million dollars if the city of Berlin could guarantee to maintain such an institution. No such guarantee was ever made, and no contract for the consummation of the offer was ever negotiated.

On February 18, 1930, President Paul von Hindenburg wrote to Rosenwald:

I have noted with deep appreciation the many magnanimous gifts which you made to German war widows and orphans, as well as to German

[3] Rosenwald did not live to see Jew-baiting in Germany become a government activity. In 1920 he also contributed $50,000 for the relief of starving children in Europe, and he took active part in a campaign by which more than $1,000,000 was raised in the state of Illinois for Herbert Hoover's European relief organization. He sent out letters and collected thousands of dollars from his friends and acquaintances for this cause. In addition to personal aid to his own relatives in Germany during this period, Rosenwald also volunteered to give funds for the continuance of the work of German and Austrian scientists and other scholars.

prisoners of war before America's entry into the World War. Since the
war you have made large donations for the benefit of the German children and have contributed liberally to endowments established for German
cultural purposes in Germany and the United States. May I assure you
not only in my own behalf but also in behalf of the German people of
my sincerest gratitude?

As an outward token of this appreciation, I have taken great pleasure
in having had forwarded to you a vase, the product of the Staatlichen Porce-
lain Works. This will be presented to you by the German Consul General
at Chicago.

I sincerely trust that there may be granted to you many years of un-
alloyed happiness in your work as a benefactor of mankind.

With assurance of my highest esteem, I beg to remain

Faithfully yours,

VON HINDENBURG.

Rosenwald was in Europe when this letter arrived in Chicago,
but on his return the German Consul General gave a luncheon
for him at the Union League Club at which President von Hindenburg's gift was presented to him in the name of the grateful
German people.

### III

The hatred which was sowed in Europe during the war resulted in a vicious crop of racial antagonisms after peace was
formally restored. The ugliest of these was anti-Semitism, which
spread with particular rapidity because it was directed against
people who were scattered and defenseless and at the same time
distinctive enough to make profitable targets for ambitious political dictators. Soon after the war the new crop of anti-Semitism
was transplanted to the United States by the Ku Klux Klan and
by Henry Ford, who kept up a virulent campaign against the
Jews in the *Dearborn Independent*.

As soon as the first anti-Semitic article appeared, Rosenwald
called it to the attention of Louis Marshall, who, as head of the
American Jewish Committee, was the leader of the efforts of

Jews to prevent misrepresentation of their activities. Marshall sent a vigorous telegram of protest to Henry Ford asking whether the scurrilous articles had his sanction and whether it was his intention to continue to publish them. In reply he received an in-sulting telegram signed by the Dearborn Publishing Co., in which he was compared to "a Bolshevik orator." The telegram contained the statement: "These articles shall continue and we hope you will continue to read them and when you have attained a more tolerable state of mind we shall be glad to discuss them with you."

Henry Ford's publication gave wide circulation to the pre-posterous forgeries against the Jews known as "The Protocols of the Elders of Zion," and among the flood of anti-Semitic articles published by the *Dearborn Independent*, was one attacking Rosen-wald, in which it was charged that he had encouraged the Negroes to settle in Chicago and was therefore responsible for the race riot there in 1919. In a German anti-Semitic newspaper these same charges were translated in 1928 into the accusation that Julius Rosenwald was helping the Negroes to arm against the white people of the United States.

The American Jewish Committee decided to face the issue of anti-Semitism in the United States vigorously, but it was cautious in its methods. Some Jews wanted to organize a large-scale boy-cott against Ford products, but the Committee advised against such tactics. Rosenwald was strongly opposed to boycott. He asked his secretary to write in answer to such a suggestion that he be-lieved two wrongs never could make a right: "He thinks revenge never is justifiable. There are much better ways to show dis-pleasure with Mr. Ford's attacks than by counter-attacks, such as you suggest."

It was not until 1927, seven years after the articles against the Jews had appeared in his magazine and had thereafter been dis-tributed in book form and in pamphlets, that Henry Ford was finally persuaded to retract his attacks. The American Jewish

Committee had continuously attempted to make him see the injustice of the articles. The Ford automobiles were being boycotted by other Jews, and Ford was sued for libel by a Jewish lawyer, Aaron Sapiro. Finally, on June 30, 1927, Henry Ford, after an exchange of correspondence with Louis Marshall, published a statement retracting the anti-Semitic charges which had been published by the Dearborn Publishing Co. and apologizing for the attacks. Rosenwald made the following statement to the Chicago *Daily News*:

> Mr. Ford's statement is very greatly belated. This letter would have been very much greater to his credit had it been written five years ago.
>
> It seems almost impossible to believe he has not been deluged with evidence on the very facts which he now seems to realize are true.
>
> But it is never too late to make amends, and I congratulate Mr. Ford that he has at last seen the light. He will find that the spirit of forgiveness is not entirely a Christian virtue, but is equally a Jewish virtue.

Ford had also agreed to withdraw from circulation all the anti-Semitic pamphlets which his publishing company had spread about the world. He encountered difficulty in stopping the publications in Europe and in South America. Damage suits were brought against him by anti-Semitic publishing houses in Germany when he tried to withdraw the foreign pamphlets that his paper had launched.

Rosenwald's attitude toward anti-Semitism was one of vigorous private opposition and cautious public activity. He refused to go to resorts or clubs where Jews were discriminated against and made it a point not to attend meetings held at the University Club of Chicago because Jews were not permitted membership there. Occasionally, he wrote letters to protest against advertisements which offered employment to Gentiles only, but on the whole the brands of anti-Semitism which he encountered during his lifetime saddened him more than they angered him. Had he lived to witness the widespread use of anti-Semitism for rabble rousing in Germany, a country which he loved and which he had helped, his sadness might have become more bitter. Many Jews felt that he, Louis Marshall and other leaders were much too cautious in their attitude toward anti-Semitism and that the problem called for aggressive retaliatory tactics. But Rosenwald could not agree.

For many years Rosenwald had been interested in the work of the Hebrew Union College, the school for rabbis of reformed Judaism in Cincinnati. Rabbi Hirsch had first aroused his interest in this institution, and he gave the college $50,000 toward a new library building in 1909. In 1923 the Hebrew Union College wished to confer on Julius Rosenwald its highest honor, the degree of Doctor of Hebrew Law, which had previously been conferred on Jacob H. Schiff, Louis Marshall and Simon Wolf. Writing to the president, Dr. Julian Morgenstern, Rosenwald expressed his appreciation of the honor and then stated:

> Knowing better than anyone how ineligible I am to aspire to such a title as "Doctor of Hebrew Law," I could not, in justice to myself and to the good name of the college, accept it. Mr. Schiff was, and the other distinguished gentlemen you name are, all truly Jewish scholars. Much to my regret, I cannot class myself as such.

Rosenwald always refused to accept honorary degrees from the universities which wished to confer them upon him in recognition of his great services. He always maintained that since he was not a man of university education, he was not entitled to accept university degrees. He consented, however, to accept the Gottheil Medal in 1929, awarded annually in recognition of the American who had done the most for Jewry during the preceding year.

At the request of his friend Adolph S. Ochs, Rosenwald agreed to give $500,000 in 1928 to a fund of $4,000,000 for the use of the Hebrew Union College. His contribution was a great impetus to the success of the campaign.

Although Rosenwald staunchly maintained his anti-Zionist position he continued to give his financial aid whenever human beings in Palestine were in danger.

In February, 1925, he had consented to contribute $50,000 for the construction of a building for the Hebrew Teachers' College in Jerusalem, of which Dr. David Yellin was the principal. This institution prepared Hebrew teachers for Palestine and the rest of the world. Although he was not himself a religious man, Rosenwald was interested in providing others with the opportunity for education in Hebrew or any other line of knowledge, and he felt it to be important that the religious education of the Jews should continue, whether it was in Jerusalem or in Cincinnati. When the cost of the building in Jerusalem proved higher than anticipated, Rosenwald increased his contribution to $75,000.

In 1929 Moslem riots broke out in Palestine over the right to worship at the ancient Wailing Wall in Jerusalem. Underneath this ritual difference, however, were basic economic and political controversies between the Arabs and the Jews. During the Arab attacks on the Jews at this time the incomplete building of the Hebrew Teachers' College was used effectively as a fort, and more than four hundred men, women and children were besieged there from Friday, August 23, until Sunday, September 1, when the attacks were finally suppressed. Mass meetings were held in this country and in England to protest against the Arab attacks and to raise funds for the Jewish sufferers. Rosenwald contributed $27,781 to this effort, and in addition he raised funds among his Chicago friends.

He was also present at a mass meeting held in Madison Square Garden, New York, at which protests were made against repudiation of British promises to the Jews in Palestine. He was incorrectly reported as having stated, "I am a confirmed Zionist." This statement was cabled to Europe and caused excitement in Zionist circles. Judge Mack, who was in Europe at the time, wrote to Rosenwald:

The news that you attended the great mass meeting, of course, reached London the next morning and created, in Zionist circles, tremendous interest. Unfortunately, I could not answer any of the questions that they put up to me in regard to it, but naturally I would greatly like to know, not only why you went, but how you now feel about the whole matter.

## Rosenwald replied:

My attending so important an event as the Zionist Protest meeting ought not to cause you the slightest surprise. You know I have always been interested in everything that pertains to the movement and to Palestine, even though I could not agree with the theories on which Zionism is based, nor the sentimental phases of the Palestine movement, which probably marks me as lacking in idealism or far too practical.

Furthermore, I have always felt that the experiment is fraught with the greatest danger, and I think I have frequently expressed to you my belief that the more successful the experiment is from the Jewish standpoint, the more dangerous it is.

## CHAPTER X

## CHICAGO AND THE NATION

I

UPON his return to Chicago after his trip to France during the war, Rosenwald threw himself once more into the diverse civic and political activities of both local and national interest for which his support was solicited.

President Wilson invited him to become a member of his Second Industrial Conference Board in November, 1919, the purpose of which was to study the problem of the growing unrest between employer and employee in the United States. Rosenwald attended the meetings conscientiously, and wrote to his wife at the time: "I get dizzy listening to and reading about 'collective bargaining' etc. Our session lasted 10 to 1 and 3 to 6 yesterday. All interesting but wearying, and very trying on the seat of one's trousers." In another letter, he wrote: "Our meeting was interesting enough, but we are all groping. A very nice group apparently and determined to do everything possible."

The conference reported in favor of collective bargaining but made no provisions for legal enforcement of such bargaining. It recommended a system of voluntary arbitration of labor disputes and a plan for employee representation by means of shop committees. The conference also reported in favor of a forty-eight-hour week for workers in mines, factories and workshops, equal pay for men and women in similar jobs, and special safeguards for the health of women in industry. State child labor laws were advocated by the conference report. It also recorded the opinion that profit-sharing plans in industry were not panaceas but merely supplements to adequate wages. It advocated a federal investigation of sickness and old age insurance plans and the establishment of municipal, state and federal employment exchanges.[1]

Rosenwald paid for the publication of the conference's report in the *Survey*. He was happy to learn six years later that F. P. Foisie, industrial relations manager of the water-front employers of Seattle, Washington, who had read the *Survey* supplement, had used the technique recommended in solving the chaotic labor problem on the Seattle water front.

Rosenwald became involved in an important labor controversy in Chicago in 1922 when he took an active part in the work of the Citizens' Committee to Enforce the Landis Award. Judge Kenesaw Mountain Landis had agreed to arbitrate between the building contractors and some of the building trades unions in June, 1921, after a long lock-out which had held up work in the entire industry. Some of the building trades unions had refused to join the arbitration and refused to accept the scales of wages fixed by Judge Landis for the entire industry. They also objected to the judge's decision that union men must consent to work on the same jobs with non-union men, and the unions claimed that this provision was contrary to the rules of their international unions. Unions comprising more than half the mechanics and laborers in the Chicago construction industry refused to accept the Landis Award and were placed on an "outlaw" list. A group of prominent citizens formed the Citizens' Committee to Enforce the Landis Award, under the auspices of the Association of Commerce of Chicago.[2]

Julius Rosenwald became a member of the Citizens' Committee and helped to raise funds for its work. Sears, Roebuck and Co. sent the committee a contribution of $25,000, and Rosenwald

[1] *Report of Industrial Conference called by the President, March 6, 1920.*

[2] For a complete account of the Landis Award controversy see *Industrial Relations in the Chicago Building Trades* by Royal E. Montgomery. Chapter XII. University of Chicago Press.

promised more funds from that source if they were needed. He also urged friends in the Chicago business world to contribute to the cause. He was strongly opposed to the conditions that had prevailed in the building industries in Chicago during his residence there, which included bribery, graft and violence. He wrote the following letter to his business acquaintances:

You will remember when the Citizens' Committee to Enforce the Landis Award enlisted in the war for decency in Chicago Building Industry, it was made clear that we faced a siege. War is expensive, but sometimes necessary.

Every citizen who has anything at stake in this community must do his part to prevent the recurrence of such conditions as existed here for years prior to the courageous position undertaken by this Citizens' Committee. The Citizens' Committee in this connection means *you*.

It means a determined public opinion facing grafters and sluggers. The army on the fighting front must maintain its lines of communication. Since the Committee began functioning, there have been no strikes, no delays in construction, no restrictions as to where material should be bought, and no graft. More building has been done in the first half of this year [1922] than any previous total for a full year, since the World's Fair.

We need your financial help to carry this fight to a successful conclusion. This will take many months and will require millions of dollars, but only a fraction of what it will cost if we lose. Hundreds of concerns have already subscribed amounts from $1,000.00 to $50,000.00 to be paid in installments as needed—25 per cent to be paid at once.

Won't your company subscribe at least $1,000.00 for this cause?

Faithfully yours,

Julius Rosenwald.

The battle between the "outlaw" unions and the Citizens' Committee went on for some years and was intense. The Citizens' Committee, maintaining that contractors who supported the Landis Award and their workmen needed protection, hired a force of 700 guards under the command of an ex-army officer, to combat the tactics of the union men. The city was divided into districts, and each district had its supervising officers and corps of guards, with a flying squad of guardsmen in fast automobiles who could reach the scenes of violence quickly. The Citizens' Committee also took out riot insurance, and according to its statements spent about $2,000,000 between 1922 and 1925 and protected property valued at $779,000,000. Some of the buildings erected under the protection of the Citizens' Committee were bombed, and two policemen were killed in the strife. The Citizens' Committee assessed contractors who agreed to work under the Landis Award one per cent on all work done in Cook County to help defray the expenses. The Committee also opened a training school for construction workers and imported workers into Chicago from other cities in order to break the control of outlawed unions.

After the Landis Award expired in 1926, strikes occurred in the building trades on the issue of the closed shop, and the unions won the battle. A new agreement was finally negotiated between the unions and the employer associations by which the closed shop was guaranteed. The Citizens' Committee helped to remedy many evils in the building industry, but some impartial citizens felt that the Committee's work was an effort to coerce workers and contractors into agreements imposed upon them and publicized and enforced by pressure exerted by men of wealth, who used their money and influence to bring about the condition most favorable to their own interests and to their conception of public welfare. Julius Rosenwald always considered the Landis Award a fair agreement, and he felt that the Citizens' Committee to enforce it had performed an important public service.

Rosenwald was always interested in general ameliorative efforts for improvement of working conditions, particularly with reference to women and children. He took an active interest in the Children's Bureau, which became a branch of the Department of Labor during the administration of President Taft. Rosenwald was largely responsible for the appointment of Julia C. Lathrop to be the first head of the Children's Bureau, and he also made special efforts to secure the appointment of Grace Abbott to succeed her. For the rest of his life he continued his interest in preventing the appointments in the Bureau from being used as a source of political patronage by professional politicians. Rosenwald wrote to President Coolidge after he succeeded President Harding offering to come to Washington if necessary to take up with him the importance of Grace Abbott's remaining as head of the Children's Bureau.

Rosenwald was a contributor to the National Women's Trade Union League of America, which aimed to improve the labor conditions of women by organizing them into trade unions and obtaining legislation in their interest. In October, 1925, Rosenwald wrote to a Chicago business man who had written to him asking for his reasons for contributing to this labor organization:

> In reply to your inquiry about the National Women's Trade Union League, please let me write that I contributed because after a thorough investigation I was convinced the people back of the movement were moderate in their attitude. While I could not subscribe to everything in their program, I felt it was a good deal better that capital should not indicate a spirit of aloofness or what might be construed as an antagonistic attitude. Furthermore, I found that men like Victor F. Lawson were assisting the League.
>
> Mrs. Pinchot's letter of endorsement came about this time and her endorsement was a factor in helping me to reach a conclusion to contribute.
>
> Our later inquiries gave further evidence that the women back of the movement belong to the conservative group.

In 1929 Rosenwald agreed to lend $50,000 to the International Ladies' Garment Workers' Union. The purpose of this loan was to enable the union to organize garment workers who were still unorganized in the New York sweatshops and thus to prevent the return of sweatshop conditions in the ladies' garment industry.

II

In his talks to Negroes during the war, Rosenwald had expressed the belief that after the war their services to the country would undoubtedly be better appreciated. This did not prove to be the case. Even during the war the discriminations against Negroes in the army continued. Rosenwald approved heartily of the letter which William G. Willcox, president of the board of trustees of Tuskegee Institute, wrote to Secretary of War Baker telling him of the great feeling of resentment among Negroes and urging the importance of not omitting them from the American parades in New York and Washington to welcome General Pershing. He also took the matter up with Secretary Baker personally. Negroes finally took part in Victory parades in the northern states and in the national capital.

During the war some Negroes were employed by the United States Railroad Administration, but two days after the Armistice that branch of the government issued an order to the railroads cautioning them against employing Negroes in any positions not open to them before the war and against employing them in white men's jobs. The Chicago Urban League protested, and the order was rescinded. The railroad brotherhoods were advising their men not to work alongside Negroes, and the American Federation of Labor discriminated against them by refusing them union privileges and then condemned them when they became strikebreakers.

The great demand for labor during the war induced the largest migration of Negroes from the South in Negro history. It was estimated that one-fifth of the ten million Negroes migrated to the northern states between 1916 and 1919.[3] They hurried from the cotton fields, rice fields and tobacco farms into the industrial centers as opportunities for jobs at high war wages opened to them for the first time. It was the Negroes' gold rush, and it threatened to empty the South of its labor supply. The Montgomery, Alabama, *Advertiser* told its readers the reason: "The Negro farm hand gets for his compensation hardly more than the mule he plows; that is, his board and shelter. Some mules

[3] *The Negro in Chicago.* Chapter III.

fare better than Negroes. This, too, in spite of the fact that the money received for farm products has advanced more than 100%. The laborer has not shared correspondingly in this advance. High rents and low wages have driven the Negroes off the farms. They have no encouragement to work." Wages in the southern states for Negroes varied in 1914 from seventy-five cents a day for farm laborers to $1.75 a day in city jobs. In the poorer counties of Alabama wages averaged between fifty and sixty cents a day. Meanwhile, the cost of living was rising rapidly during the war, and Negroes could not afford to remain in the South. In addition, the boll weevil had destroyed cotton in many sections of the South. Cotton farmers were ruined in many areas, and they had to turn to food crops, which required fewer hands than cotton, with the result that thousands of Negroes were thrown out of work.

Another motive for the huge migration was an educational one. Negroes wanted to live in areas where they could get some schooling for their children.[4]

The cessation of foreign immigration into the United States during the war and the return of many alien laborers to Europe were other important factors in the labor shortage and the consequent Negro migration. Living conditions, bad as they were for the Negroes in northern industrial centers, were better and freer than in the shacks and cabins of southern rural areas. Fear of mob violence was another motive for moving when the opportunity offered.

Wages for unskilled work in the North went up from $3.00 to $8.00 a day, and there were overtime payments and bonuses. Negroes, brought North and given better jobs, wrote home and stimulated others to follow. The Negro press helped the movement along by urging Negroes to leave for better conditions. Songs were composed comparing the movement with the flight

---

[4] The Rosenwald school building program had only begun in 1913 and was still on a small scale.

of the children of Israel and their escape from slavery into the Promised Land.

Negroes poured into Chicago, the railroad and industrial center of the Middle West. In 1910 Chicago's colored population had been 44,103 and by 1920 it had increased to 109,458. They worked in steel mills, stockyards, railroads, munitions factories and even in offices. They lived wherever they could find hovels and dilapidated buildings which white men would sell or rent to them. As there had been no building of private dwellings during the war, the housing problem and congestion were acute. Bombs were thrown into the houses of Negroes and of both colored and white real estate dealers who sold or rented property to them. Twenty-four such bombings occurred in Chicago between 1917 and 1919, and the police made no effort to find the guilty parties. Mayor Thompson had been re-elected in 1919 largely with the support of the Negro vote, and he had made demagogic appeals for that vote during his campaign. After election, however, gangs of white toughs continued their sport of attacking Negroes in parks, playgrounds and bathing beaches. As jobs grew scarcer tension increased. There were serious race riots in Washington, D. C. and Omaha, Nebraska, in the summer of 1919, and on Sunday, July 27, 1919, a race riot broke out in Chicago which kept the city in terror and disorder for three days and nights and in danger for more than ten days.

The trouble began at the crowded bathing beach on the shore of Lake Michigan on a hot July Sunday. The beach was in an area inhabited by Negroes, but it was also used by whites. Both sides had reached a tacit understanding about a boundary line, as the beach was merely the end of a street and not publicly maintained or supervised. Four Negroes who went into the water near the white section, were ordered away and left. More Negroes, however, came back to the boundary line, and stones were thrown, with a series of attacks and retreats. Meanwhile, Eugene Williams, a seventeen-year-old colored boy was swimming and had drifted into the white section of the water. Stones were landing near him, but he was afraid to come ashore into the embattled white territory. He clung to a railroad tie. A white boy of about his own age swam towards him; Williams let go of the tie, took a few strokes, sank and was drowned. The rumor spread that he had been hit by a stone and drowned, but the coroner's jury found that there were no bruises on his body and stated that fear of the battle on shore had kept him in the water. Negroes on the shore accused one of the white men of throwing a stone at the boy and demanded of a white policeman that the man be arrested. Meanwhile, both white and colored bathers dived for Williams' body, but could not find it. After this cooperative search, they divided into factions again, and excitement spread rapidly. "At this crucial point," says the report of the Chicago Commission on Race Relations, "the accused policeman arrested a Negro on a white man's complaint. Negroes mobbed the white officer, and the riot was under way."[5]

Reports of the drowning and of the policeman's action spread throughout the colored neighborhood rapidly, and police reserves were called out. James Crawford, a Negro, was said to have fired into a group of policemen and was shot to death by a Negro policeman. During the rest of the afternoon white men were attacked by Negroes, massed at 29th Street. Four were beaten, five stabbed and one shot. As darkness came on, gangs of white men and boys attacked Negroes, and from nine that evening until three the following morning twenty-seven Negroes were beaten, seven stabbed and four shot.

Monday morning men went to work as usual, and colored and white men worked side by side. That afternoon white hoodlums attacked Negroes returning from work in the stockyards. At streetcar transfer points cars were pulled from wires and taken over by mob leaders, and Negro passengers were dragged to the street, beaten and kicked. Rumors of these attacks spread quickly

[5] *The Negro in Chicago.* Report of the Commission on Race Relations, p. 4 ff.

through the Negro quarter, and there was bloodshed by both white and colored people for the rest of the day. That night mobs of both whites and Negroes, many of them boys and young men who craved the excitement, terrorized the city. Raids with men firing rifles and revolvers from automobiles going at great speed through the Negro districts occurred that night. In retaliation the Negroes took to sniping. Open warfare continued all during Tuesday and especially on Tuesday night. A general strike on streetcar and elevated lines which began Monday at midnight added to the disorder. Men, walking to work, were killed en route, and gang-rioting was prevalent throughout sections of the city. Soldiers, sailors and civilians raided the Loop district early Tuesday and killed two Negroes, beating and robbing several others, and destroying property. Negro homes were burned that night and furniture was stolen or wrecked.

It was not until Wednesday night that Mayor Thompson consented to ask the Governor for the aid of the state militia. Rain on Wednesday and Thursday drove idle people off the streets, but on Saturday the violence flared up again, when forty-nine houses near the stockyards were burned. By that time, however, the militia had control and the disorders diminished gradually and died out completely in a few days. Some of the police and militiamen testified later that white men with blackened faces had been burning houses and looting in an effort to incite further violence and get what they could of the spoils. Thirty-eight persons were killed, 537 injured and about 1,000 made homeless. Of those killed, twenty-three were Negroes and fifteen were white men, and about twice as many Negroes were injured as whites.

The Chicago race riot was particularly distressing to Rosenwald. He saw the relations between the race he had advised to be patient and many of the inhabitants of the city he loved best break down in a storm of tragic violence. While the riots were still going on, a group of leading citizens met at the Union

League Club, and a resolution was adopted to request Governor Lowden to appoint a committee to study the relations between the two races in Chicago. The Governor appointed the Commission with Edgar A. Bancroft as chairman, and Rosenwald, Victor F. Lawson, William Scott Bond, Edward Osgood Brown and Harry Eugene Kelly to represent the white people, and Robert S. Abbott, Dr. George C. Hall, George H. Jackson, Edward H. Morris, Adelbert H. Roberts, and Lacey Kirk Williams to represent the Negroes. The legislature appropriated no funds for this work, and its expenses had to be raised by private subscription. In addition to giving much of his time to the sessions of the Commission Rosenwald advanced money from time to time to pay its current expenses, until it could obtain other private contributions.

The Commission on Race Relations made a thorough study of the economic, social and political factors involved in the relations between the two races. Its report, *The Negro in Chicago,* indicated in detail the frightful standard of living the Negroes were forced to endure. It also went into the political implications of the situation and the organization of gangs by politicians for their political and personal interests. It made a valuable sociological contribution to the Negro problem in the city. Real estate agents refused to rent quarters to the Commission on the grounds that other tenants would object to the presence of Negroes in the building. It finally obtained quarters from the L. J. McCormick estate, and after the Commission had vacated the building, the agents of the estate informed the Commission that there had been no complaints from tenants.

Rosenwald took much time at a period when he was particularly busy with crucial business affairs to attend meetings of the Commission and to examine its reports. He worked closely with Charles S. Johnson, the Negro educator, whose ability he came to respect greatly. After Rosenwald's death, Professor Johnson said of this association: "What I remember most warmly of this early contact was the mellow benignity of his practical judgments, his swift instinct for sound fact, the warm and generous encouragement which he was willing to extend to a young man."

In the years after the war, Rosenwald also increased his support of Provident Hospital in Chicago, which afforded facilities for the training of Negro physicians and nurses. In addition to yearly contributions since 1911, he was active in the movement to affiliate this Negro hospital with the University of Chicago medical center. He wrote to Dr. Frank Billings in December, 1929: "The fact that one of America's greatest universities has made an affiliation with a Negro hospital seems to me one of the biggest steps in the progress of this race in America since the Emancipation Proclamation." In January, 1930, Rosenwald pledged a contribution of $250,000 for Provident Hospital and the Rosenwald Fund also appropriated $250,000 for its support.

Just before the war Rosenwald had become interested in providing housing facilities for Negroes in Chicago. He had purchased land for a low-cost housing project in 1914, but the war intervened, and the work had to be postponed. After the race riots in Chicago, which were so greatly intensified by the crowded and disreputable housing facilities, his interest in Negro housing projects increased, and he kept in mind the intention to take practical steps in that direction. When he was in Vienna in April, 1926, he inquired carefully into the municipal housing projects carried out in that city.

In 1928 his son-in-law, Alfred K. Stern, induced him to renew his practical interest in a housing project for Negroes in Chicago, and Mr. Stern took charge of the enterprise. The Michigan Boulevard Garden Apartments were planned as a yardstick to determine the possibilities of the use of private capital for model housing of persons with moderate incomes. Rosenwald had always insisted that housing projects must be practical business ventures and not philanthropic endeavors if they were to be possible on any large scale.

He invited a group of outstanding business men to serve on the board of directors of the apartment company. He invested a total of $2,700,000 in the project in the form of common stock of $1,500,000, a mortgage of $1,000,000 and an unsecured loan of $200,000. No dividends were paid to him on the common stock, but instead the unsecured loan was paid off, and the mortgage was gradually reduced.

Rosenwald purchased a six-acre city block between 46th and 47th Streets and Michigan and Wabash Avenues. On less than forty per cent of this site a five-story walk-up apartment house was constructed, containing 421 apartments of three, four and five rooms. The rest of the space was used for gardens, courts and playgrounds for children. Rosenwald took a personal interest in every detail of construction, and he stopped off at the site almost every day on his way to Sears, Roebuck to talk with the architects and the manager. One day he and Mr. Taylor, the manager, were inspecting the painting. Rosenwald asked the painter whether he was using Sears, Roebuck paint. "Hell, no," the man answered, "and I hope they never bring that stuff around here." "Why?" Rosenwald asked. "Because it ain't any good," answered the man and went on painting. Rosenwald questioned Mr. Taylor further about the paint and when he was told that its quality was not the best, he said: "That's right, don't use it unless it's up to standard." He hurried away to the Sears, Roebuck plant, and a few hours later five important executives of the company arrived at the site with instructions to remain there until they could find out how to make a paint that Rosenwald could use on his own housing project. He had assured the Sears men in charge of paint that he could not afford to have his competitors in the paint business say that Sears, Roebuck could not produce a paint which he could use.

Although he was anxious to put the Negro housing project on a business basis, he was equally anxious that the best of modern conveniences and materials should be used in the buildings.

He spared no expense, even though some of the business men on the board of directors urged less extravagance. He wanted the best of everything, not only because he took pride in this model project, but also because he wanted to give Negroes facilities which would stimulate them and their friends to live as well as they could possibly afford.

When the housing project was completed, Rosenwald's daughter, Marion Stern, who had been interested in the project from its inception, supported the child welfare work there, and under the direction of Mrs. Alfred S. Alschuler, a leading educator in that field, she organized two nursery schools and community recreation and educational facilities.

The project was completed by the summer of 1929, and all of its apartments were leased to Negroes by September of that year. The average rent of the three-room apartments was $42.13 per month, of the four-room apartments $50.70, and of the five-room apartments $58.09. Gas, refrigeration and electricity were furnished for these rentals. The lowest rent charged was $35 and the highest $61.57. The average family income of the Negro tenants was $150 a month, and sixty-five per cent of the tenants took in boarders. Bonus certificates of $2, $2.50 and $3 per month were issued to tenants of the various sizes of apartments for keeping their apartments in good condition, and these were cashed at the expiration of the leases. The tenants included families of Pullman and post office employees, waiters, stockyards workers, maids, janitors, domestic workers, chauffeurs, musicians, teachers, and a few dentists, physicians, lawyers, engineers, accountants and trained nurses. Stores located on the development were operated by four Negroes, and other stores opened there by Sears, Roebuck, Walgreen's Drug Stores and the Great Atlantic & Pacific Tea Company had colored employees.

Besides nursery schools for the children and supervised play and recreation, there were educational meetings held for the adults at Sunday afternoon forums. Sewing classes and Christmas toy manufacture were part of the community activities. A social room was provided which the tenants could hire for the evening for a fee of one dollar, at which parties, receptions and other entertainments were held. The project also included a Tenants' Cooperative Community Association with three representatives of the management and eleven representatives elected by the tenants for discussion of problems in connection with the management of the enterprise.

When Rosenwald started the project, model housing was new, and only one other development for Negroes existed, that financed by J. G. Schmidlapp in Cincinnati, which Rosenwald had inspected. There was great opposition to his plans both by white and colored real estate merchants, for the dilapidated fire traps in which Negroes were living brought in high rentals, and there were plenty of disgraceful structures in the streets of the neighborhood which could be rented to them. It was predicted that the project would be a colossal failure, and that Negroes would never keep the apartments clean or live decently in them.

After the apartments had been in operation for about a year, Rosenwald wrote to Robert Taylor, their manager, expressing his great personal satisfaction with the splendid results of the venture, and he added:

Those living in our Apartments have proven that the Negro is a law abiding citizen and a desirable tenant. In so doing they have added to the prestige of their race and have tended to encourage the investment of money in kindred projects since it is known that such property is likely to receive the sort of treatment which might be expected from the best class of people, regardless of race. I have been especially impressed with the quiet that prevailed in the Court, which is an indication that those who occupy the building must respect one another's rights.

When the project was begun, Rosenwald made efforts to interest officials of New York insurance companies in taking a mortgage on the property. He had the money to finance the project himself, but he wanted to induce insurance companies to take an interest in self-supporting ventures for Negroes. The companies declined to take a mortgage at the time unless he would guarantee it. But some years after his death, the project had proved its self-supporting character so completely that a mortgage was granted to it by the Prudential Insurance Company.

Although the Michigan Boulevard Garden Apartments were self-supporting, the project demonstrated clearly that low-cost housing for low-income groups was absolutely impossible without government subsidy. The Rosenwald project was run on the best possible business basis, and yet the return on his investment was not great enough to attract private capital. The rents, too, were necessarily too high for people with incomes below $1,500 to $2,000 a year. Rosenwald's mortgage of $1,000,000 paid him interest at 5.5 per cent, and that mortgage was reduced to $635,000 out of earnings by February of 1935. The return per share on the common stock of the enterprise was $3.93 in 1930, $4.08 in 1931, $.92 in 1932, $.09 in 1933, $.20 in 1934, and in 1935 there was a loss of $1.12 per share. The average earnings for seven years of operation amount to 1.13 per cent. On the entire investment, including the mortgage and equity, the net earnings for the seven-year period were 2.4 per cent.[6]

Alfred K. Stern, president of the building corporation, and former chairman of the Illinois State Housing Board, reported in 1937 that the problem of housing for the low-income groups was "beyond the scope of private enterprise," and that it must become a responsibility of the municipal, state and federal governments.

In November, 1929, Rosenwald offered through another son-in-law, Edgar B. Stern, of New Orleans, to match dollar for dollar, any money raised in New Orleans for a Negro housing project up to a total commitment on his part of $200,000. Because of the number of other Negro projects going forward in New Orleans at the time, and because of the depression which

[6] Seven-Year Report of the Michigan Boulevard Garden Apartments Building Corporation, Chicago, May 1937.

followed the stock market crash of the previous month, it was not possible to take advantage of this offer.

III

Rosenwald renewed his interest after the war in the general educational and cultural facilities of the city of Chicago. The University of Chicago came in for the largest share of his generosity and his gifts to it totaled more than $4,000,000. He also took a particular interest in helping the poorer students and established a student loan fund there and at other institutions to be administered by Judge Mack.

While Rosenwald was in Europe in 1914, the trustees of the University of Chicago, at the request of the faculty of the departments of Geology and Geography voted to name the new building for those departments "Julius Rosenwald Hall." Faced with an accomplished fact, Rosenwald finally consented to this use of his name, although he and Mrs. Rosenwald were always opposed to attaching their names to any of the institutions to which they had made contributions. The only other occasion on which he permitted this rule to be broken was when his friend Professor James H. Breasted, head of the Oriental Institute of the University of Chicago, insisted on calling the new library of the Institute at Luxor, Egypt, "The Rosenwald Library." Rosenwald and his wife had visited the temples and tombs at Luxor in the company of Professor Breasted in March, 1926. Mrs. Rosenwald wrote to her children: "It has been a liberal education to be with him, only we feel so poorly equipped to receive it." They had contributed about $65,000 for the work of Professor Breasted's Institute.

Rosenwald also continued his interest in Hull-House, and he remained a contributor and a trustee of that institution for the rest of his life. He took active part in defending Jane Addams when she was attacked as a radical by the head of the Illinois American Legion, and made efforts to get an apology from him.

He helped to finance the dinner given to Miss Addams by a citizens' committee in order to show their contempt for the attack.

Believing that Hull-House funds as well as other philanthropic funds should be invested more readily in common stocks, Rosenwald entered into an agreement with the settlement by which $100,000 of its endowment funds were used to purchase Sears, Roebuck stock, with a guarantee that he or his heirs would repurchase the stock at any time within five years at its purchase price and that Hull-House would receive an income of at least five per cent. He felt that the women of Hull-House, not being in business, were too conservative in their investments. Before the first year of this guarantee had passed, the stock market crash of 1929 had occurred, and Hull-House had a loss of $823.67. Rosenwald sent his check for $1,000. He continued to pay deficits until the time of his death, and the estate carried out the agreement thereafter.

On the occasion of Jane Addams' seventieth birthday, Rosenwald wrote to her:

The advent of your seventieth birthday will cause countless thousands to contemplate your exceptionally useful life and to thank a grateful Providence for being privileged to live during those years, and to have been inspired by your example.

Chicagoans are especially blessed since the reflection of your beneficence is the greater, due to your being one of them. Good fortune has permitted me a personal relation which comparatively few have had and my gratitude is correspondingly more pronounced.

May I, therefore, send as slight evidence of the affection and esteem in which Mrs. Rosenwald and I hold you the enclosed with our best wishes for as many more years as you can enjoy.

My only request is that you use it for purposes outside of Hull-House activities in which you may be interested or for your personal requisites.

He enclosed his check for $10,000.

IV

When the Rosenwald family was traveling in Europe in 1911, the youngest son, William, aged eight, wanted to go nowhere else in Munich except to the Deutsches Museum. He would disappear in the morning and watch with fascination all day long the animated exhibits showing the actual operations of industry, some of which he was allowed to manipulate himself. Rosenwald was very much impressed with the boy's interest and after visits to the museum himself, he decided that an industrial city like Chicago ought to have a similar institution.

During the war he was too much occupied with other work to do anything about an industrial museum. In 1921 Samuel Insull, then president of the Commercial Club of Chicago, wrote to its members asking for an expression of opinion on the most valuable activities for the welfare of Chicago and Illinois in which the club could engage. Rosenwald answered:

I have long felt that Chicago should have as one of its most important institutions for public usefulness a great Industrial Museum or Exhibition, in which might be housed, for permanent display, machinery and working models illustrative of as many as possible of the mechanical processes of production and of manufacture.

He went on to describe the advantages of such a museum for the stimulation of invention and the instruction and entertainment of the people. In spite of the fact that he was curtailing his contributions at that time due to the business crisis of 1921, he offered to contribute $1,000,000 for such a museum, provided additional funds could be raised among other citizens, but it proved impossible to accomplish this at the time.

Meanwhile, residents of Chicago were concerned for the fate of the old Fine Arts Building, which was considered the most artistic building of the World's Fair of 1893, and which was falling into decay. In 1922 Rosenwald made an offer to the South Park Commissioners of Cook County to pay one-half the cost of restoring the Fine Arts Building, if the board of commissioners would appropriate the other half, but without success. At a special election held in 1924, however, a proposition was adopted by the public authorizing the issue of $5,000,000 in bonds by the South Park Commissioners to pay for the restoration of its exterior and the reconstruction of its interior. At the time it was planned to use the reconstructed building for a huge municipal convention hall, combined with an industrial museum, a school of industrial arts, a Women's Memorial Hall, athletic, art and social centers, a museum of architecture and sculpture, and any other uses which might seem in the public interest. The dimensions of the original building were 320 by 500 feet, with two wings, each 120 by 200 feet. Its potential floor space was larger even than that of the Deutsches Museum in Munich, which housed 60,000 technical objects.

Rosenwald began to take up with prominent business men in Chicago his idea for the establishment of a great industrial museum there, and he asked his friend Leo F. Wormser, Chicago lawyer, to work with him on the enterprise. Wormser made careful surveys of industrial museums and carried on negotiations with the South Park Commissioners for the use of the building exclusively as an industrial museum.

During a trip abroad in 1926, Rosenwald visited the industrial museums in Munich and Vienna and discussed the problems involved with a number of experts. Upon his return he and Wormser made efforts to enlist the aid of the Commercial Club of Chicago in promoting the idea. Negotiations were also completed by which the South Park Commissioners agreed to use the bond issue of $5,000,000 to reconstruct the Fine Arts Building into an industrial museum. Rosenwald agreed to contribute $3,000,000 for exhibits and maintenance. The board of trustees of the new museum was chosen by Rosenwald and Wormser from among the members of the Commercial Club, for they wished to ensure the continued interest of business and industrial leaders in the new museum. Public announcement of Rosenwald's gift was made in the newspapers, and a flood of enthusiastic congratulatory letters came to him. Harold L. Ickes wrote: "I just want to say, apropos of your latest public-spirited act, that if Chicago has any finer citizen than yourself, I don't know who he is."

A board of directors consisting of prominent business men in Chicago was formed. At their first meeting, which was held when Rosenwald was out of town, the board decided that the corporation and the museum should be known as the "Rosenwald Industrial Museum." When he heard of this, he telegraphed:

> I appreciate more than I can tell the attitude of the committee but after full mature deliberation I have decided that my name be omitted from the Museum title and that it be the Industrial Museum of Chicago. If I were contributing the building it might be a different matter, but as that is the greater part of the investment it looks as tho I was getting a bargain. Please, therefore, make this change before the matter goes any further.

Mr. Wormser replied:

> Charter was filed before your telegram arrived but committee after hearing your telegraphic views stated that it would have disregarded your protest even if telegram had come sooner. Everyone here feels this recognition due you for your many other meritorious acts regardless of recent Museum contribution.

Rosenwald continued to insist, however, that the completed museum must not bear his name, and after an initial period when it was known as the Rosenwald Industrial Museum, its name was changed to the Museum of Science and Industry.

There was some political opposition to the use of the entire Fine Arts Building for the Museum of Science and Industry, and the proposal to make part of it a huge convention hall was considered. In 1927 Rosenwald, who was resting in California, telegraphed to the mayor of Chicago offering $500,000 toward the construction of a municipal convention hall on another site. His offer was not taken advantage of, but neither was a convention hall put into the Fine Arts Building.

In the spring of 1928 Waldemar Kaempffert was appointed director of the Museum. He made plans to make the new museum a place for the sociological interpretation of man's technical advances through the ages, instead of a mere trade exposition.

As work progressed slowly on the reconstruction and restoration of the building, efforts were made to obtain the most valuable exhibits from industry and from individuals. Rosenwald took great personal interest in the accumulation of these exhibits, and he spent considerable time and money on them. He purchased material for the Museum himself and requested friends in industry to give the Museum the opportunity to acquire historic relics and modern industrial exhibits. He declined, however, to solicit any aid for the Museum from individuals or corporations that had business relations with Sears, Roebuck or with him personally. Railways, telephone companies, oil corporations and many other organizations responded generously to his and Mr. Kaempffert's efforts. A plan was finally worked out by which the Museum would cooperate with the Century of Progress exposition which was to open in Chicago in 1933. The Museum received some of the exposition's important exhibits after it ended.

Waldemar Kaempffert resigned as director in 1931, after differences of opinion with the executive committee of the board of trustees. He felt that the committee was placing too many hampering restrictions on his activities. He deeply regretted the necessity he felt of resigning and the severance of his association with Rosenwald, who had never dictated to him in any way. In explaining his resignation to Rosenwald, Mr. Kaempffert advised that the members of the board of trustees should be men of broad scientific training and culture rather than forceful business executives, and he also urged that the president of the board should be a man of the broadest cultural background, familiar with the trends in modern visual education. Some of the trustees of the Museum felt that while a man of Mr. Kaempffert's creative imagination was of great value to the Museum, they needed more control by business executives. Mr. Kaempffert was succeeded by O. T. Kreusser and subsequently by the present director, Philip Fox, who had been director of the planetarium which Max Adler, Rosenwald's brother-in-law, had established in Chicago.

Rosenwald was anxious to have the work of the Museum brought to the attention of the public with a view to support by public contributions, memberships and legacies. In order to create such public support he considered in June, 1931, the possibility of matching public contributions up to an additional contribution by himself of one million dollars. In August, 1931, he wrote to the president of the board of trustees, W. Rufus Abbott: "The Museum is a great public project that will, I believe, enlist support in Chicago and throughout the country from individuals and corporations and possibly also from educational foundations. It was never conceived as an individual undertaking. As the Museum's merits become better known, such support should become more plentiful." In the meantime he and his family undertook its support and maintenance.

The Museum of Science and Industry did not finally open until more than a year after Rosenwald's death. It did not have its full quota of exhibits, but those which were installed won immediate public favor. There was a full size coal mine of modern type which was proclaimed the finest example of its kind in the world. Visitors were enabled to descend into the shaft of the mine and to watch and participate in the various activities of coal mining. The principle of animation in which the spectator could participate was carried out wherever humanly possible. By pressing buttons and pushing levers the men, women and children who crowded into the building in Jackson Park could make the wheels of industry turn for themselves. The processes of agriculture, chemistry, construction, transportation, printing, and the transmission of words, light and sound were illustrated in the Museum's animated exhibits. There were vivid historical exhibits giving the background of present-day processes. Hundreds of thousands of interested visitors have testified to the entertainment and educational values of the Museum which Rosenwald determined to establish for their benefit. Although it has been in operation only since 1933, it ranks in importance with the greatest of its predecessors and rivals.

In his will Rosenwald provided that his executors should use part of the money he set aside for philanthropic purposes for the Museum. The total obligation of his estate to it was more than five million dollars, and the Rosenwald Family Association made additional contributions of $1,500,000 after his death in accordance with the request contained in his will.

V

Rosenwald devoted considerable time and effort to the support of various organizations which were giving their attention to important post-war problems. The effort to combat the notorious activities of Chicago's large criminal element during the post-war years was one to which he lent active financial support. He contributed to the work of the Chicago Crime Commission and served it as a member. He was enthusiastic in his support of the efforts of Frank J. Loesch to combat crime and to break the political alliances of criminals. On one occasion he said that he would be willing to give one million dollars if a way could be found to expose the alliance between politics and crime in the city.

He also took an active part in the campaign of his friend John D. Rockefeller, Jr., to oust Colonel Robert W. Stewart from the presidency of the Standard Oil Company of Indiana in 1929. Colonel Stewart's testimony before the investigating committee of the United States Senate had revealed his part in the transactions of the Continental Trading Company. Rosenwald felt strongly that business ethics demanded that Colonel Stewart be removed. The main office of the Standard Oil Company of Indiana was in Chicago, and the fight between the forces of John D. Rockefeller and those of Colonel Stewart for stock proxies was conducted from there. Rosenwald wrote to many of the stockholders urging them to send their proxies to Rockefeller instead of Stewart, and his influence was so great that he obtained a large number of votes for the Rockefeller forces. After their success and the removal of Colonel Stewart, John D. Rockefeller, Jr., wrote to Rosenwald thanking him for his energetic public and private support in the fight. Rosenwald replied:

In reply to your very kind letter of April 25th, permit me to say that it was a privilege to publicly endorse your courageous action and it was a great surprise to me that others who represent large business interests did not take advantage of the opportunity to condemn flagrant dishonesty on the part of men who are at the head of large public corporations whose stockholders have a right to expect integrity of the highest order.

I have for some time felt that all public companies should publish with their audited statements the salaries paid to the leading officers, together with any bonuses or other indirect emoluments. I hope some day the stock exchange will demand this.

You have added one more to your long list of outstanding public services, of which all right-minded Americans are proud.

Another affair of national interest in which he participated in an indirect way was the Sacco-Vanzetti case. He had long been an ardent admirer of Felix Frankfurter, who had taken a leading part in the defense of Sacco and Vanzetti. Sentiment in Boston divided bitterly on the case, and Professor Frankfurter was attacked for his part in it, and the rumor was spread that he had received $250,000 from the Russian Soviet government to undertake their defense. As a matter of fact, the only money he had ever received for any of his activities in connection with the case was $250 paid for an article in the *Atlantic Monthly*, and of that, one half had been paid to his research assistant. His own expenses for travel and long-distance telephone calls had been considerable, in addition to the time he had devoted to the cause.

When Rosenwald heard this false rumor, he wrote to Judge Mack:

When I read your comment about Felix receiving enormous fees, I wondered whether it would not be good policy for some one of the leading Bostonians to make an offer to pay $50,000.00 if it can be proved that he ever received any fee whatsoever directly or indirectly or remuneration of any kind, except what he received from the *Atlantic Monthly* for his article. I would be very glad to risk the amount and agree to guarantee anyone who might be selected to make that offer. . . .

This offer was presented to Governor Fuller of Massachusetts in the form of a guarantee to present $50,000 to any charity in the state which the Governor might designate if proof of Professor Frankfurter's alleged fees could be presented. No such proof was ever presented, and the rumors died down.

Rosenwald also sent Professor Frankfurter $500 for the defense fund. After Governor Fuller declined to pardon Sacco and Vanzetti, the Citizens National Committee for the Defense appealed to Rosenwald to use his influence with President Coolidge to have him stay the execution. Rosenwald telegraphed to Coolidge:

Dear Mr. President. Until now I have been unwilling to intercede on behalf of Sacco and Vanzetti but I firmly believe that the wiser course would be a commutation of sentence. Any other must result in making martyrs of these men. There is surely room for doubt as to their guilt. I plead not for them but for the good name of our beloved country.

He also telegraphed to Governor Fuller asking him to commute the sentence. After the execution of Sacco and Vanzetti plans were made to publish the complete record of the case. Rosenwald and John D. Rockefeller, Jr., each contributed $10,000 toward the cost of this publication. Rosenwald also contributed $500 in March, 1929, toward the expenses of printing the record in the Mooney-Billings case.

VI

The variety of Rosenwald's community interests was so great during the later phases of his full career that it is impossible to include all of the projects for the community welfare and the public interest in which he was engaged or to which he lent aid. Business ventures he refused to engage in for the purpose of making more money. He always said that he offered financial support to business propositions, outside his own company's interests, only in order to save friends, or companies in which they were involved, from financial distress. The acquisition of more wealth never interested him in the slightest degree after he had become a rich man.

He became the financial supporter, along with other Chicago citizens, of several newspaper and periodical properties, which he was assured were worth establishing or preserving. He never took any personal part in their management or direction. As early as 1911 he was aiding his good friend H. H. Kohlsaat, who was struggling to keep the Chicago *Record-Herald* alive. In 1913, he joined Charles R. Crane, Cleveland H. Dodge, and George Porter in the purchase of *Harper's Weekly* for Norman Hapgood to edit. He also became one of the backers of the Chicago *Record*, when James Keeley edited that newspaper, and one of the financial supporters of the *United States Daily*, which David Lawrence had established in Washington, D. C., for the purpose of supplying factual interpretation of government functions and activities.

While Herbert Hoover was Secretary of Commerce in 1925, he brought to Rosenwald's attention the lack of facilities for small home owners to obtain second mortgages at reasonable rates of interest and commission. Rosenwald readily agreed to supply capital of $1,000,000 for an experiment in Chicago devoted to granting mortgages at lower rates of interest on a business basis. His friend Willoughby W. Walling, with whom Secretary Hoover had also taken up the matter, organized the effort as part of the Personal Loan & Savings Bank, of which Rosenwald was one of the largest stockholders. The result of this venture was that rates of interest for small home owners in Chicago were forced down to a more equitable level, and Rosenwald's money earned interest at four per cent during the first two years of the experiment and five per cent thereafter. He was also interested in the idea of forming an equity securities company which would enable persons of moderate means to become investors in good common stocks, but the stock market crash and subsequent depression put an end to his plans.

Rosenwald's miscellaneous ventures included a generous financial contribution to Admiral Richard E. Byrd's Antarctic expedition. When Byrd's ship was almost ready to start, Rosenwald suggested to one of the Chicago executives of Sears, Roebuck, who was making a trip to New York, that if he could find time, he should take a look at the ship. "I hear it is wonderfully equipped," he said. When the man returned to Chicago, Rosenwald asked if he had seen it. "Yes, I saw it, and Admiral Byrd certainly has excellent equipment, but I would have felt a little better about it if he hadn't bought his supplies from Montgomery Ward and Co." Rosenwald was delighted at this ironic coincidence.

Towards the end of the nineteen-twenties, people in Chicago differed on the question of their leading citizen only as to whether it was Jane Addams or Julius Rosenwald. Rosenwald had been proclaimed in October, 1928, as one of the Pioneers of American Industry along with George Eastman, Henry Ford, Thomas A. Edison, Charles M. Schwab, Orville Wright and Harvey S. Firestone. In 1931 the Chicago Rotary Club awarded him its first "Chicago Merit Award," and the citation read:

For his personal integrity and responsibility of power in the social and industrial order.

For his constant effort in the creation of opportunity for all regardless of race, creed, color, or accident of birth.

For his endowments and participation in service to all in fields of local and national education, including farm colonization in oppressed regions abroad, Negro schools, housing betterments, hospitals, universities, and the Museum of Science and Industry.

For his faith in the permanence and progress of truth to inspire mankind in the achievement of the highest ideals, and the most effective service to society.

On the evening of November 13, he was one of the guests at a banquet of 900 leading Chicago business men in honor of Secretary of Commerce Robert P. Lamont. The reporter of the Chicago *Daily News* described the scene which took place:

At the speakers' table were leaders of practically every industry known to Chicago and the middle west. These men of affairs, introduced, one by one, by Col. Robert Isham Randolph, president of the Chicago Association of Commerce, arose as their names were called, took their bows and sat down, without a word, awaiting the speaker of the evening—Secretary Lamont.

All but one—Julius Rosenwald—and when his name was called there was a thundering roar. In a moment every man of the 900 present at the dinner was on his feet in salute. Mr. Rosenwald, already back in his seat after his bow, arose once more. There was a cheer—and the little man who carries on his broad shoulders the love of all Chicago was almost overcome at the ovation. It was one of the most spontaneous recognitions of real citizenship Chicago ever has seen.

# CHAPTER XI

# POLITICS

I

IN NATIONAL politics Rosenwald remained a supporter of the candidates of the Republican Party after the war. In 1920 he was anxious to see the Republican Party nominate his friend Herbert Hoover, with whose relief work during and after the war, he was greatly impressed, and he always felt that Hoover's organizing ability and humanitarian experience would make him one of the greatest American presidents. In 1924 Rosenwald supported President Coolidge and contributed $5,000 to his campaign fund.

The Rosenwalds attended the inauguration of President Coolidge in 1925 as the guests of Secretary and Mrs. Hoover. They met many prominent people and were delighted with the attention they received from the President and Secretary Hoover. Mrs. Rosenwald wrote to her children: "I am sure that no one outside the President and the Cabinet have more the feeling of being at this moment a part of the official life of Washington than do daddy and I and it is quite thrilling."

During the 1928 campaign Rosenwald became an ardent supporter of Hoover, and he contributed $50,000 to his campaign fund, the largest contribution he ever made to a national campaign. He also worked actively to gain support for Hoover's candidacy throughout the country. In a letter to Chief Justice Taft he wrote:

I am greatly interested and actively connected in promoting the election

292

of Hoover. Smith personally is a very attractive individual, and I am quite fond of him, but I cannot picture him as the type I would like to see in the White House. To my mind the more important fact however is that continued prosperity of our country is to a great extent dependent upon retaining the Republican Party in power for at least four or possibly eight years more. I am inclined to be more optimistic over the outcome.

He also made this public statement. "I believe Mr. Hoover to be the best equipped man ever nominated by any party at any time for President of the United States." Senator Capper, of Kansas, who was also an ardent supporter of Hoover, sent Rosenwald an editorial from the Topeka *Capital*, which approved his statement but excepted Washington and Lincoln. Rosenwald answered:

I cannot agree with the exceptions taken in the editorial, even to Lincoln and Washington so far as my statement in regard to Mr. Hoover is concerned. I yield to no one in my devotion and affection for Abraham Lincoln, who was a fellow-citizen of mine at Springfield, but without detracting in the least from his ability, I feel sure you will agree with me that neither of these men when they took office were in any sense as well equipped for the duties which confronted them, either by training or experience, as is Mr. Hoover.

In a nation-wide radio address, he began by stressing the need for leadership in order to perpetuate the prevalent prosperity, and went on to say:

Herbert Hoover is by training and experience a leader. I regard him as fitted beyond any man of this generation for the presidency of the United States. I know of no man at present in public life who has displayed such extraordinary vision in dealing with many stupendous and wholly novel problems, crucially affecting human welfare. Nor do I know of any man, who, with idealism like Hoover's, has also his capacity for translating ideals into successful practice.

After Hoover's election it was rumored that Rosenwald would become Secretary of Commerce in the President's Cabinet because of his strong support during the campaign and his position as a leading business figure. He wrote in January, 1929, to one of his relatives in Germany: "The newspaper talk about my having a Cabinet position is all nonsense. There is not the slightest likelihood of such a thing being offered to me, and I would not accept it if it were." In August, 1931, Edwin R. Embree was talking with a group of southern politicians in Richmond, Virginia. They expressed regret and resentment that no southerner had been included in President Hoover's Cabinet. One man said: "If Mr. Rosenwald had been appointed to a cabinet position, we should have been satisfied: we should have felt he represented the South." The others agreed heartily.

Rosenwald and his wife attended Hoover's inauguration, although they were in poor health. Again, they were treated royally, and Mrs. Rosenwald wrote to their children:

Then to the White House for luncheon, where we met all the people on high. I wish each and every one of our children could have been with us to see the affection bestowed upon our daddy dear and to see and hear the high regard in which he is held. This was not manifested alone at the White House luncheon, but at the Capitol, in the House of Representatives, the Senate, in hotels. The President himself receives no greater acclaim. It is even a surprise to me, accustomed as I am to witnessing similar demonstrations, but nothing equal to this.

This was the last public occasion in which she participated. She had been suffering from cancer, and her life was rapidly coming to a close.

After the stock market crash of 1929 was followed by the business depression, Rosenwald wrote to Robert P. Lamont: "I feel very sorry for the Chief, although I have every confidence that in the final outcome the people will be convinced he is the great man we, his friends, believe him to be. My warmest greetings to him, if you should have an opportunity to extend them." In September, 1930, an appeal was made to him for a contribution of $10,000 toward a fund of $175,000 which was being solicited in Chicago to aid in Hoover's re-election. In his reply

he declined on the grounds that he had led the Chicago contributors to the campaign in 1928, "and I think it is up to some
others now to at least partly catch up with me." Silas H. Strawn
wrote in reply: "I know you were the leader of the contributors
in 1928. You always are, but if you wait for others to catch up,
as you say, I am afraid you will have to wait a long time."

## II

Rosenwald's most important participation in state politics occurred in 1926 in connection with the effort of Frank L. Smith
to become United States Senator from Illinois on the Republican
ticket.

Frank L. Smith, of Dwight, Illinois, had been a Republican
machine politician since 1894. He was made a colonel on the staff
of Governor Tanner in 1896 and used that title throughout his
long political career. His great ambition had been to be governor
of Illinois, and he tried several times to get the Republican nomination for that office without success. Rosenwald's first contact
with him, a slight one, had come in 1912, when Smith was manager in Illinois of President Taft's campaign. In 1918 Col. Smith
served as Representative in Congress from Illinois, and in 1920 he
was candidate for United States Senator but was defeated in the
primary election by William B. McKinley, owner of large utility
interests. Smith then became manager of the Republican campaign in Illinois in 1920, and after the easy victory of President
Harding, he was said to have aspired to a seat in the Cabinet.
In 1921 Governor Len Small appointed him to be chairman of
the Illinois Commerce Commission. Upon accepting the post, he
said:

If I should consider only personal interests and conveniences, I could
not assume the arduous duties of the position, but it becomes impossible
to refuse this call to duty, the proper discharge of which is of such vital
concern to the people of Illinois, and presents such a splendid opportunity
to give real service.

The post did offer great opportunity for service to the people of Illinois and to the utility interests, dominated at the time by Samuel Insull. Col. Smith was also chairman of the Republican State Committee of Illinois. In 1926 he decided to be a candidate again for the United States Senate. He defeated Senator Mc-Kinley for the Republican nomination in April after a contest in which large sums of money were spent by both candidates. In that same year there had also been a bitter fight in the Republican primary election in Pennsylvania, between William S. Vare, political boss in that state, and Gifford Pinchot and Senator Pepper. Vare was charged with using large sums of money for his election. The United States Senate decided to investigate the Pennsylvania election scandals, and Senator James A. Reed, of Missouri, headed a Senate investigating committee. The investigation made an inquiry into the Pennsylvania primary in May, 1926, and on June 26 Senator Caraway, of Arkansas, arose in the United States Senate, and called attention to the Illinois primary election of the previous April.

Senator Caraway said that it was openly charged that Frank L. Smith had received enormous contributions for his campaign fund from the heads of public utility corporations in Illinois, while he was still chairman of the Illinois Commerce Commission and in a position to benefit those interests. This speech focused national attention on the political situation in Illinois. When asked for a statement concerning the charges, Samuel Insull said: "My reaction to this morning's newspaper stories, which I have read, is just as though I had never read them."

The Senate investigating committee under the chairmanship of Senator Reed went to Chicago in July, and held sessions which lasted until August. Samuel Insull, who was a witness, declined to answer concerning his local political contributions, on advice of counsel, on the grounds that the committee lacked authority to inquire into them. Others of the thirty-four witnesses called maintained ignorance of what they might logically have been expected to know. Allen Moore, Col. Smith's campaign manager, testified that he kept no books, deposited whatever funds he received for Col. Smith's campaign in his own personal bank account, and that, as the expenses were greater than the contributions, he had spent much money himself. The campaign managers of Col. Smith's opponent, Senator McKinley, also kept no books, but the Reed Committee estimated that the McKinley forces had spent $514,143, mostly McKinley's own money, as he was a very rich man. When Col. Smith testified, he said that he did not know the sources of his campaign funds, but he finally made the following admission: "I think Mr. Insull contributed some money." Upon being pressed further he thought that Mr. Insull's contribution might have been around $100,000. He denied that Insull was his sole backer, but he could not remember the names of any others.

Allen Moore, Smith's manager, testified that in November or December of 1925 he had called at Samuel Insull's office at Mr. Insull's request. Insull told him that he did not think Senator McKinley, a rival of Insull's in the utility business, had made a good United States Senator, and that he admired Col. Smith, the then head of the Illinois utilities commission. Insull took $50,000 in cash from a desk drawer and handed it to Mr. Moore to be used for Col. Smith's primary election campaign. Early in March, 1926, the two men had another talk, and Insull asked Moore how he was getting along in the business of raising money for the campaign. Moore said he was having some difficulty, and added that the McKinley people were spreading the rumor that Insull had made large contributions to Col. Smith's campaign, which made others think that it was unnecessary for them to contribute. Insull said that he understood, and he took another envelope containing $50,000 out of his desk drawer and handed it to Mr. Moore. Later that month Insull gave Moore another $25,000 in cash, just a short time before the election in April.

Samuel Insull had taken this $125,000 out of the cash till of the Commonwealth Edison Company, of which he was the head, and he claimed that he had left I.O.U.'s in the cash drawer for these sums. After Senator Caraway made his speech in the Senate on June 26, Samuel Insull drew a check on June 30 to the order of the Commonwealth Edison Company for $190,000 to pay his indebtedness to the company for the $125,000 and other sums he had taken in cash. Insull had also contributed $15,000 to the campaign fund of the Democratic candidate for the United States Senate, George E. Brennan. Mr. Brennan testified:

I want to say in that connection, Mr. Senator, that the contribution from Mr. Insull he indicated to you, was given to me the day he left for Europe. He called me up on the 'phone and said, "Old fellow, don't you want to see me before I go away?" I went over to his office and he said to me, "Don't you need any money for the great Democratic organization of the State of Illinois?" I said, "Oh, we have no serious opposition. I don't contemplate anything; but nobody ever refuses money; and you always need money in political campaigns." He said, "I want to give you something. Of course, I am a Republican."

When asked about this transaction, after he had finally been forced to testify, Insull said: "Yes; I gave $15,000 to my friend George Brennan; and I feel ashamed that it was not more."

The election for United States Senator from Illinois was being fought with a background of utilities privileges and a forefront of "Americanism." Col. Smith opposed the entry of the United States into the World Court, and made his campaign on the slogan of "America First." Senator McKinley favored American participation in the World Court. The issue of whether the government power projects planned at Muscle Shoals and Boulder Dam would be privately operated or operated by the government would also be one for the Senate of the United States to decide. Samuel Insull, in addition to his contributions of $125,000 to Col. Smith's campaign and $15,000 to Mr. Brennan's, had also spent $33,735 for propaganda in foreign language newspapers in Chicago against United States participation in the World Court.

Insull testified that he was very much interested in "Americanization." But this propaganda, he admitted, also helped Col. Smith's campaign.

"There were persons elected in that contest who would fix the taxes upon the public utilities, were there not?" Senator King asked Mr. Insull.

"Oh, undoubtedly," Mr. Insull replied. "But the public utilities are owned by 40,000 stockholders . . . of whom I am one, and I put up $237,000 in this whole campaign. Would I put that up to influence the taxes for a corporation? I did it because of reasons that I have not told you and do not intend to tell you, because it involves a dead man, and other reasons, because I am very much interested in politics generally."

Besides Samuel Insull, Ira C. Copley, president of the Western United Gas and Electric Company, and its holding company, the Western United Corporation, and Clement Studebaker, Jr., president of the Illinois Power and Light Corporation, contributed to Col. Smith's campaign, while Smith was still the public official in charge of Illinois' public utility regulating commission. Mr. Copley gave Allen Moore, Smith's manager, $25,000, and Mr. Studebaker gave $20,000.

After his success in the primary campaign in April, with the aid of Insull's money and that of other public utility executives, it looked like smooth sailing for Frank L. Smith in the election campaign against George E. Brennan in November. In May Col. Smith had been a luncheon guest of President Coolidge's, and they had talked over the farm problem which was worrying the Republican Party politically and the farmers financially. Then came Senator Caraway's speech in June and the investigations of the Reed Committee in July and August. The press throughout the country printed editorials denouncing Smith for accepting money from Insull and cartoons portraying the use of money in Illinois and Pennsylvania to obtain seats in the United States Senate. The newspapers proclaimed Col. Smith to be unfit to occupy a seat in the Senate.

Rosenwald was greatly interested in the revelations brought

out by the Senate investigation, and his fervor for political reform was aroused once more. Although he was busy with his plans to establish the Museum of Science and Industry and with his business and philanthropic interests, he felt that everything possible should be done to prevent Col. Smith from representing Illinois in the United States Senate. He believed, too, that the Republican Party would be damaged by Col. Smith's candidacy. In August, 1926, he gave the following statement to the Chicago *Daily News*:

Republican Senators of force and influence, I am informed, have expressed the belief that Col. Smith, if elected U. S. Senator by Illinois voters, will not have the slightest chance of being seated. The feeling among Republican voters in other states is so strong on this subject that, in my judgment, a considerable number of Republican Senators will refuse to vote for seating Col. Smith.

What should Republicans of Illinois do in this emergency? Really they cannot afford—the national Republican party cannot afford—to permit Col. Smith's perverted ambition to lose a seat in the Senate to the party and to the national administration.

They should request Col. Smith to resign since his nomination was made by them without knowledge that he—a public official exercising judicial powers—was being financed as a Senatorial candidate by heads of great public utilities, over which he had supervision and control under the delegated authority of the State.

If Col. Smith does not accept the inevitable and resign, the Republican voters should place in the field as a protest candidate, a strong, clean Republican, on an administration and anti-corruption platform.

Personally, I should be happy to support such a candidate.

Those who were urging Col. Smith to withdraw from the campaign pointed out to him that his poor health—he had had a double operation in June—would offer a plausible excuse. Col. Smith refused even to comment on the suggestion that he withdraw. When he was told of Julius Rosenwald's statement, Smith said: "I do not feel I am called upon to answer Julius Rosenwald or any other individual." C. K. G. Billings, financier and former head of the People's Gas Light and Coke Company, one of the Insull utilities, was quoted as saying at the time of Rosenwald's statement: "Insull's all right. He has done a lot for Chicago, and he can do whatever he wants with his own money."

Shortly after Rosenwald made his statement, he went to visit President Coolidge at White Pine Camp in the Adirondacks. The President had invited him there to discuss the business situation, with particular reference to the decline in farm income, and the political situation in Illinois with particular reference to Frank L. Smith. Rosenwald left for President Coolidge's camp on the day his gift of $3,000,000 for an industrial museum in Chicago was announced.

While he was visiting the President, he had a recurrence of attacks of rapid pulse from which he had been suffering from time to time for several years and was forced to remain in bed. Secretary of State Kellogg and his wife, Senator Capper, of Kansas, and the President's friends, Mr. and Mrs. Stearns, were the other guests. Rosenwald was accompanied by his youngest daughter, Marion. He wrote to his other children:

I told Mrs. Coolidge when she expressed regret at my illness, that it was nothing of consequence, but due probably to the excitement over my invitation to visit the President which was a rare event in my life. I also told her, that going back ten years, it probably would have been true of any one who was at the camp now—that an invitation to visit the President would have produced a thrill sufficient to cause the pulse to beat faster, and she admitted that it was true in her case from an experience she herself had had.

Rosenwald presented to the President some figures on the distribution of farm income. When he left the President's camp, he gave a statement to the newspaper men, as he had promised them one, but, on the President's advice, he avoided all reference to the political situation in Illinois.

On August 22, the Chicago *Tribune* White House correspondent, Arthur Sears Henning, telegraphed to his newspaper from Coolidge's camp:

Julius Rosenwald, of Chicago, millionaire mail-order merchant, philanthropist and civic leader, started from here carrying a package of political dynamite. He is in possession of the views of Mr. Coolidge on the Republican primary campaign fund scandal in Illinois, which views Mr. Rosenwald seems to have found uncomplimentary to Mr. Smith, the Republican nominee for senator.

Mr. Rosenwald refused to say anything for publication regarding his talk with the President on the Illinois scandal, contenting himself with remarking with some significance that Mr. Coolidge seemed remarkably well informed on the details of local political situations. But Mr. Rosenwald disclosed in another quarter enough to indicate that the President has been shocked by the revelations of the sources of Mr. Smith's primary campaign fund.

The President is represented as agreeing with Mr. Rosenwald that the acceptance by Mr. Smith of public service corporation contributions while serving as chairman of the Illinois commission regulating public service corporations constitutes a disregard of moral standards that cannot be condoned. . . .

Whether Mr. Rosenwald obtained from the President any promise of support for his demand that Mr. Smith withdraw from the contest could not be learned. Ordinarily it would be unlike the President to take a hand in local party affairs.

In any event strong pressure by Republican leaders doubtless will be brought to bear upon Mr. Smith to get out of the race. In the first place, they are now convinced that no indorsement of Mr. Smith can be expected from the President under the most favorable circumstances. That will be a handicap to the success of the candidate in the election. Another handicap will be the probability that even if Mr. Smith should be elected he would not be seated by the Senate.

When it became obvious that Col. Smith would not withdraw from the election contest, Republicans who were outraged at his acceptance of Insull's money for the campaign, began to look for a possible independent candidate for whom citizens who did not wish to vote for the Democratic candidate, Brennan, could vote. Rosenwald took part in these efforts, and his favorite choice was State Senator Logan Hay. He tried to persuade Senator Hay to be a candidate, but Senator Hay found it impossible to do so. Harold L. Ickes, who was one of the leaders of the movement for an independent Republican candidate to oppose Col. Smith and Brennan, suggested Hugh S. Magill.

Mr. Magill had been superintendent of schools of Springfield, Illinois, field secretary of the National Education Association, State Senator of Illinois for two terms, and was then general secretary of the International Council of Religious Education. He was the author of the Illinois woman's suffrage bill, for which he fought until it was passed by the legislature in 1913, and he had written the resolution which resulted in unseating William Lorimer as United States Senator from Illinois.

The announcement of Magill's candidacy was released in the Chicago newspapers on September 28. Rosenwald returned to Chicago from the East on that day and was met at the station by a delegation of Magill supporters, in order to start the campaign publicity. When he stepped off the train, he told the reporters: "I am not the 'insulator' of the Magill candidacy." He added that he was only one of many leading citizens interested in decent government who were willing to defray the expenses of Magill's campaign. Although he was generally considered to be Magill's financial backer, he had merely promised to contribute not more than $5,000 to the campaign expenses, and he actually gave a total of $3,850, which was the largest single contribution. He felt that to fight the Smith forces with a huge campaign fund would be to use the very tactics of the men he was objecting to, although more experienced political strategists pointed out to him that it was hopeless to expect to win without money for an active campaign. In spite of the fact that Rosenwald did not put up large sums of money for the campaign, Magill was labeled by his opponents as the "Sears, Roebuck candidate" and the "mail-order candidate."

The Anti-Saloon League, which was in favor of the election of Col. Smith, because he had come out as an advocate of Prohibition, was not interested in political morals but merely in a successful candidate who would pledge himself to support the cause of Prohibition. Magill had been an ardent Prohibitionist. The Anti-Saloon League spread the rumor in Illinois that Magill was getting a campaign fund of between three and four hundred thousand dollars, for the one object of the League was to defeat the "wet" candidate, George E. Brennan, and it was felt that if an independent candidate drew votes from Col. Smith, Brennan might be elected. Magill testified later before renewed hearings of the Reed Committee investigating campaign contributions that the Anti-Saloon League leaders, F. Scott McBride and George Safford, had suggested that he withdraw from the race against Col. Smith, and that he had been offered the support of the League in case the Senate should refuse to seat Col. Smith. He also testified that he was offered the support of the Anti-Saloon League for the United States Senate in 1928. Magill told the Chicago newspapers: "There is one thing in Illinois worse than Governor Small or Frank Smith. That is the Anti-Saloon League." Safford, of the Anti-Saloon League, told reporters that Magill had a fund of $400,000, and the Smith forces charged that this was supplied by Julius Rosenwald. Both Rosenwald and Magill denied these charges when they testified before the Reed Committee in October of 1926.

When he was asked by Senator Reed, a Democrat, whether he was a Republican, Rosenwald replied: "I am a Republican. I would not say strictly a party Republican, for I voted three times for Grover Cleveland." To which Senator Reed remarked: "There are some bright spots in your life, then." Rosenwald testified that he had limited his contributions to $5,000 and that there was a feeling on his part and that of other Magill supporters that the entire campaign fund should not exceed $25,000.

"Did you ever hear of a proposition to raise three or four hundred thousand dollars for Mr. Magill," Senator Reed asked, "until the charge was made in an interview, by the Anti-Saloon League, that that kind of a proposition had been made?"

"That was the first intimation I had of it when I read of that in the newspapers," Rosenwald replied. "To the best of my knowledge, it is absolutely untrue."

Harold L. Ickes, who was the manager of Magill's campaign, testified before the Reed Committee that the rumor spread by the Anti-Saloon League officials was "not even a clever lie."

Less than six weeks remained between the announcement of Magill's candidacy at the end of September and the election in the beginning of November. The Magill forces were hampered by both lack of time and lack of money. Rosenwald was active in the attempt to raise the total of $25,000 which he felt should be the limit spent on the campaign. He wrote to many leading citizens in Chicago asking them to contribute money, and he received approval and contributions from many. Others felt that if they voted for or supported Magill, the "wet" Democrat, Brennan, would certainly be elected, and they refused their aid. Many replied that they were going to vote for Brennan, because they would vote for anyone pledged to repeal the Volstead Act, which they felt had an evil effect on habits and morals. Rosenwald collected a total of $23,590 for the campaign.

However, he had little faith in the ability of his candidate to win, although he believed that it might be possible to defeat Col. Smith. So strongly did he feel that Col. Smith should be eliminated from representing the State of Illinois in the United States Senate on the Republican ticket, that he took in October, 1926, the most irregular and naïve action of his entire career. Without telling anyone but his wife of his intention, he made an appointment to see Col. Smith at the Congress Hotel on Sunday, October 3.

Col. Smith did not make this interview public until five years later, and he stated at that time that he had written down the events and details of the conversation immediately afterwards. Rosenwald, according to Col. Smith, had made futile efforts to see him in Chicago in September. He finally telephoned to Col. Smith's home at Dwight, and Col. Smith agreed to see him at the Congress Hotel on Sunday, October 3. Col. Smith's subsequent account of the interview, which he wrote in part in the third person, follows:

After they had shaken hands, Mr. Rosenwald said: "You would just about as soon expect the Deity Himself here as you would me," and Mr. Smith answered: "It is said the Deity is ever present. Sit down."

Mr. Rosenwald then asked if he might take off his coat, which he did, threw it across the back of a chair and sat down in his shirt sleeves.

"May I talk plainly?" he asked.

"You sought the interview," Mr. Smith said, "so, of course, you can say what you came to say."

"I do not want to hurt your feelings," Mr. Rosenwald said, to which Mr. Smith replied: "They have already been hurt about as deeply as possible, so speak your mind."

"You know that if you are elected United States Senator you can't be seated, don't you?" Mr. Rosenwald said.

"No, I don't know that," Mr. Smith said. "I don't think anyone knows that," Mr. Smith continued, "because the only persons who have anything to say about that are the members of the United States Senate and I do not believe that they will prejudge the facts or deny a sovereign state its rights under the Constitution."

Mr. Rosenwald replied: "I have it from one very high in authority that you can't be seated."

"I don't know anyone high enough in authority to make such a statement," Mr. Smith said, "when the matter has not yet been brought to the attention of the Senate in a proper way."

"I want you to know what activity I had in the Magill matter," Mr. Rosenwald said, dismissing the question of whether Mr. Smith could be seated if elected, and went on to say that upon coming back from New York preceding this interview he had been met by a delegation, naming several of them. He stated that he and some of the members of the delegation went to his (Mr. Rosenwald's) office at the Sears, Roebuck plant.

"During the discussion of Mr. Magill's candidacy and ways and means of financing it, I told them," continued Mr. Rosenwald, "that I would support Magill, but that it would have to be a modestly financed campaign. I also told them that I would rather have supported Logan Hay but that for certain reasons Mr. Hay could not be a candidate."

Mr. Rosenwald continued that in the same week another meeting of some of the same people had been held at his office at which his secretary had been called in to act as secretary of the meeting.

"At this meeting held on Friday," Mr. Rosenwald said, "when we were discussing ways and means of financing the campaign of Mr. Magill, I told them I did not want to be the angel of the campaign, but that if I thought we could elect Magill, I would put up $500,000."

Mr. Smith broke into Mr. Rosenwald's statement to say that there was probably a law against any such expenditures for the election of a candidate for United States Senator. Mr. Rosenwald replied that he didn't understand that; that he didn't know that, and waiving the question aside, went on:

"Now I want to say something to you, not in the interest of any candidate, but just because I am a Republican and because I am interested in the Republican party and the State of Illinois.

"After the meeting the other day I went to an inner room to take a siesta upon orders from my doctor. While lying there thinking, I had a brain-storm. I thought to myself, 'If I will give $500,000 to have Magill elected, why not give Frank Smith $500,000 and have him withdraw?'

"So I acted.

"No one knows what I am about to say to you except my wife, whose consent I had to get before I could make the offer; and no one else will know from me.

"If you will withdraw from the Senatorial race I am here to offer you 10,000 shares of Sears-Roebuck stock the moment you sign your withdrawal notice. In a few months that stock will be worth three-quarters of a million dollars.

"You can give as your reason for withdrawing that your health won't permit you to make the campaign or any other reason you want to give. The 10,000 shares of stock will be deposited in escrow in any bank you name, to be turned over to you when your withdrawal occurs."

"I am astounded," Mr. Smith said, "at the turn of mind that some of you moralists have. You think that a campaign contribution by Mr. Insull has unfitted me to be a representative of Illinois in the Senate."

"Unfortunately, yes," said Mr. Rosenwald.

"But you also think," continued Mr. Smith, "that for three-quarters of a million dollars it is all right for me to sell to you for my own benefit what 650,000 people as American citizens gave me in their confidence."

To which Mr. Rosenwald replied: "Oh, you do not put it fairly. You have a perfect right to withdraw if you want to."

Mr. Smith replied, "In all probability there is no law to punish either of us for making such an agreement."

Mr. Rosenwald said, "I am not acting for any one. I speak solely for myself."

Mr. Smith replied, "I cannot understand your type of mind. From my viewpoint there is something else involved besides the election of a United States Senator. There is my personal integrity."

Mr. Rosenwald then said he did not think an election would vindicate Mr. Smith.

"I think you will be elected," he went on, "but that will not be vindication. You will always have a feeling of hurt which will be accentuated by the continuous attacks upon you. These attacks will ruin your health. Your re-election will not be worth the effort and the suffering. You can live more happily by not being a candidate; you can enjoy life and have plenty of money to do it with."

Mr. Smith declined the offer without hesitation, whereupon Mr. Rosenwald said, "Well, all my cards are on the table."

Mr. Smith replied: "There is no reason for discussing this matter further. If I believed that my candidacy would injure my party I would withdraw without consideration, but you are the first individual who has spoken to me about such action."

"What you need is a frank friend like myself," said Mr. Rosenwald.

The two sat looking at each other for a long moment. Finally Mr. Rosenwald got up, put on his coat, and walked slowly to the door. As he opened it, he said, "If you want to see me before it is too late, you have my telephone number."

"I shall not want to see you on this matter at any time," Mr. Smith replied.

When Rosenwald offered Col. Smith 10,000 shares of Sears, Roebuck stock it was worth $555,000. By November of 1928 those shares were worth $1,975,000.

Col. Smith also revealed in 1931 that he and Rosenwald met again at the Republican National Convention which met in Kansas City in 1928 to nominate Herbert Hoover for the Presidency. Col. Smith's description of the scene was as follows:

Passing through the long hallway of the Baltimore Hotel one morning on his way to the rooms of Mr. Allen F. Moore (accompanied by former Congressman William W. Wilson), Mr. Smith heard a voice out of the gloomy hallway say, "How do you do," and saw Mr. Rosenwald seated on a chair at the end of the hall. As Mr. Smith was slow in recognizing Mr. Rosenwald, the latter went on, "You remember me, don't you? We came very near being partners once."

"We did not even come close. I don't do business with sordid-minded people," Mr. Smith said and passed on.

When Mr. Smith reached the room where Mr. Moore, Mr. Garrett De F. Kinney, and others were assembled, he felt a tug at his coat and, looking around, found himself facing Mr. Rosenwald. "What did you mean by what you said out there," Mr. Rosenwald said.

"I meant that you have a sordid mind," Mr. Smith said. "You can surely understand the English language."

"Why, you don't think I had any sinister motive in trying to get you out of the race for United States Senator, do you?" said Mr. Rosenwald.

"I think," said Mr. Smith, "that I have as much right to assume that a sinister motive prompted you to offer me a million dollars to get out of the race for United States Senator (the price of Sears-Roebuck stock had gone up) as there was for you to think that there was something sinister behind contributions to my primary fund."

"Why, I want nothing from any United States Senator," declared Mr. Rosenwald.

"I don't know about that," Mr. Smith said, "but what would you have said had I told the story of your offering me 10,000 shares of Sears-Roebuck stock not to be a candidate for United States Senator, after I had been nominated by the people?"

Mr. Rosenwald said he would have admitted that he had done so, either in Mr. Smith's first campaign or in his second campaign, or that he would admit it then, but that of course he hoped Mr. Smith would not tell the story.

Mr. Rosenwald then said, "Well, everything happened to you that I told you would happen, didn't it?"

"Yes, as per schedule," said Mr. Smith.

"You are the first man I have known to refuse a million dollars," said Mr. Rosenwald.

"No, the woods are full of them, and most of them would have been less courteous in refusing you than I was," said Mr. Smith.

Rosenwald's part in this transaction was characteristically naïve, but it was also inexcusable and indicates his lack of appreciation of the democratic processes of government. He was certain in his own mind that it was morally wrong for Frank L. Smith to be Senator from Illinois after he had accepted large sums of money from Samuel Insull for his campaign fund, and he could not appreciate how even Mr. Smith could have thought otherwise. He made up his mind that he was willing to spend at least $500,000—not to elect Magill, for he refused to do that on the ground that it would be aping Insull's tactics—but to eliminate Smith. He came to the conclusion impulsively—and he often acted on his impulses—that he would be most likely to accomplish his purpose if he gave Smith 10,000 shares of Sears, Roebuck stock. He thereupon arranged to see Col. Smith and offered him what was, in effect, a bribe of more than $500,000 to act with what Rosenwald regarded as honesty. The man who was accused of taking tainted money for his primary campaign from Samuel Insull was, at least, amazed at being offered more money for his personal use to "throw" the fight. At the time of this offer Frank L. Smith was said to be in need of money, and the attempted bribe would have been useful to him. It was one of the most ironical twists in American political history, and Rosenwald never then or later realized that he had attempted to do something irregular.

This was not the only time that Rosenwald offered Sears, Roebuck stock to public officials in order to persuade them to be what he regarded as good. He once gave the chief of police of Chicago 250 shares of stock because he was impressed with the sincerity of his statement to his police captains urging them to perform their duties honestly. This stock was not delivered until the chief of police had completed his term in a manner Rosenwald regarded as entirely proper and honest. By that time the 250 shares had become by virtue of stock dividends 1,000 shares. He also once offered another official shares of Sears, Roebuck stock, provided his record in office at the expiration of his term indicated that he had carried out his pre-election pledges.

It is also true that he never attempted in any way to gain

favors from any public official for himself or for his business. However, he did not seem to realize that such action would naturally make the public officials well disposed toward his interests, and that they might be called upon to sit in a controversy in which he or Sears, Roebuck might be involved. However, no one whom he benefited in this way ever was called to sit in judgment upon him. He also never seemed to realize that it was not the business of private wealth to subsidize public officials, even if such subsidy was in the interests of what the benefactor regarded as the highest public morals.

John Graham Brooks, in his book, *An American Citizen, the Life of William H. Baldwin, Jr.,* wrote a passage concerning Baldwin which is applicable to Rosenwald in this instance:

Is an impatient ardor toward beneficence a weakness or a strength? Was Baldwin more or less of a man because he was a little headstrong in doing good? . . . Men of one type will pronounce him rash, those of another will love him better and believe in him the more because he could not brook the circumspection and delays in men of more cautious mould.

Col. Smith was elected to the United States Senate in 1926. He received 842,273 votes. Brennan received 774,943 and Magill 156,245. The leading newspapers with the exception of the Hearst press, which was in favor of Smith, supported Magill. The regular political machine, including the Anti-Saloon League, worked for Smith. The Rev. John Williams, of Chicago, a Prohibitionist, and a delegate to the Methodist Episcopal Church Conference, said: "I will hold my nose and vote for Smith." Magill had many earnest volunteer workers, but no regular political organization and insufficient campaign funds. In addition, he had entered the race only six weeks before election day. Some of the leaders of the Magill movement met with Rosenwald after the election and discussed the possibility of forming an independent Republican party in Illinois. But Rosenwald was never interested in politics for longer than one reform movement at a time, and he took no active part in state politics again.

On December 7, 1926, Senator William McKinley died. This left a vacancy in the Illinois representation in the short session of Congress, and Governor Len Small named Col. Smith on December 16 to fill it before he should take up his full term as Senator. This was the common procedure, but the circumstances were unusual, for Smith's right to a seat in the Senate was to be questioned before he took it, and by naming him to an interim appointment Governor Small had diverted the issue of the campaign contributions by Insull and other utility men. Some Republican leaders felt that this was a mistake and urged Smith to decline the appointment, but he refused to do so. As early as August, 1926, Senator Ashurst, after the first disclosures by the Reed Committee, had said that he would oppose Smith's admission to the Senate, if he were elected. On December 9, Senator Dill, of Washington, introduced a resolution declaring both Vare, of Pennsylvania, and Smith, of Illinois, disqualified as Senators.

Col. Smith went to Washington in January, 1927, surrounded by a battery of lawyers and supporters, including James M. Beck, former Solicitor General of the United States, to argue his case before the Senate. Some of the Republican Senators defended Smith. Senator Bingham, of Connecticut, said on the floor of the Senate: "The Senate has no divine right to keep itself holy and unspotted from the world." The Democratic Senators attacked Smith vigorously. Senator Reed said: "It is a plain, bald, naked question we are going to settle; that is, whether seats can be bought in the United States Senate in the interest of those who have had the right to decide as to the life and death of the interests contributing the money." Col. Smith, frail, ill and worn, waited at a seat near the door of the Senate, while the partisan debate went on for two days. Finally, he was excluded from the Senate by a vote of 61 to 23, with 10 Senators not voting. Twenty-one members of Smith's own party voted against him.

The machine politicians of Illinois determined to offer Col. Smith again as a candidate to the voters on the regular Republican ticket in the primary election of April, 1928. Governor Len Small was a candidate for renomination and State's Attorney Robert E. Crowe, the other leading political boss of Illinois, was also up for renomination. Otis F. Glenn, a lawyer, ran against Frank L. Smith for the nomination for United States Senator. Rosenwald contributed $5,000 to this primary campaign fund in 1928, and another $5,000 for the campaign of John A. Swanson, who was opposing State's Attorney Crowe. Because of the serious crime situation which was blackening the name of Chicago, the election of an honest and competent State's Attorney was of special importance. The newspapers waged a vigorous battle against Governor Small's administration of the state, Big Bill Thompson's administration of the city, and the enforcement of justice under State's Attorney Crowe's regime. They also continued to attack Frank L. Smith and urged the voters not to send him back to the Senate. It was during this exciting primary election of April, 1928, that the homes of Judge Swanson and Senator Deneen, who was supporting the reform group, were bombed, causing the election to be known as "the pineapple primary." Public feeling ran high after this outrage and the revelations of corruption in many of the branches of state and city government. The reform tickets were elected by a large majority, and the Small-Crowe-Thompson-Smith machine was put out of business. Otis F. Glenn won the nomination from Frank L. Smith by more than 243,000 votes.

After this victory for the reform group, Hugh S. Magill wrote to Rosenwald:

I know you are delighted with the results of Tuesday's primary election. I think Chicago deserved the unenviable reputation of being the worst-governed city in the world.

I cannot but feel that our campaign a year ago last fall laid the foundations for what was accomplished this week. For my part I am quite happy in the consciousness that we sowed the seed that finally bore the harvest.

In thinking over the whole matter in its relationships I feel that no one deserves more credit than yourself, and I trust you have the genuine satisfaction which comes from a consciousness of unselfish, patriotic endeavor.

## Rosenwald replied:

It is quite a coincidence that I should have received your letter this morning, as lying in bed I was thinking of the events which led up to Smith's defeat, and of course your very fine part in that achievement.

It ran through my mind that this is in many respects a unique occurrence in American political life, and all the history connected with it has not been made public. I believe a very interesting book could be written to which I could contribute some untold, and to my mind, very illuminating sidelights.

In February, 1929, Rosenwald had a conference with Professor Charles E. Merriam and Dr. Carroll H. Wooddy, of the University of Chicago, concerning a book on the history of the Smith affair. Dr. Wooddy agreed to write it, and Rosenwald agreed to finance it at an estimated cost of $6,200. *The Case of Frank L. Smith,* was published in April, 1931. Besides paying costs of publication, Rosenwald sent 1,000 copies to members of Congress, to members of the Illinois State Legislature, and to a selected group of public officials. He also sent copies to newspapers in other cities, to publicists in various parts of the country, and to the leading public utility organizations in the United States.

Dr. Wooddy's book contained no details of Rosenwald's interview with Col. Smith, and no mention of his offer to Smith. The only mention of Rosenwald's effort to get Col. Smith to withdraw was a veiled one in the following words:

This same idea [the effort to get Smith to withdraw] persisted through the campaign, and in its later stages, when it was apparent that Magill's chances were small, another effort was made to induce Smith to withdraw. The initiative in this case was taken by Mr. Rosenwald, who was greatly worried about the probability of Smith's being elected, in spite of all that was being done. When the Colonel came to Chicago to start his campaign after the primaries, Mr. Rosenwald arranged an interview with him and urged strongly that Smith abandon his candidacy on terms which would fully safeguard him from loss incurred by the effort and expense already invested in the campaign. Smith's very serious illness, it was pointed out, would offer a most reasonable occasion for this action. It would, moreover, save Illinois from disgrace and Smith and Insull from the embarrassment they would inevitably undergo when his right to a Senate seat came under scrutiny. Smith, however, had by this time definitely made up his mind to fight to the end; all efforts to bring about his elimination from the campaign were fruitless.[1]

Frank L. Smith, who had said nothing in public about Rosenwald's offer, was incensed at Dr. Wooddy's book and at Rosenwald's wide distribution of it. He made public the full account of the interview and gave it to the newspapers in the form of an open letter to Dr. Carroll H. Wooddy, suggesting that it would form an interesting additional chapter for his book. Col. Smith's account of the transaction was published in the Chicago newspapers of August 17, 1931. Rosenwald was at the time desperately ill with heart disease, of which he died within six months. He was eager, nevertheless, to issue a statement defending his action. But the advice of his lawyers and the persuasion of members of his family prevailed, and he reluctantly remained silent. The newspapers and many private individuals praised Rosenwald's impulsive act as another instance of his disinterested concern for public welfare.

### III

Rosenwald also took part in the long fight against William Hale Thompson, mayor of Chicago. In 1919 he attended a beefsteak dinner in honor of Sweitzer, who was opposing Thompson's re-election, and stirred the audience by his statement: "If this town elects this man Thompson mayor again, then this town is going to hell." Thompson retaliated in a statement in which he

[1] Wooddy, *The Case of Frank L. Smith*, pp. 220-221.

likened the beefsteak dinner of the business men to "The feast of Belshazzar," and he attacked Rosenwald as a tax dodger, a charge on which he had been exonerated in 1913. Thompson was elected again, but this time by about 20,000 votes in contrast to the 147,000 by which he had won in 1915. It was said that the Negro vote had decided the election, and Rosenwald's opinion that his influence with Negroes in general did not apply to those who voted in Chicago was sadly confirmed.

In 1920, Len Small, an associate of Thompson's in Illinois politics, became governor of Illinois by an overwhelming majority, and he held that office until the great reform wave of 1928. At the same time Robert E. Crowe was elected state's attorney, and the Small-Thompson-Crowe machine controlled both the state and the city during the lush years of prosperity and Prohibition. By 1923 the scandals were widespread. Thompson did not run for re-election, and William E. Dever, a Democrat, was elected and gave the city the rare experience of a clean administration.

When the time came for another mayoralty election in 1927, Rosenwald persuaded William E. Dever to run again. He was not inclined to do so, but finally consented. Thompson opposed him with a platform consisting largely of opposition to King George of England and a threat to "crack him on the snoot." Rosenwald came back from Santa Barbara, where he and his wife were resting, especially to work for Dever's re-election, although he was convinced that it was impossible to defeat the Thompson machine.

Dever was defeated by more than 80,000 votes, and blustering "Big Bill" Thompson was once more mayor of Chicago. Rosenwald wrote to his children just after the election:

The election was of course a terrible disappointment, although not a surprise, but as I wrote Mother, I refuse to lose faith. I still believe that regardless of the obstacles Chicago is well worth fighting for. When I got the news at Evansville about the election, I made up a new song entitled "Be it Dever so Thompson, there's no place like home."

In 1928, the machine politicians were defeated badly although Thompson's term would not expire until 1931. When Judge John A. Swanson won the office of state's attorney, in a campaign against racketeering and the affiliation of crime and politics, it became possible to begin the drive against corruption in the city and county government. Frank J. Loesch began his excellent investigations, which Rosenwald aided with loans. Police corruption, pay roll padding, election frauds, water-meter frauds and sanitary district scandals were unearthed, and a few men were punished. Business men generally were afraid to back reform movements because of the retaliation of the politicians and gangsters, who did not hesitate to bomb premises in the frantic effort to keep their control. The gangsters felt secure in the knowledge that the municipal administration would not interfere with their activities in the fields of murder and blackmail.

In the last few years of his life Rosenwald became discouraged with the effort to reform Chicago politics, and he refused to contribute to any great extent to political causes. In reply to a request for a contribution to the Business Men's Republican Organization in April, 1930, he sent $250 out of respect for those connected with it, and wrote:

For some time it has been my policy not to contribute money to campaigns. Experience has taught me that ninety per cent of all the money I have given for such purposes is wasted. But you and your associates are entitled to credit for your willingness to give up your time as you have done.

In 1931, however, when Anton J. Cermak opposed Thompson for mayor, Rosenwald supported Cermak's campaign with a contribution of $2,500 and wrote letters asking other citizens to support him. He also wrote to Melvin A. Traylor:

It is deplorable that men who represent large interests in our community are rarely willing to take the risk of publicly condemning the Mayor, regardless of his sins of commission or omission, because of the fear of reprisal.

I am therefore greatly delighted to know that you and others have come out boldly to work for the defeat of the present administration. It is cause for the greatest satisfaction to all who have the good of Chicago at heart to read the encouraging reports which seem to assure the election of Mr. Cermak.

Our City would not survive another four years of Thompson. We are now disgraced in the eyes of the world morally and politically and our financial condition looks like bankruptcy. The small tax payer is desperate. His home is taxed beyond his ability to pay and, in common with every citizen, he is compelled to pay indirectly the very large cost of racketeering and robbery as well as of waste of public funds.

Mr. Cermak's long record in the administration of the County encourages his supporters to believe that with his election Chicago's reputation will be redeemed. I shall be happy to aid to that end.

During the bitter mayoralty campaign of 1931 the forces opposed to Mayor Thompson had all of his speeches taken down in shorthand, for he was in the habit of making extempore remarks. Late one night Mayor Thompson delivered the following anti-Semitic outburst against Rosenwald:

Rosenwald is a Jew and is trying to edge his way out of hell by giving part of the money he steals. He is the greatest hypocrite that ever came to my attention. Cermak has that great Jewish fakir philanthropist still for him. Julius Rosenwald is a slave driver of Sears, Roebuck and Co. All this bird of a philanthropist is doing with the money he is giving away is trying to edge his way out of hell. That is all he is doing that for.

In another campaign speech Mayor Thompson said: "They went to England and got you a president, Herbert Hoover; they went to Czecho-Slovakia and got you a mayor, Tony Cermak; and they went to Jerusalem and got you a governor, Henry Horner." These two statements were taken up by the opposition and printed widely, and it was estimated that they cost "Big Bill" Thompson more than 50,000 votes.

The people were tired of horseplay, indignant at their high taxes, worried by rising unemployment and the approach of municipal bankruptcy, and ashamed of the reputation of their

city as a nest of crime. They could no longer afford the political
irrelevancies of "Big Bill" Thompson, and they retired him to
private life in 1931 by giving Cermak a plurality of 200,000 votes.

After the campaign was over, Rosenwald received from Judge
Henry Horner, who was treasurer of Mayor Cermak's campaign
fund, a check for $152.52 as a refund on the $2,500 he had contributed, for the campaign managers had not needed to spend
all of the funds they had collected. The letter with the refund
was sent to Rosenwald's sick room in June, 1931, by one of his
secretaries, with the notation: "I think this is the only letter of
its kind in captivity. Do you want to send Judge Horner any
special message?" "Write him," Rosenwald marked on the memorandum, "this almost gave me a relapse."

CHAPTER XII

# A PHILANTHROPIST AND HIS MONEY

I

IN THE course of a long career of giving, Rosenwald gradually developed some principles, out of which he fashioned an effective science of philanthropy. He did not start with any philosophy, but developed one as he went along, which was flexible enough to meet circumstances and opportunities as they were presented to him.

In the beginning he did all of his giving personally, with advice and solicitation from friends and acquaintances. As his wealth increased, he found the demands upon it too great for his unaided personal attention. In 1912, William C. Graves, who had had wide experience in charities in Illinois, became his assistant. Mr. Graves occupied an office next to Rosenwald's at Sears, Roebuck, and he sifted the hundreds of requests which constantly poured into that office from all over the country and from various parts of the world.

In 1917, Rosenwald formed the Julius Rosenwald Fund, which, at first, was a distributing organization for his many benefactions. As his interest in Negro education broadened, he used the Fund more and more as the clearing house for funds to be used in the building of rural schools and in aiding institutions of learning for colored people.

Writing to his son William in November, 1926, he said:

You will realize, as I have, that it is a very difficult thing to give away money in a way which is entirely satisfactory and one cannot be critical of oneself, especially after a decision is made. As you know, we never give money from this office, without a thorough investigation, and we do not pretend to investigate anything like all the appeals which come to us, but try to confine ourselves to interests of a certain kind, with of course considerable latitude.

National organizations are usually turned down without much investigation, because our experience is they spread very thin, and claim great results which as a rule are largely exaggerated, possibly not intentionally, but due to enthusiasm and lack of ability for proof.

In several instances he gave large sums of money to individuals whom he trusted so that they might use them for any philanthropic purposes they thought worthy. In 1924, upon the occasion of the ninetieth birthday of Dr. Charles W. Eliot, of Harvard University, Rosenwald offered to contribute $100,000 to any department or work at Harvard University for which Dr. Eliot might wish to use the money. He had refused to contribute to the endowment fund campaign, for he felt that Harvard had a large body of wealthy men among its alumni who ought to support the university and who could well afford to do so. Rather than contribute to general American educational institutions, except those in his own city, he preferred to reserve his money for those causes, educational and otherwise, which were not so commonly supported by rich men, such as elementary and advanced education for Negroes. But his admiration for Dr. Eliot as a man and as an educator was so great that he made an exception in this case. Dr. Eliot used the $100,000 for the department of chemistry, and he wrote to Rosenwald: "I have chosen the department of chemistry because I believe that from that science, especially in its connection with biology, is to be expected in the near future great improvements in human well-being." He added: "I avail myself of this occasion to tell you how greatly I have admired your use of your wealth for the promotion of the public welfare and particularly of the welfare of oppressed races."

The greatest contribution which Rosenwald made to the philosophy of philanthropy was his insistent practice and propaganda against the abuse of perpetual endowments. Men used in ancient times to bury a man's property with him after his death. The practice of dictating its use unto many generations was a more modern form of this interment. Instead of burying his goods in the ground, a man often buried them just as effectively in a perpetual endowment, the purpose of which he assumed would continue to be useful forever. Men also used to leave their wealth to priests who would say prayers for their eternal rest. In modern times men left money to institutions whose continuance perpetuated their names, no matter what other purpose they may or may not have served. More often than not such institutions served wider purposes than the glory of their founders, but in some instances, they were as little needed as graven images, and not nearly so artistic. Rosenwald showed both the good sense and the modesty to eschew both the perpetuation of his own philanthropic wishes or notions and the glorification of his own name. There is only one building in the United States named after him, and that was done against his will. The more than five thousand public schools for Negroes in the southern states are frequently referred to as "Rosenwald Schools," but that is a sobriquet and not an official designation.

From the days when he first began to think of his gifts in terms of philanthropy instead of individual charity, Rosenwald was as much opposed to the effort of the donor to perpetuate his ideas by means of frozen money as he was to the use of his name in connection with institutions which he had aided. His own foundation had as its only expressed purpose "for the well-being of mankind," but even this he did not consider a sufficient safeguard against perpetuity. He stipulated in 1928 when he gave the Fund 20,000 shares of Sears, Roebuck stock that all of its funds must be spent within twenty-five years of his death.

As early as 1909 in his annual address as president of the Associated Jewish Charities of Chicago, Rosenwald urged that donors give money to the Associated Charities rather than to special Jewish institutions which were at the moment part of the association but which might outlive their particular usefulness. He repeated this advice annually, and in his address of 1913, he added: "Give without hampering restriction or condition. Give so that your gift can be progressively applied by living minds to meet the changing needs of a progressive community. The man who bases future expenditure of his fortune on the needs of today must have blind eyes, in respect at least to the changes that come with progress."

In a discussion before the American Academy of Political and Social Science on "Private Benefactions," he said:

This is the today of our generation. Today has its own needs, which private benefactions should serve. I am opposed to the permanent or what might be styled the never-ending endowment. Permanent endowment tends to lessen the amount available for immediate needs; and our immediate needs are too plain and too urgent to allow us to do the work of future generations. . . .

When the time comes—as it does come—when a philanthropic enterprise no longer is needed, it should not be kept alive by a perpetual endowment pulmotor operated by a dead hand.

"Owners of property frequently feel as if they have a natural right to provide for its bestowal in perpetuity, but why people should expect to be allowed to manage their property after they are dead and can no longer use it themselves, is hard to see, and it is even harder to see why a community should be bound to accord to them the privilege that is to make them legislators in perpetuity regarding the disposition of a certain amount of wealth which they happen to have at the time of death."[1]

In this address Rosenwald cited as an example of the changes in ideas that took place from one generation to another, the present effort to take care of orphans and the aged in private homes instead of in asylums. He had taken a leading part in that effort, not only in Chicago, but in other cities, making several large offers to contribute to the care of orphans provided the institutions for them were abolished and home finding societies substituted. But

---

[1] This last paragraph was a quotation from Warner's *American Charities.*

the bricks and mortar were there, and so were the directors and trustees. It was impossible for Rosenwald to convince them that they ought to abolish themselves.

When he became a trustee of Tuskegee Institute in 1912, Rosenwald discovered that Andrew Carnegie had given Tuskegee $750,000 with the stipulation that only the income should be used. He urged his fellow trustees to ask Mr. Carnegie to change this condition and to permit the trustees to use part of the principal at their discretion. Seth Low, president of the Tuskegee board, wrote to Carnegie a few years later, telling him of Rosenwald's suggestion, and of Rosenwald's willingness to give $100,000 to the Booker T. Washington Memorial Fund provided the trustees would use a percentage of the Memorial Fund each year for current purposes. Seth Low added: "It is always possible that within the lifetime of the next generation industrial training for the Negro race will be assumed by the State or National Government. Should any such change, or any unforeseen change in conditions take place, a fund so firmly tied up in perpetuity that the principal cannot be touched, except possibly through an act of the Legislature, might be a disadvantage rather than an advantage." Andrew Carnegie consented to the use of a percentage of the principal of his gift annually.

Writing to Harvey L. Simmons, one of the trustees of Fisk University, Rosenwald said:

My observation is that most endowments average an income of about 4½ per cent, exclusive of losses. The same amount, consuming itself over a period of 25 years, would result in producing fully 9 per cent per annum during that time, and those are the years which the contributors believe are the most important ones for the institution, since they can see its needs for at least the greater part of 25 years. On account of the increased income the institution is enabled to do far better work, and by that means would have a much stronger hold on the thinking public and consequently enlist their support.

I am a great believer in the fact that institutions which deserve support, will find supporters, and when the time comes that an institution is not needed it should not be hampered by endowment funds to prevent it from going out of existence.

In 1925, he was instrumental in having the trustees of the Baron de Hirsch Fund encroach on the capital of the fund to the full extent permitted by Baron de Hirsch's original deed of trust. Baron de Hirsch had foreseen the possibility that future needs might change the usefulness of his Jewish agricultural philanthropy, and in his original deed of trust he had permitted the trustees of the fund to use their discretion to the extent of spending ten per cent of the original fund of $2,400,000 each year, as well as the income from that fund, after the first ten years. When the immigration of Russian and Rumanian Jews had diminished as a result of the change in conditions in Russia and the restrictions of the United States immigration laws, the original purposes of the fund had to be altered. There was, however, great need for helping Jews already living in the United States, who were immigrants or descendants of immigrants from Russia and Rumania. The Baron de Hirsch Fund was thus enabled to spend some of its capital and to aid the Jewish Agricultural Society to the extent of $500,000.[2]

In January, 1929, the *Saturday Evening Post* published an interview with Rosenwald by Elias Tobenkin entitled "The Burden of Wealth," in the course of which he said:

I feel confident that the generations that will follow us will be every bit as humane and enlightened, energetic and able, as we are, and that the needs of the future can safely be left to be met by the generations of the future. Second, I am against any program that would inject the fortunes of today into the affairs of the nation five hundred or a thousand years hence. Like the manna of the Bible, which melted at the close of each day, I believe that philanthropic enterprises should come to an end with the close of the philanthropist's life, or, at most, a single generation after his death. . . .

It is trite to speak of the burden of wealth, but there are few possessors of large fortunes in the country to whom the worthy disposal of their

[2] Joseph, Samuel. *History of the Baron de Hirsch Fund*, p. 168.

wealth has not become a genuine concern. Viewing the matter in retro-spect, I can testify that it is nearly always easier to make $1,000,000 honestly than to dispose of it wisely. . . .

We are in the midst of the greatest era of public giving that the world has ever known. Few of the monumental fortunes in the country today pass on to new owners undivided, and there is a growing total of un-counted billions in prospect for the purposes of organized public welfare. It is the consensus of opinion among students of our social order that unless this money is quickly used for contemporary philanthropic needs, it is almost certain to stagnate within a comparatively short period. I hold to this opinion. . . .

The generation which has contributed to the making of a millionaire should also be the one to profit by his generosity. Contemporary needs are the only needs of which we can be certain, and it is those needs that we must seek to serve. They are too plain and too urgent to permit us with good conscience to overlook them, or even slight them, and to at-tempt to provide for the unknowable problems of the future. . . .

In May, 1929, the *Atlantic Monthly* published an article called "Principles of Public Giving, the Danger of Perpetual Endow-ments," by Julius Rosenwald. This essay, to which several people contributed their advice and aid, gained much attention through-out the country. It contained Rosenwald's fundamental ideas on the theory and method of giving. Thomas Cochran, a partner in J. P. Morgan & Co., wrote:

It is one of the most constructive contributions to the subject I have ever read, and should be productive of much good. It has changed my conception of how I ought to handle a substantial gift that I am planning to make in the near future. Thus, I am indebted to you.

Commendation for this article poured in from philanthropists, college presidents, lawyers, educators and laymen. Mr. Robert Brookings, founder of the Brookings Institution, told Rosenwald that in his opinion, regardless of how much money Rosenwald had ever given away, it was insignificant compared to the value of this idea, and that he was convinced of the soundness of the principle.

Some prominent attorneys wrote to Rosenwald for extra copies of his article to hand out before they made their wills to wealthy clients with philanthropic tendencies. One correspondent cited the will of Charles W. Fairbanks, which provided for a fund in memory of his wife of fifty thousand dollars to be given to the city of Indianapolis on condition that the city keep the fund safely invested at compound interest for a period of five hundred years. At the end of the first fifty years the city might use the accumulated interest for parks and playgrounds; at the end of the second fifty years for buildings for the worthy poor; at the end of the third fifty years for buildings for labor, art, science and charity. At the end of the five hundred years the principal and accumulated interest could be used for the various purposes already enumerated. It was estimated that the fund, being exempt from taxation, would have amounted to approximately three hundred billion dollars at the end of five hundred years.

Rosenwald's article aroused so much interest that the editor of the *Atlantic Monthly* requested a second article, which appeared in December, 1930, under the title, "The Trend Away From Perpetuities." In it Rosenwald cited the influence of his ideas on the Near East Colleges campaign and added:

The argument for not tying up funds in perpetuity is particularly strong in the case of these American-controlled institutions in foreign countries. Who can tell what the situation in the Near East will be in another hundred years or even in twenty-five years? Political conditions may be such that it will be undesirable or even impossible for foreign institutions to continue in these countries. . . .

In view of the rapid change in political conditions throughout the world since his death, his prophetic insight in the matter of perpetuities has all the more value.

In his second article Rosenwald mentioned instances of foundations which had altered their policies on perpetuities or which had been established without perpetuities. He cited the change in attitude of some of the Rockefeller boards, the practice of the

Falk Foundation and the case of Senator James Couzens, who had set up a fund of ten million dollars for the welfare of children and had insisted that it must be spent within twenty-five years of its establishment in 1929. Senator Couzens' action had been directly influenced by Rosenwald's views.

"The Trend Away From Perpetuities" went on to point out that it was not only unwise to set up perpetuities, but also impossible. The Egyptians had tried it, and so had the Greeks and Romans, but their funds had succumbed to conquest, confiscation, expropriation and the decline in the purchasing power of money.

Real endowments [Rosenwald wrote] are not money, but ideas. Desirable and feasible ideas are of much more value than money, and when their usefulness has once been established they may be expected to receive ready support as long as they justify themselves. We may be confident that if a public need is clearly demonstrated, and a practicable way of meeting that need is shown, society will take care of it in the future.

Some university presidents and heads of other large educational institutions thought that he went too far in his theories. They felt that his opinion that future needs would be taken care of by future generations was not always borne out by experience. They maintained that in years of business difficulty it was almost impossible to raise fresh money no matter how worthy the projects were, and that in such times the existence of endowment funds was vital. Rosenwald, however, was not opposed to adequate financial reserves for universities and other large educational institutions. He was merely opposed to the attempt to tie up such funds in perpetual endowments. Even those who were critical of the extremes to which he carried his idea believed that his propaganda against endowments was of great value in bringing the subject prominently before the public for intelligent and liberal consideration. Trustees of universities and presidents of institutions also believed that by his own generous example and by his opinions Rosenwald had succeeded in influencing many other donors to lift the restrictions on their gifts. Others felt that by setting a time limit when all the funds of a foundation must be spent, he was doing in principle what he objected to, taking discretion away from trustees. However, Rosenwald's long experience as a trustee of several outstanding institutions had made him more fearful of the timidity of trustees than of their daring.

His views influenced John D. Rockefeller, Sr., to release some of the funds he had donated to the University of Chicago and other institutions for current expenditures. In June, 1930, John D. Rockefeller, Sr., wrote to the University of Chicago trustees and stated that he realized that it was unwise to make gifts in perpetuity except in the broadest terms. Rosenwald wrote to Harold H. Swift, chairman of the board of trustees of the University of Chicago:

I greatly appreciate your thoughtfulness in sending me copies of your correspondence with Mr. Rockefeller in regard to endowments, and to say the least, I am highly gratified with the changes that have been made. If it only contained the one sentence "I am realizing increasingly that it is unwise to make gifts in perpetuity unless in the broadest terms and for the most general purposes" that one statement coming from him will be instrumental in preventing untold millions having strings tied to them which, in many cases, would result in dry rot and misuse.

In 1931 the Rockefeller General Education Board decided that in future the income from gifts it had made to specific educational institutions should be used for a period of ten years for the specific purposes for which the gifts were made, and that thereafter the income could be used for any other purpose the trustees desired and that after fifty years the principal might also be spent. Gifts could also be transferred at any time to other institutions which the trustees felt might better serve the purposes of the original donations.[3]

In 1938 the Rockefeller Foundation and the General Education Board both freed from restrictions, gifts made in the past, and

[3] General Education Board, Annual Report, 1931-1932.

permitted the money to be used in whole or in part for "new purposes to be as reasonably related to the original purposes as may be found practicable, having regard to intervening changing conditions." In a statement issued at the time of this action, the trustees of these two largest foundations in the world remarked: "These liberalizing provisions represent the belief that the wisdom of this generation cannot be substituted for the wisdom of the next in the solution of problems hidden from our eyes." Institutions were also notified by both Rockefeller boards that five years after the date of the gifts they had received they might use five per cent of the principal each year "for any purpose for which income may then be used." These changes in philanthropic policy were influenced by Rosenwald's ideas.

## II

In 1929 Rosenwald was asked to participate in a unique distribution of philanthropic funds. Conrad Hubert, a Russian Jewish immigrant, died in February, 1928. He left a will appointing the Bankers Trust Company and his friend and former business associate, C. Bertram Plante, executors of his estate, which was thought to be worth more than six million dollars. The will provided that after one-quarter of the estate was given to Mr. Hubert's relatives, the remaining three-quarters should be distributed by a committee of three eminent American citizens to religious, educational, charitable and benevolent institutions recognized as valid under the laws of the State of New York.

Conrad Hubert started his career a penniless Russian immigrant. He sold cigars at retail, operated a restaurant, and later a boarding-house, worked as a farmer and a retail milk dealer, and went into the watch business. During his spare time he devoted himself to inventions. One of these was the electric flashlight for which he took out a patent in 1898. His friends told him that it would never be worth anything. It was said that had there been a difference of one word in Hubert's patent papers, he would have had a complete monopoly of the entire flashlight industry. In order to market his flashlight, Mr. Hubert formed the American Ever-ready Company. Besides originating the flashlight, Hubert also developed the miniature incandescent lamp, a vacuum cleaner, a pocket cigar lighter, an electric vibrator, a check protector, a rotating machine, automatic tools, vulcanizing equipment and other articles.

When he suffered an ailment, which doctors thought would be fatal, his friend and lawyer, C. Bertram Plante, urged him to make a will, which he did just before sailing for France, where he died. The Bankers Trust Company appointed a committee to select the committee of three eminent American citizens provided for in the will. This committee nominated Calvin Coolidge, Alfred E. Smith and Julius Rosenwald. On June 21, 1929, Thomas Cochran, of J. P. Morgan & Co., wrote to Rosenwald, telling him of his selection and requesting him to serve, Mr. Coolidge and Mr. Smith having already consented. Mr. Cochran added: "I think Mr. Coolidge was somewhat influenced to do so by the hope that you, too, might serve with him, because he realizes that, with your long experience, you have expert knowledge in constructively giving away money." Rosenwald accepted and expressed himself as "greatly flattered by this mark of confidence on the part of the Committee, and especially to be associated in the task suggested with two such eminent gentlemen as Ex-Governor Smith and Ex-President Coolidge." He added: "I use the word task advisedly, because I realize how difficult it is to dispose wisely of so vast a sum as six million dollars. However, I do not underestimate the agreeable side."

Rosenwald made careful preparations for his part in the distribution of Conrad Hubert's fortune. The Bankers Trust Company made a preliminary survey and sifted out numerous appeals which had already begun to pour into its offices. The news that three eminent men would begin to distribute six million dollars of another man's money seemed too good to be true to the hundreds of churches, schools, colleges, charities, hospitals, fraternal orders and individuals throughout the United States and in other countries. No general publicity had been given to the event, but the news spread rapidly.

The first meeting of the three men was held on July 25, 1929. Alfred E. Smith suggested that some of the money might well be used for the removal of a block of tenements on the East Side of New York and the construction on the site of a model housing project. He also suggested that the return from this project might well be placed in a limited dividend corporation, and the money used for another project after the first one began to earn money. Lawyers finally decided that under the terms of the will it would not be possible to carry out Smith's plan, as such a limited dividend corporation would not be a religious, educational, charitable or benevolent institution as provided in the bequest.

At this first meeting, Rosenwald expressed one of the main tenets of his own philanthropy. He called to the attention of the Committee that Conrad Hubert's money could be made to yield between fifteen and twenty million dollars of philanthropic money, if it were given to projects with the understanding that additional funds be raised from others. He declared that he himself would be willing to make substantial gifts to institutions receiving money from the Conrad Hubert estate. He also urged that no money should be given for running expenses of institutions, because such a grant would only relieve others who had been in the habit of contributing from continuing to do so. He felt that this new money should be allotted for improvements which could not otherwise be carried out, wherever it was possible to do so.

Coolidge, Smith and Rosenwald allotted $500,000 to Provident Hospital, the Negro institution in Chicago, to which Rosenwald had already been a heavy contributor. They also allotted $500,000 to St. Vincent's Hospital, in New York, in which Governor Smith was interested. They gave $500,000 to the Boy Scouts of America and $500,000 to the Girl Scouts. Beekman Street Hospital in New York received $500,000 and the Children's Aid Society of New York, $200,000. The American Red Cross received $375,000 for a new chapter house in New York, and the Y. M. C. A. of Jersey City, where one of Conrad Hubert's factories had been located, was granted $250,000. The New York Foundling Asylum, which had taken care of the children of unmarried mothers since the time of the Civil War, received $50,000. Other large grants were made to the Jewish Mental Health Association, the National Committee for Mental Hygiene, the Jewish Theological Seminary of America, the International Migration Service, the Young Men's Hebrew Association, and New York University.

A list had been presented to the committee of those institutions to which Conrad Hubert had contributed during his lifetime, and some of these obtained grants. The Conrad Hubert will was an example of just the kind of philanthropic carelessness to which Rosenwald was ordinarily opposed. In a series of four monthly meetings in October, November and December of 1929, and January of 1930, three men had to decide quickly how another man's millions should be distributed. Of the three men chosen, Rosenwald was the only one with professional experience in philanthropy.

### III

"Benevolence today has become altogether too huge an undertaking to be conducted otherwise than on business lines," Rosenwald once wrote. During the later years of his career as a philanthropist he felt more and more the need to organize his efforts. He also realized the importance of devoting much of his philanthropic activity to the field of Negro education and the improvement of health among the under-privileged Negroes of the South. Abraham Flexner wrote him in 1925: "You have acquired a prestige in the field of Negro education, which ought not to be wasted and which perhaps no one else will ever again acquire. There is no more important single field, whether looked at from the standpoint of the Negro himself or from the standpoint of our international well-being. There exists no agency with funds or personnel capable of exercising the influence which the development of the Negro race and the evolution of public opinion have now rendered feasible." In his reorganization of the Julius Rosenwald Fund, Rosenwald created such an agency, and he selected Edwin R. Embree, of the Rockefeller Foundation, to direct its activities.

Edwin R. Embree had had wide experience in the field of Negro education, as well as training in general philanthropic endeavors. He was associated with the Rockefeller Foundation from 1917 until 1927, when he became a vice-president of that organization. On January 1, 1928, he took up his duties as president of the Julius Rosenwald Fund. At the same time the Fund was reorganized with new trustees, who included some members of Rosenwald's family as well as prominent educators and executives.

The Fund, as we have seen, had been organized in 1917 as a convenience. Under the late Francis W. Shepardson it had developed into an instrument devoted to the supervision of Rosenwald's program of rural schoolhouse construction for Negroes. After his original gift of 20,000 shares of Sears, Roebuck stock Rosenwald added from time to time gifts of dividends from stock which he owned in other companies, and more Sears, Roebuck stock. In the latter part of 1928 the Fund owned 227,874 shares of stock in Sears, Roebuck, valued at more than $40,000,000. The Fund also received small gifts from a few other donors. Theodore Max Troy, of Jacksonville, Florida, who admired its principles and program, gave $20,195; the Rosenwald Family Association, gave $69,119; and the Carnegie Corporation contributed $200,000 for the support of the Fund's program of library extension in the South.

The general principles of the Fund were stated by Edwin R. Embree in his report for 1929:

Our aim is to give as little as possible for as short a time as possible. Should any of our projects become permanently dependent upon our help, we should feel that we had failed.

The Fund is not attempting to create institutions of its own, but to give stimulus and help in the building up of schools and health agencies and welfare activities by those properly responsible for them.

Mr. Embree added:

In the diversified programs which we have supported the unifying threads are our belief in education as an effective means of personal and social growth and our belief that society can make real progress only as the several groups of the population advance together and work together for the common good.

The rural schoolhouse program for Negroes was still an important part of the Fund's work. By the time of Julius Rosenwald's death in 1932 the Fund had contributed to the construction of 5,357 schoolhouses and other buildings in fifteen southern states. These schools had a pupil capacity of 663,615. The report of the Fund for 1931-1933 stated that the total number of buildings aided exceeded the total number of schools of every sort which existed for Negroes in the southern states at the time of the beginning of the program. The total expenditures for building and equipment of Rosenwald schools alone by 1933 was nearly twice the total amount invested in rural schools for Negroes throughout the South twenty years before, when Rosenwald first offered to aid Booker T. Washington in a rural school program in Alabama.

In 1931 the Fund decided to discontinue further construction of rural schools for Negroes. The more than five thousand schools already constructed and operating were ample demonstration of what could and should be done. The trustees and officers decided that any further work in that direction would make the outside aid of the Fund "a crutch rather than a stimulus." Rosenwald's tentative goal had been 5,000 Negro school buildings, and that goal had been exceeded. He and the trustees felt that the rest was up to the public of the southern states, and the Negroes themselves.

In addition to its rural schoolhouse program, the Fund made efforts to improve the quality of instruction in those schools by setting up experimental public schools in the South and by offering Negro teachers opportunities for improving their qualifications. The Fund also fostered higher education for Negroes by aiding in the development of four important university centers for them. It appropriated one and a quarter million dollars for these Negro university centers at Washington, D. C., Atlanta, Nashville and New Orleans. It also contributed to fourteen smaller Negro private colleges, seven state colleges for Negroes and industrial high schools in five cities, as well as summer institutes for teachers, preachers and agricultural workers. Rosenwald also contributed to the work of the Jeanes and Slater Funds, which aimed to improve the qualifications of Negro teachers and to bring about the extension of the school term for colored children.

In ten counties of seven southern states the Julius Rosenwald Fund supplied library service for colored children, and once the great educational value of this work was demonstrated by the Fund's activity, the county governments supported library service with public funds. The Fund, with some aid from the Carnegie Corporation, succeeded in establishing four thousand libraries in connection with rural schools in the South.

The Julius Rosenwald Fund also maintained an active interest in race and educational problems in other countries, and it initiated studies on education in American Samoa, the Dutch East Indies and Mexico.

IV

A story frequently told about Rosenwald concerned his innate habit of personal economy. It was said that one colored Pullman porter was overheard on the platform of the limited train between Chicago and New York asking another who was on his car that day. The second man's face beamed as he said, "I've got Julius Rosenwald!" When the train arrived at its destination, the first porter asked the second: "Well, how did you make out?" The man replied thoughtfully: "I guess Mr. Rosenwald is more for the race than for the individual."

However characteristic this may have been of his tipping habits, it was not characteristic of him as a philanthropist. During his long career of giving he did not concentrate entirely on institutions, and movements. His aid to innumerable individuals is evident in the loan folders in his personal files. When the Fund was reorganized in 1928, it paid some of its attention to the lot of the individual student and scholar and granted almost four hundred fellowships, amounting to $437,612, mainly to Negroes, between 1928 and 1936.

Previous to this work of the Fund, Rosenwald personally had undertaken to aid men to obtain a college education and to help them in various ventures, intellectual and personal, in which they were engaged. Many of these individuals were a source of great concern and difficulty to him, and some of them were a source of pride and satisfaction. As in his large philanthropic enterprises, so in the matter of personal loans, he had definite theories of giving. If he felt that an individual showed signs of recognizing the responsibility and was sincerely anxious to discharge the obligation, he was lenient. But he hated to be imposed upon, or to be regarded, because he was a rich man, as an easy mark for individuals who were willing to take his money, no matter how small a sum. He feared, too, that he would do harm to individual stamina if he did not insist rigidly upon fostering a sense of responsibility in the debtor.

The result of Rosenwald's aid to individuals was often hard feelings on both sides. The debtors were conscious of the fact that he was a very rich man, and many of them felt that it could not mean much to him to help them freely in the desperate efforts some of them were making to keep their heads above water while preparing themselves for a professional career. Rosenwald, on the other hand, tried firmly to limit his individual loans to as short a period as possible, in line with the principle he held to in his larger philanthropies that the object of his generosity must become self-supporting rather than dependent. Some of the men whom he aided with loans for their undergraduate, collegiate tuition fees, resented his attitude bitterly when, after having loaned them the money to get through their undergraduate courses, he refused to take financial responsibility for their professional work. In some cases he was accused by those whom he had aided in the beginning of ruining their careers by refusing to see them through to the end. As he had never promised to do so, Rosenwald felt that they were ungrateful for what they had received and eager to get whatever they could from him. Seldom were the loans he made actually returned although continuous efforts were made by his office to collect them.

When this work was taken over by the Fund, it was done on a different basis. Aid was never given in the form of loans but always in the form of outright grants to students who showed promise in their scholastic work or to mature creative workers in the sciences and arts. Among those who were aided by Julius Rosenwald personally or by the Fund were James Weldon Johnson, the Negro writer; Professor Morris R. Cohen, the philosopher; Professor Jean Perrin, French physicist, who later won a Nobel prize; Dr. E. E. Just, the Negro biologist; Samuel Reshevsky, the chess prodigy; Dr. Nathaniel Reich, the Egyptologist; Marian Anderson, the singer; W. E. B. Du Bois, Langston Hughes and Claude McKay, the Negro writers; Augusta Savage, the Negro sculptress; Professor Charles Johnson, sociologist of Fisk University; and many others, both white and colored, who received grants for work in sociology, music, painting, biology, medicine, history and literature.[4]

In 1920, Rosenwald was approached by a member of the National Research Council on behalf of Dr. E. E. Just, Negro biologist, who was doing excellent work and who was painfully in need of funds to carry it on. After consulting Abraham Flexner, Rosenwald agreed to contribute $2,000 a year for Dr. Just's biological work for three years, and this offer was subsequently renewed for another two years. Dr. Just, besides working on fertilization at the Marine Biological Laboratory at Woods Hole, Mass., taught at Howard University. Other biological scholars recognized the great importance of his work, and some maintained that if he had been born with a white skin, he would have occupied an important post at a great university with facilities for carrying on his unique research. Dr. Just wrote to Rosenwald in 1922 that with the $2,000 a year he had received from him, he had been enabled to do more work in two years than in the ten years previous. He added: "Your generosity came at a time when I was rather despondent; it really gave me a new grip." Dr. Just was recognized as a leading scientist in Germany, England, France, Japan and Denmark, and he was asked to be associate editor of a new biological journal published in Germany in 1926 and to contribute to other publications there. His investigations were considered to have special value in the fields of eugenics, population, anatomy, physiology and pathology.

Dr. Just continued teaching at Howard University despite the help he was getting, although such work interfered with his pure research. He wrote to Rosenwald that he felt the Negro needed scientific training more than anything else, for it tended to make him harder and more realistic rather than sentimental and emotional. He added: "I am thus trying to use myself in the teaching and at the same time carry on what may result in scien-

[4] None of those mentioned above falls into the category of individuals who resented Rosenwald's attitude or in whom he was in any way disappointed.

tific work of more than passing grade. If I ever make any really great contribution to science, I shall have you to thank." In September, 1926, he asked Rosenwald's permission to dedicate to him the scientific book he considered his most important contribution.

In spite of international recognition of Dr. Just's work and the fact that he was invited to international scientific congresses—he did not have the money to go—he was never invited to scientific congresses in the city of Washington, where he worked and lived, though scientists there gave him private recognition for his work. Because Howard University was poor, he could not obtain proper equipment or assistance, and he was forced to work at Howard because he was a Negro. In January, 1927, he wrote to Rosenwald's secretary, detailing his difficulties, the first statement he had ever made of them in the five years of Rosenwald's interest in his work. He wrote that he knew that he never would get the recognition or position his work ordinarily would have brought to him and added:

I should like to have some kind of assurance for the proper conduct of my work. I feel that I have now proved my worth and that I have as good scientific work in progress now and as promising a program for the next ten years as any biologist I know. What I want is the chance to put this work over in a way that is in keeping with its importance. I do not want to do shabby work. And yet situated as I am, I can't do my job as I think it ought to be done.

He added that he needed sufficient money yearly to publish his work so that its merit could be recognized, and that the nervous strain of living from year to year without assurance of being able to continue his work was distracting. He said that he did not expect ideal, but merely workable conditions, "a little better than the present."

The General Education Board took over the support of his work in March, 1927, and appropriated $2,500 a year for five years to enable him to continue it. Rosenwald had carried it for seven years. Dr. Just wrote to him that no matter what he might accomplish in the future, "everything will date back to these last seven years of work, thanks to you," and added:

I well remember the first time that I saw your picture in the office of Dr. J. E. Moorland when he was here in Washington. From then on I wanted to know you for that face made a lasting impression on me. You will never know how much you have meant to me and what an abiding light you and your life have meant to me. I do not want to seem to be sentimental and I have no need to be. But as I write these lines my heart is full. I do so want in some way to measure up to something for what you have done not for me alone but for the Negro race. . . .

In 1919 Rosenwald offered six fellowships in medicine for exceptional Negro students. Among them was Dr. W. S. Quinland, who had been compelled through poverty to work in the Chicago stockyards. He was brought to Rosenwald's attention by Abraham Flexner, received one of the Rosenwald fellowships and studied for three years at Harvard Medical School. He proved an exceptional pathologist and subsequently became professor of pathology at Meharry Medical College.

Rosenwald also contributed toward two research fellowships which Professor Felix Frankfurter had established at the Harvard Law School with the aid of Judge Julian W. Mack. The aim of these fellowships was to further legal scholarship and to provide adequate recruits for the teaching of law, as well as provide an opportunity for men of scholarly tastes to obtain post-graduate work before going into the actual practice of law. Among the individuals who received these fellowships were James M. Landis, who later became secretary to Justice Brandeis, head of the Securities and Exchange Commission and dean of the Harvard Law School; Thomas Corcoran, later counsel to the Reconstruction Finance Corporation and adviser to President Franklin D. Roosevelt; Malcolm Sharp, who became a member of the faculty of Wisconsin Law School. The men who occupied the fellowships also did important legal studies which were published in the *Harvard Law Review* and in book form. The book by Professor

Frankfurter and James M. Landis, *The Business of the Supreme Court,* was also a by-product of these fellowships. Rosenwald, as he did in many other cases, distributed a large number of copies of this book to libraries and to individuals who might be interested. In addition to contributing to a fund raised to enable Professor Morris R. Cohen to write his work *Reason and Nature,* Rosenwald also distributed many copies of the book.[5]

When Rosenwald was seriously ill in April, 1931, he read an article in the *Atlantic Monthly* called "The Unintellectual Boy" by Frederick Winsor, headmaster of Middlesex School, of Concord, Mass. He was so enthusiastic about it that he offered to distribute 100,000 copies of the article in pamphlet form. Mr. Winsor's article impressed him by virtue of its distinction between the boy who was not intellectual, but who was not therefore unintelligent. The thesis was that the secondary schools were merely fitting their pupils to pass examinations which entitled them to enter colleges, regardless of whether they were fitted for academic education or not. Mr. Winsor suggested giving attention to special aptitudes of those boys who did not have inclinations for formal learning, and he was in favor of giving them cultural and ethical stimuli which might make them more congenial to themselves and to others in their maturity.

Frederick Winsor wrote: "Now the activities of a man's life, for which a school should prepare him, fall into four main classifications: his vocation, his civic relations, his family responsibilities, and the recreative occupations of his free time." Rosenwald had certainly been successful in his vocation, which was business; in the performance of public duties and in the family life which he loved. His recreations he found pleasant, although he was conscious at times that he had lacked the time and the stimulus to develop cultural activities which might have given him fuller

[5] Rosenwald was also greatly interested in the book published by his friend and adviser, Abraham Flexner, *Universities,* and he distributed copies of that book widely to university libraries and to individuals.

enjoyment of life. This feeling showed itself in the faith he had in intellectuals and in his respect for their pursuits.

Perhaps Rosenwald saw a reflection of himself as he read in Mr. Winsor's article:

The political, social and business leaders of the next generation are rather more likely to be drawn from the class of men who are not academic-minded than from the class which has special talents for learning. Leadership depends on traits of character, not on intellect. It arises from an inborn urge to lead, and it is successful in operation in proportion to the strength of purpose, the tact, the determination, and the will power of the individual. It has nothing whatever to do with scholastic aptitude. Indeed, the very traits on which successful leadership depends are promoted by the overcoming of obstacles, and the school experience of the less intellectual among the school population, and the very struggle they have to make in their competition with their better-endowed schoolmates, is likely to result in the growth of the very qualities required for leadership.

Rosenwald could recall as he read these sentences that he himself had become an accepted business, social and civic leader without the advantages of an intellectual or an academic training. He had had the urge to lead—whether or not he recognized it in himself—and his strength of purpose, determination and will power were great. In spite of his admiration for scholastic aptitude and for intellectual traits in others, he had succeeded eminently without them. He had been thrown early into a competitive maelstrom and had come out on top. Perhaps there were thousands of others with the same potentialities. In any case, he was eager to see to it that as many people as possible who were responsible for the training of youth, should see this article, which had stirred him so deeply.

Before distributing the article Rosenwald had it submitted to a few educators, for on such subjects he never felt justified in depending on his own judgment. Most of these experts were enthusiastic about it, but two of them denounced it roundly as inadequate and reactionary. One of these suggested that it would hurt the future activity of the Fund if Rosenwald sent out such an article. This was the kind of challenge which always aroused Rosenwald to fight. On the margin of this paragraph in the educator's letter, he wrote: "Bunk." On the margin of a memorandum suggesting that the article "may damage the vocational point of view," Rosenwald wrote: "Perhaps that would be highly desirable." In a memorandum to Rosenwald, summing up certain expressed objections to the article, Edwin R. Embree wrote: "I think we need not worry that the sending of these reprints by you will be regarded as 'reactionary.'" Rosenwald wrote in the margin: "I have been accused of many worse things—so am entirely willing to take my medicine if necessary." Fifty thousand copies of the article were finally sent out, and they received grateful and enthusiastic acknowledgment by educators throughout the country, who were stimulated by Mr. Winsor's statements however powerless they felt to change their own curricula.

V

One of the outstanding activities of the Fund after its reorganization was its health program. Although some of the features of this program met with vigorous opposition from organizations in the medical profession, Rosenwald was stirred to increased activity and interest by the type of criticism directed against his efforts to stimulate lower cost of medical care throughout the country and to demonstrate the extent of venereal disease in rural areas of the South.

When the Fund came to the conclusion that medical services were often too expensive and inefficient, it began to plan a campaign for pay clinics and other self-supporting organized medical services for the poor and those with moderate means. Mr. Embree warned Rosenwald from the beginning that he would receive much criticism and abuse from some members of the medical profession. Rosenwald, who was sixty-seven years old at the time and in poor health, told Mr. Embree: "If it's a good thing to do, go ahead. People have said hard things about me before. I guess I can stand anything the doctors say." This was not a speech made for effect, because when the attacks came, which they did shortly, he never winced nor did he ever ask the officials of the Fund to curtail their plans in any way. The attacks made him only all the more determined to fight.

The medical program was worked out under the direction of Dr. Michael M. Davis. Dr. Davis had previously made a study of dental clinics in schools, which Rosenwald had financed, and was the leading authority in the country on the cost of medical care. He began work on the medical program late in 1928. In the spring of 1929 the Chicago Medical Society expelled Dr. Louis Schmidt, and he was expelled from the American Medical Association as well. He was expelled because he had a nominal connection with the pay clinic organized in Chicago by the Public Health Institute for the treatment of venereal diseases. The Public Health Institute advertised in the newspapers, and the Medical Society opposed advertising. The controversy over Dr. Schmidt's expulsion rapidly became nation-wide. Rosenwald took active part in his support. When he was warned that there might be retaliation against Sears, Roebuck as a result of his part in this controversy, he brushed aside the warning and declared himself ready for any fight that might result. He became a director of the Public Health Institute, which was managed by prominent Chicago citizens of wealth and standing, and he embarked generously on his own program for public health among the Negroes, who could least afford expensive medical service, and who needed medical attention most.

The Fund used part of its resources to cooperate with hospitals, clinics, medical and dental organizations on the problems of efficient medical care at moderate costs. Just as it did with the many problems involved in Negro education, it planned to act as a stimulus for further and greater activity on the part of public and semi-public institutions and organizations. The investigators studied existing pay clinics, in which the patients paid fees approximating costs, including reasonable fees for physicians. They also became interested in hospital projects, and took part in initiating and aiding medical, dental and nursing services in small and large communities and among special groups. Rosenwald and his advisers wished to avoid charity for patients of moderate means, and they aimed to contribute to projects which would become self-sustaining. There were precedents in the practical operation of the Mayo Clinic in Minnesota, where patients paid according to their means, and the clinics operated by Cornell Medical School in New York and the University of Chicago.

During the first year the Fund made an appropriation to the Committee on the Cost of Medical Care to enable it to study the entire problem, and another appropriation to the Institute of Medicine of Chicago for a survey of clinics and hospitals in that city. It gave $150,000 to the Massachusetts General Hospital for its experiments in hospital care for people of moderate means and $250,000 to the clinics operated by the University of Chicago. In addition, it supported efforts to obtain colored public health nurses in Arkansas, Tennessee, North Carolina, Mississippi and Louisiana. It also made gifts to Negro hospitals in Chicago, Philadelphia, New Orleans, Raleigh, Greensboro, and Savannah.

The important survey of the economics of medical care made by the Committee on Cost, to which the Fund contributed $90,-000 was finally completed in 1932, after five years of intensive work. The survey included descriptive material on existing medical service and data on plans and experiments in organized medical care. It went into physicians' incomes and family incomes with reference to the costs of illness. Twenty-six volumes of special studies were published by the committee, as well as a large summary volume of factual findings, in addition to technical reports. The work was acknowledged to be the most important contribution on the subject ever made in any country, and it formed the basis for further investigations by governmental bodies and other associations. This work was finally incorporated in 1936 into the work of the Committee on Research in Medical Economics, of which Dr. Michael M. Davis became chairman. The Fund pledged $165,000 over a period of five years for the cost of the continuation of the work. The Fund also made an appropriation of $100,000 to the American Hospital Association for its studies of sickness insurance and group hospitalization. In line with its policy of initiating projects and stimulating others to continue them, the Fund liquidated its medical work after it was firmly established and had won the support of other foundations and individuals.

The Committee on the Cost of Medical Care discovered that the incomes of doctors were alarmingly low even in prosperous times, and that the unmet medical needs of the population were great. The doctor and the patient could not find each other because of lack of public facilities for information and the fear of medical costs among people of low incomes. The committee recommended forms of voluntary sickness insurance and group hospitalization. Its findings were denounced as socialistic and communistic by the American Medical Association, although Dr. Ray Lyman Wilbur, Secretary of the Interior in the Cabinet of President Hoover, was its chairman and the other members were men of cautious views. Three years later the American Medical Association adopted some of the recommendations which it had previously denounced as "inciting to revolution."[6]

The Public Health Institute in Chicago had given approximately 2,700,000 treatments for venereal disease between 1920 and 1929. Its important work, performed in spite of the opposition of strong forces both within and without the medical profession, resulted in greater public attention to the subject, and its pioneer

---

[6] "Eight Years Work in Medical Economics, 1929-1936," Report of the Julius Rosenwald Fund, pp. 17-21.

work resulted in the wider treatment of the problem by the U. S. Public Health Service in later years.

So much disgrace has been attached to venereal diseases that they have been particularly difficult to combat. Public bodies were reluctant to appropriate money to fight them and philanthropists who would not hesitate to give money for the control of leprosy or cancer were timid about entering the field of the so-called social diseases. Rosenwald had no such inhibitions, and he welcomed wholeheartedly this great opportunity to do something of importance in a field neglected by other men.

In 1929 Dr. O. C. Wegner, of the U. S. Public Health Service, made the first authoritative study of syphilis among rural Negroes. He gave about 3,000 Wassermann blood examinations to Negroes in Mississippi and more than twenty-five per cent showed a positive reaction to syphilis. This sample seemed to indicate that syphilis among Negroes was an even greater problem than malaria, pellagra or hookworm. Dr. Thomas Parran was then assistant surgeon general of the U. S. Public Health Service in charge of the division of venereal diseases. He presented the facts of the survey to Dr. Michael M. Davis.

The U. S. Public Health Service submitted to the Julius Rosenwald Fund a series of recommendations for a demonstration of the control of syphilis among Negroes in the South, by means of the cooperation of the Fund, the federal health service and the state and local health departments. It was planned to confine the work to syphilis because of the opportunity to achieve prompt results with that disease. The responsibility for the control of the disease was acknowledged as that of the public health services, but the Fund was willing to devote itself to "developing and popularizing effective methods by temporary assistance to official health agencies." The health officers of the southern states were informed of the service and told to apply for aid in selected areas. Demonstration units were organized and the Fund paid approximately one-half of the expenses of the work, the states appropriating the remainder.

In Mississippi the area selected was at Scott, on the cotton plantations owned by a syndicate of cotton spinners of Manchester, England, where a company hospital was maintained jointly by the company and its tenant farmers. In North Carolina an area was selected in Pitt County, where skilled Negro laborers and tobacco growers lived. Conditions of living in this section were better than the average and educational facilities greater. Glynn County, Georgia, which was predominantly industrial and where there were turpentine camps, was also chosen. There was considerable illiteracy in this community and lower than average economic conditions. Macon County, Alabama, in which Tuskegee Institute was located and where the first Rosenwald Schools had been constructed, was selected because it was located in the deep South, was predominantly rural, and had poor housing, low wages, a high percentage of illiteracy and a high percentage of disease. Tipton County, in the western part of Tennessee, was selected because conditions were intermediate between the extremes of other areas. Albermarle County, Virginia, where the University of Virginia had operated a venereal disease clinic for many years, was chosen because economic, health and educational facilities were unusually high for Negroes. Thus practically every type of Negro community was represented in the six demonstration areas.

The work was carefully explained to the local medical society, individual physicians, county officials, planters, industrial interests, educators and other influential individuals and groups, both white and colored. Speeches were delivered in Negro churches and schools. Handbills were distributed suggesting that people who wished to do so could have their blood tested free of charge at designated places. The Negroes took advantage of the opportunity willingly and without embarrassment, because they had not learned to associate syphilis with immorality, but regarded it as the result of "bad blood" and as a particularly virulent form of "the misery." In addition to the blood tests which they gave, the health officials prescribed for other ailments whenever possible, gave typhoid inoculations to 3,500 persons in Macon County, Alabama, immunized 600 children from diphtheria and vaccinated 200 against smallpox in that locality.

Three general subjects were investigated by the six demonstration units: the prevalence of syphilis among a given population group; the amount of treatment possible; the cost of finding the cases and of their treatment. The prevalence of syphilis was found to vary directly with the economic and cultural conditions in the areas selected.

In the six counties 27,131 blood tests were given, and of these almost 6,000 showed positive reactions. The patients received some treatment, but not much, because the work was not on a permanent basis. Dr. Parran wrote: "Although from the treatment point of view, the Rosenwald demonstrations in syphilis control were not more than a gesture, nevertheless, six years after they were finished, in every community where the rate has been rechecked, the rates are down. Spending money for this purpose is not pouring sand down a rat hole. Every honest effort is productive." The results of the demonstration also indicated that for every Negro treated for syphilis there were twenty-five Negroes with the disease who were receiving neither treatment nor observation.[7] Dr. Clark added that the demonstrations also indicated "that it would appear to be possible to reduce the prevalence of syphilis at least 50 per cent with the maintenance of permanent clinics in these counties."[8] The demonstrations also exploded the superstition that the Negroes were more susceptible to venereal disease racially than white men. Dr. Parran wrote:

[7] Clark, Taliaferro, *The Control of Syphilis in Southern Rural Areas.* Fund, 1932, p. 32.
[8] Clark, p. 34.

"An environment approximating that of the white man produced a syphilis rate approximating his."

Unfortunately, the financial depression began soon after the work was started, and funds were not available in ensuing years for large federal and state-wide programs of syphilis control, which the six demonstrations had indicated were both necessary and practical.

When Congress passed the Social Security Act of 1935, provision was made for funds for the Public Health Service, and it was possible to continue the campaign on syphilis, which became nation-wide in its publicity and state-wide in its activities in many areas. Rosenwald and his Fund had started something of incalculable importance, and the government at last took it up with energy and support.

After the depression began to lift, the Fund concentrated on providing Negro physicians and nurses for an ailing population, and on supplying opportunities for study and improvement to those already engaged in health work in the South. It enabled well-trained Negro physicians and surgeons to act as members of state health departments in the South by paying part of their salaries, and it aided Negro nurses to obtain postgraduate courses in public health.

VI

The Fund also made efforts to contribute toward the improvement of race relations between the Negroes and the rest of the population. It supported special university courses on race relations for teachers and other educators, and through the Social Science Research Council, the Fund granted aid to professors in southern universities for work on regional problems. It also supported the work of the Commission on Interracial Cooperation which attempted to bring colored and white people together in cooperative efforts in the South. On the branch of the work dealing with race relations the Fund spent a total of $331,289 between 1928 and 1936.

The Fund was able to accomplish little toward the improvement of economic opportunities for Negroes. It paid the expenses of conferences on economic conditions in which both white and colored leaders took part. It also made some studies of the depressed economic situation of the Negroes in farm tenancy and in trade-unions. During the depression it did whatever it could to obtain consideration for the Negro in relief allotments.

The task of obtaining equal opportunity for work and earnings with white people was beyond the power of any fund, just as it had proved impossible earlier for Rosenwald to obtain equal opportunities for Negro employees even in his own enterprises.

The economic destitution of the Negroes was a problem which long concerned Rosenwald, but he felt that there was little that he or his fund could do to change their status except by offering educational opportunities and improved sanitary and social welfare facilities. Whenever a chance offered to get Negroes jobs or to take up their economic status with influential persons Rosenwald was quick to do so. On December 12, 1929, he wrote to his friend President Hoover:

At this time when you and the members of your administration are giving such constructive attention to the economic well-being of the nation, would it not be well to give careful study to the conditions of life and employment of the Negroes, which vitally affect the prosperity of the country?

These twelve million colored people constitute one of the great potential markets for American industry. At the present time the standards of consumption of goods in this group are substantially below the prevailing national average. And yet these people speak the English language and are easily reached by existing retail outlets—a market far more accessible than many that have been cultivated in the development of foreign trade.

The problems of opening this market more fully would involve the

increase of standards of consumption and the development of higher earning power. The measures to be adopted are many, but three stand out
conspicuously. First, educational programs should be accelerated, with
particular reference to the elimination of illiteracy. Second, health activities
should be restudied to make sure that this group of people, whose conditions of life are in many ways different from those of whites, are
receiving the aid in the elimination of disease that is desirable for their
health and for the protection of the rest of the population. Third, the
improvement of opportunities for employment should be made the serious
concern of the government and such agencies as chambers of commerce
and farm boards. No case can be made for employing an inefficient black
man in preference to a more efficient white, but when employment can be
given to the colored man on a sound basis, the national welfare and
prosperity are promoted since on the whole the opportunities for employment for the Negro are much more restricted than for the white.

Several philanthropic agencies, including the Julius Rosenwald Fund,
are helping in Negro education and health. But private groups can do
little in the fundamental matter of employment and economic well-being.

It seems to me that the Federal Government and business agencies
could be helpful in urging this point of view from time to time when
educational, health and employment progress are under consideration. Results of economic importance would probably come slowly. But the development of this large market would have substantial and favorable con-
sequences for the prosperity of the country.

The President replied thanking Rosenwald for his letter and
stating that, as usual, he was most wise in his suggestions. No
action was ever taken on these suggestions by any governmental
bodies or business agencies, and at the time of Rosenwald's death
the economic status of the people for whose educational and
social welfare he had done so much was far below that of other
sections of the community.

### VII

The severity of the depression caused a great shrinkage in the
value of the Fund's capital. Rosenwald had always believed firmly
in the stock of his own company, and he had been reluctant
to have his philanthropic foundation sell any of it and put its

assets into other investments. Along with the other good common stocks of the country, that of Sears, Roebuck declined drastically. The shares which had been worth almost $200 each in 1928 fell to a price of $30 a share in December, 1931. Income had practically ceased for the Fund. It was compelled to avoid any new philanthropic commitments for the time being, and some of the projects which it had initiated were aided by larger and wealthier foundations. The Carnegie Corporation, which had been a pioneer in library work, appropriated $200,000 in order that the Fund might carry out its county library projects in the South. The General Education Board made grants to Negro institutions which the Fund had been aiding during this emergency. Edwin R. Embree reported:

> At a time when the pattern was fright, timidity, rigid hoarding of whatever one might still have left, the Fund, while necessarily reducing new appropriations, did not withhold payments due, did not cut important personnel, did not cease contributing leadership and also money to the movements it was sponsoring. It is in fact probable that the Fund's influence was greater during the depression era than during any other period in its history.[9]

In order to preserve its dwindling resources and to avoid selling stock at an unnaturally depressed price, the Fund arranged to pay interest of five per cent per annum on some of its commitments instead of making the payments of the principal in full. Loans were also obtained from banks with Sears, Roebuck stock as collateral. As economic conditions gradually improved, the Fund was able to pay all of its philanthropic commitments in full by 1936, as well as its loans at banks.

From 1928, when Rosenwald organized his fund on a large scale basis it became one of the most important influences for public welfare in the United States, and its influence has continued to be felt ever since. Its activities affected beneficially the lives of colored men, women and children in all of the southern

[9] Embree, Edwin R. *Review of Two Decades.* Julius Rosenwald Fund Report, 1936, p. 6.

states and in many northern communities. Creative ideas in education and health for both colored and white people of under-privileged groups received from the Fund the financial aid and intellectual consideration necessary to prove their worth to the community. Julius Rosenwald, who had started out in the first years of the century as a rich man with charitable instincts, had become by virtue of his own generosity and philanthropic courage the creator of one of the most useful and flexible welfare agencies in the country. James Weldon Johnson said of him in a memorial address at Fisk University:

> Julius Rosenwald used his brains in disposing of money. Had he used them only in acquiring it, we should not be gathered here.

## CHAPTER XIII

## PERSONAL

ROSENWALD'S personality was characterized by its vigor and amiability. He made a great success in life both as a farsighted merchant and as a warm-hearted humanitarian. Whatever he gave of himself or his resources he gave fully and freely, and he won the love as well as the respect and admiration of thousands of his friends and of millions of his beneficiaries.

He was always regarded as one of the most modest rich men in the United States. He liked to attribute a large part of his own business success to luck, and his engaging manner of presenting this thesis endeared him to the hearts of millions who had been accustomed to more pomposity and less frankness.

"Counsel, then, is useless from a master of money to a candidate seeking a place in the ranks?" an interviewer asked Julius Rosenwald in 1917.

"Wholly," Rosenwald replied. "The commonest and shabbiest thing in the world is advice. A normal man does not require it. His conscience or intellect is sufficient. What he wants is an opening. He may seek it or he may find it. Often it will meet him face to face when he is thinking about something else. In that event, his heart should not be filled with arrogance."

"But you have had a programme?" the interviewer insisted.

"None whatever," Rosenwald replied. "Had I followed a programme, I would still be in the clothing business."

"Anyway you have a policy?"

"Only so far as trying to feel that I am always selling merchandise to myself. I would stand on both sides of the counter, if we had a counter."

In later years he made the following statement to a newspaper reporter in New Orleans, and the words went around the nation:

I believe that success is 95 per cent luck and 5 per cent ability. I never could understand the popular belief that because a man makes a lot of money he has a lot of brains. Some very rich men who made their own fortunes have been among the stupidest men I have ever met in my life. There are men in America today walking the streets, financial failures, who have more brains and more ability than I will ever have. I had the luck to get my opportunity. Their opportunity never came. Rich men are not smart because they are rich. They didn't get rich because they are smart. Don't ever confuse wealth with brains. They are synonyms sometimes, but none too often.

He was fond of an anecdote told to him by his friend, Solomon Levitan, about a man who won a million dollars on number 14. When asked how he had figured it out, he said: "I had a dream. One night I saw in my dream a great big 9, and next I saw a 6, so I used my brains and figured that 9 and 6 is 14."

In January, 1929, Rosenwald was asked to appear in a Fox Movietone reel and make a short statement. He consented, and said:

It was Ingersoll who said: "I hate a stingy man. If you have only a dollar in the world and you have to spend it, spend it like a king. I'd rather be a beggar and spend my money like a king than be a king and spend my money like a beggar." Most people believe that because a man has made a fortune his views on any subject are valuable. For my part, I have always believed that most large fortunes are made by men of mediocre ability who tumbled into a lucky opportunity and could not help but get rich and in most cases others given the same chance would have done far better with it. Hard work and attention to business are necessary, but they rarely result in achieving a large fortune. Do not be fooled into believing that because a man is rich, he is necessarily smart. There is ample proof to the contrary.

Rosenwald's statement was like a fresh breeze in an atmosphere of stale platitudes. From various parts of the country friends and strangers wrote to him expressing gratitude and praise for his pleasing frankness. Many people asked for copies of the talk, saying that it was the finest thing they had ever heard a rich man say.

In answer to a statement in March, 1929, by Dr. Clark, of Teachers' College, that a college education is a detriment to the earning capacity of American youth, and that it "is likely to make a man too pensive and hesitant for the task of money-making when daring and courage are the prime necessities," Rosenwald said:

Although I am convinced that many who go to college would be far better off if they went to work, I believe in college education. If I did not I should not have served for many years as a trustee of the University of Chicago nor taken so much interest in the growth and development of that institution.

It is true that many men have achieved greatness in various lines without ever being inside a college, as for instance Abraham Lincoln and Grover Cleveland and Thomas Edison, and because they are in the majority a large number of non-college men have made fortunes as compared with those equally lucky in business who have had an education. But this does not seem to me to prove the lack of value of colleges.

We must remember that many of the great fortunes in America have been made in part at least simply by taking advantage of the great natural resources of this new country and by reaping the almost inevitable rewards of developing these resources in the presence of a rapidly growing population. It required only energy, imagination and courage to turn oil into millions and billions of dollars, or to amass great wealth by building railroads over a vast and rich country, or to roll up fortunes from automobiles as millions of people began almost overnight to demand them, or to take advantage of good transportation and communications to develop national mail-order businesses.

As we pass the pioneering period in America, and as the great natural resources of this new country become more nearly balanced by the increasing population, it may not be so easy to build up huge fortunes by these relatively simple means. Increasingly business is becoming complex; and success in it is tending more and more to require special and general training. Colleges and technical schools are likely to be called upon in increasing measure to train men for industrial leadership, while they continue to serve to broaden and enrich the lives of their students.

Rosenwald possessed energy in great abundance; he also had sufficient imagination to envision the future of the novel method of merchandising with which he became associated in its early history; and he possessed to an unlimited degree the courage to support and develop that enterprise in times of crises.

The great energy with which he was endowed expressed itself not only in his business but in his philanthropy and his recreations. He played tennis vigorously until he was more than fifty years old when he was forbidden to continue because of the effect on his heart. He then took up golf and played that game until illness prevented him from doing so any longer. He hated inactivity, and he could not abide rest resorts, although he was frequently compelled to visit them. After he had been at Hot Springs, or Santa Barbara or Atlantic City for a few days, he became avid to get into the busy swim of large affairs which was his daily life in Chicago. He did not feel completely alive, unless he was active, and he was particularly exhilarated when he had a good fight on his hands in which he believed himself to be wholly in the right or an exciting crisis to cope with, such as the 1929 stock market crash. His favorite sport of those in which he could not participate was football, and he went to all the games he could possibly attend when he was in Chicago.

Until he was about forty-five years old he was rather stout, of middle height, jolly and fond of play with his children. He also gave way to occasional tantrums and was stubbornly insistent on some of his own views and ways of doing things. He loved to catch trains at the last moment, and in the heyday of his later activities he was so anxious to participate in as many things as possible that he frequently changed his clothes in his automobile en route to still another appointment. Mrs. Rosenwald made efforts, without much success, to persuade him to read less newspapers and more books; he had little time for long books; for painting and sculpture he had no taste, and the meditative effect of music bored him.

He was congenitally optimistic, and he was reluctant to take illness seriously until it was acute. He neglected his own health and preferred to attend to it only when it became absolutely necessary. He shook worry off quickly and lost little energy in fretting over decisions and occurrences which could no longer be remedied. In his later years he grew more impatient as he grew conscious of the lack of time he had in which to accomplish the largest possible number of important things.

His relations with his family were always delightful to him. His family circle was something set apart, and he never permitted the disturbances of a busy existence to mar the happiness of his home life. Whenever he was separated from his wife, he wrote her daily letters, and whenever they were together he took her into his complete confidence. He was exceedingly fond of his children and took time continuously to write them long accounts of his activities, no matter how many other efforts he might be engaged in at the moment. For his grandchildren he had an enthusiasm that was sometimes terrifying to them, as he tossed them about with energetic affection. The Rosenwald home was always full of people, and Sunday dinners were large family events. Although he had little interest in formal society, he loved people, and he enjoyed entertaining them in his home in a considerate and open-handed way. Men who worked with him and noted how disagreeable he could be on the way home from the office if he disapproved of the way something had been done in his business or in his philanthropies, were surprised to find that just as soon as they had stepped across the threshold of his home, all irritability and impatience had disappeared, as if he had taken off an itching garment. He loved to wander about his large, wooded estate at Ravinia in the outskirts of Chicago, and one day he remarked with wonder to one of his daughters: "Who am I to live in a park?"

He was full of pat phrases, such as, "I never want to own much property—I only want the place next to mine," and he enjoyed repeating the quips and phrases of newspaper philosophers and other popular thinkers.

In later years Rosenwald suffered from Paget's disease, a gradual calcification of the bones, which caused him to bend as he walked, and his entire appearance grew gradually more shriveled as he reached old age. When his heart became seriously strained during the years following the war, he was forced, much against his strong will, to attempt to curtail his activities. In 1925 after an examination by the specialists of the Rockefeller Institute, he was advised to walk slowly, use the elevator going upstairs and to give up golf over hilly courses. He was also advised to take frequent rest journeys abroad and at home, and the effort was made to persuade him to leave Chicago for long periods because of the demands upon his attention there and his desire to participate in everything that was taking place. The doctors wrote him after their examination in 1925 urging him to have no office except in his home and to use a secretary only for about three hours a day. That was an injunction he was never to obey. "In short," the doctors wrote, "we think that you should lead a simple quiet Godly life so far as possible." "We are moved to write all this," they added, "solely from our desire to see you have many more years of comfort and usefulness—not usefulness in accomplishing things rapidly and effectively but usefulness through employing your accumulated experience in guiding others in proper directions."

For a short time he tried to carry out the injunctions of his doctors and sincerely planned to heed the wishes of his wife. But before long he was rushing again into the momentum of his activities and before he realized it was carried along at a terrific pace. Luncheon meetings, conferences, dinners, social, philanthropic, civic and business gatherings were his routine in Chicago and whenever he visited New York. Demands followed him wherever he went, and he loved to consider and answer them personally. The only thing he hated to do for philanthropy was to make a speech, which he avoided whenever possible, although he was always willing to do so if necessary.

Mrs. Rosenwald, who also kept up an active nervous pace in philanthropic and social work and in family activities, became seriously ill in 1927. She had to undergo several severe operations, and her suffering was great. In 1928 Dr. W. J. Mayo, of the Mayo Clinic, came to Chicago to examine her. Upon his return to Rochester, he wrote to Rosenwald asking to be permitted to make no charge, and he added:

> I went down because I knew something about your wife's condition and knew how vital the problem was to your future happiness. I would not have you feel under an obligation, but I have been much interested in your altruistic undertakings, and I wish you would let us consider that such service as I was able to be to you was a slight token of esteem and sympathetic recognition of your work for a better America.

Rosenwald answered:

> Never have I been so at loss to know how to reply to a letter as I am yours of August 13th. Mrs. Rosenwald and I have been the recipients of some beautiful letters but this surpasses anything that has come to us. I must confess that it brought tears to our eyes. That you and your brother, who have been so prominent in your service to mankind not only professionally but in every other way, should recognize in so beautiful a manner my comparatively slight achievements, touches a tender chord. It is needless to assure you that the generous tribute you so kindly pay to me is highly prized. I hope always to merit your esteem and sometime to have the opportunity to demonstrate my appreciation. . . .

In May, 1929, his wife's condition became worse, and she died on May 23, at the age of sixty.

The couple had been married for thirty-nine years. In addition to the fact that Mrs. Rosenwald was the most influential person in her husband's charitable and philanthropic work, she had also engaged in her own charities and causes over a long

period of years and made annual contributions and special donations to a large number of institutions and individuals.

Rosenwald conducted simple funeral services himself for his
wife, and they were attended only by close members of the
family. When the family assembled, he was sitting in the room,
and he remarked that he had jotted down a few things which he
would like to speak of to them. He first spoke of the great love
which had always existed between his mother and his wife.
He then spoke of his wife's great love for her family and of her
kind deeds to her friends and those who worked for her and of
her interest in their lives. At his request his wife's coffin was
placed directly underneath the portrait of his mother which hung
in the room.

Upon the occasion of their twenty-first wedding anniversary on
April 9, 1911, Rosenwald wrote to his wife, who was then in
Europe:

> Your endless devotion to me and our dearest ones, your encouragement
> in my work, your self-sacrifice through all the years of married life has
> multiplied many times the love I felt for you twenty-one years ago. . . .
> Twenty-one years of true womanly devotion have resulted in accomplishing
> this and in making us to one another the loving couple that we are. What
> I am of Jew or Citizen or any honors which have come to me would not
> have come but for your co-operation and helpfulness.

Writing to a friend of his and Mrs. Rosenwald's after her death,
he said: "My children and I are endeavoring to live up to our
philosophy of being as cheerful as possible over events that cannot be changed, and trying to create an atmosphere of happiness
for our own sakes as well as those with whom we come in contact. There is nothing to be gained by any other course."

In the fall of 1929 he planned a trip to Japan, where he wished
to attend the sessions of the Institute of Pacific Relations, in
whose work he was interested and to which the Fund had made
a contribution. But his children objected to the strain on his
health, and he gave it up.

On January 8, 1930, he married Mrs. Adelaide R. Goodkind, the mother of Lessing Rosenwald's wife. The wedding took place at his son's home in Philadelphia and was conducted by Rosenwald's good friend, Judge Horace Stern. After the wedding they went to New York, where Rosenwald had a final meeting with Calvin Coolidge and Alfred E. Smith for the purpose of disposing of the Conrad Hubert Fund. They then sailed for the Mediterranean and Egypt.

In the fall of 1930 Rosenwald and his wife visited Springfield, where Rosenwald showed her the scenes of his boyhood and youth. He saw again some of those with whom he had played and gone to school, and on the streets he met and remembered many of his early associates. He attended the Mid-Day Luncheon Club of Springfield, and when he was asked to speak on "Business," he replied: "There is none!"

In December, 1930, Mr. and Mrs. Rosenwald went to Honolulu, so that he might rest and recuperate. His heart was in bad condition, and he became exhausted after slight effort. The disease of his bones, which caused them to become brittle and his legs to swell, was also getting worse. In January he felt better and was able to go about more. He visited the Royal School for mixed races in Hawaii, where Japanese, Chinese, Filipino and Hawaiian pupils were educated, and he considered it "a glorified Tuskegee." He was much interested in the work of this school and made a contribution to it before leaving Hawaii.

After his return to Chicago he was confined to his home almost continuously. He was cheerful and resigned to his position as an invalid, but insisted that he did not wish to be a burden to others. He still loved to keep in touch with his affairs, and he spent some time each week in consultations with Mr. Embree and his secretaries. Memoranda were submitted to him on many of his large philanthropic interests. It was at this time that he wished to defend his action after the disclosure of his offer of

10,000 shares of stock to Frank L. Smith, but the doctors insisted on his conserving his health.

Requests for his aid poured in constantly during the severe period of the depression. While he had been resting in Honolulu, he received a cable from Cyrus H. McCormick urging him to make a contribution to the campaign for five million dollars for the relief of unemployment in Chicago, which had by that time become, as Mr. McCormick stated in his cable, "disaster relief." Sears, Roebuck had already made a large contribution to this fund, but Rosenwald cabled back a personal contribution of $25,000. In October, 1931, he offered to give $250,000 to the Joint Emergency Relief Fund for Unemployment Relief in Cook County, provided five other individuals would give a like amount. It was found impossible to find five others willing or able to do so, and Rosenwald made an outright contribution of $100,000 and pledged an additional $50,000, provided the entire $10,000,-000 aimed for was raised. In addition, he gave $15,000 to the special unemployment relief campaign conducted by the United Charities of Chicago during 1930.

During the depression many bewildered and some frantic people, strangers to him, wrote for money or advice. Many friends and former employees also appealed to him for aid and advice. His great wealth and his reputation had spread throughout the country, and numerous pathetic and distressing appeals came from individuals, while organizations, finding their other support dwindling, flooded his office with requests for increased or renewed contributions.

As his health grew worse, friends and strangers throughout the country expressed their appreciation of his character and their concern for his life. Older employees of Sears, Roebuck who had been in the habit of seeing him at the plant almost every day for many years, drew up letters telling him how much they missed him and wishing him speedy recovery. Negro groups in the South telegraphed their hope for his health, and prayed for him. People with nostrums and people with faith in miracles wrote their advice when they read in the newspapers that he was critically ill.

Rosenwald died in his sleep on the afternoon of January 6, 1932. The intimate members of his family were present at his bedside. Relatives in Germany, Negroes in the southern states, and Americans throughout the country listened with sorrow to the radio announcement that night that one of the world's great humanitarians was dead. In the Russian Jewish colonies of the Ukraine and in the Zionist settlements in Palestine mourning was proclaimed for him. He was buried in Rosehill Cemetery beside the graves of his mother and his first wife.

A tremendous outpouring of praise filled the newspapers of this country and of many other countries upon the occasion of his death. He was universally acclaimed as one of the greatest benefactors to humanity of his time, and he was missed as a warm friend by those who had known him.

Rosenwald had given away most of his wealth during his lifetime to his philanthropies and to his family. His will made a bequest of eleven million dollars to the Rosenwald Family Association, which was organized shortly before his death to carry on contributions to organizations, so that those in the habit of depending upon his aid for many years would not suddenly be embarrassed by his death. The remainder of his estate was bequeathed to his children. The estate at the time of his death had a net worth of $17,415,450 without deductions for taxes. At one time the value of his fortune had been more than $200,000,000. During his lifetime he had distributed approximately $63,000,000 to causes, organizations and individuals, exclusive of his gifts to members of his family and to friends.

During the last years of his life, although Rosenwald saw his large fortune dwindling on paper, he never lost confidence in the enduring importance of the business institution which he had developed. His son Lessing and tried executives who were also his friends were in charge of the great business of which he was proud.

Even as he lay ill, he deprecated to his doctor what he had done in the field of philanthropy. He said that it was no more than his duty, and he regretted that he had not been able to do more. He had the satisfaction of knowing that the important projects in which he had taken a part were proving of great spiritual and practical value to millions of people throughout the world. Negroes in the South were enjoying the opportunity to go to school because Julius Rosenwald had lived. Jews in the south of Russia were able to exist because he had helped them. A great Museum of Science and Industry was rising in Chicago. Innumerable institutions, causes and movements were flourishing because they had arrested his attention. He also had the satisfaction of knowing that his philanthropic interests would be faithfully carried on after his death. He had established the formal aspects of them carefully, and the Julius Rosenwald Fund was continuing its useful work. From their earliest years he had imbued in all of his children a respect for and an interest in the art and science of giving. He could feel that he had lived well, happily and usefully during the entire course of a constructive career in a vital period of American history; that the things he had built would not quickly decay; that he was not attempting to force them upon future generations by immuring them in perpetual endowments; and that the impress which his personality and his intelligence had stamped upon them would endure long after his death.

Professor Charles S. Johnson, speaking in his memory, said:

Whatever else may be said, we here today can bear witness above all else that he had "faith and force enough to form generous hopes of the world's destiny," and that he moved with courage and brilliant effectiveness toward the accomplishment of these hopes.

# BIBLIOGRAPHY

The basic source material of this book was contained in the files of correspondence, memoranda, speeches and statements kept by Julius Rosenwald throughout his lifetime, in addition to family letters and papers.

The following list of books and documents were used as well:

ADDAMS, JANE. *Twenty Years at Hull-House.* New York. Macmillan Co. 1910.

——. *The Second Twenty Years at Hull-House.* New York. Macmillan Co. 1930.

ADLER, CYRUS. *Louis Marshall.* A Biographical Sketch by Cyrus Adler, Memorial Addresses by Cyrus Adler, Irving Lehman and Horace Stern. New York. The American Jewish Committee. 1931.

——. *Jacob H. Schiff. His Life and Letters.* 2 vols. New York. Doubleday, Doran & Co. 1928.

AMALGAMATED CLOTHING WORKERS OF AMERICA. *The Clothing Workers of Chicago,* 1910-1922. Published by the Chicago Joint Board of the Amalgamated Clothing Workers of America. Chicago. 1922.

AMERICAN JEWISH HISTORICAL SOCIETY. Publications. 1909-1932.

AMERICAN JEWISH YEAR BOOK. Vol. 34, Oct. 1, 1932 to September 20, 1933. Article on Julius Rosenwald by Pauline K. Angell.

ANGLE, PAUL M. *"Here I Have Lived." A History of Lincoln's Springfield.* Springfield, Illinois. 1935.

ARTHUR, GEORGE R. *Life on the Negro Frontier.* New York. Association Press. 1934.

AYRES, LEONARD P. *The War With Germany, A Statistical Summary.* Washington, D. C., Government Printing Office.

BARUCH, BERNARD M. *American Industry in the War.* A Report of the War Industrial Board. Washington, D. C., Government Printing Office, 1921.

BOGEN, BORIS D. *Jewish Philanthropy.* New York. Macmillan Co. 1917.

BREGSTONE, PHILIP P. *Chicago and Its Jews.* Privately Published. 1933.

BROOKS, JOHN GRAHAM. *An American Citizen, the Life of William Henry Baldwin, Jr.* Boston. Houghton Mifflin Co. 1910.

CABOT, RICHARD C. *Social Service and the Art of Healing.* New York. Moffat, Yard & Co. 1909.

CLARK, TALIAFERRO. *The Control of Syphilis in Southern Rural Areas.* A Study by the United States Public Health Service and Certain States and Local Departments of Health, in Cooperation with the Julius Rosenwald Fund. Published by the Julius Rosenwald Fund. Chicago. 1932.

CLARKSON, GROSVENOR B. *Industrial America in the World War, The Strategy Behind the Line.* 1917-1918. Boston. Houghton Mifflin Co. 1934.

COMMONS, JOHN R., AND ASSOCIATES. *History of Labor in the United States.* 2 vols. New York. Macmillan Co. 1926.

COON, HORACE. *Money to Burn.* New York. Longmans, Green & Co. 1938.

CURREY, J. SEYMOUR. *Chicago: Its History and Its Builders, A Century of Marvelous Growth.* 5 vols. Chicago. The S. J. Clarke Publishing Co. 1912.

EMBREE, EDWIN R. *Brown America, The Story of a New Race.* New York. The Viking Press. 1931.

———. Julius Rosenwald Fund Reports, 1928-1936.

FORBES, B. C. *Men Who Are Making America.* New York. B. C. Forbes Co. 1917. Sketch of Julius Rosenwald, pp. 310-318.

*General Education Board. An Account of Its Activities.* 1902-1914. New York. General Education Board. 1930. Also annual reports of the Board since 1914.

GOODSPEED, CHARLES TEN BROEKE, AND OTHERS. *Loring Wilbur Messer.* Chicago. The Young Men's Christian Association. 1934.

GOODSPEED, THOMAS W. *The Story of the University of Chicago.* Chicago. University of Chicago Press. 1925.

HARDY, JACK. *The Clothing Workers.* New York International Publishers.

HARRISON, CARTER H. *Stormy Years. The Autobiography of Carter H. Harrison, Five Times Mayor of Chicago.* Indianapolis. The Bobbs-Merrill Co. 1935.

HIRSCH, EMIL G. *My Religion.* New York. Macmillan Co. 1925.

HUMPHREY, EDWARD FRANK. *An Economic History of the United States.* New York. The Century Co. 1931.

*Illinois, The Centennial History of,* edited by Clarence Walworth Alvord. Vol. IV. *The Industrial State,* 1870-1893, by Ernest Ludlow Bogart and Charles Manfred Thompson. Springfield, Ill. 1920. Vol. V. *The Modern Commonwealth,* 1893-1918, by Ernest Ludlow Bogart and John Mabry Mathews. Springfield, Ill. 1920. Published by the Illinois Centennial Commission.

ILLINOIS. Report of the Senate Vice Committee, Created under the Authority of the Senate of the Forty-ninth General Assembly. 1916.

———. Reports of the Factory Inspectors of Illinois. 1894-1916.

JOHNSON, CHARLES S. *Shadow of the Plantation.* University of Chicago Press, 1934.

JOHNSON, JAMES WELDON. *Negro Americans, What Now?* New York. The Viking Press. 1934.

JOSEPH, SAMUEL. *History of the Baron de Hirsch Fund.* Printed for Baron de Hirsch Fund by the Jewish Publication Society. 1935.

KALLEN, HORACE M. *Frontiers of Hope.* New York. Horace Liveright. 1929.

KING, HOYT. *Citizen Cole of Chicago.* 1931.

LEVINE, LOUIS. *The Women's Garment Workers. A History of the International Ladies' Garment Workers' Union.* New York. B. W. Huebsch, Inc. 1924.

LEWIS, LLOYD AND SMITH, HENRY JUSTIN. *Chicago, The History of Its Reputation.* New York. Harcourt, Brace & Co. 1929.

LINDEMAN, EDUARD C. *Wealth and Culture. A Study of One Hundred Foundations and Community Trusts and Their Operations during the Decade 1921-1930.* New York. Harcourt, Brace & Co. 1936.

LINN, JAMES WEBER. *Jane Addams.* New York. D. Appleton-Century Co. 1935.

MARTIN, DR. FRANKLIN H. *Digest of the Proceedings of the Council of National Defense During the World War.* Washington, D. C. Government Printing Office. 1934.

MASTERS, EDGAR LEE. *Levy Mayer and the New Industrial Era.* Privately Printed. New Haven, Conn. 1927.

———. *The Tale of Chicago,* New York. G. P. Putnam's Sons. 1935.

McCORMICK, J. SCOTT. "The Julius Rosenwald Fund." Article in the *Journal of Negro Education,* vol. III, No. 4, Oct. 1934.

McDOWELL, MARY. *Mary McDowell and Municipal Housekeeping.* Chicago. Privately Printed.

MEITES, HYMAN L. *History of the Jews of Chicago.* Chicago. Jewish Historical Society of Illinois. 1924.

MERRIAM, CHARLES EDWARD. *Chicago, a More Intimate View of Urban Politics.* New York. Macmillan Co. 1929.

MILLER, KELLY. *Race Adjustment. Essays on the Negro in America.* New York. The Neal Publishing Co. 1908.

MONTGOMERY, ROYAL E. *Industrial Relations in the Chicago Building Trades*. Chicago. University of Chicago Press. 1927.

MOORE, EDWARD C. *Forty Years of Opera in Chicago*. New York. Horace Liveright. 1930.

*Negro, The American*. Annals of American Academy of Political and Social Science. Philadelphia. 1928.

*Negro, The, in Chicago. A Study of Race Relations and a Race Riot*. By the Chicago Commission on Race Relations. University of Chicago Press. 1922.

O'HARA Report. *See* Illinois.

PALMER, FREDERICK. *Newton D. Baker. America at War*. 2 vols. New York. Dodd, Mead & Co. 1931.

PARRAN, THOMAS, M.D. "The Next Great Plague to Go." In *Survey Graphic*, July, 1936.

——— "No Defense for Any of Us." In *Survey Graphic*, April, 1938.

PECK, HARRY THURSTON. *Twenty Years of the Republic, 1885-1905*. New York. Dodd, Mead & Co. 1906.

*Philanthropy, Intelligent*. Edited by Ellsworth Faris, Ferris Laune, Arthur J. Todd for the Wieboldt Foundation. Chicago. University of Chicago Press. 1930.

POPE, JESSE ELIPHALET. *The Clothing Industry in New York*. University of Missouri Studies. Social Science Series. Vol. 1. Published by the University of Missouri. 1905.

RAPER, ARTHUR F. *Preface to Peasantry, A Tale of Two Black Belt Counties*. Chapel Hill, N. C. University of North Carolina Press. 1936.

ROSENFELT, HENRY H. *This Thing of Giving*. The Record of a Rare Enterprise of Mercy and Brotherhood. New York. Plymouth Press. 1924.

ROSENWALD, JULIUS, FUND. Annual Reports. 1928-1936. Chicago. Published by the Julius Rosenwald Fund.

SCOTT, EMMETT J. AND STOWE, LYMAN BEECHER. *Booker T. Washington, Builder of a Civilization*. New York. Doubleday, Page & Co. 1917.

SHARPE, HENRY G., MAJOR-GENERAL. *The Quartermaster Corps in the year 1917 in the World War*. New York. The Century Co. 1921.

SHEPPLEY, HELEN EDITH. "Camp Butler in the Civil War Days." In *Journal of the Illinois State Historical Society*, January, 1933, vol. XXV, no. 4, pp. 285-317.

STEAD, W. T. *If Christ Came to Chicago*. Chicago. Laird & Lee. 1894.

STEIN, LEONARD. *Zionism*. London. Ernest Been Ltd. 1925.

SULLIVAN, LOUIS H. *The Autobiography of an Idea*. New York. 1926.

UNITED STATES. Industrial Commission. Final Reports of the Industrial Commission. 1902. vol. XIX.

—— *Minutes of the Council of National Defense*. Printed for the use of the Special Committee Investigating the Munitions Industry. 1936. 74th Congress, 2d Session.

—— *Minutes of the General Munitions Board*. Printed for the use of the Special Committee Investigating the Munitions Industry. 1936.

—— *Minutes of the War Industries Board*. Printed for the use of the Special Committee Investigating the Munitions Industry. 1936.

—— Senate. Subcommittee of the Committee on Manufactures, March, 1892. *Investigation of the Sweating System*.

—— Senate. Committee on Military Affairs, U. S. Senate, 65th Congress, 2d Session, *Investigation of the War Department*. Hearings. Eight parts. Washington, D. C. 1918.

—— Report of Industrial Conference Called by the President, Washington, D. C. March 6, 1920.

—— *Senatorial Campaign Expenditures*. Hearings before the Special Committee Investigating Expenditures in Senatorial Primary and General Elections. U. S. Senate, 69th Congress, 1st Session. Parts 2, 3, 6. July and October 1926. Washington. 1926. Reed Committee.

VICE, CHICAGO, COMMISSION. *The Social Evil in Chicago. A Study of Existing Conditions*. Chicago. 1911.

WASHINGTON, BOOKER T. *Up From Slavery, An Autobiography*. New York. Doubleday, Page & Co. 1901.

WIEBOLDT FOUNDATION. See *Philanthropy, Intelligent*.

WILSON, HOWARD E. *Mary McDowell, Neighbor*. University of Chicago Press. 1928.

WOODDY, CARROLL HILL. *The Case of Frank L. Smith. A Study in Representative Government*. University of Chicago Press. 1931.

WRIGHT, FRANK LLOYD. *An Autobiography*. New York. Longmans, Green & Co. 1932.

ZARETZ, CHARLES ELBERT. *The Amalgamated Clothing Workers of America*. New York. Ancon Publishing Co. 1934.

In addition newspaper clippings collected in fourteen scrapbooks by Julius Rosenwald's secretaries have been used, as well as newspaper accounts during various years, dates of which are given in the text or in footnotes throughout the book.

# INDEX

Aaronsohn, Aaron, 97-100, 172, 173
Abbott, Grace, 93, 94, 266, 267
Abbott, Robert S., 273
Abbott, W. Rufus, 285
Abt, Jacob J., 93
Adams, Lewis, 110
Addams, Jane, 90-94, 147, 148, 158, 279, 280, 290
Adler, Dr. Cyrus, 98, 99
Adler, Max, 68, 79, 284
Advisory Commission, 186-206
Agricultural Foundation, 63
Agro-Joint, 246, 247, 252, 253
Alabama schoolhouses for Negroes, 131, 132
Albion and Wurth, 20
Alexander, Governor Moses, 185
Allen, General Henry T., 255
Alschuler, Mrs. Alfred S., 276
Alvah Manufacturing Company, 38
American Academy of Political and Social Science, 323
American Commission for Restoration in Europe, 219, 220, 221
American Ever-ready Company, 331
American Federation of Labor, 268
American Hospital Association, 347
American Jewish Committee, 167, 173, 174, 176, 245, 257, 258
American Jewish Congress, 176, 177, 248
American Jewish Relief Committee, 174, 176, 177, 185
American Medical Association, 345, 347
American Missionary Association, 109, 136
American Red Cross, 333
American Relief Administration, 245
Amir of Afghanistan, 58, 59
*An American Citizen, the Life of William H. Baldwin, Jr.,* 107, 311
Anderson, Marian, 338
Anti-Saloon League, 303, 304, 305, 311
Anti-Semitism, 255-260
Armstrong, General Samuel Chapman, 110
Arthur, George R., 121

Asher, Louis E., 68
Ashurst, Senator, 312
Associated Jewish Charities of Chicago, 86, 90, 103, 166, 322
Association of Commerce of Chicago, 264
Atlanta Cotton States and International Exposition, 116, 117
Atlanta University, 109
*Atlantic Monthly,* 287, 288, 326, 327, 342
Automobiles, cheap, 65
Avxentieff, Nicholas D., 244

Baker, Newton D., 179, 187-195, 204, 205, 206, 210, 215, 216, 217, 219
Baldwin, Judge Jesse A., 104
Baldwin, Mrs. William H., Jr., 107
Baldwin, William H., Jr., 107, 108, 113, 114, 311
Balfour Declaration, 100, 101
Bamberger, Governor Simon, 185
Bancroft, Edgar A., 273
Bankers Trust Company, 330, 331
Barondess, Joseph, 248
Barrett, Oliver H., 92
Barron, C. W., 231
Baruch, Bernard M., 191, 197, 202
Base Sorting Plant, 203, 204
Bastedo Pneumatic Tube Co., 40
Beck, James M., 312
Bedford, E. T., 70
Beekman Street Hospital, 333
Beilis, Mendel, 166, 167
Benjamin, Alfred & Co., 21
Bernstorff, Count, 182
Billikopf, Jacob, 183, 208, 253
Billings, C. K. G., 300
Billings, Dr. Frank, 274
Bingham, Senator, 312
Biro-Bidjan, 251
Blackstone, Rev. William E., 95
Blackstone Hotel, 121, 146
Boll weevil, 113
Bond, William Scott, 273
Booker T. Washington Memorial Fund, 324

373